THE GERMAN
PACIFIC LOCOMOTIVE
ITS DESIGN AND DEVELOPMENT

THE GERMAN
PACIFIC LOCOMOTIVE
ITS DESIGN AND DEVELOPMENT

David Maidment

PEN & SWORD
TRANSPORT

First published in Great Britain in 2017 by
Pen & Sword Transport
An imprint of Pen & Sword Books Ltd
47 Church Street
Barnsley
South Yorkshire
S70 2AS

ISBN 978 1 47385 249 5

All royalties from this book will be donated to the Railway Children charity [reg. no. 1058991] [**www.railwaychildren.org.uk**]

Typeset in Palatino by Pen & Sword Books Ltd
Printed and bound in China by Imago

Pen & Sword Books Ltd incorporates the imprints of Pen & Sword Archaeology, Atlas, Aviation, Battleground, Discovery, Family History, History, Maritime, Military, Naval, Politics, Railways, Select, Social History, Transport, True Crime, and Claymore Press, Frontline Books, Leo Cooper, Praetorian Press, Remember When, Seaforth Publishing and Wharncliffe.

For a complete list of Pen and Sword titles please contact:
Pen and Sword Books Limited
47 Church Street, Barnsley, South Yorkshire, S70 2AS, England
E-mail: enquiries@pen-and-sword.co.uk
Website: www.pen-and-sword.co.uk

Previous Publications:

Novels (Religious historical fiction)
The Child Madonna, Melrose Books, 2009
The Missing Madonna, PublishNation, 2012
The Madonna and her Sons, PublishNation, 2015

Novels (Railway fiction)
Lives on the Line, Max Books, 2013

Non-fiction (Railways)
The Toss of a Coin, PublishNation, 2014
A Privileged Journey, Pen & Sword, 2015
An Indian Summer of Steam, Pen & Sword, 2015
Great Western Eight-Coupled Heavy Freight Locomotives, Pen & Sword, 2015
Great Western Moguls and Prairies, Pen and Sword, 2016
The Urie and Maunsell 2-cylinder 4-6-0s, Pen and Sword, 2016
Great Western Small Wheeled Outside Frame 4-4-0 Tender Locomotives, Pen and Sword, 2017

Non-fiction (Street Children)
The Other Railway Children, PublishNation, 2012
Nobody Ever Listened To Me, PublishNation, 2012

Cover photo: Preserved 3-cylinder oil-fired Pacific 01.1100 ready to depart from Osnabrück with an enthusiasts' railtour to Altenbeken, 11 May 1995. (David Maidment)

Back cover:
Top left: 01.0510-6 at Leipzig waiting to depart with E807 to Saalfeld, 24 April 1979. (David Maidment)

Top right: East German reboilered three-cylinder 03.10 Pacific, 03.0077-2 at Stralsund with a relief D-Zug, D10513, for Berlin Lichtenberg, 12 April 1979. (Alastair Wood)

Bottom left: 18.630, formerly 18.543 built by Henschel under licence in 1930, the last 18.5 to be rebuilt with all-welded boiler and combustion chamber in April 1957, at Lindau Depot where it was stationed until its withdrawal in April 1965, 21 June 1962. (Herbert Schambach)

Bottom right: Preserved Baden four-cylinder compound Pacific 18.314, as rebuilt by the East German DR for use at Halle Research & Test Centre, and converted in the late 1960s to oil-burning, in Saalfeld, September 1969. It is now preserved and in the Auto & Technikmuseum, Sinsheim, in West Germany. (Eisenbahnstiftung Collection)

ACKNOWLEDGEMENTS

I have drawn on the knowledge and experience of many previous authors, whose books and articles are listed in the bibliography. I have added my own experience of German Pacific locomotives in the last two decades of their existence, when I travelled in both East and West Germany, building on my three years at London's University College German Department and attending Munich University for a term in the summer of 1959.

I have had extraordinary help in compiling the photographs for this book. I therefore wish to thank a large number of German, Australian and British photographers who have allowed me to publish their images free of charge as all the royalties from the sale of the book will be donated to the Railway Children charity (**www.railwaychildren.org.uk**) which I founded in 1995, a charity which supports street children living around railway stations and transport hubs in India, East Africa and runaway children in the UK. The charity is widely supported by the British professional and heritage railway industries. In addition to my own photographs, I have, therefore, relied on the photographs of several other expert photographers and their collections, in particular, assistance and permission from the publishers Eisenbahn Kurier Verlag of Freiburg for use of photos by the famous German photographer, Carl Bellingrodt; German photographers, Helmut Dahlhaus, Herbert Schambach, Ulrich Budde, Robin Garn, Hans-Jürgen Wenzel, Gerhard Gress and the Eisenbahnstiftung Gallery of over 20,000 photos administered by Joachim Bügel; Australian photographers Malcolm Holdsworth, Robert Kingsford-Smith and their friend, the late George Bambery; the collections of the Manchester Locomotive Society and their photo archivist, Paul Shackcloth, of MLS member Mike Bentley, and colleagues and friends Richard Spoors, Colin Boocock, Roger Bastin, Graham Stacey, and my college friend and partner on many journeys, Alastair Wood. Alastair has also allowed me to publish many of his logs of locomotive performance throughout Germany which supplement my own and those from the archives of the Railway Performance Society, of which I am a member.

It has been difficult tracing the owners of the copyright of some of the oldest photographs in various collections and if I have missed anyone, please contact the publisher so that the omission can be rectified.

I also acknowledge the help of the editors and staff of Pen and Sword, and their Commissioning Editor, John Scott-Morgan, in particular.

A side view of reboilered East German 03.162 with the 13.03 Hamburg Altona to Berlin, June 1967. (MLS Collection/J. Davenport)

CONTENTS

Chapter 1

OVERVIEW

The first railway in Germany was the short line from Nuremberg to Fürth in Bavaria in 1835, followed by a rapid expansion into a vast network of railways throughout the independent States and Princedoms. These were run by a variety of companies over very different terrain and with different political allegiances, served by a number of engineering companies and works pursuing their own policies and practices. It was not until after the Franco-Prussian war in 1871, and the increasing dominance of the Prussian State, that the beginning of some order began to arise, although the independence of the State systems lasted well into the twentieth century.

At the turn of the century, express passenger trains of the various companies were in the hands of Atlantic 4-4-2 and 4-6-0 locomotives – of the State railways of Bavaria, Baden, Saxony and Württemberg in the south, and Prussia, Oldenburg and Mecklenburg in the north. With the pressure to increase train speeds and loads for the more affluent

Preserved Bavarian four-cylinder compound 3673 (DB 18.478) restored in Bavarian Royal State Railway livery and in active operation at Meiningen Works, 1999. It is standing next to the unique Pacific, 18.201, used for rolling stock testing at Halle Research Centre and since preserved. (Richard Spoors)

The January 1926-built 001.008-2 (since preserved) departs from Neuenmarkt-Wirsberg under the B303 road with a Nuremberg-Hof train, September 1972.
(Richard Spoors)

travellers during the first decade, the railways began to look for larger and more powerful locomotives and the Munich firm of Maffei produced Germany's first Pacific 4-6-2 for the Baden system in 1907, one year before Britain's first, the Great Western's *Great Bear,* and just a few months after the French Pacific 4500 built by the Paris-Orleans (PO) Railway. The Baden IV f (DR 18.2), was followed in rapid succession by the Bavarian Royal State Railway's famous four-cylinder compound S3/6 Pacific (DR 18.4) also built by Maffei, and the smaller Württemberg class 'C' (DR 18.1) built at the private Esslingen Works in 1909. The Baden Company produced an improved version of their Pacific, the IV h (DR 18.3) in 1918, and the Saxon Railway, their

XVIII H (DR 18.0), built by the Hartmann Engineering Company a year earlier during the war in 1917.

Only after the First World War was there pressure to unify and standardise railway systems and locomotive policy – the financial state of the main State railways after so much railway equipment had been handed to the victors as war reparations made the nationalisation of the State railways inevitable, which happened on 1 April 1920, with all the State railways incorporated by April 1921. With a shortage of capital, the nationalised railway struggled and, within a short time, efforts to privatise the railway were being advocated. Initially there were continuing problems, as the French military still occupied the

Ruhr industrial area and inflation was rising rapidly. However, under the American Dawes Plan, a loan of 800 million Goldmarks was provided to enable German industry to recover and improve exports, and, on 24 February 1924, the *Deutsche Reichsbahn Gesellschaft* (DRG) took responsibility for the national railway system outside state control.

When the amalgamation of the State railways into a national system took effect on 1 April 1920, the new *Deutsche Reichsbahn* inherited 275 different classes of steam locomotive. The Transport Minister, at a conference in Oldenburg in May 1921, asked three key questions re future locomotive policy:

    1. Which existing locomotive

The preserved and re-streamlined three-cylinder Pacific, 01 1102, as built in 1940, on a Sunday special from Cologne to Kreuzberg in the Ahrtal. Here, she is awaiting a path at Huerth-Kalscheuren on the way to Remagen, October 1999.
(Richard Spoors)

classes should be further constructed?

2. What new locomotive types should be created?

3. How should all the new locomotives to be created be allocated?

There followed a long series of debates between the former chief engineers over the merits of the Prussian S10.1 4-6-0s for lighter work, the Saxon XX HV compound 2-8-2s for heavier work, issues of axle-weight, length compared with turntables available. In the meantime, a number of German manufacturers put forward a host of 4-6-0, 4-6-2 and 2-8-2 simple and compound designs for consideration for new standard express engines.

The DRG was formed in 1924, and the new numbering and classification system of the State locomotives was then introduced, with all the Pacifics receiving the class 18 designation, the numbers 01-10 being reserved for possible future DRG standard locomotive developments. The construction of State railway designs continued for a few years, with the Bavarian S3/6 Pacific and the Saxon XX HV 2-8-2 in particular, as capital for new investment was in short supply until preparations for new standard locomotives were completed. Then, at the end of 1925, the two-cylinder DRG 01 designed by the new chief engineer, Head of Locomotive Construction, Richard Paul Wagner, appeared, built by Borsig and AEG.

The locomotives continued to be built by a variety of firms until 1937, when the class numbered 231 examples.

The Bavarian S3/6s were the last State design to be built by the DRG, forty class 18.5s being constructed by Krauss-Maffei and Henschel between 1926 and 1930, some twenty or more years after the introduction of the prototype, while a version of the 01, the class 03, was developed with lighter axle-loads for secondary main lines. The DRG experimented with four-cylinder compound variations of the 01, but quickly opted for the simplicity and reliability of the two-cylinder simple 01 and 03s for all main line express passenger work. Then, in the 1930s, the worldwide

interest in high-speed rail travel to compete with the burgeoning air and auto industries led to experimentation with high pressure and streamlining. The German Nazi regime, interested in demonstrating their power and supremacy, encouraged the development and high-speed exploits of a streamlined three-cylinder 4-6-4, the 05, in 1935, built by Borsig in Berlin, the second example of which, 05.002, set a world record of 200.4km/hr (125mph) on 11 May 1936, the record standing until just eclipsed by the British A4 Pacific *Mallard* in 1938.

With this experience behind them, the DRG developed the three-cylinder streamlined 01.10s for regular express passenger work, the first of which was built in 1939 in competition with the high-speed diesel train concept of the early 1930s – the *Flying Hamburger*. It was planned to build 400 of these locomotives, although only fifty-five had been completed before the impact of the Second World War caused construction to cease. Experiments had been conducted to assess the effects of streamlining on examples of the 03 class and

the building of 140 03.10 three-cylinder streamlined lightweight Pacifics was planned, although only sixty had been built before their construction also ceased in 1941.

The German railways suffered enormous damage during the final years of the war and many of the old State Pacifics were either destroyed or were in such a bad condition at the end of the war that they were stored as unserviceable, pending decisions on possible repair, rebuilding or withdrawal. Many of the streamlined standard Pacifics were also in a very

Preserved three-cylinder de-streamlined and reboilered oil-burner 01.1100 on a railtour special at Velden, 25 May 1985. (Roger Bastin)

Oil-burning 01.523, rebuilt from standard 01.191 by the East German DR in 1964, climbs through Ronshausen to Hönebach Tunnel with a Frankfurt–Bebra–Erfurt express, 16 September 1968.
(Richard Spoors)

damaged condition and as post-war track allowed no possibility of the immediate restoration of high-speed working, the 01.10s and 03.10s were de-streamlined and reboilered.

As the German economy recovered and post-war reconstruction commenced, the West German Federal Railway (*Deutsche Bundesbahn* – DB) began to equip their locomotive fleet for post-war conditions, rebuilding many of the 01s, and all of the 01.10s and 03.10s, with all-welded boilers and combustion chambers. Also, thirty of the 1926-30-built S3/6 Bavarian

compound Pacifics were rebuilt between 1953 and 1957, with higher performance welded boilers, and reclassified 18.6. In 1956, 01.1100 was equipped for oil-burning and thirty-four of the fifty-five-strong class were similarly modified and a dozen examples remained on the Rheine-Emden-Norddeich route until 1975 as the last DB steam main line passenger engines.

The West German examples of the 03.10s were reboilered between 1956 and 1958, but remained coal-burning and were all stationed at Hagen in the Ruhr, until their mass

withdrawal in 1966. The post-war administration designed a new series of standard locomotives in the mid-1950s, but the only Pacific design, the semi-streamlined class 10, built as a three-cylinder simple locomotive by Krupp in 1956, consisted of only two prototypes before dieselisation and electrification of the main routes made the design redundant.

The Communist East German State inherited a similar number of 01, 03 and 03.10 Pacifics (although no 01.10s) and also proceeded to equip them for the post-war era.

The 03s and 03.10s received new boilers with feedwater heaters, and thirty-five of the two-cylinder 01s also received new boilers with semi-streamlining, being reclassified as 01.5s. Locomotives of all four Pacific types – 01, 01.5, 03 and 03.10 – lasted until the early 1980s, with all bar two of the 03.10s and most of the 01.5s becoming oil-fired for their last decade of operation.

All the former State railway Pacifics had been withdrawn by the early 1960s in West Germany, apart from the reboilered 18.6s which lasted until 1965 and three Maffei Pacifics kept at Minden research headquarters for testing purposes (ex-Bavarian 18.505 and Baden 18.316 and 323). The Saxon State engines 18.001-010 (apart from 18.002, destroyed during the war) lasted on the Berlin–Dresden route until the early 1960s, and one other State Pacific, Baden's 18.314, and two DR Pacifics, 03.1010 and the unique 18.201, rebuilt from a pre-war high-speed 4-6-4 tank, were housed at the Halle Research Centre.

However, both administrations allowed a series of *Plandampf* projects when diesel or electric services on secondary routes were replaced by steam engines on selected trains for two or three days for the benefit of enthusiasts. In West Germany this mainly occurred in the Rhine/Moselle area, with standard 01 Pacifics and smaller engines, but in East Germany in the 1990s there were more ambitious events on the Magdeburg–Berlin and the Bebra–Erfurt–Dresden–Görlitz corridor between the West German and Polish borders. Five former DR Pacifics were the stars for these events – 01.137, 01.531, 03.001, 03.204 and 03.1010 –

and *Plandampf* events have continued into the twenty-first century although the appearance of the Pacifics has been less frequent, except on the occasional enthusiast railtour.

A large number of German steam locomotives have been preserved, most 'plinthed' in the cities where they were built or domiciled, but German enthusiast societies have been active in establishing some excellent museums and ensuring some of these large engines are fit to run on the main line. In fact, one locomotive, 18.201, is the only steam locomotive in the world still authorised to run at a maximum of 160km/hr (100mph) and 03.1010 is allowed 140km/hr (87½mph). A few of the State railway engines existed for some time capable of

operating on the main lines, the main examples being the Baden 18.316 and the Bavarian 18.478 (as Bavarian Railways 3673), both in the former West Germany.

The following chapters will recount the history of the construction and operation of each class of German Pacific, their development and modification in East and West Germany after 1945, my personal experiences of seeing and travelling behind many of the Pacifics in both parts of Germany between 1958 and 1979 and experiencing the main line *Plandampfs* in 1993 and 1994, and finally a brief description of each Pacific that has been preserved in either museum or running condition.

Preserved three-cylinder 03.1010-2, built in 1940 as a streamlined light axleweight pacific, was de-streamlined and reboilered after the war in East Germany at Halle, converted to oil-burning in 1967, and reconverted to coal fuel after preservation, at Görlitz with D1854 to Dresden during a *Plandampf* event, 30 April 1994.
(David Maidment)

Chapter 2

GERMAN EXPRESS PASSENGER LOCOMOTIVES AT THE START OF THE TWENTIETH CENTURY

Express locomotive power at the turn of the century in Britain, France and Germany consisted of a large assortment of different classes of 4-4-0s and 4-4-2 Atlantics, with some of the more progressive companies beginning to see the 4-6-0 wheel arrangement offering more power and adhesion to cope with the fast increasing market of leisure travel by the newly affluent middle classes. Some of the leading engineers, such as Churchward and De Bousquet, were sharing ideas and looking to the United States as well, whilst many of the smaller private or local State companies were more insular and were introducing myriad designs by different builders, of varying success.

The main State railways of Germany were thriving in the century's first decade and new designs were coming forth almost every year, with the Baden State Railway leading the field with the class IVe 4-6-0 four-cylinder compound of 1894. The Bavarian, Württemberg and Saxon Railways all produced 4-6-0 designs between 1898 and 1910, with the Bavarian and Saxon Railways producing several designs, each an improvement on the earlier. The vast Prussian network relied on 4-4-0s and 4-4-2s until the first of the S10 group of 4-6-0 locomotives entered the scene in 1911.

The Baden State Railway

The Baden State Railway had contracted for a 4-6-0 as early as 1894, type IVe four-cylinder compound of the De Glehn system, similar to its French sisters, for use on the Black Forest Railway. Despite its small boiler, it seems to have been successful. However, in 1902, the firm Maffei produced the first of its powerful four-cylinder compounds that were to become the hallmark of many designs for the southern states of Germany over the following two decades. The 4-4-2, type IId, was built for the flatter stretches of the Rhine Valley and was the most powerful locomotive in Germany at the time, with boiler pressure of 227lbpsi, grate area of 41.6sqft and heating surface of 2,258sqft. With large driving wheels of 6ft 10in it was a fast runner, capable of reaching 90mph, and on a test between Offenburg and Freiburg, over a 120-yard stretch at a speed of 72½mph, recorded an output of 1,850 horsepower. It had the sleek outline with conical smokebox door and windcutter cab that became the trademark of later

Baden 4-cylinder compound IVe 4-6-0 of Bw Wilna, c1918.
(Eisenbahnstiftung Collection)

designs. However, train loads in the first decade of the new century soon outgrew the Atlantic wheel arrangement.

The Bavarian State Railway

The Bavarian State Railway produced a De Glehn 4-6-0 four-cylinder compound in 1898, class CV, similar to a Württemberg design and, at the same time, a two-cylinder saturated steam 4-4-2 built by Krauss for the Bavarian Pfalz Railway, class P3.1. In 1899, the Bavarian State Railway ordered two four-cylinder compound 4-4-2s from the Baldwin Company, delivered in 1900, to learn from American practice. In 1903 Maffei produced simultaneously a 4-4-2 S2/5 and a 4-6-0 S3/5,

both four-cylinder compounds built with bar frames using the Baldwin locomotive experience, which became standard practice for following types. The locomotives were virtually interchangeable and

only ten Atlantics were built, as loads were becoming too much for that wheel arrangement. The high

Bavarian Maffei four-cylinder compound 4-6-0 of 1899, No.2842 (later 17.326) of class CV, at the turn of the century.
(MLS Collection/Carl Bellingrodt/EK-Verlag)

Bavarian State Railway's S2/5 4-4-2, 3007 (later numbered in series 14.141-145) ready to depart from Munich Hbf, 1919. This locomotive was withdrawn in 1927. (Kallmünzer/ Eisenbahnstiftung Collection)

point of the Atlantic type was the Baden IId. In the search for more speed, in 1906 Maffei produced a unique 4-4-4 S2/6, No.3201, with 7ft 2in diameter coupled wheels, which many decreed to have been the most handsome locomotive ever produced in Germany. On test with a 150-ton train between Munich and Augsburg, it reached the speed of 154.5km/hr (96½mph) which remained the German speed record for steam traction until beaten by the streamlined 05 4-6-4 in 1936. However, the Bavarian Railway needed to combine the speed potential of this machine with the haulage capacity of its 4-6-0 S3/5s.

The Bavarian State Railway imported a couple of American Baldwin bar-framed 4-4-2s at the turn of the century which influenced the railway's Pacifics later, as bar frames became their standard. Here is the second of the pair, 2399, later renumbered 14.132, at Munich Hbf, 1910. (Eisenbahnstiftung Collection)

Bavarian S3/5 four-cylinder compound 4-6-0 17.419 of 1903, with saturated steam, at Lindau Depot, c1925. (MLS Collection/Carl Bellingrodt/EK-Verlag)

The Württemberg State Railway

The Württemberg Railway also procured a De Glehn 4-6-0 four-cylinder compound from Esslingen Works in 1898, especially for the hilly parts of its system. It was classified type 'D', and was capable of hauling 250 tons up a gradient of 1 in 100 at 37½mph. The large low-pressure cylinders of 23.6in diameter could no longer be contained within the frames and were placed outside. For main line work in less hilly parts of the system, the Railway still relied on the 4-4-0 wheel arrangement, the class AD two-cylinder compound of 1899 and ADh two-cylinder simple superheated version of 1907. This was the last 4-4-0 built in Germany.

Württemberg ADh 4-4-0 of 1907 as DRG 13.1711, was used for express services outside the most mountainous areas, but was inadequate for the loads and was soon superseded by the 1909-built class 'C' Pacifics. (MLS Collection/Carl Bellingrodt/EK-Verlag)

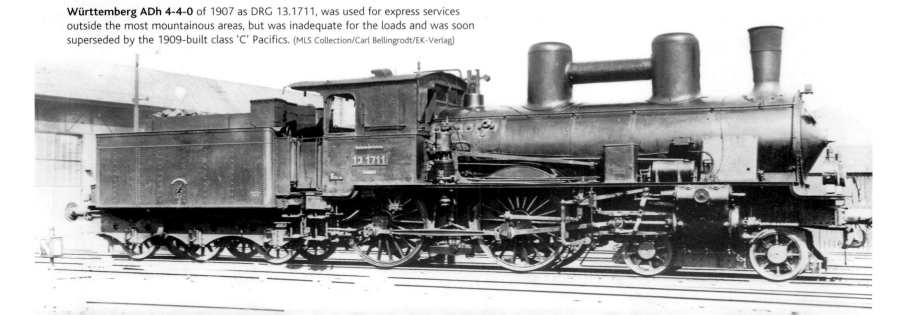

A Württemberg State Railway two-cylinder compound class D 4-6-0, used on the steep gradients of the State Railway's main lines in south-west Germany in the Stuttgart area, prior to the introduction of the Class 'C' Pacifics (18.1) and the later influx of former Prussian P10 2-8-2s, c1914. 428 was built at Esslingen in 1901 and later became DR 38.105. (MLS Collection)

422, a Württemberg Class D 4-6-0, heading D59, a Strasbourg–Munich express, at Esslingen (the site of the R ailway's main workshop), 1910. (Eisenbahnstiftung Collection)

The Saxon State Railway

The Saxon State Railway struggled to find suitable engines for its mountainous terrain, and, impressed by the French De Glehn compound Atlantic exhibited at the Paris World Exhibition in 1900, ordered a similar design from Hartmann, the Saxon XV type (DRG 14.2 class), delivered the same year. It was, with the Baden engines, the first to adopt the 'windcutter' cab. The main change from the De Glehn practice was the Joy valve gear to the inside cylinders. However, the engine was a disappointment and fell short of the French locomotives in performance. The fifteen engines had all been withdrawn by the 1920s.

A group of new designs emerged in quick succession from Hartmann between 1906 and 1909. A 4-6-0, XII H (DRG 17.6), a four-cylinder superheated simple engine with 6ft 3in coupled wheels, 170lbpsi boiler pressure, 16.9in x 24.8in diameter cylinders and 16.4 ton axleload was better than the XVs, but still not satisfactory; a compound version with higher boiler pressure, 213lbpsi, appeared a year later in 1907. Forty-two locomotives of this type XII HV (DRG 17.7) were built and lasted into the 1930s. Whilst these engines were suitable for the areas with severe gradients, the Saxon State Railway ordered an Atlantic 4-4-2 two-cylinder superheated simple engine from Hartmann, delivered in 1909 as class XH1 (DRG 14.3). Boiler pressure was down to 170psi again, but with two 20in x 24.8in diameter cylinders and 6ft 6in diameter coupled wheels, it was capable of hauling 440 tonnes on the level at 100km/hr (62mph). Eighteen of these locomotives, the last Atlantics in Germany, were built and all had been scrapped by 1930. A similar 4-6-0 version with 6ft 2in coupled wheels was built in the same year, class XII H1 (DRG 17.8). These seven locomotives with 24in x 24.8in diameter cylinders were the last Saxon design before the Pacific in 1917 and four survived to be part of the DRG fleet.

DRG 14.315, former Saxon XH1 1909 Hartmann-built two-cylinder 4-4-2, the last Atlantic built in Germany c1925.
(MLS Collection/Carl Bellingrodt/ EK-Verlag)

Saxon XII H four-cylinder compound 4-6-0, 17.604, built in 1906 and withdrawn by the 1920s, here seen partly dismantled after withdrawal.
(MLS Collection/Carl Bellingrodt/EK-Verlag)

Saxon 4-6-0 17.717 (formerly XII HV-31) built 1912, withdrawn December 1933, photographed in May 1932.
(MLS Collection/Carl Bellingrodt/EK-Verlag)

The Prussian State Railway

The Prussian State Railway was still introducing 4-4-0s in 1902; the S4 built by Borsig with high superheat. Prussian locomotive developments were being hindered by rivalry and bad feeling between their great engineers, von Borries and Garbe, particularly over the issue of superheat. Von Borries had locomotives built by Hanomag in Hanover, whereas Garbe would not countenance locomotives built outside Prussia. Thus Garbe's S5 4-4-0 was a saturated simple steam locomotive, but the von Borries S7 4-4-2 built by Hanomag in 1902 was a four-cylinder compound. Although smaller than the Baden IId Atlantic, its performance was excellent, capable of moving 318 tons on the level between Berlin and Hanover at 67½mph, and reaching 89mph on test. A similar machine with the De Glehn system was built at Grafenstaden in 1903, also receiving the S7 class name.

Then, belatedly, the S6 introduced in 1906 was the last and largest 4-4-0 built in Germany. Unlike the Württemberg ADh, the Prussian engine had 6ft 10in coupled wheels and was of altogether heavier construction – at 17-ton axleload it was the heaviest 4-4-0 on the continent. The machine could pull 600 tons on the level at 50mph, but within a year the Prussian Railway developed the most powerful Atlantic 4-4-2 of all for its flat main lines in northern Germany. The S9 was an unsuperheated four-cylinder compound machine and was undoubtedly the best of the Prussian express engines of its time. The grate area was 43sqft, had a heating surface of 2,462sqft and could haul 570 tons on the level at 62mph. Two examples, built later with superheater and feedwater heater, were the most economical locomotives of their period. However, disaster struck these locomotives when 96 of the 99 engines were taken from Germany under the Versailles Treaty in 1919 and the remaining three examples were soon withdrawn.

When the minds of the other

Saxon XII H1 2-cylinder 4-6-0, No.17, (later 17.803) in the last days before the take-over by the DRG, c1922.
(MLS Collection/Carl Bellingrodt/EK-Verlag)

Prussian four-cylinder compound 915 *Hannover*, of the S9 class, built for fast work over the level plains of the Prussian main lines in the north, later DRG 14.036, one of the few to remain in Germany when most of the class became war reparations to the First World War victors, 1920. (MLS Collection/R Kreutzer)

State Railways turned to the Pacific locomotive to solve the increasing load/speed problems of the first decade of the century, the Prussian Railways moved only to the 4-6-0 wheel arrangement with the S10 series of locomotives. Von Borries had died and Garbe had departed, and the new technical director was Lübcken who, whilst a capable engineer, had the isolationist Prussian mentality. He, however, developed three different varieties of 4-6-0 for express service. A four-cylinder superheated 4-6-0 S10.0 (DR 17.0) was built by Schwartzkopff in 1910. It had von Borries valve gear, and combined bar-(front) and plate frames. The boiler was developed from the Prussian P8 at 199lbpsi, with coupled wheels of 6ft 6in, and four cylinders of 16.9in x 24.8in. Maximum authorised speed was 110km/hr (69mph) and calculated

horsepower available was 1,500. However, it was heavy on fuel compared with the compound Pacifics in southern Germany. The last example was scrapped in 1948, apart from 17.008 which was retained for the national museum.

In 1911, Lübcken produced a four-cylinder compound on the De Glehn principle, the S10.1 (DRG 17.10) built by Henschel, which was at last successful. It had coupled wheels of 6ft 6in diameter, inside cylinders of 15.8in x 26in, low-pressure outside cylinders 24in x 26in and boiler pressure of 213lbpsi, and a maximum authorised speed of 110km/hr. However, the engine was heavy and at the limit of the permitted 17-ton axleload (in fact over it at 17.8 tons), and was therefore not fitted with a feedwater heater. A second series was built by Henschel, again in 1914, and

ultimately 264 were built in addition to the 202 S10.0s. The last in normal traffic was withdrawn in 1952, but experiments with pulverised fuel (17.1055) and a condensing steam system (17.1119) lasted until 1968. 17.1055 was preserved and restored in Prussian dark green lined livery for display at the Dresden Altstadt Museum.

Finally, a superheated three-cylinder simple version of the S10 was built in 1914, the S10.2 (DRG 17.2). It had 6ft 6in coupled wheels, the same as the other S10s, a 199lbpsi boiler and three 19.7in x 24.8in cylinders. Not as powerful as the S10.1, it rode as well as the compound machine, but was not as economical. The locomotives could haul 450 tonnes on the level at 62mph and 400 tonnes up a 1 in 100 gradient at 31mph. It showed some superiority over the S9 when

the track was undulating rather than flat throughout. 127 of these S10.2 machines were built, making 593 S10s in total. However, the 1918 Armistice forced 153 of the S10 machines to be sacrificed to the war victors, although after the fall of France in 1940, a number were reclaimed.

Prussian Railway four-cylinder 'simple' S10.0, 17.024 (Bw Osnabrück), working international express FFD 211 Hook of Holland–Hamburg, 1928. (Werner Hubert/Eisenbahnstiftung Collection)

Prussian 4-cylinder simple 4-6-0 No.1006 (later 17.007) shortly after construction, c1912. 17.007 was withdrawn from service in 1933. (MLS Collection)

17.1016, Bw Stargard, a Prussian Railway S10.1 4-cylinder compound 4-6-0, built in 1911, at Berlin Stettiner Bhf on a train for Stralsund, 1931. (Hermann Otte/ Eisenbahnstiftung Collection)

17.1026, a four-cylinder compound S10.1, hauling E168, Stralsund–Stettin, near Düsterförde in Mecklenburg, 23 August 1934. (Carl Bellingrodt/Eisenbahnstiftung Collection)

S10.1 four-cylinder
compound 4-6-0 17.1089
in Hanover with express
D1, Cologne–Berlin, 1929.
(R Kreutzer/ Eisenbahnstiftung
Collection)

17.203, a Prussian three-cylinder simple 4-6-0, built 1914, seen
here c1925. 17.203 was stored at the end of the Second World
War and withdrawn without being repaired in September 1948.
(MLS Collection/Carl Bellingrodt/EK Verlag)

17.258, a Prussian three-cylinder simple S10.2 4-6-0 in passenger service, c1930. 17.258 was one of the many S10s stored in damaged condition after the war and withdrawn in September 1948, although it had not turned a wheel for several years. (MLS Collection/Photomatic)

Prussian Railways three-cylinder simple S10.2 17.219, at speed on D47 near Boppard travelling north towards Koblenz. Carl Bellingrodt's first wife is standing by the fence beside the locomotive, 9 May 1931. (Carl Bellingrodt/Eisenbahnstiftung Collection)

Preserved Locomotives
17.008
The S10s were four-cylinder 4-6-0s built by the Prussian Railways. 17.008 was built by Schwartzkopff in 1911 and is sectioned in the Deutsches Technik Museum (German Technical Museum), Berlin.

17.1055 (Prussian Railways 4-6-0, 1135)
A subsequent set of four-cylinder 4-6-0s were built between 1911 and 1916 as compound machines. 17.1055, previously Prussian 1135, was built in 1913 and is currently displayed in Prussian dark green lined livery as 1135 in the Verkehrs

Museum (Transport Museum), Dresden Altstadt. 17.1055 outlived most of its sisters still at work post-war in the DDR, and was used as a test bed for burning pulverised fuel, being converted between 1949 and 1951, and withdrawn from regular service in January 1963.

Other State Express Locomotives at the turn of the century

Already mentioned are some Atlantic P3.1s built for the Pfalz Railway, but this came under the Bavarian State Railway. Similarly, the Lübeck-Buchen Railway owned a number of S10s of Prussian design. The only other notable express engine in Germany of this period was the Oldenburg State Railway 2-6-2, also described as class S10 (DRG 16.0). However, this was built much later by Hanomag in 1917, constructed to replace the Prussian P4 4-4-0s and S5 4-4-2s which had been their previous passenger locomotive fleet. They had two 22.8in x 24.8in cylinders, 6ft 6in coupled wheels, and a 199lbpsi boiler, but were restricted to 100km/hr (62mph). Only three locomotives were built and, although they were capable of hauling 300 tons on the level at 62mph and 520 tons on 1 in 100 at 19mph, they were really a luxury that this small state railway could not afford. After only a ten-year life, they were cut up in 1926.

The four-cylinder S10 17.008, that was withdrawn in 1935, and later preserved and sectioned in the Berlin Technical Museum. (MLS Collection/Carl Bellingrodt/EK-Verlag)

Prussian four-cylinder compound S10.1 No.1135 (later 17.1055), built in 1913 to the 1911 design, restored to Prussian dark green lined livery, at Dresden Altstadt Railway Museum. (MLS Collection)

Chapter 3

THE BADEN PACIFICS – THE IV f&h (18.2 & 18.3)

The Baden IV f Pacifics, DR 18.2

Maffei's Chief Engineer, Anton Hammel, was the first German to propose a further enlargement to the 4-6-2 Pacific layout as early as 1905. The Baden Railway had still nothing more powerful than a fleet of 1894 De Glehn compound 4-6-0s for the heavily-graded Black Forest route and Maffei 4-4-2 IId express passenger locomotives for the Mannheim–Basle Rhine Valley line and as train weights increased in the latter years of the decade before the First World War, their engineers looked to Maffei to develop a locomotive to meet both needs. In 1907, three four-cylinder compound

Baden IV f locomotives appeared on the scene, numbered 751-753, just after the Paris-Orleans (PO) Pacific No.4500, the first in Europe, and beating the Great Western Railway of Britain's first 4-6-2, *The Great Bear*, by only a few months.

They combined American and German practice, having 4in-thick bar frames and the Pacific wheel arrangement, the trailing wheels under a wide firebox, with the German-originated von Borries four-cylinder compound system. Because the Baden network included main lines in the heavily-graded Odenwald and Schwarzwald regions, as well as the flat Rhine Valley, they were equipped with 6ft 1½in-diameter driving wheels,

a decision that was later regretted as they proved unsuitable for the fast Rhine Valley services. Boiler pressure was 227psi, grate area, 48.4sqft, a total heating surface of 2,244sqft and superheater capacity of 538sqft. Inside-cylinder dimensions were 16.7in x 24in stroke and outside 25.6in x 26.4in. Maximum axle load was 16.7 tons and the total locomotive weight in service was 88.3 tons (excluding tender). A further thirty-two locomotives of this type, numbered 754–765 and 833–852, were delivered to the Baden Railways up to the year 1913, all the later ones constructed under licence by the Maschinenbau-Gesellschaft (Machine-building Company) of Karlsruhe.

The first German Pacific type, the Baden IV f of 1907, No.763 (later 18.216) in Works Grey, of the second batch built in 1910. 18.216 was one of the last survivors of this prematurely withdrawn class, being taken out of service in 1927. (MLS Collection/Carl Bellingrodt/EK-Verlag)

IVf 757 (later 18.214) in steam at Karlsruhe shortly after delivery in 1909, withdrawn in the mid-1920s. (Eisenbahnstiftung Collection)

Their maximum speed was stipulated as 100km/hr (62mph), although on a successful test in 1907 they proved capable of hauling 460 tons on the level at 69mph and 194 tonnes up a gradient of 1 in 61 at a sustained 34mph. They were powerful engines with the high boiler pressure and small wheels, capable of exerting 1,850 horsepower, but the use of the locomotives on D-Züge on the Basle–Offenburg–Mannheim trunk route caused many problems with overheating and damaged motion and failures, and their test results were not reproduced in everyday running. In 1914, twenty-six of these machines were based at Offenburg and nine at Karlsruhe. The decline in maintenance standards during the First World War, shortage of

materials and the despatch of over 5,000 German locomotives to the victors as war reparations created further problems, and the Pacifics needed assistant engines to help the heavy trains out of Basle, Offenburg and Mannheim stations, and double-heading on heavy international trains on the trunk route became the norm.

In the mid-1920s, the Prussian P8s, then being built in large numbers, took on the working of trains over the Offenburg–Konstanz Black Forest Railway, and the building of twenty IV h Baden Pacifics between 1918 and 1920 for the Rhine Valley route led to their withdrawal.

The *Deutsche Reichsbahn* took

Micro Feinmechanik model of Baden IVf Pacific 847 (later 18.253) built in 1913. (Badische Eisenbahn)

A works photograph of Baden Pacific IV h 95 in delivery condition in 1918, taken by the J.A. Maffei Company.
(DB Museum Nuremberg/J.A. Maffei)

An official photo of No.95 (later 18.303) on delivery from the Maffei Works at Munich-Hirschau.
(Krauss-Maffei/Siemens AG)

over all thirty-five locomotives in 1920, but by 1925 just twenty-two of these machines were still in traffic, reclassified as DRG class 18.2, the remaining locomotives being numbered 18.201, 211-217, 231-238 and 251-256. The frequent damage to the valve gear, excessive repair costs and a reputation for poor steaming led to their early demise, just twelve remaining at the end of 1925, eight in December 1926 and the last four were withdrawn by the end of 1927. None were preserved.

The Baden IV h Pacifics, DR 18.3

The Baden State Railway commissioned the building of twenty locomotives of a much improved version, identified originally as class IV h, for higher speed running over the level main-line of the Upper Rhine Valley from the Swiss border at Basle as far as Offenburg, at the edge of the Black Forest, and onto Mannheim or Karlsruhe. The IV f was the last Baden engine intended for use on both the level high-speed line and the mountainous gradients between Offenburg and Konstanz, which in fact had suited neither. Although planned and ordered in 1915, because of late changes in the design specification and the post-war shortage of materials, the prototype IV h was not constructed until June 1918. The production

locomotives were built in three batches between 1918 and 1920, and were authorised initially to run up to a maximum of only 110km/hr (69mph) because of restricted braking capacity – later after brake-strengthening, raised to 140km/hr (87½mph), the only German locomotive type permitted to run at this speed until the early 1930s.

They were four-cylinder compounds like the earlier 18.2s, but many other dimensions were enlarged. The driving wheels were 6ft 11in in diameter, boiler pressure was slightly reduced to 213lbpsi, but the grate area was increased to 53.2sqft and the total heating surface had risen to 2,377sqft with a

18.302 on an RAW Offenburg-organised test of its newly-fitted electric headlamps at Emmendingen in 1928. This locomotive was destroyed in an accident at Klecken in January 1942, 31 March 1928. (Eisenbahnstiftung Collection)

superheater capacity of 880sqft. The inside cylinders were 17.3in x 26.8in and the outside cylinders 27in x 27in. Unlike the earlier IV f Pacifics, the high-pressure inside cylinders drove the front coupled axle and the low-pressure cylinders, the second coupled axle. The bar frames were similar, 4in thick. The axle-load was now much heavier at 17.9 tons (increased axle-loadings had been authorised) and the total locomotive weight in service (minus tender) was 97 tons. The tender had an unusually short wheelbase to fit the Baden Railway 20-metre turntables with water capacity of 6,500 gallons and 9 tons of coal. Total weight in service was, therefore, 160 tons.

Imposing rather than elegant, they were powerful locomotives, designed to achieve 1,950hp, capable of hauling 650 tons on the level at 62mph, and were successful

18.326 at its home depot, Koblenz-Moselle, in the 1930s. This locomotive was destroyed by bombs in the Second World War, being condemned and scrapped in 1944. (MLS/Carl Bellingrodt/EK-Verlag)

Portrait of Baden IV h Pacific 18.319 as built, and running between Mannheim, Offenburg and Basle in the 1920s.
(MLS/Carl Bellingrodt/EK-Verlag)

18.324 in the shed at Offenburg, 1932.
(Gerhard Gress Collection)

18.318 in original condition in the immediate post-war period, at Soltau, 20 April 1946. These locomotives had been based at nearby Bremen when displaced by the 01 Pacifics on their former Baden main line work and were stored in the area before withdrawal of the majority in 1948.
(MLS Collection)

on the road, particularly on the main line from Mannheim down to Basle where their high-speed capability could be exploited. They could also, on test, haul the same 650ton load up a 1 in 186 gradient at a sustained 44mph, eighty tons more than the later 03 standard Pacific could haul on a 1 in 200 gradient. However, on shed they had drawbacks, access to the motion and valve gear being particularly difficult, especially the inside motion which required the skill of only the slimmest of fitters to maintain. They were also tricky engines to drive, with their complex compound system; only their regular drivers could get the best out of them and in general traffic their fuel consumption was higher than the later standard two-cylinder Pacifics.

The first locomotives entering service were numbered 49, 64 and 95, and later ones 1000–1016, and were initially based at Offenburg, and worked express services on the main line between Basle and Frankfurt (Main). All the locomotives passed to DRG ownership, becoming 18.301-303, 18.311-319 and 18.321-328 (the latter group being built with the DRG numbers adopted after 1920). 18.302 was involved in an accident in 1942, and 18.326 was bomb-damaged and withdrawn during the Second World War. The other locomotives were withdrawn in

1948, apart from three retained at the Minden Test Centre and one at the East German Research Centre at Halle. Two of these locomotives, 18.316 and 323 remained at Minden until withdrawn in 1969, but were retained subsequently for special working and preservation.

Meanwhile, 18.314, after initial working in the Stendal area, moved to Halle and was equipped with the tender from Pacific 07.1001 (the former SNCF Pacific 231E 18). It was then utilised for high-speed tests, similar to those of its West German sisters, and authorised for 140km/hr (87½mph). In 1958 it went into the Zwickau Works and was rebuilt by the DR authorities

with a new enlarged boiler (of the modernised type fitted to the P10s-class 39, the modified engines being reclassified as class 22), a larger smokebox, 'Caledonian'-style chimney, 'witte' smoke deflectors, larger sandboxes, counter-pressure brakes and a standard large tender holding 10 tons of coal and 7,500 gallons of water.

Some dimensions were modified during the rebuilding, the new boiler having 227lbpsi, the outside low-pressure cylinders being lined up to 21.7in diameter, the grate area reduced to 45.5sqft and heating surface to 2,145sqft. It emerged in 1960, part-streamlined, painted in a striking livery of green

with white horizontal stripes and the authorised speed raised to 150km/hr (94mph). Its weight was increased to 105 tons. In 1967 it was equipped for oil-firing (capacity 3,000 gallons of fuel) and undertook tests between Halle and Berlin and Halle and Saalfeld. It was withdrawn in 1971 and retained for preservation.

Operation

Their main sphere of activity was on the Baden State Railway's key route from Basle to Offenburg and Mannheim over which many international expresses ran. From their construction until the late 1920s they regularly took over the

18.323 as modified with counter-pressure brakes for testing of rolling stock at Minden Research Centre, 23 August 1967. (MLS Collection/J.Davenport)

The Minden Research 18.3 with extended smokebox, 18.316, at Osnabrück, 8 April 1963. (MLS Collection/A.C.Gilbert)

18.316, at Minden Research Centre, photographed during the stop of a railtour hauled by sister locomotive 18.323. 18.316 differs by having an extended smokebox. It was also preserved and used on railtours for a few years before being retired and displayed at the Technoseum (Mannheim), 14 October 1967. (Helmut Dahlhaus)

Minden research engine 18.316, with extended smokebox, leaving Hagen with a test train, May 1967. (HD Kremer/Eisenbahnstiftung Collection)

running of the *Rheingold* prestige service between Mannheim and Basle, exchanging locomotives at Mannheim with the Bavarian S3/6 class which operated the service to and from the Dutch border. They were noted on special occasions achieving speeds nearing that of the famous unique Bavarian S2/6 4-4-4 No.3201, which held the German speed record at that time of 96mph. They also operated the *Orient Express* between Frankfurt and Basle, and a number of other prestige international services including L19/20 *Riviera-Neapel Express*, L91/92 *Skandinavien–Schweiz Express* and FD 5/6 Basle–Berlin, FD 163/4 Holland–Geneva and FD 191/2 Italy–Mannheim–Hamburg–

18.316 at Baden-Oos with the *Rheingold* (FD 101), composed of six Pullman cars and Baden Railway luggage van, c1929. The Baden Pacifics operated the *Rheingold* between Basle and Mannheim, the Bavarian S3/6 between Mannheim and the Dutch border at that time.
(Carl Bellingrodt/ Eisenbahnstiftung Collection)

Berlin over the Upper Rhine Valley section. Average speeds over the 40-mile section between Mannheim and Karlsruhe varied from 45mph with the 600-ton D4 to 50mph on the 430-ton *Rheingold*. However, speeds rarely in everyday practice exceeded 62mph because of line speed restrictions and signalling/braking distances until their braking system was strengthened.

Annual mileages of these engines ranged from 30,000 to 35,000, but by the 1930s this had significantly increased to 50-60,000, with 18.302 averaging 6,400 miles a month and 18.314 7,200 miles a month in 1929-30. However, in April/May 1930, their main activity over this route was taken over by 01 standard Pacifics, of which a batch was allocated to Offenburg (01.077-81), with many of the 18.3s being transferred further north. Most of the Offenburg-allocated locomotives were sent to Darmstadt and Koblenz in 1933, Hamburg in 1934 and Bremen in 1935. The actual allocation in 1935 was:

Darmstadt: 18.311, 18.317 (to Hamburg 1934), 18.321.
Koblenz: 18.312-18.316, 18.318, 18.319, 18.323-18.326, 18.328.
Bremen: 18.301-18.303, 18.311 from 3/1935, 18.322.
Hamburg Altona: 18.317, 18.327.

Offenburg lost its last 18.3 Pacifics in May 1935 (18.303), September (18.301) and November (18.302). The Koblenz-allocated locomotives replaced that depot's three-cylinder class 17.2 former Prussian 4-6-0s.

In the summer of 1933, after the authorised speed was raised, 18.328 on test hauling 250 tons reached a speed of 97mph, the fastest speed achieved by a former State railway locomotive, just beating the previous record. At Koblenz, one of their duties included acting as standby for the *Rheingold*, as well as Saarbrücken–Frankfurt services. Those sent to Bremen were mainly used on secondary services on the flat northern plains and took over a number of diagrams previously operated by 03 standard Pacifics. The two Hamburg Pacifics,

supplemented by 18.312 and 313 transferred from Koblenz, replaced the four-cylinder compound S10.1s on special services to Cuxhaven as well as regular services to Westerland, Flensburg, Kiel and Berlin.

Some data available on the comparative economics of the 18.3s shows a surprising advantage over the newly-delivered 01s. On the Upper Rhine section between 1930 and 1933, the 18.3s' repairs between L4 major works visits cost on average some 200 to 220 RMs per 1,000kms (650 miles), although there were wide variations, with 18.303 costing 306 RMs and the exceptional 18.324 only 123 RMs per 1,000kms. 01.077 and 01.078 between 1930 and 1936 averaged 232 RMs for the same distance. And coal consumption was some 10% lower on these longer runs, though the figures would have reversed in later years when the 18.3s performed more varied work and war conditions reduced the quality of maintenance.

In 1939, five IV h Pacifics were allocated to Bremen (18.301-303, 311 and 322), but in 1942 all the Koblenz and Hamburg engines of the class were transferred there, replacing six 03s and five 17.10 4-6-0s. The Bremen-based Pacifics covered a wide range of work – local passenger and freight as well as D- and E-trains. Their monthly mileage ranged from around 6-8,000, although this reduced towards the end of the war as track and locomotives were bomb damaged; by 1947 all were in store, apart from 18.314. 18.302 was out of action for over a year in 1942-3 because of its involvement in

an accident – a head-on collision with 03.259. The 03s had been struggling in wartime conditions with heavy trains between Bremen and Hamburg, often running short of steam, and the twenty-five-year-old State Pacifics, once the staff became used to them, were an improvement and became, despite the difficulty of maintaining them on shed, well liked. The Bremen crews nicknamed them the '*Maffeis*'. After major overhauls in 1943-4 for most of the 18.3s, their reliability and performance left the 03s in the shade. One example recorded was with a late-running heavy E143 from Halberstadt which a Bremen engine took over in Hanover. With the same load, crew and weather, Bremen's 03.109 recovered six minutes, but 18.322, fifteen! War damage to water supplies in Bremen in August 1944 led to untreated hard water being used, and an increase in boiler damage and failures.

In 1945 all the locomotives – bar 18.326, which was destroyed in an attack on Bremen Hbf in the autumn of 1944, and 18.314 , which was exchanged with the East German DR's 18.434 – were retained by the West German *Bundesbahn* (Federal Railway). A few struggled on in 1945 and 1946, 18.314 and 315 both exceeding 20,000 miles in a twelve-month period. However, all were redundant after the war, when they were in poor condition from wartime damage and neglect, and were stored at Soltau, Buchholz and Flensburg, pending a decision on whether they should be repaired. Eventually they were deemed

18.317 arrives in Mannheim from Basle with the northbound FFD 101 *Rheingold* where it will exchange engines with a high-wheeled Bavarian S3/6 for the onward run along the Rhine Valley to Cologne and the Dutch border, 15 May 1930.
(DLA Darmstadt/Maey/ Eisenbahnstuiftung Collection)

18.316, a Koblenz-based locomotive, heads a stopping train (P1290) on the left bank of the Rhine at Oberwesel, 17 April 1938.
(Carl Bellingrodt/ Eisenbahnstiftung Collection)

too small and complex a class for modernisation for post-war conditions, and in 1948 all the West German ones were withdrawn from service. The star – 18.314 – exceeded 3 million kilometres (1.9 million miles) in its active life, including its transfer to the Soviet Zone and test work at Halle, and five more exceeded 2 million kilometres (1.25 million miles) including the three that were retained at Minden. 18.322 and 18.324 were the two that reached this figure despite

withdrawal in 1948. There was the possibility of a brief respite in 1950 as train mileage increased and a number of older State Pacifics were considered for repair, but only some Württemberg 18.1s were reprieved, and the 17.10s, 18.3s and the older Bavarian S3/6s were scrapped in 1951 and 1952.

However, locomotives capable of high speed were required at the Göttingen Research and Test Centre, and three of the locomotives were subsequently

reprieved – 18.316, 319 and 323. Initially the Centre had acquired a three-cylinder 01.10, 01.1056, but at the continuous high speed demanded by some of the tests, it failed frequently with overheating of the inside motion. High-wheeled S3/6 18.451 was commandeered from Augsburg in 1950 and then the decision was made to repair the three IV h Pacifics. 18.319 received a boiler with an extended smokebox (which was transferred to 18.316 when the former was withdrawn)

and a few defects were repaired, and the three locomotives were transferred to the jurisdiction of the Minden Test Centre, where they were fitted with counter-pressure brakes and authorised for speeds of 165km/hr (103mph). In 1951 18.451 was utilised on a test with an FD train right through from Hamburg Altona to Freilassing, a distance of 616 miles, a German long-distance record for a single locomotive performance, stopping only to take water and more coal. The four compound Pacifics, with 18.505 replacing 18.451, worked on test trains all over Germany, from Minden to Freiburg and

Saarbrucken in the south, to Bebra, Kiel and Lübeck in the north. In 1956, on test with new electric multiple units between Kufstein and Wörgl, 18.316 achieved 101mph, breaking the record previously held by the class and their power, exerting up to 2,000 PS counter pressure, was utilised in testing the new-build DB Pacific, 10.001. They were required in the mid-1950s to test the rebuilt 01.10s and the new diesel V200s.

In 1957, a review of the Minden requirements was made, with the initial intent of replacing the 18.3s, but the assessment found in favour of their continued use. Their

2100mm-diameter driving wheels, the reliability of the four-cylinder compound valve gear and motion, their smooth riding characteristic at speed and their large grate area, enabling them to maintain steam over long distances,, gave them advantages over the alternatives considered – the two-cylinder 01s and 03s were restricted to 120 or 130km/hr and rode roughly at speed in comparison, the three cylinder 01.10s and 03.10s suffered frequent overheating of the inside motion at sustained high speed, and the Bavarian S3/6s, whilst as economical and reliable as the 18.3s, had a maximum speed of 120km/hr.

18.316 (Bw Koblenz) on the 11.16am Koblenz–Wiesbaden (P1006) on the right bank of the Rhine near Kaub, 1938. (Carl Bellingrodt/ Eisenbahnstiftung Collection)

Only the three destreamlined 4-6-4 class 05s could match or better the 18.3s, but there was a shortage of spare parts for these three engines and they were withdrawn by 1958.

Throughout the 1950s, with many new engines requiring testing, the three 18.3s were clocking up between 20,000 and 35,000 miles a year. After completion of new steam locomotive building in 1959, a further review of requirements was undertaken and, in 1963, the need for five test locomotives at Minden was confirmed to test the new traction and rolling stock. Coal-fired 01.10s were considered for the role, but the expense of fitting them with the Riggenbach counter-pressure brakes and the

need of the traffic department for the 01.10s as traffic grew and further electrification was slower than anticipated, led to a decision to overhaul the 18.3s once more. 18.319 suffered a major failure to its inside cylinder and was withdrawn in July 1963; it was then used for spare parts to keep the other two 18.3 Pacifics in use. Coal-fired 01.1090 replaced 18.319, but 18.316 and 323 survived at the Test Centre along with 18.505 until 1969 when they were withdrawn and used on railtours and other special trains before final preservation.

The other extant Baden Pacific, 18.314, was the last in normal traffic operation in March 1948. The DR in the east had no suitable

locomotive for their high-speed tests and exchanged the only S3/6 in their territory, 18.434, for 18.314 which, after initial operation at Stendal, moved to Halle and was coupled with the large SNCF tender from 231E 18 (07.1001). 18.314 was regularly used for tests throughout the 1950s and was putting up annual mileages ranging from 15,000 to 45,000. New 100mph rolling stock and 87mph locomotives needed higher-speed test locomotives, and 18.314 was reconstructed in 1960 with a Reko-boiler; improved axle-loading; a standard 2′ 2′ T34 tender; a rebuilt cab and semi-streamlining, and authorised for 150km/hr (94mph) running. With the rebuilt 18.201 reconstructed from

18.323 of Minden Research & Testing Station, on a test train at Löhne, 23 August 1967. (MLS Collection/J.Davenport)

18.323, while still a Minden Research Centre engine, at Löhne with a DGEG railtour special train, 14 October 1967.
(Helmut Dahlhaus)

the high-speed tank engine, 61.002, for test work also, 18.314 was itself running up to a maximum of 50,000 miles annually (180,000 miles over a seven-year period) on test trains, and regular passenger diagrams between Halle and Berlin from 1961 to 1967, when it was converted to oil-burning. Its boiler life was extended beyond its limit of January 1972, but it was then withdrawn and utilised on special trains before a surprising purchase in the west in 1983 and transfer in 1986 to the Auto-Technik Museum in Sinsheim. It had run 3,045,555 kilometres (1.9m miles) in its life, 359,762 (224,850 miles) of them during its residence as test locomotive at Halle.

The Preserved Locomotives: 18.314

18.314 was a Baden Railway IVh built in 1919. It was exchanged with the sole Bavarian compound Pacific, 18.434, that had remained in the east after the war when that was withdrawn from traffic in 1948. 18.314 was subsequently rebuilt by the DR authorities in 1960 with increased boiler pressure of 227lbpsi, reduced grate area and heating surface, increased axle-load of 18.5 tons and total engine weight of 105 tons. It was semi-streamlined and was authorised for 150km/hr (94mph) maximum speed. It was stationed at the Halle Research Centre and was one of the handful

of locomotives used for testing new rolling stock. Renumbered by the DR as 02.0314-1, it was withdrawn in 1971, and sold in 1984 to the Verein Historische Eisenbahn Frankfurt (Railway Historical Society of Frankfurt) and subsequently displayed, under cover in the Auto & Technikmuseum Sinsheim in West Germany.

18.316, 18.323

Three remaining four-cylinder compound Baden Pacifics, 18.316, 319 and 323, were retained at the Minden Testing and Research Depot after the Second World War. 18.319 was withdrawn in 1963, but 18.316 and 323 were

The Baden four-cylinder compound coal-burning Pacific, 18.314 (02.0314-1), rebuilt by the DR in the 1950s for use at the Halle Research & Testing Station, at Halle c1960. (MLS Collection)

Preserved Baden four-cylinder compound Pacific 18.314, as rebuilt by the East German DR for use at Halle Research & Test Centre, and converted in the late 1960s to oil-burning, in Saalfeld, September 1969. It is now preserved and in the Auto & Technikmuseum, Sinsheim, in West Germany. (Eisenbahnstiftung Collection)

retained after their useful life at the testing station was over in 1969 and both were preserved. 18.316 (018.316-0) was initially displayed in the 'Potts Park' at Dützen, near Minden, then at the Landesmuseum für Technik & Arbeit, Mannheim (State Museum for Technology & Work). After twenty years in the open it was restored for active operation, and operated special trains between 1995 and 2002, but was eventually returned in 2007 to its museum place. 18.323 (018.323-6) was also used on railtours for a few years after preservation and is now part of the national German Railway Museum collection, based at Offenburg and displayed outside the Technical High School.

18.316, with extended smokebox, powers a railtour at Oberkatzau, 17 May 1996.
(Roger Bastin)

Chapter 4

THE WÜRTTEMBERG 'C' (18.1)

Design & construction

The exact history of the development of the first Württemberg Pacific is lost in documents destroyed or missing over the years, but the German State railways in the south were leading the way in seeing a Pacific locomotive as fulfilling their needs for a more powerful locomotive to deal with increasing traffic levels. The Baden State Railway had produced their IV f in 1907 and the Bavarian Railway their famous S3/6 in June 1908, leaving the Württemberg Railway in between with its well-known and challenging *'Geislinger Steige'* on the mainline from Stuttgart to Ulm. There was without doubt co-operation of the railway's headquarters engineers with the chief engineers of the Esslingen Works, with contacts each week in the railway company's offices in Stuttgart about the new construction taking place.

The Württemberg Railway Inspector Dauner described the new locomotive in the newspaper of the Society of German Engineers in December 1909 thus:

'As a result of ever-increasing loads in the express passenger service, the Company's Board decided to create a locomotive class capable of hauling fast passenger trains on the main line from Heidelberg through Bretten and Mühlacker to Stuttgart and Ulm without the need for double-heading. Only on the four-mile 1 in 44 gradient from Geislingen to Amstetten would there be a need for a banking locomotive. The following specification was demanded for the new locomotive: to haul 350 tons on the level at 100km/hr (62mph) and up long stretches of 1 in 100 gradient at 60km/hr (37½mph) with a maximum speed of 110km/hr (69mph). The performance on the main bank at the specified performance level would require at least 1,500 horsepower to be developed. To keep the axleweight down to 16 tons, and provide the necessary heating and grate area, the weight would have to be spread over three coupled axles and three bogie/trailing axles… For the higher speed and power, a four-cylinder drive with compound working was chosen with the hindsight of the economy of working.'

The Württemberg Class 'C' Pacific, introduced in 1909, was one of the more successful express locomotives of this period. Although it was the smallest of the Pacifics built in this era, it was efficient and economical. In addition, it was a good-looking and elegant machine.

As it was to operate in the hilly countryside of the Württemberg State, the driving wheel diameter of 5ft 11in was considered appropriate. Boiler pressure was 213lbpsi, grate area was 42.6sqft. The four-cylinder compound Pacific had inside cylinders measuring 16.5in x 24in, outside cylinders of 24.4in x 24in, it had a total heating surface of 2,204sqft and superheating surface of 585sqft. The maximum axle-load was a light 15.9 tons and the engine weight in service was just 85 tons, 132 tons with a tender holding 4,400 gallons of water and 5.5 tons of coal (the locomotives later received a larger tender holding 7 tons of coal and 6,600 gallons of water). Maximum permitted speed of the engines was initially 115km/hr (72mph) raised later to 120 (75mph). Despite their apparent small size, they packed a punch, in practice capable of achieving 1,840hp in service, belying their comparatively low tractive effort of 17,504lb, this being the calculation for a compound locomotive starting from rest initially in 'simple' mode.

Forty-one of these locomotives were built by Maschinenfabrik Esslingen between 1909 and 1921,

numbered 2001-41. Five were built initially in 1909, and in the initial tests on the 84-mile stretch of line between Mühlacker and Ulm, hauled 408 tons up a six-mile-long 1 in 100 gradient at 44mph, 478 tons on an eight-mile gradient of 1 in 270 at 56mph with indicated horsepower ranging between 1,800 and 1,860. In an article in the newspaper of the Society of German Engineers of 27 May 1911, Railway

Inspector Dauner described the outcome of the tests which had been conducted with locomotive 2003 (later 18.102), which had just been run in on light passenger work and had accumulated just 2,000 miles before the tests took place. The tests had taken place over four consecutive days when the weather was dry and wind speed was insignificant. After the tests the condition of the

A works photo of the second 'C' Pacific, 2002 (later DR 18.101 – the prototype 'C' Pacific, 2001, was transferred to the SNCF in 1918 as one of the three war reparation Württemberg Pacifics), built in 1907, and withdrawn in 1953. It is seen here with the small tender type that was attached to the first series – a larger tender was supplied with engines from 2027 onwards, and later standard for all the class.
(MLS Collection/Postcard)

18.126, formerly class 'C' 2030, when based at Heilbronn, 25 July 1949. The locomotive is one of the second series with large bogie tender, and was withdrawn from Ulm Depot in October 1954. The famous German photographer, Carl Bellingrodt, is visible on the footplate.
(MLS Collection/Carl Bellingrodt/EK-Verlag)

18.127 of the second series at Bw Heilbronn, in 1934. It was stored after the war at Heilbronn and condemned in December 1950, and was removed to Ulm for scrapping in May 1953.
(DLA Darmstadt/ Eisenbahnstiftung Collection)

locomotive was excellent with no failures, axleboxes remaining cold. On the third test, in climbing the Geislinger Bank at 19mph, it demonstrated over 20,000lb tractive effort. A further test with 2005 (18.104) on five passenger coaches and the research vehicle, weighing 220 tons, climbed the bank at a minimum of 25mph, including slipping twice as the rails were damp. In the 1909-10 winter timetable, the five locomotives ran 194,227 miles at an average of 38,845 miles each, consuming an average of 8.3lb per mile run, including standing time.

2006-2011 were built in 1910,

2012-2015 in 1912, 2016-2020 in 1913 and 2021-2024 in 1914. 2025-2029 were built in 1915, with the larger tender holding 7 tons of coal and 6,600 gallons of water, 2030-2036 after the war in 1919 and finally 2037-2041 in 1921. 2041 was the 4,000th engine to be built at the Esslingen Works. The cost of the locomotives ranged from 118,000 Reichsmark to 123,000 for the last batch after the war. Four were sacrificed to the war reparations programme in 1919 (2010 going to Poland and three, the prototype 2001 and the 1915-built 2026 and 2027 to France) with thirty-seven being taken over by the DRG and

renumbered 18.101-137. All the class on building were allocated to the Company's main Depot at Stuttgart Nord. The last examples of the type, 18.133 and 18.136, were withdrawn by the *Deutsche Bundesbahn* from Ulm Depot in 1955.

Operation

The first five class 'C' Pacifics, after running in, were given a special set of diagrams of heavy passenger trains between Bruchsal and Ulm, with two turns starting from Heidelberg. Average train weight in their first winter timetable was 254 tons, 291 tons in the summer, with average train speeds between 50 and 56mph. With train strengthening in the summer, loads could increase to 360 tons, which a class 'C' could manage. By the beginning of the First World War twenty Pacifics had been built, all based at Stuttgart Nord Hbf.

Loads increased further and D19 (Bruchsal–Stuttgart–Ulm–Friedrichshafen) was booked for eleven coaches, 450 tons. Other services booked for the Pacifics included the seven-coach D3 Bruchsal–Munich, the nine-coach D4 Munich–Bruchsal, the seven-coach D56 Munich–Karlsruhe and the eight-coach D57 Karlsruhe–Munich with through coaches from Paris and Luxembourg to Vienna, Salzburg and Nuremberg. For other services the State Railway had to rely on fourteen D 4-6-0s, seventeen ADhs and twenty-six AD 4-4-0s at Stuttgart, while the depots at Heilbronn, Ulm and Tübingen only had AD 4-4-0s. Off the main-line there were no heavy D-Züge, just semi-fasts with a maximum load of 150 tons. The peak of the class 'C' working was the luxury pair L62/63, the *Orient Express*, which needed a banker up the Geislinger Incline and had a timetabled stop at the summit to detach it.

As more Pacifics were built, despite the loss of four as war reparations, they were able to replace Stuttgart Depot's 4-6-0s and 4-4-0s, which were transferred to Heilbronn, Crailsheim and Tübingen. In October 1919, the Stuttgart Pacifics had a dozen D-Züge and one Eilzug over the Ulm–Stuttgart main-line, although loads had fallen compared with the pre-war period. In 1920, the

Reichsbahn was created, bringing together a number of the State railways. The influence of the Prussian management became apparent, though in locomotive affairs it was initially in the mixed traffic 4-6-0 class P8 (38.10-40) and the Prussian freight G10s. By 1925, eighty-two P8s had been built to replace the Württemberg AD, ADh and Ds and in 1922, four Saxon class 19 2-8-2s and two Prussian P10 2-8-2s were in service on the former State railway. This increased to fourteen P10s by 1926, although the Saxon engines had disappeared. By 1930, the former Württemberg system had thirty-seven class 'C' Pacifics; eighty-three P8 mixed traffic engines; fourteen P10s; twenty-two of the new Standard class 24 light 2-6-0s; and just eight of the old State ADh 4-4-0s. The Ds had gone by 1923 and the last ADs went in 1927.

As traffic increased in the 1920s there was a need for more power, especially on the Geislinger Incline. Three options existed – to increase the power of the train engine; to employ two bankers; or increase the power of the banking engine. The third option was selected and two Prussian T20 2-10-2 tank engines, 95.001 and 95.002, were allocated as bankers there in 1922. Three more, 95.011-13, appeared later and the five locomotives solved that problem until electrification of the route in May 1933. Trials were also made with the 2-8-2s mentioned above. 39.009 and 39.010 arrived from Elberfeld, and Saxon 2-8-2s numbered XXHV 206-209 were present for just a year. The P10s had difficulties on the Ulm–Munich high-speed section, but performed

well in the hill country and were to remain sharing duties with the class 'C' Pacifics. On test results used by the DRG to assess locomotive loadings, it would appear that the P10 could pull heavier loads on the steep gradients at slow speeds, but that the Pacifics performed better at the higher speeds – for example on a 1 in 50 gradient, a P10 and C were nearly identical at 30mph (both capable of hauling 200 tons at this speed), but at 37½mph, the P10 could only manage 135 tons, whereas the C was allowed 170 tons. However, the heavier axleload of the P10 was a big disadvantage on the Württemberg system where most lines were only fit for a 16-ton axleload locomotive. Between 1923 and 1925 the Stuttgart–Ulm and the Black Forest lines were strengthened to take greater axleloads, and the P10s returned, especially to the Karlsruhe District and the Black Forest. In 1925 the Stuttgart 'C' Pacifics still had Stuttgart–Ulm-Munich expresses and the *Orient Express* at weekends, although a Bavarian S3/6 (18.4) worked this on weekdays. Workings out of Ulm were more suited to the 'C' (18.1) and the 18.4s, and the P10s were largely kept out of the working here.

Transfers of the 18.1s from Stuttgart to Ulm started in 1925 with six locomotives (18.108, 112, 115, 117, 118 and 126). Six more followed in 1927, four more in 1928, and, by 1930, eighteen Württemberg Pacifics were based at Ulm. At this time, Stuttgart had ten P10s and eighteen 18.1s, of which four were stored, as only nine diagrams existed for them. There were, however, frequent examples of

18.109 climbs the 1 in 44 gradient of the Geislinger Incline in the Swabian Alps on a stopping passenger train, P900, banked by former Prussian T20 2-10-2T, 95.011, 19 June 1931. The banking engine seems to have a coach attached – reason unknown. (Carl Bellingrodt/ Eisenbahstiftung Collection)

the Pacifics being used as pilots to the P10 train engine, as well as on occasions to the Bavarian 18.4s. Unfortunately, most of the records of the 1930s have been destroyed and the main workings can only be assessed from photographs, many of them taken by Carl Bellingrodt. It would appear that in 1931-2 most of the diagrams for the 18.1 Pacifics were on light trains, although the eleven-coach 448-ton D176

Stuttgart–Friedrichshafen was an exception. Other trains noted in that period with 18.1 haulage were D119 Munich–Cologne (Munich to Ulm, 9 coaches); D185 Friedrichshafen– Frankfurt (Friedrichshafen– Stuttgart, change 18.1s in Ulm, 6 coaches); D208 Stuttgart–Innsbruck (18.1 Ulm–Friedrichshafen, 10 coaches); D215 Stuttgart– Neuenmarkt-Wirsberg (18.1 Stuttgart–Nuremberg, 6 coaches);

E221 Stuttgart–Crailsheim (18.1 Stuttgart–Crailsheim, 5 coaches); D245 Stuttgart–Backnang (18.1 Stuttgart–Nuremberg, 3-coach relief to D45 Strasbourg–Nuremberg); and D337 Friedrichshafen–Crailsheim (18.1 throughout).

In 1928, 18.107 was involved in a serious train accident overspeeding at a crossover before single-line working, derailing at 50mph instead of slowing to

the required 28mph. The line between Ulm and Friedrichshafen was being strengthened with new rails to take 20-ton axleloads and the engineering work was at Ummendorf Station. Thirty-one passengers were injured. Another

tragic accident occurred in 1934 when two 18.1-hauled trains collided head-on between Backnang and Crailsheim killing ten people. 18.134 was so badly damaged that it was scrapped.

The line from Munich to

18.137 (Bw Stuttgart Rosenstein), the last locomotive of the class built in 1921, accelerates through the wintry Rohrer Forest, near Stuttgart, 1934. This, as C 2041, was the 4,000th locomotive built at Esslingen Works, and was stored and not repaired after the war, being condemned in December 1950. (RVM/Eisenbahnstiftung)

18.137 piloting sister engine 18.132 on D9 in the Neckar Valley on the stretch of line between Immendingen and Stuttgart, 21 July 1937. (Carl Bellingrodt/ Eisenbahnstiftung)

Augsburg was electrified in 1931 and the whole route to Stuttgart including the notorious 'Geislinger Steige' was electrified by May 1933. In that year Stuttgart gave up some of its Pacifics to Tübingen, working semi-fast and slow trains to Stuttgart and Horb with possibly a loco change in Sigmaringen, although the turntable there could not cope with the Pacifics. However, by 1935 the Tübingen engines were back at Ulm. Between

1933 and 1939 there were few changes in allocation of the 18.1 Pacifics – minor single engine exchanges only, mainly between Stuttgart and Ulm. At the end of the 1930s, the main line work of the 18.1s was restricted to pilot work plus D-, E-, and P-Züge on the Ulm–Friedrichshafen line and to Donaueschingen, Aalen and Crailsheim. Ulm now had twenty-four of the thirty-seven locomotives.

A surprise was the allocation to

Ulm of five new streamlined three-cylinder Pacifics, 03.1075–1079, in 1940 which shared six D- and E-train diagrams with 18.1s – the Württemberg Pacifics having nine turns also on semi-fast and stopping passenger trains. However, the new engines were not popular with the Ulm crews, and the 18.1s frequently had to stand in for them. Within a couple of years, two of the 03.10s left for Kattowitz and the other three for Munich, being replaced by more 18.1s. Three Ulm 18.1s went to Heilbronn to replace P8 4-6-0s which were needed in the extended Germany to the east.

By 1944, the timetable was introduced by the words 'until further notice', and was disrupted by bombing destruction and temporary repairs. The Stuttgart District suffered badly from Allied bombing, attacking the rail junctions at Ulm, Bruchsal and Reutlingen, and especially the freight yard at Kornwestheim. All that was left of passenger work were four D- and one E-train pairs to the west of Stuttgart, three Stuttgart–Crailsheim pairs of D-trains, a number of trains over the electrified Stuttgart-Ulm main line, a couple of D-train pairs to Friedrichshafen/Lindau, and two semi-fasts and one express from Ulm or Stuttgart to Tuttlingen. From 25-29 July 1944, the American and British air forces led a concerted attack, leaving Stuttgart in ruins. The engine shed collapsed and two 'C' Pacifics,

including 18.125, were caught in the destruction. Many others suffered enough damage to put them out of action until the end of the war and some were withdrawn without further running. 18.122 and 18.133 were moved to Heilbronn, and 18.127, 129 and 137 moved to the relative safety of Lauda. Later, a further six locomotives moved from Ulm to Heilbronn and another to Lauda. A number of P10s from Erfurt were sent to Stuttgart to replace the 18.1s and P10s that had been damaged. On 1 January 1945, there were twenty-one 18.1s at Ulm, nine at Heilbronn, five at Lauda and one of the bomb-damaged unserviceable engines at Süssen. The depots where the remaining 18.1s stood fell to the invading Allied armies in April 1945.

Disputes between the French and American occupying armies caused uncertainty over the boundaries of the French and American Zones, and caused chaotic administration with uncertainties over the location and state of damaged

and destroyed railway facilities, locomotives and rolling stock. At the end of the Second World War, only seven 18.1s were undamaged and active: 18.107, 108 and 109 at Ulm; 18.119 and 122 at Heilbronn; 18.133 at Lauda; and 18.137 at Stuttgart. Six weeks after the end of the war, the Zone boundaries were eventually agreed and were divided along the Stuttgart-Ulm-Munich axis, the American Zone to the north and French to the south. In August 1945, six 18.1s were stored at Rottweil, Freudenstadt and Tübingen. Five other Pacifics found their way from the French Zone in Aulendorf and Friedrichshafen to the American Zone and were stored at Ulm, just one, 18.103, capable of working. The Pacifics in the French Zone remained in store, the local services between Friedrichshafen, Aulendorf and Ulm being worked by a few T5 Württemberg 2-6-2Ts.

It was not until April 1948 that any plans were made to bring some of the 'C' Pacifics back into service. In the American Zone,

18.101 Bw Ulm, (former C 2002 built in 1909) heads D185 past Amstetten, 19 June 1931. (Carl Bellingrodt/ Eisenbahnstiftung Collection)

18.137 pilots Prussian 3-cylinder P10 2-8-2, 39.203, on D369 at Geislingen Station, June 1930.
(DLA Darmstadt/ Eisenbahnstiftung Collection)

a decision was made that seven Pacifics - 18.106, 111, 114, 119, 121, 129 and 135 – would be withdrawn as the cost of repair was too high. They were officially withdrawn in November 1948. 18.127 and 18.137 were taken into the Esslingen Works, but neither emerged and were withdrawn in December 1950. At the end of 1948, sixteen Pacifics had been brought back into service and were located at Ulm and Heilbronn. The five Pacifics in the French Zone – 18.104, 105, 112, 122 and 123 – were given a full overhaul at the Munich-Freimann Works and returned to Ulm at the end of 1949 or early 1950.

Ulm used its 18.1s on local stopping services to Friedrichshafen and Immendingen. Only one pair of faster trains, D513/514, was booked for 18.1 haulage from Ulm to Friedrichshafen. All other D- and E-trains in the area from Ulm to Friedrichshafen, Donaueschingen, Crailsheim and Kempten were booked to be hauled by Lindau's Bavarian 18.4-5 Pacifics, P8s or P10s. The Heilbronn-based 18.1s fared better. They were rostered for D7/D8 Stuttgart–Würzburg and back, and semi-fast services between Heilbronn, Mannheim and Stuttgart. However, they were replaced by P8s at the end of 1952

and the remaining Pacifics were transferred to Ulm. Ten were withdrawn in 1953, eight more in 1954, leaving just four at the beginning of 1955, although only two of those – 18.133 and 18.136 – were in active service. Although 18.133 had initially been stored pending withdrawal in August 1953, it received an overhaul in February 1954 and was the last 18.1 to haul a train – a semi-fast train from Ulm to Freiburg on 13 February 1955. Its official condemnation date was 23 May 1955 and then the class was extinct. Unfortunately, no members of the class were preserved.

War Reparations Locomotives

Four Württemberg 'C' Pacifics were decreed to be part of the large number of German locomotives to be sent to other countries under the Armistice at the end of the First World War. 2010 was allocated to the Polish State Railways, the PKP, and was identified there as Om 101-1. In 1937, it was in the Warsaw Motive Power Division and during the war it was moved eastwards as the German troops advanced through the country. By 1943, however, it was under German control in the Lemberg area, and in 1946 was observed between Erfurt and Sangerhausen, although no trace of the locomotive in official records can be found since then.

The other three Pacifics, the prototype 2001, built in 1909, and 2026 and 2027, both built in 1915, were deployed on the Etat system of France, where they were renumbered 231.997-999. All three were stationed at Le Mans and apparently were mainly used on trains between Le Mans, Angers and Nantes, duties which in the early 1930s included some express passenger work for which they had a good reputation. They were painted black, with only the buffer beams red.

By 1934, they were out of service and by 1938, although allocated the SNCF numbers of 231A 997-999, two, 998 and 999, were reconditioned as stationary boilers at Le Mans Depot, 997 (the former 2001) being cannibalised for spare parts. Both were destroyed during an Allied bombing raid on railway installations at Le Mans in March 1944.

Württemberg 'C' Pacific, built as 2026 in 1915, ceded to French Etat Railway along with 2001 and 2027 after the First World War, and here seen stored out of use at Le Mans, c1935. 231.998 was stationed at Le Mans in service between Le Mans and Angers until around 1934. It was later used as a stationary boiler at Le Mans until it was destroyed in an air raid in March 1944. (MLS Collection)

Chapter 5

THE BAVARIAN MAFFEI PACIFICS – S 3/6 (18.4-5)

The Bavarian four-cylinder compound S3/6 Pacifics were a famous and successful design built over a twenty-two-year period from 1908 to 1930, but in four distinct phases with variations in design between each. Undoubtedly, they were the most successful of the State railway Pacifics and were perpetuated alongside the building of the new Reichsbahn standard Pacifics in the 1925-1930 period. In all, 159 were built, a number finishing their lives in France and Belgium as war reparations after the First World War, a few lasting to 1962, and thirty being rebuilt with all-welded modernised boilers and lasting until 1965 (see Chapter 6).

18.401-435, 461-478: Design & Construction

The Royal Bavarian State Railway had a difficult physical and economic environment. Much of its network was in the mountainous areas – the foothills of the Alps with heavily-graded lines – and the Bavarian economy, without much heavy industry, was weak. The railway therefore had to balance its needs for more power to cope with increasing traffic in the first decade of the twentieth century with the need for efficiency and low running costs. The Munich firm of Maffei had built thirty-nine saturated steam 4-6-0s, class S3/5, in 1903 and ten Atlantics, S2/5, in 1904. In 1906, it built a further ten S3/5s, but with superheaters. These were capable of hauling 350-400 tons on the level, but struggled on the many 1 in 100 or steeper grades that abounded on the system.

In 1907, Maffei had built the first German Pacific locomotive for the Baden State Railway, the class IV f (18.2), which aroused much interest and the Bavarian railway authorities discussed the development of a similar locomotive with Anton Hammel and Heinrich Leppla of the Maffei firm. By July 1907, a decision to build the S3/6 four-cylinder compound Pacific was made, but with a larger boiler than the Baden engine. The first engine, 3601, emerged from the Maffei Works on 16 July 1908 and four days later, 3602 astonished everyone in its yellow ochre livery displayed at an exhibition in Munich. 3618, in grey/blue livery, made an impact worldwide when presented at an international exhibition in Brussels in 1910.

3601 immediately began a series of trial runs between Munich, Rosenheim and Salzburg, and coped with a 400-ton load without any fuss. The performance of the larger boiler was particularly impressive, and the engine held 44mph with this load on a 1 in 100 gradient and 56mph on 1 in 200. Its top authorised speed of 120km/hr was easily reached and on test 135km/hr (85mph), when the ride of the engine was described as very smooth. 3601 achieved times on the test runs on this stretch that were only matched thirty years later by the fastest electric trains over the same section! All this was achieved at an economy of water and coal that met all expectations.

Between October and November 1908, Maffei delivered the remaining five locomotives of the first order, with a few small adjustments gained from the experience of the test runs with 3601, one of which was to improve

S3/6 3608 (later 18.406), built by Maffei in September 1909, seen here in 1911. It was based at Bw Munich until 1923 and its final depot from 1943 was Treuchtlingen where it was stored needing repair in 1945, was withdrawn in 1946 and scrapped in 1949. (Eisenbahnstiftung Collection)

the air flow to the ashpan. Ten more locomotives were ordered immediately, and 3608-3617 were delivered between September and November 1909. The engines entered service in record time and 1911-built 3621 was noted on the day after its delivery to Kufstein already working a D-Zug.

Between 1908 and 1918, seventy-one of these machines were built with a distinctive 'wind-cutting' arrow-shaped cab, bar frames after the American practice, and bullet nose. Because much of the Bavarian

system ran through the foothills of the Alps, driving wheels of 6ft 1½in were chosen. The inside cylinders measured 16.7in x 24in whilst the outside cylinders measured a huge 25.6in x 26.4in. Boiler pressure was 213lbpsi, a wide firebox with grate area 48.4sqft and heating surface of 2,885sqft. The engine was superheated, 537.5sqft, and had an axle-load of 16 tons, making it a useful engine for secondary lines as well as the main routes. The total engine weight was 88.3 tons and, with a tender holding 5,800

gallons of water and 7½ tons of coal, weighed in total 143.9 tons. The series from 3650-3679 had an increase in both heating surface and superheater to 2,954sqft and 599sqft respectively, a four-ton greater weight and an axle-load of 17 tons.

Initially they were numbered 3601–3623 and 3642-3679, and painted in the Bavarian passenger livery of apple green with yellow and black lining, and ten numbered 341–350 of the Pfalz system. In 1815, Bavaria absorbed the former Palatinate (Pfalz) State and in

A Bavarian S3/6 of the first batch built in October 1909, 18.412, at Augsburg in 1927. It was then based at Regensburg before being reallocated to Hof the following year. It was withdrawn in 1950 as were so many war-damaged State railway Pacifics. (Rudolf Kallmünzer/Eisenbahnstiftung Collection)

January 1909 the Pfalz State Railway was taken over by the Bavarian State Railway and formed its Ludwigshafen Division. It had 500 miles of standard-gauge track and its locomotives retained their Pfalz Railway numbers until the Bavarian Group Administration was disbanded by the DRG in October 1933. Forty-two Bavarian engines of this series were taken into DRG stock, painted black with red wheel centres, and numbered 18.401-424 and 18.461-478. The Pfalz

One of the first series S3/6 Pacifics, built in 1909, renumbered 18.408, with Bavarian 0-8-2T 98.1118, at Bamberg, 16 June 1939. It operated for a short while from Treuchtlingen and Bamberg after the war, but was condemned in 1948 and scrapped in 1950. (MLS Collection/Carl Bellingrodt/EK-Verlag)

Company remained a separate system outside the DRG until 1938, but their numbers were incorporated as 18.425-434. Their maximum speed was fixed at 120km/hr (75mph) and the design tractive effort was calculated as 20,017lb, 1,660 horsepower (1,715 for 3650-3679).

However, nineteen of this series were sent as war reparations in 1919, sixteen to France and three to Belgium. These included two from the very first order, 3602 and 3605, and most from the 1918 latest build numbered between 3665 and 3679. Many of the early engines were damaged during the Second World War and were stored unserviceable at a number of depots, especially Nuremberg and Hof, before being withdrawn without re-entering service in 1949-50. The last survivor of the DR/DB engines of this series was 18.478 (the former 3673), built in 1918 and withdrawn from Ulm Depot in the summer of 1960, and stored at Lindau Depot after purchase by a Swiss engineer and enthusiast, Serge Lory. However, it was found to have exchanged frames with the withdrawn 3645 (18.422) in 1948, so the identity of the preserved engine is really the 1914-built S3/6.

18.441-458:
(The high-wheeled S3/6) Design & Construction

In 1911, the State Railway introduced two pairs of especially fast expresses between Munich and Nuremberg, 124.3 miles in 135 minutes (D79/80 Munich–Berlin), and Munich and Würzburg, 173 miles in 200 minutes (D57/58 Munich–Cologne–Hamburg), requiring average speeds between stops of 56-62mph and regular attainment of 69-72mph over long distances. There had been failures on this service from overheating, and the water capacity of the tender was insufficient for a proposed new non-stop service from Munich to Halle, 196 miles. Therefore a new series of the Maffei S3/6, 3624 -3641, was constructed in 1912 with larger-diameter driving wheels specially for routes where these train schedules demanded higher speeds – not only from Munich to the north and Nuremberg, but also to the east–west route through Munich from Passau and

High-wheeled 3630 (later 18.447) on delivery to the Bavarian State Railway at Munich Hirschau, 13 May 1912. It was based at Wiesbaden for a short time in 1928 when it was one of the S3/6s rostered for the *Rheingold* and withdrawn from Augsburg in 1949. (Krauss-Maffei/Siemens AG)

3641 (later 18458), the last of the high-wheeled S3/6s, as delivered brand new by the Maffei Works, Munich, 1913, withdrawn from Nuremberg in 1946 and scrapped in 1950.
(DB Museum Nuremberg/ J A Maffei)

Regensburg to Ulm and Stuttgart. Dimensions were identical to the first series, 3601-3623, apart from 6ft 7in-diameter driving wheels and enlarged outside cylinders of 26.4in x 26.4in. The engine had a conventional straight-fronted cab, and was just 2ft 3in longer and 1.2 tons heavier. Because of the larger wheels, the centre of the boiler was seated at a height of 9ft 7in. An enlarged tender with higher sides and two rear axles was provided, with 7,150 gallons of water and 8 tons of coal. Total engine weight with tender and fully watered and coaled was 155.6 tons. The new locomotives were capable of exerted 1,815 horsepower and these were the pride of the Bavarian express locomotive fleet.

This batch of locomotives was numbered 18.441-458 after the formation of the *Deutsche Reichsbahn* and lost their striking green livery for the standard DRG black with red wheel centres. However, one in full Bavarian livery, 3634, which became 18.451, can still be viewed in the main exhibition hall of the Deutches Museum in Munich.

Most of this batch of locomotives were stored after the damage and

18.454, built as 3637, in October 1912, after assimilation by the *Deutsche Reichsbahn*, c1925. It is still minus smoke deflectors, and is in the condition it would have run the *Rheingold* immediately after construction and in the early 1920s before the building of the 18.509-548 series.
(MLS Collection/Carl Bellingrodt/ EK-Verlag)

neglect of the Second World War, and withdrawn during 1949-50 with one, 18.451, becoming one of the Minden Test Centre engines along with 18.505 and three Baden 18.3 Pacifics, and later preserved as noted above.

1923/24 Series, 18.479-508
Design & Construction
After the war, reparations had required the release of nineteen S3/6s to France and Belgium in 1919, the former Bavarian State Railway territory found itself short of express motive power to cater for the build-up of post-war passenger traffic. While the new management team was researching the development of new standard classes, new locomotives were urgently needed and the Krauss-Maffei Company was given the order to build thirty new engines to the 1908 basic design. They reverted to the 6ft 1½ in driving wheel diameter, but with an increased boiler pressure of 227lbpsi, a higher tractive effort of 21,340lbs and 1,830 hp was realised. Other dimensions were unchanged – cylinder and grate size, heating surface. The tender held 6,000 gallons of water and 8½ tons of coal. The higher boiler pressure and larger tender increased the weight of the total locomotive to 153.2 tonnes and the axle weight to 17.9 tons. The locomotives, numbered 3680–3709,

1923-built Maffei four-cylinder compound Pacific 18.483 at Augsburg on a P-Zug for Buchloe, August 1959. 18.483 was one of seven unrebuilt Bavarian S3/6 locomotives still operational, all from Augsburg Bw in 1959. It was withdrawn in 1960. (David Maidment)

18.481, one of the two last survivors of the 18.479-18.508 series constructed in 1923-4, at its home depot, Augsburg, 15 September 1959. It was withdrawn from Lindau in the summer of 1961. (Herbert Schambach)

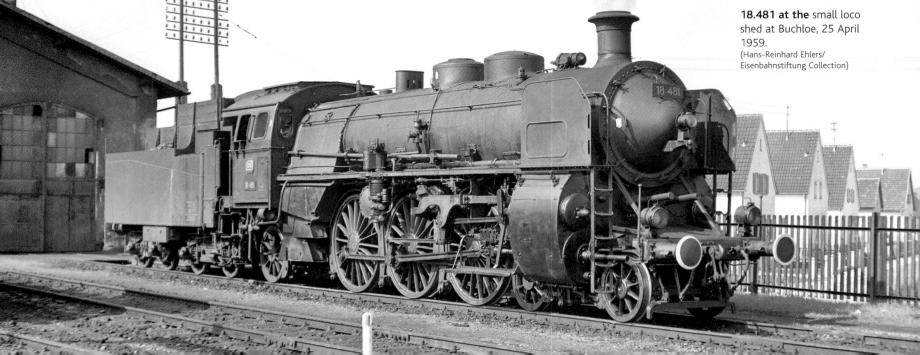

18.481 at the small loco shed at Buchloe, 25 April 1959.
(Hans-Reinhard Ehlers/ Eisenbahnstiftung Collection)

18.504, one of the 1923-4 series ordered by the Bavarian State Railways to replace S3/6s sent to France and Belgium as war reparations, at its home Depot, Bw Lindau, in 1935.
(DLA Darmstadt /Maey/ Eisenbahnstiftung Collection)

DR 18.479–508, were built in 1923-4 and entered traffic at the sheds traditionally associated with the Bavarian engines.

The last engine of the batch, 3709, built in 1924, was displayed at the engineering exhibition held at Seddin, Berlin, painted especially in a royal dark blue livery with silver bands. Several of these locomotives survived until the early 1960s, 18.483 being withdrawn from Augsburg in the summer of that year, 18.481 in June 1961 and 18.508 itself (the former 3709) lasting

until the autumn of 1962 at Lindau Depot.

18.509-548
Design & Construction

Although Richard Wagner and the new *Deutsche Reichsbahn* engineering team developed the standard DR Pacific, class 01, in 1925, because of its 20-ton axle-load it was prohibited from a number of important main line routes. In order to increase the number of express locomotives capable of improving train speeds

on these lines, and while a light-weight version of the 01 (the class 03) was still under development, the DRG management decided to order twenty more examples of the Bavarian S3/6, the most economic and efficient of the former State railway Pacifics. The Krauss-Maffei Company of Munich was given the order and the new locomotives, numbered 18.509-528, were built between 1926 and 1928. A further twenty were then ordered from the same Company, but the Wall Street crash, rapidly escalating inflation in

Krauss-Maffei-built 18.520, painted a dark green livery, poses at the Munich Works location immediately after its construction in June 1927. This locomotive was rebuilt with an all-welded higher performance boiler in December 1954 as 18.612, and is the only 18.6 that has been preserved. (Krauss-Maffei/Siemens AG)

18.528, built in March 1928 by Krauss-Maffei, at its allocated depot, Augsburg, 3 April 1961. 18.528 was one of the ten 1926-30 DR built series that was not reboilered in the 1950s and it was the last original 18.4-5 to survive, being withdrawn from Lindau depot in October 1962, before being retained on display at its birthplace. (MLS Collection/Konzelmann)

the German Weimar Republic and the resultant worldwide financial crisis, created major difficulties for the Munich firm and only 18.529 and 530 were completed. The remaining eighteen engines, 18.531-548, were then built in 1930 by Henschel, under licence.

The dimensions of the new locomotives were almost identical to the 1923-4 series, with a slight increase in the inside-cylinder size to 17.3in x 25.6in, increasing the weight of the engine and tender in traffic to 153.9 tons, and the maximum axle-weight to 18.5 tons. The Henschel engines, by a slight redistribution of weight, reduced the maximum axle-weight to 18.1 tons, but with a larger 7,000 gallon capacity tender holding 10 tons of coal, the engine's total weight in service was 165.2 tonnes.

All these engines survived the Second World War apart from 18.515 and 18.533, and were retained in West Germany, repaired and allocated to their traditional area of the former Bavarian State Railway. In the early 1950s, the *Deutsche Bundesbahn* developed a programme of rebuilding many of their express engines with high-performance all-welded boilers and a decision was made in 1953 to equip thirty of the most recently built S3/6s with the new boilers. Sixteen of the twenty-two Krauss-Maffei-built engines were converted and fourteen of the eighteen Henschel locomotives, all being renumbered in the 18.6 series. This left the following locomotives unaltered in the post-war period – 18.512, 513, 516, 519, 528, 537, 538 and 541 – which remained until withdrawal in the

late 1950s with three, 18.512, 516 and 528, lasting until the 1960s and 18.528 as the final survivor, being withdrawn from Lindau Depot in the autumn of 1962, before external restoration and display at the Krauss-Maffei Works in Munich-Allach.

Operations 1908 – 1920 (Bavarian State Railway)

All the first batch of the Bavarian S3/6s were allocated to the main Munich Depot, as were all further locomotives up to and including the 1911-built series (3601-3623). They appeared on all the main Bavarian routes from Munich: west to Augsburg, Ulm and Stuttgart; north to Würzburg and Nuremberg; east to Passau and the Austrian border; south-west to Lindau and the borders with Austria and Switzerland. They were good hill climbers

and exceptionally economical in operation.

The eighteen S3/6s constructed with 6ft 7in coupled wheels for higher speed work were primarily utilised on the fast Munich–Nuremberg–Aschaffenburg runs, 229 miles, Nuremberg–Halle (on Berlin services), 196 miles, and Nuremberg–Lindau, 206 miles. In 1914, ten were built to the initial design for the Pfalz network of the Bavarian Royal State Railway, which were all allocated to Ludwigshafen. Their longest route was from Metz to Stuttgart, 195 miles.

In 1909, S3/6s ran 473,000 miles in passenger service and in 1910, 1,063,194 miles. By the year 1914, forty of these locomotives were in service based at Munich, from which city virtually all D-Züge were S3/6-hauled, with an annual 2.075m miles. Some very long non-stop runs were scheduled, including D57/58 between Munich

The last unrebuilt S3/6, 18.528, built by Krauss-Maffei in March 1928, poses at Röthenbach whilst working a Kempten:Lindau P-Zug, 8 June 1962. It was withdrawn from Lindau in October 1962 and retained by its builder at the Company Works at Munich-Allach.
(Herbert Schambach)

and Würzburg, and D79/80 between Munich and Nuremberg. Nine of the 1912-built 6ft 7in coupled wheel engines were allocated to Nuremberg, the rest to Munich.

The nine large-diameter wheeled S3/6s (3624-3627 and 3637-3641) allocated to Nuremberg from their introduction in 1912, were specifically for the Nuremberg–Halle (-Berlin) and Nuremberg–Lindau trains. A journey in July 1912 behind 3624 on a 430-ton Nuremberg–Lindau train recovered a three-minute late start, after taking water at Buchloe, on the 1 in 100 gradient to Günzach. The locomotive half slipped twice in the early morning mist, but recovered to hold 25mph on the gradient. The return journey in the evening on a 415-ton train held the scheduled time exactly on the 1 in 100 climb to Günzach from the Kempten direction. In August 1913 an overloaded 3638, with 480 tons, including heavy sleeping cars, working D70, fell to 19mph losing three minutes on the climb but in a hurried (and illegal) descent caught up and arrived in Lindau precisely on time.

During the First World War, the number of fast passenger services was substantially cut back and as a result some of the Munich and Nuremberg S3/6s were redistributed to Hof, Aschaffenburg and Würzburg. Some of the locomotives were operational on military specials including eight in the war zone in the former French territory behind the German lines. By the end of 1918, the first series up to 3679 had been completed and put into traffic, but then in 1919 the fleet was much depleted by the Armistice obligation to send nineteen of these locomotives to the French and Belgian railways as war reparations.

At the nationalisation of the State railway systems in 1920, sixty of the seventy-nine Bavarian S3/6s passed to the new *Deutsche Reichsbahn* and fifty of them were numbered between 18.401 and 18.478. Ten were still based in the Pfalz system (numbered 341–350, later DRG 18.425–18.434).

Operations 1920-1945 (*Deutsche Reichsbahn*)

As traffic levels recovered after the war, many S3/6s gravitated back to Munich again and by 1923 there were thirty-three allocated there. This included three of the 1923-4 built series with 17-ton axleloads, numbered 18.479-508. Many of the earlier 16-ton axleload engines were drafted to the depots with operations over the lighter rail routes, especially to Regensburg. By 1926, the Munich fleet dominated the luxury and fastest expresses out of Munich, including two return D-Züge Munich-Lindau, two return D-Züge and the pair L62/63 (the *Orient Express*) Munich-Stuttgart, three train pairs Munich-Würzburg, four D-Züge and F80 Munich-Nuremberg, three return D-Züge Munich-Salzburg, two return D-Züge Munich-Freilassing and six D-Züge Munich-Kufstein.

By 1925, Nuremberg's allocation of 18.4s had risen to twenty-five units and by 1928, thirty-five engines. The main services covered included all the main expresses from Nuremberg to Saalfeld and Leipzig via Bamberg and Hof, Nuremberg to Passau, Stuttgart, Würzburg, Frankfurt and Munich. These included L51/52 (the *Ostende-Wien-Express*) and a pair of Berlin expresses non-stop between Nuremberg and Halle. The Bavarian S3/6s were now regularly working way beyond the confines of the Bavarian State, in Thuringia, Saxony, Hesse and Württemberg. The locomotives, especially the 1926-built 18.5s, were working 312 miles a day, 8-9,500 miles a month – 18.505 achieved a record 12,500 miles in one month in 1937 with an average of 481 miles per day over a twenty-seven-day period!

However, electrification was spreading rapidly through South Germany, and the Munich-Rosenheim, Regensburg and Kufstein routes were electrified by 1927, Salzburg by 1928, Augsburg by 1931, and the main lines from Augsburg to Stuttgart and Nuremberg by 1933 and 1935 respectively. This led to a significant reduction in the presence of S3/6s at Munich, which had reduced to just twelve by 1933. Left were just the main lines from Munich to Würzburg via Ingolstadt and Treuchtlingen and Munich-Lindau. At Nuremberg, although the allocation held up, their turns, especially of the earliest engines, increasingly included semi-fast and stopping passenger trains, and four were transferred to Bamberg in 1935. In the same year, seven new standard 01 Pacifics took over the main Nuremberg-Berlin services.

As well as the routes listed above, initially the high-wheeled 18.441-458 series, then the latest 18.5s were drafted to operate the famous *Rheingold* international

Pullman car train from the Dutch border at Zevenaar down the Rhine Gorge as far as Mannheim (307 miles) where the S3/6 would be exchanged for a Baden IV h 18.3 Pacific (later Offenburg 01s). Wiesbaden-based 18.4s and brand-new 18.521, 523 and 524 operated the luxury train from 1928, six hours allowed with four intermediate stops. By 1929, the older 18.4s had been replaced by the 1926-1928-built 18.5s, 18.520-528. Mainz Depot took over these turns and locomotives in 1931, with additionally, 18.536 and 537. Eight diagrams a day were operated by these locomotives until 1936, including FD 101/102 Emmerich (instead of Zevenaar)-Mannheim and return (the *Rheingold*), FD 263/264 Frankfurt-Zevenaar and return, eight D-Zügen, six semi-

fasts and five main-line stopping trains. After October 1936, the 18.5 diagrams reduced to five with the arrival of new standard 03s, but the S3/6s kept their diagrams for the *Rheingold* until May 1937.

As electrification and the spread of the standard 01s and 03s occurred in the 1930s, the 18.4-5s replaced the earlier Bavarian S3/5 4-6-0s on semi-fast and stopping services in the Munich, Nuremberg and Augsburg areas, as well as maintaining their hold on main lines in the south that were heavily graded and needed light axleweight locomotive power.

The other main area of 18.4 operation in the 1920s and 1930s was the former Pfalz network, radiating from Ludwigshafen, Kaiserslautern, Neustadt, Landau and Zweibrücken on fast services to

Basle, Metz, Stuttgart, Heidelberg and Wiesbaden. In 1931 there were thirteen turns for S3/6s, most, but not entirely, the Pfalz machines. In March 1935, the Ludwigshafen Depot received five brand new 03 standard Pacifics and this was the beginning of the end for the Bavarian Pacific allocation there. An interesting example of a run recorded in the archives of the Railway Performance Society is typical of work by these Pfalz-based locomotives in the early 1930s. A heavy (525 ton) 13-coach Stuttgart-Cologne D-Zug was hauled on 30 July 1930 by a Ludwigshafen-based S3/6, 18.433, assisted as far as Mühlacker by P8 38.1680. At this time, much of the route was still restricted to 62mph (100km/hr) and over the twenty-nine-mile heavily-graded section, speed did

High-wheeled 18.448 departs Nuremberg Hbf with D54, Ostend-Bucharest, on its next leg to Regensberg and the Austrian border at Passau, 5 May 1927. (DB Museum Nuremberg)

High-wheeled 18.447 draws the *Rheingold* (FD 102) into Mainz after its run from Cologne, May 1928. It was based at Wiesbaden for this service just between April and June 1928.
(Werner Hubert/ Eisenbahnstiftung Collection)

not exceed more than the mid-50s, with one section between Sersheim and Vaihingen getting a momentary 60mph, the section time being just over 45 minutes. At Mühlacker, the load was reduced to nine coaches (365 tons) and the fifty miles to Landau, calling at Bruchsal, Graben-Neudorf and Germersheim with 18.433 now unassisted, took 84 minutes, including seven minutes station time and one section of planned engineering single-line working. The top speed was again just about the maximum 62mph allowed, with ten miles between Ruit and Gandelsheim being

covered at an average of 58mph. At Landau, the S3/6 was replaced by a Prussian S10, 17.103, for the run up the Rhine Valley through Boppard and Koblenz, with speed in the 50s for most of the way with station to station start-to-stop average speeds hovering around 42-48mph.

Other locations in the 1930s which received their own allocation of S3/6s working over much of the routes served by the Munich and Nuremberg Pacifics were Würzburg, Aschaffenburg, Augsburg, Hof and Regensburg, the latter in the late 1930s having large-wheeled 18.444, 447 and 449

for the politically important main line to Passau and Vienna. Lindau, which was to become the last stronghold of the class, received its first S3/6 at the end of 1923 with newly-built 18.479 and 480, then in the late 1920s four of the former Pfalz engines and, in 1928, two of the new Krauss-Maffei Pacifics, 18.525 and 526. These had gone by 1933 but been replaced by 18.473, 481, 503, 504 and 506 which joined 18.479 and 480 for the rest of the decade. An example of typical work of a Würzburg-allocated S3/6 was also found in the Railway Performance Society archives. On 20

July 1930, D254, 04.45 Wiesbaden/ Frankfurt to Munich, was hauled from Wiesbaden by P8 38.1632, and after the reversal at Frankfurt (Main), the load was made up to 13 coaches, 575 tons, with P10 2-8-2 39.084. The twenty-nine miles to Aschaffenburg took 50 minutes with two intermediate stops and afterwards the train was banked to the summit at Laufach, averaging 27mph over the six miles from the start at Aschaffenburg. The twenty-six miles on to Gemünden took just under 41 minutes, with a top speed of 55mph and the twenty-four miles to Würzburg, a further 35 minutes, with a top speed of 52mph. At Würzburg, locally-based Pacific 18.494 was added as pilot for the 173 mile run to Munich via Treuchtlingen and Augsburg. The thirty-six-mile run to Steinach took 58 minutes, with no speed higher than the mid-50s, and the twenty miles to Ansbach, 31 minutes with 52mph being averaged over a five-mile section. The eighty-mile non-stop section onto Augsburg took 118 minutes including a two-minute signal stand and one permanent, way slack, 112 minutes net, with speeds hovering between 52 and 56mph for much of the way. The final thirty-eight-mile main line run onto Munich took four minutes under the hour, including a signal stop for several minutes between Pasing and Munich Hbf, net time approximately 50 minutes, an average start-to-stop speed of 45mph, top speed about 60mph.

For a brief period between July 1930 and October 1931, eight of the 1930 Henschel-built 18.5s were drafted to Osnabrück to operate on the Hamburg-Cologne 'Rollbahn'

until more standard 03 Pacifics with light axleloads could replace them. When 03.058-071 arrived, the 18.5s were transferred to Wiesbaden and Mainz for operating in the Rhine Gorge and in the Frankfurt-Wiesbaden-Heidelberg-Darmstadt and Ludwigshafen area. Their North German duties included D93/94 from Hamburg Altona to Cologne via Hamm, which the 18.5s worked throughout without engine change, a distance of 286 miles.

By the summer of 1939, the complete fleet of 241 01s and 298 03 Pacifics had been built and distributed throughout the network, yet the 18.4s still had two return express workings between Munich and Würzburg including FD 264 (which had been worked by a Mainz 18.5 between Zevenaar and Frankfurt). They were still active in the Nuremberg-Würzburg and Nuremberg-Hof areas right up to the electrification of the line to Hof and Berlin in 1939 and, despite the influx of 01s and 03s as well as the electrics, Nuremberg still retained twenty-five 18.4-5s right through to the 1940s.

Big changes occurred during the Second World War. The invasion and occupation of France saw the sixteen war reparation Pacifics (SNCF 231A class) returned to the German Reich, and split between the Munich and Würzburg depots, where they remained until the end of the war when they were reclaimed by the French national railway. Despite the recent appearance of the streamlined three-cylinder 01.10 and 03.10 locomotives, and the reduction in fast passenger services as the war ground on, Munich still had fifteen

operational 18.4s of the first series in 1943 and Nuremburg twenty-five, split between the various tranches of the Pacifics. Obviously, the movement of military and freight traffic increased during these years, more than offsetting any reduction in civilian passenger traffic.

In the latter stages of the war, as the Allies prepared for invasion and then advanced into Germany, railway installations in 1944 and the early part of 1945 were subject to extensive bombing raids, and the locomotive depots and the engines in them suffered considerable damage, so that at the end of the hostilities very few of these compound Pacifics – or any other class of German locomotive – were capable of active service. Large numbers of the 18.4s and 18.5s were stored unserviceable pending decisions on possible repair or withdrawal.

Operations 1945-1962 (*Deutsche Bundesbahn*)

At the end of the war, civilian passenger traffic was very slow to be restored in the Zones under control of the British, American and French military. Such passenger trains that ran in the 1945-7 period were mainly a few stopping trains serving local communities. The repair and return of express passenger locomotives was not a priority, and decisions were not made until 1948-50 about which engines to repair and which to withdraw, apart from the locomotives completely destroyed in the bombing raids. Many engines that had been stored since 1944-5 were therefore not shown

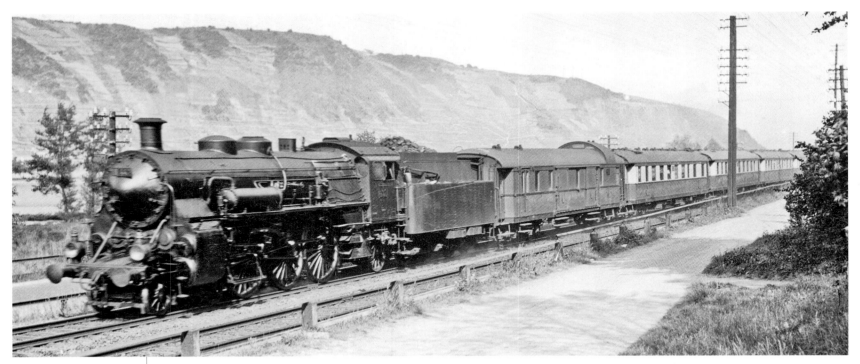

High-wheeled S3/6 18.443 working FFD101 *Rheingold* northbound past Andernach, in the Rhine Valley, 3 July 1929. (DLA Darmstadt/ Eisenbahnstiftung Collection)

18.466, built in 1917, hauling D39 Munich–Berlin at Falkenstein in the Frankenwald, c1930. These Maffei Pacifics regularly were diagrammed to these services between Munich, Nuremberg and Halle with some turns throughout to Berlin. 18.466 was based at Nuremberg for nineteen years between 1928 and 1947, and continued operation during and in the immediate post-war years, being withdrawn from Ulm in October 1955. (Eisenbahnstiftung Collection)

as withdrawn until 1949 or 1950, although most had not turned a wheel in the intervening period.

A decision was clearly taken to concentrate repairs on the 18.4s and 18.5s built after 1923, with most of the earlier engines based at Munich and Nuremberg, including many stored at stations throughout Bavaria, being withdrawn. A total of forty-four 18.4s were withdrawn in 1949-50, including all the large-diameter wheeled 18.4s with the exception of 18.451 which went to the Minden Research & Testing Centre, where it was equipped with a standard 7,500-gallon water capacity large tender to extend its range on test trains. On 2 May 1951, it broke the long distance record for a single run with steam

power – 512 miles - from Hamburg to Munich.

In the 1950s, the remaining Bavarian Pacifics undertook some prestige passenger turns again including long-distance F3/4, F19/20 and F51/52 (Passau-Regensburg on the *Vienna-Ostend Express*). Munich had lost all its 18.4-5 turns by 1950, although Nuremberg retained some diagrams until 1953. Munich's last significant turns were via Ingolstadt to Treuchtlingen. Nuremberg engines worked on express trains to Stuttgart and Würzburg, plus a number of semi-fast and stopping trains to Crailsheim, Bayreuth and Würzburg. Their last three locomotives of the class, 18.487, 501

and 505, were transferred to Ulm and Lindau in September 1953.

Hof had been the location for many of the stored locomotives that were withdrawn in 1949 and 1950, but in May 1950 the Depot received eight 18.5s, which – as well as semi-fast and stopping passenger trains – operated the following expresses: D11/12, D115/116 and D337/338, all between Hof and Bamberg, averaging some 220 miles a day until replaced by rebuilt 18.6 Pacifics and the standard 01s. Regensburg had ten 18.5s, although some were reappearing as rebuilt 18.6s, until the summer of 1955. On similar turns, the standard 01 and 03s were burning some 10-30% more coal than the compound

18.444 at its home Station, Passau in Bavaria, 1933. It still sports the chimney decoration that dates from the time these machines were the regular locomotives for the *Rheingold* and has also a small swastika at the top of the smokebox door showing the allegiance of much of this part of Bavaria to the recently elected Nazi Government, 1933. (MLS Collection)

1924-built 18.500 with D57 at Heigenbrücken, on the line between Nuremberg and Aschaffenburg, 8 September 1934. (Carl Bellingrodt/Eisenbahnstiftung Collection)

18.534, built by Henschel in 1930, passing Hagen-Haspe in the Ruhr with D94 Hamburg-Cologne, 11 February 1934, when eight of these Bavarian-designed engines were allocated to Osnabrück as 'stopgaps' until the new 03s, 03.058-071, were allocated there. (DLA Darmstadt/Eisenbahnstiftung Collection)

Pacifics. However, when total running costs were taken into account, including maintenance, the more complex compound Pacifics were more expensive overall. In 1955, Regensburg had eight 18.5s and two 18.6s. By June 1956, this had fallen to just two 18.5s and five 18.6s. From 1957-9,

the remaining former Bavarian Pacifics there were all DRG-built 18.5s and DB-rebuilt 18.6s.

The last years of the lives of the 18.4s and 18.5s were concentrated in the Augsburg-Lindau-Ulm area. In 1949, Ulm Depot had seven to eight locomotives of the 18.461-478 series, most of which were

withdrawn between 1953 and 1955, and replaced by engines in the 18.479-546 series, working mainly to Friedrichshafen, Lindau, Kempten and via Ingolstadt to Regensburg, the latter a run of 201kms (126 miles). They were replaced at Ulm by the P10 2-8-2s in 1955.

Augsburg had a large fleet

Henschel-built 18.545 (Bw Mainz) with E112 at Wuppertal-Unterbarmen, April 1937, shortly before being displaced by the 03 4-6-2s when the remaining S3/6s based in the Rhine Valley and Ruhr were sent to depots in the south.
(RVM Berlin/Eisenbahnstiftung Collection)

ranging between fifteen and seventeen locomotives of the type between 1950 and 1954, working to Aulendorf via Memmingen, Lindau via Kempten, Garmisch and Ingolstadt. This reduced to seven locomotives for five diagrams from 1954 to 1960, involving eight semi-fast and eight local passenger trains, and just two D-Zug turns over the short distance between Augsburg and Buchloe. The most

18.524 on FFD 102, the southbound *Rheingold*, at Boppard, 1930.
(DLA Darmstadt/ Eisenbahnstiftung Collection)

important turns were heavy semi-fast trains from Augsburg to the Alpine resort of Oberstdorf, the train splitting at Immenstadt, with the S3/6 continuing with a light load to Lindau. 18.483 and 18.516 were withdrawn in 1960, and the last four

unrebuilt Bavarian Pacifics, 18.481, 508, 512 and 528, remained working local services to Weilheim and Kempten until May 1961, when 481, 508 and 528 were sent to Lindau.

After the Second World War, Lindau had seven active S3/6s for

its main line work to Munich, Ulm and Radolfzell, and received three more from Nuremberg in 1953. The older locomotives were withdrawn in the mid-1950s and were gradually replaced by Pacifics built in the 1920s. After electrification in the

18.527 with the southbound *Rheingold* FFD 102, at the famous Rhine photographic spot of Oberwesel with its castle, including the Ochsenturm (Ox tower), 16 April 1938. (RVM Berlin/Eisenbahnstiftung Collection)

18.536 (later rebuilt as 18.613) works the *Rheingold* (FD 101) near Trechtinghausen on the Rhine, autumn 1932. (Carl Bellingrodt/ Eisenbahnstiftung Collection)

18.476 enters Nuremberg Station with an express from Augsburg (its home depot) passing a class 50 2-10-0 standing at the next platform, 1951. 18.476 (the former 3667 of June 1918) was one of the few of that batch that were not taken as war reparations (3665/66 and 3668-70/72/74-79). It was withdrawn from Augsburg in May 1954.
(Fritz Söltner/Eisenbahnstiftung Collection)

Darmstadt area in 1957, more 18.4s and 18.5s came to Lindau, although they were replaced by 18.6s as rebuilding took place and by 1959, all the remaining 18.4-5s had gone to Augsburg, with Lindau's fleet being made up entirely of 18.6s. In May 1961, however, Lindau received the last three from Augsburg, 18.481 being withdrawn in August 1961, 18.508 in July 1962, and the last survivor, 18.528, in November 1962, its official condemnation date not being until November 1963.

However, just one other 18.5 survived, but out of the normal traffic operating stock. 18.505 had gone to Minden Research Centre in 1955 and remained there until withdrawn in 1968, and was then preserved.

War Reparations Locomotives

As part of the Armistice Treaty at the end of the First World War, the German railways were required to send over 5,000 locomotives to the systems of the victor nations to repair the losses sustained on their railways through the damage and harsh use incurred during the war years. Included in this number were nineteen Bavarian S3/6 Pacifics,

three going to Belgium, 3620, 3646 and 3649, renumbered 5920/46/49. They were allocated to the Tournai District, and worked between Brussels and Ostend among other duties, but their condition was rumoured not to be good and all three had been withdrawn from service by 1924.

Most of the other sixteen destined for France were in much better condition; indeed, thirteen of them were virtually brand new, having been being built at the Maffei Works in 1918,

One of the surviving unrebuilt Bavarian Pacifics of the 1926-30 series, 18.528, heads a local P-Zug towards Lindau, while 0-8-2T 98.1026 shunts at Röthenbach S tation in the foothills of the Bavarian Alps, 8 June 1962. (Herbert Schambach)

Bavarian S3/6 Pacific 3668, built in July 1918, was passed to the French Etat Railway in 1919 as part of the Armistice agreement and was numbered 231.987, and 231A.987 after 1938. The locomotive, with others of the class, was based at Le Mans, Niort, Nantes and Saintes, recovered by the DR in March 1942 and allocated to Munich, and returned to the SNCF in 1945, but withdrawn immediately. The last examples were withdrawn in 1949. It is probable that this photo was taken at Nantes in the early 1930s. (MLS Collection)

numbered between 3665 and 3679 (they would have received DR numbers in the series from 18.476 onwards had they remained in Germany). They were all allocated to the Etat system of France, later the Ouest Region of the SNCF, receiving the numbers 231.981-996 (3602/05/18/22/65/66/68-70/72/74-79) in that numerical order. In February 1919, most were allocated to Le Mans with a few to Thouars. A few were at Niort and La Rochelle between 1927 and 1931. After 1931 all were reallocated to Nantes and in 1935 were stationed at Saintes. Their duties at the height of their use in the 1920s and 30s included passenger trains between Paris-Le Mans-Rennes / Angers, Thouars-Niort-Royan, Thouars-Bordeaux, Nantes-Bordeaux and Saintes-Royan. At the end of the 1930s, their diagrams included *rapides* between Nantes and Bordeaux via La Rochelle and Saintes. Although the economy and performance of these locomotives was good, it can't have been easy as the French railways were unable to purchase spare parts from the DRG.

There were obvious changes in appearance – French air-pump brake cylinders replaced the German ones, flat smokebox doors replaced the distinctive Maffei 'bullet noses', and short stovepipe chimneys, as some Bavarian engines sported in the early days, were never replaced by the flared taller chimneys of the German engines. Smoke deflectors of French design were fitted and the engines received the dark green livery, becoming SNCF 231A 981-996 in 1938.

During the German invasion of France, the DR recovered the sixteen SNCF locomotives in

High-wheeled S3/6 18.451, retained at Minden Research Centre for rolling stock trials, seen here at Minden in 1951 just before withdrawal and subsequent restoration in 1958 as Bavarian State Railway 3634 in Bavarian State Railway green livery in the Deutsches Museum, Munich. It was damaged during a storm in 1967 and restored again, and is currently displayed in the State Transport Hall of the Museum.
(Carl Bellingrodt/MLS/EK-Verlag)

February/March 1942, and divided them between Würzburg and Munich until the end of the war, when all sixteen were reclaimed by the SNCF, although the condition of most of them, including war damage, meant that they were at first stored at Achères, Versailles and Saintes, and then withdrawn as the imported rugged American 141R 2-8-2s were more suited to the post war traffic situation than the complex four-cylinder compounds. Most were officially withdrawn in 1945 and 1946, although 231A 983, 984, 989, 995 and 996 lasted (at least on paper) until 1949, and 231A 987

and 993 were actually not broken up until the early 1950s.

Preserved Locomotives
18.427
18.427 was built by Maffei in 1914 as No. 343 for the Pfalz State Railway system and stationed at Ludwigshafen. After a spell at Hof from 1926 to 1928, it returned to Ludwigshafen for another ten years before being stationed at Treuchtlingen during the war. It was stored out of action there for several years before returning to Munich in 1948, but only to be officially withdrawn there in

April. It was cut up in August 1950, but the cab and backplate of the locomotive were restored and exhibited in the Deutsches Museum Transport Hall in Munich from 1951 until 1969, when lack of space there allowed it to be on permanent loan to the Deutsche Gesellschaft fur Eisenbahngeschichte (DGEG) Museum in Bochum-Dahlhausen.

Preserved four-cylinder compound Pacific 18.478, restored in Bavarian State Railway livery as 3673, double-heading a railtour with preserved 01.2066-7 at Dresden Altstadt. (Roger Bastin)

18.505 at Minden Research Centre, 23 August 1967. It is equipped with a ten-wheel tender from a class 45 2-10-2 giving it more coal capacity and a longer range than its own Bavarian Railway tender. (MLS Collection)

18.451 (3634)

18.451 was one of the 1912-13 built eighteen S3/6 Maffei Pacifics with 6ft 7in driving wheels designed for high-prestige trains such as the *Rheingold*. It was initially stationed at Munich, then from 1923 to 1935 it was based at Würzburg. It was based at Treuchtlingen for most of the Second World War, then afterwards, still operational, it was at Kempten and Augsburg before going to Minden Research & Test Centre from 1950 to 1952, and stored until 1954 pending cutting up. However, after withdrawal it was restored between May 1957 and June 1958 as an exhibit in full Bavarian State Railway green

livery as 3634 in the Deutsches Museum Munich. Because of lack of space, it was kept in the open and suffered storm damage and, after further restoration, was found a place in the Museum Hall of Transport in 1968.

18.478 (3673/3645)

18.478 was the last of the first series design of Maffei four-cylinder compound Pacifics built in 1918 and retained on the DR system, and the last to be withdrawn in June 1960 from Ulm Depot, although it had been stored out of service since March 1959. It was initially allocated to Munich and spent most of the pre-war

years there before moving between Lindau, Ulm and Augsburg in the 1950s. It was purchased by Swiss enthusiast, Serge Lory, in 1962 and stored at Lindau during initial steps towards restoration in running order. Although given the number 18.478, an engine built as 3673 in 1918, Lory discovered that it had the frames and Maffei Works number of 3482, which was built in 1914 as 3645 and subsequently renumbered as 18.422. It is thought that the frames were exchanged during Works visits after the war, when some engines were being repaired and others cut up in the Munich-Freimann Works between 1948 and 1953. It was moved from

The preserved 18.505 hauls Pullman cars on the fiftieth anniversary of the introduction of the *Rheingold* between Amsterdam and Basle. It is seen leaving Cologne in pouring rain, 14 April 1978.
(Peter Schiffer/Eisenbahnstiftung Collection)

Lindau to Switzerland in 1966 for restoration. After Lory's death, Christoph Oswald purchased it in 1981 and restored it to Bavarian livery numbered 3673 (in both apple green and blue liveries) in running order and for use on railtours, until 2004. It is based at the Bayrische Eisenbahn Museum in Nördlingen in Bavaria.

18.505
18.505 (018.0505-8) was built by the DR in 1924, but numbered as Bavarian State Railway 3706. After being stationed at Nuremberg for nearly thirty years, and a couple of years at Lindau, it was allocated to the Minden Research Centre in 1955 and coupled to a ten-wheel large-capacity tender from a class 45 2-10-2 freight locomotive. It remained there until withdrawn in 1968. It was repaired and restored at Neuenmarkt-Wirsberg, and then was transferred to the DGEG Museum (the German Society for Railway History) at Neustadt Weinstrasse in the Pfalz/Saarland area on long-term loan.

18.508
18.508 was built in 1924 and was the last to bear the Bavarian Railway number, as 3709. It appeared at the railway engineering exhibition at Seddin near Berlin the same year in a blue livery with silver boiler bands. It took part in a display of locomotives in Friedrichshafen in June 1962 and was withdrawn from Lindau Depot two months later, and was saved from the line of stored condemned locomotives standing at Lindau-Reutin by the Swiss architect

18.508, operating out of Lindau Depot, at Kempten, 27 March 1962. It was then working mainly stopping services between Lindau and Kempten via both Oberstaufen and Memmingen. It was nicknamed '*Saunalok*' by its crews because of its habit of filling the cab with leaking steam. (MLS Collection)

Otto Fiechter. Many items had been stripped from the stored locomotive, but the new owner obtained the necessary parts from East Germany, Italy and Austria. 18.508 was hauled to Switzerland in 1973 and is now based at Romanshorn.

18.528

18.528 was the last of the twenty S3/6s ordered from Krauss-Maffei in 1925, built in March 1928 and spent most of the pre-war years at Mainz where it would have included haulage of the *Rheingold* among its duties. After the war it was based at Darmstadt, then Hof, moving to Lindau in 1957, Augsburg from 1958 to 1961 and being withdrawn from Lindau in November 1962. In 1963 the firm Krauss-Maffei purchased the last working 18.5, which had been stored after its withdrawal. It was moved to the Company Works in Munich-Allach in January 1964, sandblasted and restored externally, and displayed outside the main offices as a memorial to the most famous product of the firm. It was restored in 1968 so that it could be seen by people in the street outside the Works boundary. It began to deteriorate in the open air, but a club initially called Railway Club 18.528, renamed later as the Munich Railway Club, took regular care of it to maintain it in good external condition.

Chapter 6

THE REBUILT MAFFEI PACIFICS – 18.6

Design & Construction

As described above, the *Bundesbahn* engineering management got authority to modernise a significant number of their express passenger locomotives with large high-performance all-welded boilers and combustion chambers to equip them for post-war conditions, including all the three-cylinder 01.10s, the 03.10s remaining in West Germany, and a good proportion of the two-cylinder 01s. After the mass withdrawal of the unserviceable older S3/6s in 1949/50, there were 86 of the 159 former Bavarian Pacifics aged between twenty and thirty-eight years old still in traffic. It was decided to rebuild the younger members of the class with new boilers, cabs and cylinder blocks. 18.521 was selected as the first, due for a L4 overhaul in 1951, and Krauss-Maffei built five new boilers. Then followed a substantial number of tests at Minden Research Centre; improvements were made to strengthen the boiler, then, because of costs, a decision was made not to include new cylinder blocks in the rebuilding. There were also investigations into the possibility of equipping the rebuilds with Kylchap exhausts, but delivery and licence problems with the builder in France led to that idea being abandoned. Had all these projected improvements been incorporated, the result could have been not only the most economical of German express locomotives, but also one of the most capable in service.

18.521 was finally equipped with the strengthened all-welded boiler with combustion chamber in March 1953 at the Munich-Freimann Works and renumbered 18.601. The remaining new boilers were then fitted to 18.547 as 18.602 in June 1953, 18.525 (18.603) in July and 18.522 (18.604) in November. Because of Munich-Freimann's workload with the construction of new electric locomotives and multiple units, the rebuilding programme for the 18.5s was switched to the Ingolstadt Works, and 18.530 received the last of the five new boilers there and emerged in January 1954 as 18.605. The expected improvements in boiler performance were realised and further rebuilding was authorised, the intention at that time of the Stuttgart motive power division being to rebuild forty-five of the newer machines. However, electrification was progressing apace, the Nuremberg-Würzburg section being the latest, and the decision was reversed with an edict in 1954 that no more of the 18.461-478 series were to receive L4 overhauls, and the 18.479-508 series were not to receive new boilers. The decision was still to rebuild the thirty-eight remaining 1926-30-built engines (18.515 and 533 had been destroyed in the war), but as further electrification took place, the rebuilding ceased with the conversion of 18.543 as 18.630, which was released back into traffic at Lindau in April 1957. After 18.605, all the rebuilding took place at Ingolstadt at the rate of approximately one a month. The cost averaged out at 130,000 DM per locomotive.

Key dimensions remained – still a four-cylinder compound with 6ft 1½in driving wheels, 227lbpsi, total heating surface of 2,111sqft, superheater 797sqft. The engine was

The first all-welded boiler S3/6, 18.521, at the Krauss-Maffei Works at Munich-Allach in February 1953, renumbered a month later as the first of a new series, 18.601. (Krauss-Maffei/Siemens A6)

heavier at 169.3 tons (if equipped with the larger 7,000-gallon tender) and maximum axle-load was now increased to 19.1 tons. The performance was significantly upgraded with the indicated output upped to 2,250hp, the theoretical tractive effort remaining at 21,362lb.

After its rebuilding, tests were conducted at Minden with 18.601. These included an extraordinary test at 75mph with 800 tons for over forty minutes between Karlsruhe and Offenburg when, it was said, the spectacle put the fear of God into any observer at the intermediate stations! Further tests took place on the Frankfurt-Hamburg trunk route, initially

with 18.608 and 18.609 in similar diagrams to two 01s, 101 and 151. The prime purpose was to compare fuel economy and the rebuilt S3/6s averaged 13.82 tons of coal per 1,000 kilometres (625 miles) compared with the 01s' 14.15, although it was admitted that the crews' familiarity with their own 01s probably gave them a 10% advantage. However, the trials were only for a few weeks, and it was felt that six months would have been necessary to come to fair and firm conclusions. In September 1954, trials were made in service on a pair of long-distance trains on the route F41/42. 18.606 was tested at first, but there were a number of mechanical failures of the

motion and 18.601 was substituted before 18.606 returned. Boiler pressure held up well, and the S3/6 showed superior acceleration in recovering from slacks and delays, but the maximum speed of 75mph compared with the standard Pacifics' 81mph left them little in reserve. It was finally concluded that their 6ft 1½in coupled wheels made them unsuitable for fast expresses on the flat lands of northern Germany and their most appropriate areas remained in the heavily-graded routes in the south. The mechanical problems experienced by 18.601 and 606 were repeated at first by the Darmstadt engines working in the Heidelberg, Karlsruhe

18.601, with new number identification, the first S3/6 rebuild with all-welded boiler and combustion chamber at Munich-Freimann Works, 16 March 1953.
(Georg Steidl)

1930 Henschel-built 18.535, converted and renumbered 16.606 in February 1954, ex-works after its last L4 overhaul at its home depot, Bw Lindau, 1960.
(W. Grange/Eisenbahstiftung Collection)

and Ludwigshafen area, with damage caused by overheating until lubrication problems were addressed.

The first rebuilt locomotives to be withdrawn, as V200 diesels made redundant by electrification were drafted to Kempten Depot to power the Munich-Lindau D-Zug services, took place in 1961, the first to go being 18.625 in January and officially condemned in May. This was followed over the next three months by 18.604, 18.618 and 18.628 as their overhauls became due, as the imminent dieselisation of key trains on the Lindau-Munich route became clear. The engines were steadily withdrawn as they were due for heavy overhaul and stored at Lindau-Reutin pending scrapping through 1962-4, with the last survivors, 18.603, 614, 617, 622 and 630 eking out their last days on semi-fast and stopping services, with 18.630 being withdrawn in April 1965 and 18.622 finally being withdrawn in September.

One of the recently rebuilt S3/6 Pacifics, 18.527, reboilered in 1954 and renumbered 18.607, at its home depot, Darmstadt, 2 June 1954. (MLS Collection/ Carl Bellingrodt/EK-Verlag)

18.620, formerly 18.514, built by Maffei in 1926 and rebuilt with all-welded boiler and combustion chamber in July 1955, at Aulendorf Depot, 6 May 1964. (Herbert Schambach)

18.620 on the turntable at its home depot of Lindau, 1962
(Herbert Schambach)

Operations

The initial allocation of the rebuilt S3/6s was to Darmstadt where they performed on the services that the Pfalz locomotives 18.425-434, and later 1926-30-built 18.5s had operated, particularly on express services to Frankfurt, Wiesbaden and Heidelberg. There were a number of mechanical failures caused by lubrication problems, especially when working light fast trains. Reduced coal consumption expectations were fulfilled, burning around one ton less per 1,000 kilometres than the 18.5s. 18.6s allocated to Hof for the Nuremberg-Bamberg-Hof services experienced no problems and 18.611, in December 1954, handled heavy Christmas traffic where its superior boiler performance was useful. 18.615 also worked in the area and, because of their performance, 18.6s were rostered to the Hof-Stuttgart expresses. Nuremberg used 18.6s in its summer 1955 01 diagrams successfully until, in 1956, there began to be welding failures in the new boilers that caused all locomotives to be stopped and returned to Ingolstadt while investigations were made and the boiler faults corrected.

Initially, as a temporary measure, their boiler pressure was reduced from 227lb to 199lbpsi, although restoration to the former pressure was authorised in 1957, by which time the teething problems of the

18.630, formerly 18.543 built by Henschel under licence in 1930, the last 18.5 to be rebuilt with all-welded boiler and combustion chamber in April 1957, at Lindau Depot where it was stationed until its withdrawal in April 1965, 21 June 1962.
(Herbert Schambach)

18.611, rebuilt from 18.509 in December 1954, and based at Nuremberg, standing at the head of a Nuremberg-Stuttgart D-Zug into the latter station, 17 August 1958. (Joachim Claus/ Eisenbahnstiftung Collection)

new boilers had been resolved. However, their opportunity for high-performance work was rapidly diminishing as further electrification was introduced, the Hof engines becoming redundant in October 1957 as 01s were transferred which were not needed elsewhere. In May 1959, the Regensburg-allocated 18.6s were made superfluous by electrification and in 1961, 18.6s were no longer required at Ulm. Despite the mechanical and boiler problems that the 18.6s had had since their conversion, the engines were popular on the road with their crews, who were sorry to see them go.

Other rebuilds quickly found their way to Ulm and Lindau, operating between Lindau, Friedrichshafen and Ulm, and Lindau-Munich via both

Oberstaufen and Memmingen. The first allocation to Lindau was of 18.609 in April 1957. They hauled all the international services from Munich to Austria and Switzerland via Lindau, and many of the semi-fast heavy services (shared with unrebuilt 18.5s and ex-Prussian class 39 2-8-2s) between Munich/ Augsburg and Oberstdorf/Lindau.

Finally, all the 18.6s, with one solitary exception (18.628, which stayed at Ulm until withdrawal) were allocated to Lindau until V200 diesels began to infiltrate in 1961 and the V200.1s in 1963. During a visit I made with colleague Alastair Wood in the summer of 1962, the named trains D92/93 *Bavaria* and D96/97 *Rhône-Isar*, formed of lightweight Swiss stock, were hauled by V200s based at Kempten

– we had runs on D91, D95 and D98 which were still 18.6-hauled. By April 1963, they were limited to a few Eilzug and P-Zug diagrams between Lindau and Kempten via Oberstaufen and Memmingen, Aulendorf to Munich, Buchloe to Lindau, and a couple of turns to Friedrichshafen and Ulm. No more major Works repairs were carried out after 1962 and by the summer service of 1964, just six were left – 18.603, 614, 617, 620, 622 and 630. The last to operate out of Munich main station was 18.620 on E766, 7.37am Munich – Freiburg, on 26 September 1964. 18.603 and 617 were withdrawn in September, 18.620 in November, 18.614 in January 1965 and 18.630 in April, leaving just 18.622.

However, in the summer of

18.616 on the turntable at Bw Nuremberg, freshly rebuilt in March 1955 from 18.517, April 1955. (Eisenbahnstiftung Collection)

1965, the Austrian main line (the *Arlbergbahn*), used by the *Orient Express* and a number of other international sleeping car expresses, was blocked by flooding and some trains were diverted via the Munich-Lindau route, causing 18.622 to experience a last flowering on some of these high-prestige services. Along with Kempten V200s and a few 01s, 18.622 is known to have worked a number of international named expresses including the *Rot-Weiss Kurier, Arlberg Express* and the *Wiener Walzer*, and on 10 August 1965 hauled a Touropa-Zug between Radolfzell and Lindau. Its last run was made on 1 September 1965. 18.622 had previously had a 'farewell' railtour from Munich to Ingolstadt and Treuchtlingen in May that year, so the resurgence in the summer was unplanned and unexpected.

Although 18.622 languished for sometime after withdrawal in case of possible preservation, it was an earlier withdrawal, 18.612, that was preserved. Because the 18.6 boilers were relatively new, several were retained for stationary boiler duties, and one, 18.610, went to Minden for research and experimentation on a central automatic-coupling device. When the research and tests had been completed, it was again possible that it would be preserved, but eventually it too was scrapped. 18.602 acted as a stationary boiler at Saarbrücken until it was scrapped in January 1983, although its wheels were retained and are on display at Saarbrücken Hbf.

For logs of my own personal experiences behind the rebuilt S3/6 18.6s between Lindau and Munich, see Chapter 18, pages 125.

18.608, rebuilt from 18.518, on an Ulm-Friedrichshafen-Lindau train at Aulendorf, alongside former Württemberg 2-6-2T 75.007, c1957. (MLS Collection)

18.615 (18.529 built by Maffei 1930) at Munich Hbf with a D-Zug for Lindau and Switzerland, 1960. (MLS Collection)

Lindau Locomotive Depot roundhouse, the home of nearly all the reboilered S3/6s from the late 1950s until their final demise in 1965. From left to right, reboilered 18.608, locos in original condition 18.481 and 528, P8 38.3364 and reboilered 18.616, May 1961. (MLS Collection)

A group of S3/6 Pacifics at the roundhouse in Ulm, from left to right, 18.601, 18.607, the unrebuilt and later to be preserved 18.478 and 18.629, 1960. (Kronawitter/ Eisenbahnstiftung Collection)

Lindau Station on arrival of D76 from Kiel, finding 18.629 (formerly 18.539) on the evening D97 for Munich, and 18.607 (ex-18.527) on the D75 to Kiel which it will run only as far as Friedrichshafen where it will be replaced in a reversal movement by an 03 Pacific for the next section to Ulm, August 1961. (David Maidment)

18.605, the former Maffei 18.530 rebuilt with an all-welded boiler, backs onto an evening Eilzug (E765 to Munich/Augsburg via Memmingen) at Lindau Hbf, July 1962. (David Maidment)

18.611 (18.509 built by Maffei 1926) at Singen with a Lindau-Konstanz Eilzug, 22 January 1963. (MLS Collection)

Two rebuilt Bavarian Pacifics, led by 18.623 (Henschel 1930 18.531), depart from Lindau with a D-Zug for Munich, 9 June 1962. (Herbert Schambach)

18.620 leads 18.611 with D92 (Geneva – Lindau – Munich express) at Bühl-bei-Alpsee in the Alpine foothills between Lindau and Immenstadt, April 1962. (H.Navé)

A Lindau-Kempten stopping train, composed of former Bavarian State Railway four-wheel coaches, halts at Röthenbach behind 18.613 (the rebuilt 18.536), 8 June 1962. (Herbert Schambach)

18.612 (Maffei 18.520, rebuilt December 1954) on a stopping train near Nonnenhorn, between Lindau and Friedrichshafen, 5 June 1962. 18.612 is now the only preserved rebuilt 18.6 and is displayed at the museum at Neuenmarkt-Wirsberg. (Herbert Schambach)

18.615 (Henschel 1930, rebuilt March 1955) stopping at Nonnenhorn Station with a Lindau-Friedrichshafen P-Zug, 22 June 1962.
(Herbert Schambach)

18.630 (Henschel 1930 18.543, rebuilt April 1957) approaching Nonnenhorn with a Lindau-Friedrichshafen P-Zug, 7 June 1962. (Herbert Schambach)

18.617 crosses the Bodenseedamm, departing from Lindau with a D-Zug for Munich, 22 May 1964. (Herbert Schambach)

18.620 (Maffei 1926 18.514, rebuilt July 1955) with train E766 from Aulendorf at Kisslegg, 6 May 1964.
(Herbert Schambach)

The decorated 18.622 stands in the pouring rain at Solnhofen on the occasion of its 'farewell' railtour, 29 May 1965, from Munich to Ingolstadt and Treuchtlingen. 18.622 was reprieved for a few further months after flooding and a serious earthslip on the Arlberg route in Austria, and a number of international expresses were diverted via Munich and Lindau.
(Helmut Dahlhaus)

18.604 (formerly 18.522), after withdrawal in the autumn of 1961, stands alongside the withdrawn 18.618 (18.510) at Lindau-Reutin, 25 April 1963. It was hauled to Offenburg Works in 1963 and given an overhaul to fit it for stationary-boiler duties at Cologne until 1969. (MLS Collection)

Preserved Locomotives

18.610

18.610 (18.523 Maffei 1927) was withdrawn from Lindau Depot in November 1962 and initially used as a stationary boiler in Lindau. In 1965, it was experimentally equipped with automatic central couplings and took part in tests at Minden Research Centre from 1967. Most of the locomotive was scrapped in 1976, but the wheel sets, cylinders and smokebox were retained and put on display at the Deutsches Dampflok Museum at Neuenmarkt-Wirsberg.

18.612

18.612, built as 18.520 by Krauss-Maffei in 1927, and rebuilt with an all-welded boiler in 1954, was withdrawn from Lindau in 1964 and acted as a stationary boiler at Kempten until 1969, when it was selected by enthusiasts Gerhard Böck and Steffen Lüdecke for possible preservation in preference to 18.610 and 18.602 that had lingered on with stationary-boiler duties. Helped by railway official and 'friend' of the S3/6s, J.B. Kronawitter, it was rescued and taken initially to Munich in

18.612, built by Maffei in 1927, and rebuilt with all-welded boiler and combustion chamber in December 1954, destined for preservation at the Deutches Dampflokomotiv Museum in Neunmarkt-Wirsberg, at work on a D-Zug at Nonnenhorn between Lindau and Friedrichshafen, 12 June 1962. (Herbert Schambach)

1973 and then in 1974 moved to the Deutsches Dampflokomotiv Museum in Neuenmarkt-Wirsberg in West Germany, where it was cosmetically restored by a group of railway enthusiasts from the Munich area who spent over 3,500 hours between them until it was capable of being displayed in gleaming condition in 1975.

Preserved 18.612 (18.520 Maffei 1927) on D95, 9.47am Lindau-Munich, before preservation at the Deutsches Dampflokomotiv Museum Neuenmarkt-Wirsberg, 27 September 1962. This is the only example of an 18.6 that has been preserved. After withdrawal in 1964, it was retained as a stationary boiler in Kempten until 1969. It was moved to the Museum in August 1976. (W.A. Reed/Eisenbahnstiftung Collection)

Chapter 7

THE SAXON PACIFICS – XVIII H (18.0)

Design & Construction

At the turn of the nineteenth century the Royal Saxon State Railway, whose main lines radiated out from Dresden to Leipzig, Chemnitz and Berlin, had their express trains running at planned speeds no higher than 56mph. Their VIII VI 4-4-0 of 1897 could haul just 210 tons on the level at that speed and rarely ran further than fifty miles before stopping or engine change. The lines to Berlin and Leipzig were relatively flat in contrast to the main line to Chemnitz and Hof, which had heavy gradients through the Erzgebirge, or the line through Bautzen to the Polish border that ran close to the edge of the Lausitzer mountains. In their search for more powerful and appropriate locomotives for their terrain, the Saxon Railway Board had worked closely with the engineering firm of Hartmann, and built Atlantic 4-4-2s (X H I – later DRG 14.3) for the level routes and XII H V four-cylinder compound 4-6-0s (17.7) for the more difficult lines.

As loads grew and their Bavarian, Württemberg and Baden State Railway neighbours moved to four-cylinder compound Pacifics to ease their problems, the Saxon Railway began to debate the merits of two- or three-cylinder superheated 'simple' engines compared with the compounds used elsewhere in the more mountainous parts of southern Germany. Neighbouring Austria had experimented with oil-firing, with fuel from the Galicia oil field. The most numerous Saxon passenger class in the first decade of the new century were forty-two 4-6-0s – the XII HV (DRG 17.7) built between 1908 and 1914. One of these was experimentally fuelled by oil, but import taxes for the fuel were high. Tests were carried out in 1915 between a Bavarian S3/6 (3654), a Prussian S10.1 4-6-0, and one of their own 4-6-0 four-cylinder compounds, seeking an engine that could haul 430 tons up long 1 in 100 gradients on the Leipzig-Chemnitz-Hof route at 44mph, but none of the test engines could do this. Both Prussian and Saxon engines were under-boilered for this specification. The Bavarian engine could do this for short uphill gradients, where its performance was outstanding, but this was not sustainable for long stretches. The Saxon 4-6-0s had better coal consumption figures than the Saxon Atlantics, but the compound engines were more expensive to maintain.

Initially, the Company resolved to contract the firm of Hartmann to build a number of locomotives to the Bavarian Maffei S3/6 design under licence, but after this proposal had been aborted, Hartmann built ten three-cylinder superheated simple steam Pacifics, of class XVIII H between 1917 and 1918, numbered XVIII H-196-205, later given the number series 18.001-010 by the DRG. These were designed for the level routes from Dresden to Berlin and Leipzig whilst a 2-8-2 four-cylinder compound design was being pursued simultaneously for the Leipzig-Hof route. Rapid acceleration from rest was also important for the Saxon routes as stops were frequent, key cities being only fifteen to twenty miles apart compared with much longer non-stop sections in Bavaria and

Saxon Pacific XVIII H-201 (renumbered DR 18.006 in 1923) as delivered in 1917 by the firm Hartmann. It was withdrawn from Riesa (Elbe) in 1962 and acted as a stationary boiler at Reichenbach until 1964, and scrapped in 1965. (MLS/Carl Bellingrodt/EK-Verlag)

Baden. Up to this stage the Saxon passenger engines were restricted to 62mph, whilst the Prussian S10s were authorised for 69 and the Bavarian Pacifics 75.

The Pacifics had 6ft 3in coupled wheels, three cylinders of 19.7in x 24.8in, boiler pressure of 199lbpsi, grate area of 48.4sqft, heating surface of 2,320sqft and superheater 774sqft. The maximum axle load was 17.2 tons and the engine weight in service was 93.5 tons. It was attached to an eight-wheel tender, the capacity of which was 6,800 gallons of water and 7 tons of coal. Maximum speed was initially 62mph because of the overall maximum line speeds on the Saxon rail network, though this was raised to 75mph as line

speeds improved through track relaying in the 1920s. Maximum indicated horsepower was calculated as 1,700. The cost of the new locomotive was 144,000 Reichsmark, 20,200 for the tender.

Tests in the 1920s between all the main State passenger locomotives as the new *Reichsbahn* administration sought to establish whether any of the designs should be continued or replaced by new standard locomotives, produced interesting and important comparative performance data. At 75mph on level track, the most modern designs of each State railway were led by the Bavarian S3/6 which could haul 640 tons at this speed, followed by the Saxon XX HV (19.0) 2-8-2 which appeared a year after

the Saxon Pacific, at 630 tons, the Baden IV h at 600 tons, then the Prussian P10 and the Saxon XVIII H (18.0) Pacific at 550 tons, and finally the Prussian S10.1 4-6-0 at 400 tons. On a sustained gradient of 1 in 100 at 37½mph, the Bavarian Pacific maintained its superiority with the Baden Pacific and the Saxon 2-8-2, being capable of hauling 380 tons, followed by the P10 at 360 tons and the 18.0 at 310 and finally the S10.1 at 285 tons. Improvements in the main line track was raising line speeds, and the XVIII H was the first Saxon locomotive able to take advantage of the new 75mph limit on the Dresden-Berlin/ Leipzig routes. Coal consumption was 13.8 tons per 1,000 kilometres working 450-ton trains on the

18.001 at Dresden Altstadt
Depot, 3 June 1936.
(MLS/W Hubert)

Berlin-Dresden route, which was higher than the 03 standard Pacifics which replaced them in the 1930s. With its three-cylinder layout, the 18.0 rode at speed as well as the four-cylinder compounds and better than the two-cylinder standard Pacifics. However, the engines were notorious for their inclination to slip on starting.

Nine of the ten locomotives survived the Second World War but were retained in Saxony in East Germany after the Country's partition at the end of the war. The first withdrawal was of 18.002 which was destroyed in the Dresden bombing of April 1945. 18.004 was withdrawn in 1951 to provide spare parts for the overhaul of the other Pacifics, but the other eight then lasted to 1965, with most withdrawals taking place in 1967, although several were stored out of use long

18.010 (previously XVIII-H 205) renumbered and fitted with smoke deflectors, c1925.
(MLS Collection/ C. Bellingrodt/EK-Verlag)

An unidentified Saxon Pacific withdrawn and awaiting scrapping, circa 1965. (MLS Collection)

before official withdrawal and some found later use as stationary boilers. 18.005 was the last to be withdrawn in February 1968, but it had been stored out of use from April 1963. The last active Pacifics were 18.006 and 18.010 which were not withdrawn until May 1965, and were both condemned in 1967. 18.010 was stored until 1971 as it had been earmarked for preservation and display at the Dresden Railway Museum, but a

decision was made to preserve the Saxon express 2-8-2 19.017 instead, and 18.010 was cut up in 1974.

Operations

All ten of the Saxon Pacifics were allocated to Dresden initially and most throughout their entire lives. (18.006 was at Reichenbach and 18.007 at Riesa for the last few months of their existence.) Their immediate work, which they retained until the advent of the 03s

in 1937, was on the Dresden-Berlin main line, and on other routes spreading out from Dresden to Leipzig, Chemnitz, Zittau, Breslau (Wroclaw), Cottbus and Stettin, Magdeburg and via Berlin as far as Wittenberge and Schwerin. In the late 1920s and early 1930s, until the 01s and 03s were available in significant numbers, the 18.0s ran some very long daily mileages, the longest single journeys including the 296 miles to Stralsund on the

18.010 on a D-Zug from Dresden to Görlitz in Dresden-Klotzsche, 1930. Post war in East Germany it was destined for the Dresden DR Museum, but was passed over in favour of Saxon 2-8-2 19.017. It was stored at Dresden-Altstadt Depot awaiting a possible overhaul in September 1964, and withdrawn in March 1967. It was stored at Dresden-Pieschen pending a decision about its fate. It was finally scrapped in February 1974.
(Werner Hubert/DLA Darmstadt/Eisenbahstiftung Collection)

North Sea coast via Frankfurt (Oder); 262 miles to Schwerin via Berlin; 212 miles to Wittenberge; and 146 miles to Frankfurt (Oder).

These long-distance passenger services for civilian personnel were cut back severely from 1943, the maintenance of the track worsened and all long-distance day trains were withdrawn from June 1944. Dresden Altstadt Depot was flattened in the Dresden bombing

raids of 1945 with many of the 18.0s damaged as well as the total destruction of 18.002, and the rail network collapsed with the destruction of the rail bridges over the Elster and Elbe rivers. At the end of the war only one 18.0 Pacific was in working order.

Because of the absence of passenger expresses in the Soviet Zone of Germany in the aftermath of the war, the repair of the damaged 18.0s was not a priority. Of the larger engines, the class 39 2-8-2s were the first to be repaired, then the 18.0s and finally the 19.0s

that had been war-damaged. At least two 18.0s (18.001 and 18.003) were operational by 1948 on stopping passenger services, and by 1954 four of the eight remaining engines were active. They were all still based at Dresden and resumed working expresses on the Berlin

18.004 at Berlin Anhalter Terminus with a D-Zug for Dresden, c1929. (MLS Collection)

Ost-Dresden route from 1953/55 until 1958 when reboilered class 39 2-8-2s (class 22) were rostered to these services, and the 03s in 1960 and even later Dresden 01s and Berlin 01.5s. Some 18.0s had been stored unserviceable between six and eight years before restoration to active use. For a while in the early 1950s, the few operational locomotives worked again, as pre-war, on the long turns to Wittenberge and Schwerin, and Frankfurt (Oder) and Stralsund, and also worked Prague expresses as far as Bad Schandau.

After displacement on the Berlin route, they worked mainly stopping passenger services between Dresden and Elsterwerda, Chemnitz, Riesa and Leipzig, and towards Zittau and Frankfurt (Oder). 18.006 was based at Riesa for six months in early 1962 and then spent just over two years at Reichenbach. 18.007 also spent a few months active at Riesa in early 1963 before being stored unserviceable there until formally condemned in February 1967. 18.010 spent eight months based at Bautzen in 1963-64 before returning to Dresden Altstadt Depot, where all the remaining engines were then based or stored.

18.002 departing from Dresden Hbf with D65, 8 June 1929.
(Werner Hubert/Eisenbahnstiftung Collection)

18.001 on a stopping train from Berlin to Bad Schandau, at Pirna, 17 February 1948. The locomotive will return on the only D-Zug between Dresden and Berlin at that time, D101 Prague-Dresden-Berlin. Because of the need to burn 'brown coal', its tender sides have been built up. (MLS/Thiel)

18.006 entering Dresden Hbf with a stopping train to Elsterwerda, c1960. The Saxon Pacifics lost their main line turns between Dresden and Berlin to the standard DR 03 Pacifics in the winter of 1960. (MLS/Thiel)

Chapter 8

THE *DEUTSCHE REICHSBAHN* 01

The decision to build a new standard Pacific

After the nationalisation of the German State railways in 1921, a number of key appointments were made which shaped the future locomotive policies of the new *Deutsche Reichsbahn*. Richard Paul Wagner, born in 1882 in Berlin, studied engineering at the Technical High School in Charlottenburg and entered to employment of the Prussian State Railway Company in 1906. After a very promising early career there, he worked in Dortmund for the railway headquarters and was appointed as Head of Locomotive Construction in April 1923, following the DR's initial Chief Locomotive Engineer, Heinrich Lübkens, when the latter retired three months later. A Standardisation Office was set up under the leadership of August Meister, who had been in charge of locomotive construction at the firm of Borsig from 1903. A third key appointment was that of Hans Nordmann to the post of Head of Locomotive Testing at

Richard Paul Wagner, Head of Locomotive Construction, *Deutsche Reichsbahn* & *Deutsche Reichsbahn Gesellschaft*, 1922-42.
(A. Gottwaldt Collection)

the same time. He had worked at Halberstadt on the Prussian State system before various other senior engineering positions. In January 1923, he was also appointed as Professor for Engineering Construction at the Technical High School, Charlottenburg. To these three men fell the responsibility and opportunity to develop new standard designs for the nationalised railway.

The new *Reichsbahn* inherited 275 different classes of steam locomotive from the State railway companies, the vast majority of locomotives, 26,148, from the largest, the Prussian State Railway; as explained earlier, that Railway had no passenger engines bigger than the S10.1 4-cylinder compound 4-6-0s. The Royal Bavarian and Saxon Railway Companies had 2,672 and 1,743 engines respectively, and the Baden and Württemberg railways just under 1,000 each. In 1921, the German Railway Ministry held a conference to determine future rail transport policy including locomotive developments. This stimulated debate over the best existing designs to continue as well as setting in train a vast amount of research and development work by the main German locomotive manufacturers. A committee of engineers selected those existing designs for consideration: the Prussian S10.1 (DRG 17.10-12); the Bavarian S3/6 Pacific (DRG 18.4); the Baden IV h Pacific (DRG 18.3); the Württemberg 'C' (DRG 18.1);

the Saxon XX HV 2-8-2 (DRG 19.0); and the Oldenburg S10 (DRG 16.0).

The Oldenburg S10 was quickly eliminated from the considerations, and the 4-6-0 wheel arrangement was believed to be inadequate to cope with the boiler and wide firebox developments which demanded the 4-6-2 or 2-8-2 wheel arrangement. The Saxon XX HV four-cylinder compound found favour, but had the disadvantage of its length and axle-weight, and also difficulty without radical redesign of increasing the diameter of the 6ft 3in driving wheels. Therefore, the Bavarian and Baden Pacifics came back into the reckoning, especially as most turntables were limited to 20-metre lengths. Although some locomotives of State design continued to be built in the 1921-24 period (especially the Bavarian S3/6s to replace the nineteen war reparations), a decision was made to go for a completely new design, although a further forty S3/6 Pacifics were built between 1926 and 1930 before a lightweight standard design Pacific was ready.

The first efforts were 1921 outline designs by Borsig for a 2-8-2 and 4-6-0, followed by Borsig and Henschel designs for a four-cylinder compound Pacific (see drawing, Appendix x). Further ministerial discussions in 1922 laid down that track must at least be able to allow 17 ton axle-weights with the main trunk routes a minimum of 20 tons, larger freight locomotives being as important as new express passenger designs. In the south, turntables were already 22 metres to cater for their Pacifics; the main problems were in Prussia where the S10 4-6-0 had been the largest locomotive.

Parallel to the Pacific four-cylinder compound designs, both Borsig and Henschel prepared proposals for two-cylinder simple superheated Pacifics. Both designs had 213lbpsi boilers and there was pressure to include a combustion chamber along American locomotive design practice – Richard Wagner and the Minister, Friedrich Fuchs, had both had the opportunity to make visits and study USA locomotive policy. It was only after the Second World War, however, that this element of boiler design was incorporated in German locomotives.

There was eventually a long debate over the merits of the competitive proposals of Borsig's two-cylinder simple and Henschel's four-cylinder compound Pacifics. In the end, it was decided to build and compare both, the four-cylinder compound being heavier and more costly, but expected to be more economical in traffic. Maffei also produced a belated four-cylinder compound proposal and with their experience of building such designs, could have been the most efficient design, (see Appendix x) but the Borsig and Henschel designs won the approval of the railway board.

The Standardisation Office set up at the Borsig Works, led by August Meister, became functional on 1 October 1922 and all the drawings were under the direction of the Head of Locomotive Construction, Richard Paul Wagner. In July 1923, he was appointed to the German Railways Board in charge of all new locomotive building in succession to Heinrich Lübkens, and promptly expedited the development of the Borsig and Henschel Pacific designs, sidetracking various other

proposals that were still on the table to develop the Baden IV h Pacific and the Prussian P10 2-8-2 further. The development and introduction of the first standard Pacifics, the two-cylinder 01 and the four-cylinder compound 02, was, therefore, very much the work of Wagner, who frequently visited the Standardisation Office in Berlin-Tegel, worked in close harmony with August Meister, and was present during much of the construction of the prototype locomotives. The availability of 330 million Reichsmark via the Dawes Plan for investment in engineering to recover from the First World War helped at this time, and before the designs were complete, the nationalised *Reichsbahn* was privatised in 1924 to form the *Deutsche Reichsbahn Gesellschaft* (DRG).

The Standard 01 Design & Construction

The standard express locomotive of the new *Reichsbahn* series was the two-cylinder 4-6-2, designated the '01' class, but built almost simultaneously with the compound 02s – in fact the first 02 appeared in October 1925 and was exhibited at a transport exhibition in Munich, whilst the first 01 did not appear until January 1926. Surprisingly, the second 01 to appear in the same month was 01.008 which was the 12,000th locomotive constructed by the Borsig Company. 01.001-008 were built by Borsig and AEG constructed 01.009 and 01.010, and the successful class continued to be built by a number of companies right up to 1937 by which time the class numbered 231. Although the prototype 01s were to be tested against the compound 02s, Wagner made no secret of his preference for the simplicity and robustness of the simple machine, following the principles of the Prussian engineer, Garbe.

The dimensions of the standard 01 as initially built included coupled wheels of 6ft 7in diameter, two outside cylinders of 25.6in x 26in, boiler pressure set at 227lbpsi, although 199lbpsi had been originally proposed for the two-cylinder version; grate area of 47.4sqft; heating surface of 2,554sqft; and a superheated surface of 1,075sqft. The cab design used the form of the Prussian P10 2-8-2. The maximum axle load was 20.2 tons and the engine weight was 108.9 tons. With the original tenders holding 10 tons of coal and 7,000 gallons of water, the total engine weight in service was 184.4 tons. Tractive effort (at 80 per cent) was 39,352lb, indicated horsepower 2,240. Maximum authorised speed was 75mph. The first ten locomotives (01.001-010) were built to this specification. The cost for each was 160,020 Reichsmark. Although originally a standard livery of olive green for boiler, cab and tender had been decided, Wagner changed this to black to avoid the costs of obtaining the paint from overseas.

The 01 was designed to haul 15-16 coaches, weighing 800 tons, at 69mph on the level – indicated horsepower 2,400, edhp 1,800. The first ten locomotives were allocated to Grunewald, Hamm, Hof and Erfurt, and the first ten 02 compound Pacifics similarly allocated for comparison in early 1926. Therefore, they were tested on both level and heavy gradients, and

were operated on similar diagrams as far as possible. Early experience showed the compound locomotives had no advantage over the two-cylinder engines, but tests were set up between Bebra and Erfurt, 64.3 miles, involving two moderate inclines from Bebra/Gerstungen to Hönebach (both directions) and Eisenach to Leinakanal. Testing was not so thorough as later developed at Grunewald, Minden and Halle with counter-pressure brake locomotives, but the compound locomotive did not show the advantages expected by many of the engineers. 01.001 was tested against 02.002, the 01 with both 199lbpsi and 227lbpsi boilers, and the 02 with just the higher boiler pressure. Both produced edhps of 1,750, 01.001 with the lower pressure, 1,700.

In 1929, when looking at whether the lighter axle weight 03 should be a simple or compound locomotive, the experiences of the 01s and 02s at the Hamm, Erfurt and Hof depots were analysed. Despite higher construction costs of 15,000 RMs per locomotive and even higher maintenance costs, the 02 compound's economy compared to the 01 was virtually indistinguishable. In test runs the 1.5 per cent improvement in coal consumption was not repeatable in normal traffic. When worked very hard, the compound showed a slight advantage, but with normal and easy running the 01 was more economical. On the Berlin-Leipzig/Halle routes, the 01 was more economical up to power outputs of 875hp, above that power output the compound showed a 3.6 per cent advantage. The shedmaster of Erfurt stated

that the coal consumption of the 01 was about one ton less than the 02 per 1000 kilometres. The manager of the Brunswick Works stated that the overhaul costs of the 01 was approximately 26,000 RMs per loco, the 02 cost 31,200. In fact, for a similar mileage, the cost of overhaul of 1927-built S3/6 18.520 was lower than either – by a considerable margin! However, the 02 gave a smoother running ride than the 01. Later, with a longer boiler that Wagner had designed and tested on 02.010, and which was subsequently fitted as standard to the 01s, tests at Grunewald in the 1930s with counter-pressure brake locomotives gave an even more favourable result for the 01. All 01s from 01.077 onwards had the longer tubes and shorter smokebox as fitted to 02.010.

Despite the performance specification, the 1931 working timetable only allowed the 01 to haul 430 tons at the expected speed of 69mph on the level, upped to 480 tons in 1932. In 1938 this was raised to 650 tons, the higher performance a result of experience and continuing research and testing. In fact, the later DB Chief of Research & Testing (1948-61), Theodor Düring, in hindsight criticised the initial lack of proper testing of the standard Pacifics and the less than satisfactory design elements that could have been improved, particularly the thermodynamic proportions of the boiler.

There were many teething problems with the prototype machines and up to 270 minor modifications were made. Most problems were corrected at the first overhaul. For the main production run, begun in 1927 (01.012-101), the cylinder size was reduced to 23.6in

Newly-built Reichsbahn standard two-cylinder Pacific 01.003, with small smoke deflectors and original tender, at Hamm, 1926.
(Hermann Maey/Eisenbahnstiftung Collection)

x 26in, and boiler dimensions were modified, increasing the heating surface to 2,658sqft and reducing the superheater area to 914sqft. As a result of the cylinder size reduction, the tractive effort was reduced to 33,510lb. Some locomotives were fitted with a tender of 7,500-gallon water capacity, increasing the total locomotive weight in traffic to 185.3 tons. The cost per locomotive had already increased to 207,900 RMs. The production series construction programme was shared between Borsig, AEG, Henschel, Hohenzollern and Schwartzkopff.

The number 01.011 was retained at first for an experimental high-pressure version of the 01 of the Schwartzlopff/Löffler type, which was later numbered H02.1001 (see Chapter 9). The vacant number, 01.011, was filled in 1937 by the rebuilding of 02.001 as an 01.

From 01.102, the size of the front bogie wheels was increased in diameter from 2ft 9in to 3ft 3in, a slight readjustment of weight distribution reducing the maximum axle load to 19.9 tons and a strengthened braking system all leading to an increase in the authorised maximum speed to 81mph. The 'fourth' series of construction went to three firms – Henschel, Krupp and Schwartzkopf. The fifth series (01.191-232), built in 1937 and 1938, was constructed by Krupp and Henschel. Detail diffences were small. Finally, the 02 compounds were rebuilt as two-cylinder 01s between 1937 and 1942, receiving the numbers 01.011 and 01.233-241.

After the war and the restoration to service from the neglect and war damage, a number of minor changes were made on the 01s that remained in the west; these were mainly cosmetic. The large straight-sided smoke deflectors

01.009, built by AEG in 1926 and allocated at first to Erfurt, seen here in the 1930s and probably in the Saar area (SNCF coaches in the background). (MLS Collection)

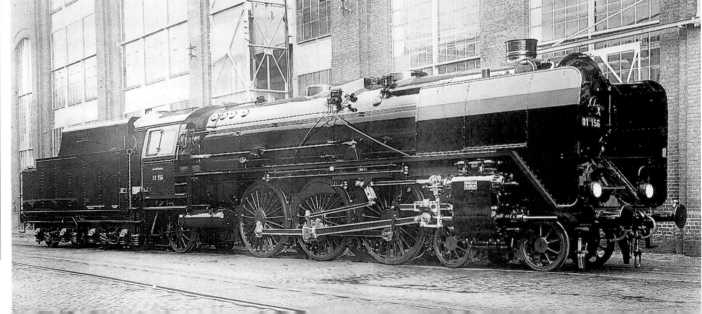

01.156, newly turned out by the Henschel Company with larger-diameter bogie wheels and large smoke deflectors, 1935. (Henschel Works photo/Robin Garn Collection)

were replaced later by the smaller 'witte' deflectors either side of the upper half of the smokebox. 01.199 appeared experimentally with small 'witte'-type smoke deflectors high on the smokebox either side of the chimney. A new smokebox door design removed the central wheel release mechanism and lights were fixed at the front in triangular formation. On some 01s the front 'skirt' was removed, giving access to the front end for easier maintenance. Those remaining in the east retained their original external appearance.

The prototype 01.001 was withdrawn from service after a frame fracture was experienced in October 1958; it was officially withdrawn on 31 December 1958, the first withdrawal for other than war or accident damage reasons. The last survivors in West Germany were based at Hof and withdrawn in 1973, East German versions lasting in traffic until 1979 at Berlin, 1980 at Magdeburg and 1981 at Saalfeld.

01.199, fitted experimentally with high-side smoke deflectors, on test in 1946. (J.Kronawitter/Robin Garn Collection)

01.199, uniquely fitted with high 'witte' smoke deflectors, standing at Bamberg at the head of a D-Zug to Hof, 1946. (Kronawitter/Eisenbahnstiftung Collection)

01.123 stands at Trier, 3 July 1965.
(MLS Collection)

001.168-4 stands ready for departure at Hof Station with a train for Bamberg, 23 June 1969.
(Graham Stacey)

Standard **01.067** at Hof Depot, August 1970.
(Richard Spoors)

19.9 tons, engine weight 111.1 tons plus either a 7,000-gallon or 7,500-gallon water capacity tender. Authorised maximum speed was 81mph and calculated indicated horsepower 2,450.

01.042 was withdrawn in 1957 after involvement in an accident which cracked its frames, and its boiler was passed on to 01.046. 01.192, at a Works repair after damage, exchanged its boiler with a new-build all-welded boiler in 1958. 01.112 was withdrawn in November 1967 and 154 in September 1966. 01.046 was the last survivor retaining the feedwater heater and was withdrawn in October 1968 (for photo of 01.046 without the front 'skirt', see Chapter 18, page 303).

01.112, one of the five 01s fitted with Heinl feedwater heaters placed very distinctly above the smokebox, giving the locomotives a 'top-heavy' appearance, standing here at Frankfurt/Main Hbf, 1957.
(Dr Feissel/Eisenbahnstiftung Collection)

With Feedwater Heater

Between 1950 and 1951, the *Deutsche Bundesbahn* rebuilt five standard 01s with feedwater heaters operated by turbo-pumps, which were very visible atop the front part of the smokebox, giving the locomotives a 'top-heavy' appearance. The equipment was made by Henschel using the Heinl type. Five locomotives were rebuilt, nos. 01.042, 046, 112, 154 and 192. They received new inner and outer fireboxes, shortening the tube lengths by 3ft 3in. However, most dimensions were the same as the standard 01s, although the grate area was slightly reduced to 46.3sqft, the heating surface to 2,324sqft and the superheater area increased to 1,027sqft. Some of the steam was condensed and provided an extra 5-10% water capacity. The maximum axle-load was

With large all-welded boiler

After 1957, as part of the modernisation of the DB locomotive fleet, some fifty of the standard 01s were provided with new high-performance all-welded boilers with combustion chambers, similar boilers to those with which the 01.10s had already been equipped. A similar type 2 boiler was developed for the class 03, 03.10, 39 and 41s, although only the 03.10s and some 41s were equipped. The 01s so fitted could easily be recognised because of the low wide chimney, as also fitted latterly to the coal-burning 01.10s, which gave the optical illusion that their boilers were much larger in diameter. The feedwater heater was incorporated within the smokebox and was not visible, unlike the five 01s equipped with feedwater heaters in 1950. The 01s receiving the new boiler received new cylinders. The front part of the footplating was removed, providing better access to the cylinders, bogie and front of the frame, giving the locomotive a powerful, imposing or ugly

01.115, rebuilt with an all-welded large boiler in 1957, stands at Bremen Hbf, 28 July 1967.
(MLS Collection)

01.192-4 at Hof, June 1968. This locomotive was one of five 01s that received a boiler with feedwater heater above the smokebox door, this being the first in October 1950, although this was replaced in 1958 by the larger all-welded boiler seen here. (MLS Collection/J.Davenport)

01.223 on Hanover Depot, 23 August 1967.
(MLS Collection)

appearance according to your taste.

The boiler had some dimension variations to the standard 01s; the grate area was just 42.6sqft, which reduced fuel consumption when standing idle, heating surface 2,076sqft, but the superheater covered a large 1,081sqft area. Maximum axle-load was 19.8 tons and engine weight 108.3 tons. With 7,500-gallon water capacity tender, the total locomotive weighed 182.5 tons. Calculated horsepower was 2,330, tractive effort 33,510lb.

It is surprising that only three of the last remaining 01s at Hof in 1973 had the modernised boilers, but once a decision was taken to undertake no more heavy repairs as dieselisation and electrification spread rapidly, it was pure chance which locomotives were last through Works before the edict of no more heavy repairs was promulgated.

Operations 1925 – 1945

The first ten locomotives, as stated previously, were initially dispersed to Hamm, Hof and Erfurt to get experience of different working in comparison with the ten compound 02s. By 1927 some twenty-nine 01s were in operation, and of these, the first four and 01.031-034 were stationed at Hamm; 01.005-7 at Hof; 01.008-010, 01.022-030 and 01.035/6 at Erfurt; and 01.037- 040 at Magdeburg. The Hamm engines were working between Aachen and Hanover, the Hof engines from Regensburg through Hof to Leipzig and Dresden, and the Erfurt 01s between Frankfurt-am-Main and Leipzig/Berlin. 01.012-021, built the following year, were all immediately allocated to Berlin

Anhalterbahnhof, and the rest of the 1928 build to Kassel, Hanover, Hamburg Altona and Frankfurt-am-Main. By the end of 1928, the 01s were running on main lines all over the centre and north of the country, leaving the State compound Pacifics still holding their own on main lines radiating from Munich, Stuttgart and Basle, with S10s still in the far north and east.

No 01s were built during 1929, but the next batch of twenty-five locomotives built in 1930-31 included five, 01.077-081, that invaded the south, allocated to Offenburg, when they took over running of the *Rheingold* from the Baden IV h Pacifics between Mannheim and Basle. Five, 01.072-076, were allocated for the first time to Bebra, and the fleets at Hamm, Frankfurt, Hanover, Erfurt and Berlin were all strengthened.

In 1933, the DRG possessed one hundred 01s, ninety-three 03 standard Pacifics, ten 02 compounds and two 04 four-cylinder high-pressure compound locomotives. Against this, they still had 634 former State railway 4-6-2s and 4-6-0 express locomotives in active service, and 260 former Prussian P10 2-8-2s that operated many D-trains in hilly areas. The *Reichsbahn* was still in financial difficulties in the world depression following the German hyper-inflation, and it was only from 1933 onwards that the recovery began to take effect and the Company could accelerate its replacement of older stock with the new standard classes, develop its high-speed capacity and experiment with high pressure and more powerful experimental designs.

The next set of 01s, built in 1934-5, from 01.102, now authorised to run at 81mph, comprised sixty-two locomotives. Three more, 01.113-115, went to Offenburg; a number invaded the east at Leipzig West (01.118-121); at Schneidemühl (01.133-136 and 01.156-157); at Breslau (01.137–140 and 01.154-155); and Halle (01.162-165). The rest went to depots with existing fleets. Hamburg Altona lost its 01s, as they were replaced by new 03s for the lines north of Hamburg to Lübeck, Flensburg and Westerland. Building was now continuous, and in 1936, Königsberg, Göttingen, Paderborn and Dresden received their first 01s and in 1937, Cologne-Deutzerfeld. The final series built in 1937-8 were all distributed to depots which already had a fleet of the standard Pacifics. The highest concentrations of 01s were at Hanover with twenty-two engines, Erfurt with eighteen and Hamm with fifteen.

It is probably easier therefore to see from these allocations on which routes the 01 Pacifics did not hold sway. Hof was still the main stronghold of the 02 compounds on the Munich-Hof-Halle-Berlin run until they were augmented by some of the later series of 01s to displace the remaining 18.4-5s on that trunk route. In the south, there was a famine of 01s, leaving the field largely to the former Bavarian S3/6 (18.4-5) compounds and the smaller Württemberg 'C's (18.1s), plus a few of the new 03 light standard Pacifics, most of which went to the east and north to replace the Prussian S10s. They would only begin to spread further afield as the three-cylinder 01.10s came on stream for the Cologne-

01.004 departs from Hagen with train D4 in the year of the engine's building, 1926. A former Prussian Railway G7 0-8-0 is standing on the left. (Carl Bellingrodt/Eisenbahstiftung Collection)

The prototype DRG standard two-cylinder Pacific 01.001 at Letter on a Warsaw-Paris through express, 1926. (Carl Bellingrodt/ Eisenbahnstiftung Collection)

Hamburg and Berlin-Leipzig/ Halle-Munich F- and D-trains. In 1935, they displaced the Prussian S10s in the Berlin area, and further east at Königsberg and to the Polish borders. In 1938, they took over the running of the *Rheingold* from the Maffei/Henschel 18.5s between Mannheim and the Dutch border at Zevenaar. They challenged the Saxon Pacifics on the Berlin-Dresden main line and worked to the Polish border.

Until 1932, main line speeds were relatively low with some lines still restricted to 62mph; only eighteen services were timed at an average of over 55mph. From 1933 onwards, however, there was a rapid advance in scheduled speeds. The prime time or highpoint of the 01 operation was between 1934 and 1937 when many of the expresses were accelerated. They were hauling 11-12 coaches weighing 550-600 tons (03s on the same schedules could only take 7-9 coaches). Many of these services were scheduled start to stop at over 60mph. The high demands were not without consequences. There were frequent failures affecting boiler, valve gear and frames. For example, 01.156 allocated to Schneidemühl, only delivered in 1935, was out of service with defect repairs eight times between January 1936 and February 1938, five times with necessary boiler repairs, once with coupled wheels moving on the axles, once to reprofile wheels and renew bearings, and one intermediate repair in Works after just fourteen months in service. The research centre at Grunewald blamed not the workload, but the poor conditions on shed and lack of skills of some of the crews. The 1936 Olympics put particular stress on services, when the Nazi regime was determined to show the rest of the world its superiority and demonstrate some of the fastest train schedules in the world. There were many runs with Grunewald test vehicles and inspectors on the Mannheim-Basle route with Offenburg 01s. The Head of Testing, Professor Nordmann, came to the conclusion that on the Mannheim-Heidelberg-Basle test trains with heavy and fast D-Züge, the limit of performance was scarcely reached. On one trip with a 626-ton train on

01.016 departs from Berlin Anhalter Bhf with an express while new three-cylinder streamlined 01.1053 stands on the left with a D24 for Munich, 1940. (Eisenbahnstiftung Collection)

9 September 1935, an 01 did reach a boiler output of 61k/sqm/hr. (evaporation rate of 31,900lbpsqft/hour), although on the return journey only 45.2k/sqm/hr (23,540lbpsqft/hour) was necessary. Professor Nordmann concluded that only rarely did the current schedules require a maximum steam output of 57k/sqm/hr (just under 30,000lbpsqft/

hour) and then only momentarily. There are few logs of 01 Pacifics in this period, but one was recorded over the 100 miles between Schneidemühl and Küstrin Neustadt in 87½ minutes with a 525 tons gross train, an average of 68.8mph, with a top speed of 88mph.

At this time there were also some very long single locomotive mileages

achieved on a regular diagrammed basis. In 1911, a Bavarian S3/6 ran the 173 miles from Munich to Würzburg without an intermediate stop. Later, a Baden IV h Pacific was diagrammed for a 195 miles diagram from Mannhein to Konstanz without engine change. In 1927, Hamm 01s ran the 251 miles Aachen-Cologne-Hanover, and Erfurt used its 02s on a 337-mile Berlin-Halle-Erfurt-

A staged publicity photograph of eight of the 01s newly allocated to Bw Hanover in February 1928. The new BMAG-delivered engines, 01.053-066, were all allocated here from new. (Eisenbahnstiftung Collection)

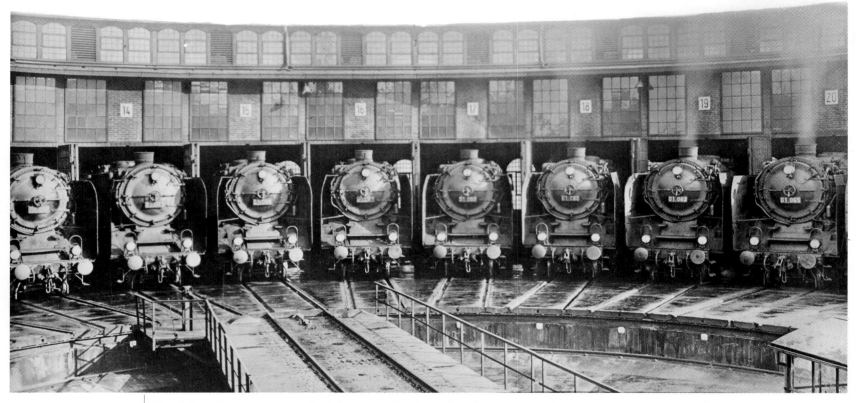

Frankfurt diagram. 01s worked the Berlin-Halle-Munich D39/40 and FD 79/80 without loco change. Berlin-Nuremberg, (273 miles) was a routine diagram. Göttingen's 01s worked Kassel-Berlin (249 miles). One of the fastest expresses covered this mileage in 293 minutes – an average of just over 50mph including stops. A racing stretch was the Berlin-Hanover section, 147 miles, with FD 26 in 181 minutes, FD 112 in 179 minutes (both 55mph). These trains started from Berlin Schlesische Bahnhof (today's Ostbahnhof), and stopped at Berlin's other stations of Friedrichstrasse and

Zoologischer Garten, then after 12 miles at Spandau, before the racing section began. Average speeds of 60-62mph were required between Spandau and Hanover with heavy trains. In the Rhine Valley, the fastest trains went from Basle to Karlsruhe at around 50mph including stops, the *Rheingold* the fastest, averaging 54mph. Many locomotives were turning in a round trip of 375 miles a day. The fastest trains were worked by high-speed diesel railcars, but these stopped abruptly in 1939 at the outbreak of war because of shortage of fuel.

By 1941 all 231 standard Pacifics were in service plus the ten 02s rebuilt as 01s. They were distributed thus:

Berlin (3 depots):	30
Breslau (Wroclaw):	8
Dresden:	8
Erfurt/Saalfeld:	18
Hamm:	16
Frankfurt (Main)/ Bebra:	21
Halle/ Leipzig:	13
Hanover/Brunswick/Magdeburg:	32
Offenburg:	21
Kassel/Göttingen/Paderborn:	21
Cologne-Deutzerfeld:	10

Newly-delivered
01.146, allocated to
Würzburg, but delivered
to Nuremberg as part of
the centenary of German
railways celebration,
1935.
(MLS/Carl Bellingrodt/EK Verlag)

Königsberg (Kaliningrad):	8
Würzburg:	11
Schneidemühl (Pila):	8
Hof:	16

(incl two 02s still to be converted)

The vast majority were thus in control of the centre of the country, the lines to the east and the Rhine Valley. There were none at Osnabrück, whose 01.10s and 03s dominated the Cologne-Hamburg route, but they were active throughout the Ruhr region and operating from the Hanover district in the State of Hesse.

As the war progressed, the most urgent need was for freight traffic and even the streamlined 01.10s found themselves hauling freights, as did the 01s. As the Red Army advanced, the DRG pulled back its express locomotives into West Germany to avoid them falling into the hands of the Russians. At the end of the war, there was no immediate need for express locomotives and most were stored, many in deplorable and damaged condition. Six 01s suffered war damage that caused their scrapping – 01.038, 053, 145, 155, 201 and ex-02, 01.238. 165 of the 241 locomotives were in the west at the time of the split of Germany between the Western Allies and Russian occupying forces.

Operations DB 1945 - 1973

The 165 x 01s available after the war to the West German railway, the *Deutsche Bundesbahn*, were distributed over the following motive power districts and were brought back into service after overhaul at Brunswick and Nied Works:

Essen (Bw Hamm):	18
Frankfurt & Bebra:	29
Hanover & Brunswick:	45
Cologne:	12
Munich:	14
Münster:	7
Nuremberg (Bw Würzburg):	33
Regensburg (Bw Hof):	7

During the 1950s the allocation remained static apart from a few withdrawals following mishaps or damage or exceptionally poor condition – 01.001-004 inclusive, 01.012, 042, 097, 101 and 241 (ex-02.004). By 1961, the remaining 156 locomotives were broadly in the same locations although the Mainz District had gained sixteen, mainly at the expense of the Nuremberg District where there had been substantial electrification. Further electrification on both banks of the Rhine south of Cologne in 1959-61 and the receipt of V200 diesels by Hamm from 1957 onwards saw further redistribution and in the early 1960s, a steady withdrawal of engines needing the most costly repairs. In 1964, they invaded the last stronghold of the rebuilt S3/6s at Lindau.

The fleet had dropped to 103 locomotives by June 1966, and the

Frankfurt, Kassel, Cologne, Mainz and Munich Districts had given up their engines, some of which had gone to the Augsburg and Trier Districts. A year later, the class had been virtually halved, the remainder being shared between the Essen (Hamm), Hanover, Regensburg (Hof) and Trier Districts.

On 1 January 1968, all remaining DB steam engines received new computer numbers – the 01s became 001 + former identification number + computer check-digit. Sixty-eight new numberplate sets had been made for the 01s, but many were never fixed. Three, 01.150, 199 and 227, were based at Ehrang for the Moselle services in 1970, but by June 1971 only twenty-seven 01s still remained in West Germany, 01.164 at Brunswick and the rest at Hof.

The Hof locomotives with the

original standard boilers were: 001.008, 088, 111, 150, 168, 173, 202, and 234 (the latter ex-02.003).

The Hof locomotives with the all-welded high-performance boilers were: 001.103, 126, 131, 169, 180, 181, 187, 190, 192, 200, 210, 211, 217, 229 and 230.

Despite the preponderance of 01s with the modernised boiler (15 to 8), at the very end in April 1973 it was the engines with the old standard boilers that predominated, 001.008, 088, 111, 150, 168 and 173 all lasting until the very end. Only three of the all-welded boiler 01s were still extant by this time – 001.131, 180 and 211. Most of the steam diagrams ended at the commencement of the summer timetable in June 1973. Just four 01s were retained as reserve locomotives, all members of the

001.073-6 at Cochem with an Eilzug in the Moselle Valley, 31 August 1970. (MLS Collection)

Munchberg-Bamberg 1971
E1794 15.52 Hof-Stuttgart-Tubingen
001.111-4 Bw Hof
5 chs, 163/170t

Munchberg	00.00	mph	T	0 miles	
Stambach	09.10	44/51/45			1 in 90/100R
Falls	14.29	45		
Marktschorgast	18.07	49		
Neuenmarkt-Wirsberg	24.32		2½ E	17.8
	00.00		T	0
Ludwigschorgast	03.19	65		
Untersteinach	04.51	58/73		
Kulmbach	08.51		1L	7.7
	00.00		T	0
Mainleus	04.12	66/72		
Mainroth	06.56	73/76½		
Bergkunstadt	10.17		1E	10.1
	00.00		T	0
km 41	-	63		
Hochstadt -Marktgeuln	04.52		T	3.5
	00.00		T	0
Michelau	03.28	66/69½		
Lichtenfels	06.20		½ L	5.1
	00.00		T	0
Staffelstein	04.29	68½		
Ebenefeld	07.13	78		
Zapfendorf	10.00	81		
Breitengussbach	13.05	78		
Hallstadt	15.04	82/75		
Bamberg	17.33		½ E	19.8

class with the original design standard boilers – 001.008, 111, 150 and 173 (all of which have since been preserved). They were kept in use on a pair of stopping trains between Hof and Regensburg until the end of the seasonal timetable at the end of September. The last run by an 01 in service on the DB was with 001.150 on 29 September 1973.

There were some high-mileage diagrams for the 01s still in the 1950s and early 1960s. The longest was a diagram from Hamburg right through to Aachen, 327 miles, and several Hamburg to Cologne, 299 miles, although it was normal for the latter to be worked by two 01.10s changing engines at Osnabrück. There was a Munich-Bebra diagram in 1951 of 278 miles with a Würzburg 01, and Munich-Frankfurt diagrams between 1952 and 1957, 259 miles with Würzburg 01s. After electrification from Würzburg through Aschaffenburg to Frankfurt in 1957-8, Würzburg 01s still had regular turns between Munich and Würzburg with Frankfurt D-Züge; indeed, the author travelled behind Würzburg's 01.046 from Munich on D673, the *Tirol Express*, in August 1959, though this train was electric from Munich to Treuchtlingen and a V200 diesel on to Würzburg by 1962. More details, including some logs of runs behind 01s, are described in the chapter of the author's own personal reminiscences (Chapter 18).

The two longest through runs by an 01 post-war were isolated

Lichtenfels-Bamberg, January 1973

	E1648 Hof-Mannheim, 7.1.73 001.111-4 Bw Hof 8 chs, 265/275t				E1648, 8.1.73 001.150-2 Bw Hof 8 chs, 265/280t			E1648, 10.1.73 001.187-4 Bw Hof 8 chs, 265/275t		
Lichtenfels	00.00	mph	4L	0 miles	00.00	mph	1½ L	00.00	mph	1½ L
Staffelstein	05.03	67			04.54	72½		05.13	68½	
Ebenefeld	07.49	79/82			07.42	78/69		08.02	76½	
Zapfendorf	10.35	81			10.42	78/82		10.54	78½	
Breitengussbach	13.44	81/75			13.57	78/72		14.17	75/70	
Hallstadt	15.48	79			16.00	79		16.34	74	
Bamberg	18.30		3½ L	19.8	18.46		1½ L	19.08		1½ L

	Bamberg-Munchberg, 1973 E1863, 05.36 Tubingen-Hof, 9. 1.73 001.111-4 Bw Hof 6 chs, 190/200t				**E1863, 10.1.73** 001.180-9 Bw Hof 6 chs, 190/195t				**6.1.73** E1649, 12.02 Ludwigshafen-Hof 001-088-4 + 001.180-9 Bw Hof 7 chs, 237/245t		
Bamberg	00.00	mph	T	0 miles	00.00	mph	T		00.00	mph	T
Hallstadt	03.50	60½			04.01	53			03.52	52	
Breitengussbach	06.11	70/78			06.25	70½			06.17	74	
Zapfendorf	09.31	76/79			09.49	75/73			09.36	78/75	
Ebenefeld	12.25	75/80			12.50	74/72			12.35	73	
Staffelstein	15.02	78/81			15.38	75			15.17	80	
km 30	-	80			-	73			-	76	
Lichtenfels	18.46		T	19.8	19.36		1L		19.26		½ E
	00.00		T	0	00.00		1L		00.00		T
Michelau	04.15	pws 30*			04.33	pws 31*			04.18	pws 35*	
H-Marktgeuln	07.06	65½			08.38	52			07.17	63½	
km 44	-	72½			-	67½			-	70½	
Bergkunstadt	10.38		½ L	8 .65	12.30		3 ½ L		11.02		T
	00.00		T	0	00.00		3L		00.00		T
Mainroth	04.41	63½ / pws 47*			05.06	57/pws 45*		04.50	60½ / pws 57*		
Mainleus	08.04	63/70			08.21	63/68			08.08	59/67	
	-	pws 15*			-	pws 15*			-	pws 15*	
Kulmbach	12.04		T	10.05	12.25		3 ½ L		12.26		½ L
	00.00		T	0	00.00		3L		00.00		T
Unsteinachach	05.09	62/53			05.38	57/47			05.23	59/53	
Ludwigschorgast	06.48	54½			07.20	52/49			07.05	50/52	
N-Wirsberg	09.55		T	7.7	10.58		4L		10.30		½ E
	00.00		T	0	00.00		1L		00.00		T
km 77	-	40½	1 in 57R		-	34½			-	33½	
(Schiefe Ebene)			1 in 44R								
km 79	-	38/34½			-	26½			-	30	
km 81	-	33			-	21½			-	29	
Marktschorgast	08.10	34			11.03	21½			09.32	30	
Falls	12.24//20.14 sig stand			7.45	15.55//18.48 sig stand				12.16	46	
Stammbach	27.00	47/44			25.28	38			19.12	45/easy	
Munchberg	35.36		2 ½ E	17.8	34.56		2E		28.10		3E

occurrences for the duration of one timetable. In 1954, a Treuchtlingen 01 had a 344-miles turn between Treuchtlingen and Mönchen-Gladbach, and in 1960, a Bebra 01 worked right through from Lübeck in the far north to Würzburg on the key north/south trunk route via Hamburg, Hanover and Göttingen (354 miles). In the late 1950s and early 1960s, the author experienced 01s on the Cologne-Hanover/Brunswick and Frankfurt-Kassel-Hanover-Hamburg routes. Before the electrification of the section of line between Munich and Treuchtlingen in 1961, the Treuchtlingen 01s, which seemed to be maintained in excellent order, were very active on the Treuchtlingen-Munich section of Nuremberg-Munich fast expresses.

The very last stronghold of the 01s was, as stated above, at Hof; many German and British railway enthusiasts experienced energetic running from some of the last survivors between Hof and Bamberg, via Neuenmarkt-Wirsberg, which included the five miles of the 1 in

57/44 gradient of the '*Schiefe Ebene*'. I include below some of the most interesting logs of such running, courtesy of a college colleague, Alastair Wood, who made several visits to the line at that time. The last steam turns covered a pair of expresses, D853/854, and semi-fast trains E658/9, E1648/9 and E1791. Hof-Bamberg trains were mainly the standard-boilered 01s, whilst Hof-Regensburg was the prerogative largely of the modernised-boiler 01s, though mainly on stopping trains.

Alastair Wood commented that 01.111 seemed to be, with 01.150 and 01.008, the best of the 01s, consistently better and faster away than the reboilered Pacifics. Acceleration between the stops was lightning fast and the average start-stop speed over the last section was 67 ½mph.

None of the trains were banked on the *Schiefe Ebene*, where six coaches was the maximum allowed unless double-headed or banked. 01.111 was worked practically flat-out to sustain 34mph on the 1 in 44. E1649 was booked to be double-headed.

For logs of my own personal experience of 01s between Munich, Würzburg, Göttingen, Hanover and Hamburg, see Chapter 18, pages xxx.

01.086, with cut-away front running plate, arrives at Bremen Hbf with an Eilzug, 26 August 1967. (MLS Collection)

A reboilered 01 leaves Bullay in a spectacular sunset and crosses the Moselle River with an Eilzug from Koblenz to Trier, September 1971. (Richard Spoors)

Reboilered 001.199-9 near Neef with an Eilzug from Koblenz to Trier, next stop Bullay, September 1971. (Richard Spoors)

001.111-4 at Oberkotzau, approaching Hof with an afternoon D-Zug from Regensburg, August 1970. (Richard Spoors)

001.230-2, rebuilt with all-welded boiler, climbs to the summit of the 'Schiefe Ebene' (1 in 44) with a Nuremberg-Hof train, August 1970. (Richard Spoors)

An unidentified 01, rebuilt with an all-welded boiler, climbs through the woods up the 1 in 44 of the '*Schiefe Ebene*' bank to Marktschorgast, banked by a 110 class diesel locomotive, with an Eilzug from Nuremberg to Hof, August 1970.
(Richard Spoors)

001.111-4 drifts down the '*Schiefe Ebene*' incline with an afternoon Hof–Bamberg train, September 1972.
(Richard Spoors)

001.202-1 en route from Bamberg to Hof with a D-Zug , September 1972.
(Richard Spoors)

01.062 comes off the Hohenzollern Bridge entering Cologne Main Station with a Cologne Deutz-Gerolstein Eilzug, 2 July 1968.
(Helmut Dahlhaus)

01.081 with a Cologne Deutz-Trier E556 at Cologne Main Station, 6 July 1968.
(Helmut Dahlhaus)

Large-boilered 001.180 blows off steam as it tackles the 1 in 44 of the *Schiefe Ebene* bank with the seven-coach D853 banked by a V60 diesel shunting locomotive, 30 October 1972.
(Fell/Eisenbahnstiftung Collection)

Operations DR 1945 – 1981

At the end of the war, despite the attempts to keep as many express locomotives as possible away from the territory being occupied by the advancing Russian Army, seventy 01 Pacifics were in the eastern Russian sector. 01.007, 082, 083, 115, 147 had already been destroyed by enemy action and although their carcases were in the Soviet Zone, they were not included in the seventy counted above. However, five of this number were so badly war-damaged that they were promptly withdrawn and cut up – 01.026, 030, 035, 110 and 214 (four of these were at Erfurt Depot, one at Leipzig West Depot). At least half of the others were out of action, war-damaged, and had to be repaired at the Meiningen Works before they could be used. Initially, around twenty-five became 'Kolonnenlok' (engines commandeered by the Soviet Military Command) and remained in that service until the last was returned to the DR in July 1954. Despite the fraught economic situation in post-war Eastern Germany, the remaining 01s were

Hof's 001.111-4 leaves Lichtenfels in a hurry for Neuenmarkt-Wirsberg and Hof on E1863, passing DRG electrics 194.132 and 144.070, 10 January 1973. (Wolfgang Bügel/ Eisenbahnstiftung Collection)

01.162, one of the 01s prepared for use by the Soviet military authorities and fitted with a red star on the smokebox door, at Karlshorst, 1948. (R. Garn Collection)

back in DR active service by 1950.

The allocation in 1949/50 was as follows:

Berlin Anhalter Bhf: 01.014, 016, 018

Berlin Lehrter Bhf: 01.116, 117

Erfurt: 01.005, 022-025, 027-029, 036, 084, 114, 142-144, 152, 153,163, 218, 219, 221

Halle: 01.048, 050, 057, 069, 089, 118, 119, 127, 129, 135, 136, 156, 157, 174, 175, 191, 204, 207

Magdeburg: 01.054, 065, 066, 158, 160, 203, 224

Leipzig West: 01.085, 120, 121, 137, 139, 162, 165, 185, 205, 225

Wittenberge: 01.107

Grunewald: 01.184, 186, 226

At that time, the 01s were supported by thirty-seven S10.1 four-cylinder compound 4-6-0s (17.1005 -1199) for secondary duties, nine of the Saxon Pacifics (18.0)

01.023, a 'Kolonnenlok' used by the Soviet military authorities immediately after the Second World War, 1949. It is equipped with a 2'2'T26 tender from a class 50 2-10-0. (TZA/R. Garn Collection)

and most of the Saxon 2-8-2 Class 19.0. The Soviet-installed Minister of Transport, Dr Erwin Kramer, decreed that, because of the difficulty of obtaining spare parts, the different classes of locomotive should be concentrated each in one specific motive power district to minimise this problem, and the Erfurt and Magdeburg Districts took responsibility for the 01s, Halle for the 03s and Berlin for the remaining class 17s.

As a result of this decree, by the early 1950s, all the East German 01s were operational and back under the control of the DR administration. They were then split between just two depots – Magdeburg had twenty-two, numbered between 01.005 and 01.089, and Erfurt the other forty-three (01.107-226). The subsequent changes to this did not occur before October 1960, when at last the DR introduced some accelerated services between Berlin and their main cities. In consequence of this, 01s were allocated to Wittenberge and Rostock in addition to Erfurt and Magdeburg. After August 1961, twenty-five 01s were transferred to Berlin Ost Bhf Depot, when the route from the West German border at Helmstedt was transferred to Berlin rather than operating Magdeburg diagrams.

After 1962 some of the Erfurt 01s were rebuilt as 01.5s (see Chapter 10). Before that time the Erfurt 01s were working fast passenger services and three sample diagrams were:

Diagram 1:
Erfurt-Leipzig (D-Zug)
Leipzig-Berlin (Fast City Service)
Overnight in Berlin

Berlin-Erfurt (Fast City Service)
Diagram 2:
Erfurt-Probstzella-Berlin (D-Zug)
Overnight in Berlin
Berlin-Erfurt (D-Zug)
Erfurt-Bebra (International Train)

Diagram 3:
Leipzig-Bebra (International Train)
Bebra - Leipzig (International Train)
(possible change engines at Erfurt)

Other diagrams included Erfurt- Sangerhausen-Magdeburg; Erfurt-Gera; Erfurt-Dresden; Erfurt-Meiningen, this last in conjunction with class 22 2-8-2s - reboilered Prussian class 39s.

Madgeburg 01s worked the international Helmstedt-Berlin trains until 1961, then Berlin-Magdeburg-Halberstadt, also a Cologne-Görlitz international train over DR metals until 1969. By 1970, Magdeburg's allocation had dropped to seven 01s, when Magdeburg became a diesel depot. Wittenberge handled trains between Berlin and West Germany at Hamburg through the international corridor. In 1960, it had thirteen 01s and later acquired six of the rebuilt 01.5s for the Berlin-Hamburg trains. Eventually, thirty-five 01s of the series with larger bogie wheels (01.102 onwards) were rebuilt, leaving only eight of that latter series as unrebuilt 01s, although they received new steel-welded cylinders not needed for further 01.5 conversions – Nos. 01.114, 118, 120, 137, 165, 204 and 207. The other twenty-two 01s were all of the earlier series with 2ft 9in-diameter bogie wheels. By this time, the DR steam locomotives had also received computerised numbers, but in a different format to the

Bundesbahn. Oil-burning locomotives had a zero placed before their number with a computer check-digit at the end, coal-burning engines of the 01 and 03 class acquired a '2' before the number, thus: 01.2137-6 (formerly 01.137).

At the end of the winter timetable in 1972, the allocation of the remaining unrebuilt 01s in East Germany was as follows:

Magdeburg: 01.2022, 2025, 2036, 2085
Wittenberge: 01.2014, 2018, 2027, 2054
Berlin Ost: 01.2016, 2029, 2065, 2084, 2114, 2165, 2226
Dresden: 01.2050, 2057, 2066, 2069, 2118, 2120, 2137, 2204, 2207
Rostock: 01.2048 (reserve locomotive)

However, the Magdeburg allocation was on paper only as all four locomotives were standing ready for withdrawal. Also, three of Wittenberge's allocation, 01.2018, 2027 and 2054, were already out of active service. 01.2014 was overhauled but only to become a stationary boiler at Schwerin Depot, before being scrapped in 1976. Similar fates threatened 01.2048 and 2069, but 2048 became for a while the standby locomotive at Rostock, whilst 2069 was overhauled and allocated to Dresden where it entered into the Berlin-Dresden express diagrams before being withdrawn in 1977.

Dresden was the depot for former Saxon and Prussian locomotives until some 03s arrived in 1962, but it was not until 1967 that Dresden acquired any 01s. These were for heavy international trains between

	D378 *Istropolitan*, 26.8.75 23.55 Bratislava-Berlin 01.2118-6 Bw Dresden 8 chs, 329/340t				D1274 *Metropol*, 6.9.77 22.05 Budapest-Rostock 01.2066-7 Bw Dresden 12 chs, 457/480t			D678, 13.4.77 Dresden-Berlin 01.2165-9 Bw Berlin Ost 9 chs, 291/295t		
Dresden Hbf	00.00	mph	16L	miles	00.00	mph	11 ½ L		mph	
Dresden Mitte	04.03	37			04.25	34				
Dresden Neustadt	06.00		16L	2.4	06.20		12L			
	00.00	15½ L		0	00.00		14L	00.00		1L
Radebeul Ost	06.01	55			06.47	59		06.20	58	
Neucoswig	10.29	70/65			11.17	69/62		11.25	62/53	
Weinböhla	13.01	59			13.56	57		15.30	50/sigs 2*	
km 22	15.59	56			16.54	54		21.30	43	
Böhla	18.21	74			19.10	72/74		24.16	67	
Grossenhain	22.13	76		21.4	25.25	pws 21*	10½ L	29.11		8L
		72			00.00		10L	00.00		8L
Zabelitz	25.09	78			06.26	62		05.43	63	
Frauenhain	27.06	75			08.43	68		08.02	68	
Prosen-Wainsdorf	29.24	80			11.11	73		-	71	
Elsterwerda	31.15	75/77		33.05	14.07		6L	13.44		6½ L
		75			00.00		6L	00.00		6L
Hohenleipisch	34.40	67			07.12	47		06.21	48	
Rückersdorf-Oppelhain	38.23	80			11.40	68/70		10.40	72	
Doberlug-Kirchhain	41.19	75		45.45	15.24	72	6½ L	14.36	73	4L
		77			00.00		7L	00.00		4L
Brenitz-Sonnewalde	46.00	74			08.02	64/68		08.13	56	
Walddrehna	50.22	65			12.30	63		14.18	sigs 43*	
Gehren	52.49	75			14.55	75		17.33	pws 45*/62	
Uckro	55.16	82			17.18	83		20.15	72	
Drahnsdorf	58.45	84/79			20.40	85½ /78		24.07	72	
Golssen	61.58	75/72			23.44	82/77		27.41	68/71	
Klasdorf	65.04	75			26.39	76		30.45	72	
Baruth	67.21	77			28.49	79/76		33.08	72	
Neuhof	72.00	79			33.40	72/70		38.00	70/77	
Wunsdorf	73.58	pws 56*		85.4	35.28	pws38*		39.29	68	
Zossen	77.33	70			41.23	44½		42.52	72/67	
Rangsdorf	82.01	75			46.57	64		44.00	69/67	
Dahlewitz	83.53	72			49.10	54½		47.38	62	
Blankenfelde	84.31	69			50.10	pws 41*		49.00	sigs 20*	
Ringbahn	-	sigs 29*		-	60			-	58	
Berlin-Schönefeld	93.36		4L		102.9	57.26	6½ L	59.04		10L

Hungary, Czechoslovakia and Bulgaria, replacing the 03s which could not cope with the train loadings. On average, Dresden retained eight 01s during this era,

kept in excellent condition. They also shared with Berlin Ost the fast Dresden-Berlin services after the demise of the Saxon Pacifics. The performances over this section

became outstanding, and again I am indebted to Alastair Wood for the logs recorded above as examples of their work between 1975 and 1977. The star locomotives for these services were Dresden's 01.2050, 2066, 2069, 2118, 2120, 2137, 2204 and 2207. The number of '*Magistrale*' fast inter-city services diagrammed to these 01s fell in 1977 and ended at the start of the 1977/78 winter timetable on dieselisation. The last run was performed by 01.2207-7 on 25 September 1977. However, 01.2204-4 was given a major overhaul at Meiningen, and became a heritage locomotive for special trains and on 11 June 1978, as 01.204, double-headed 01.2118 on a special train from Dresden to Wolkenstein.

The first two runs, on the previous page, were of exceptional quality, 01.2118 achieving a start-stop average of just over 66mph, whilst 01.2066, with a very heavy load, achieved an average of just over 60mph start-stop from Doberlug to Berlin. The run with 01.2165 is shown to demonstrate a more normal run, operating as well as loco performance.

A couple of 01s, 01.2029 and 01.2065, were stationed at Jüterbog for heavy trains to the Soviet border at Frankfurt-Oder. 01.137, later to be preserved, was based at Seddin, then moved to Rostock, then finally became one of the Berlin (Ost) 01s, then a Dresden engine, both for the Berlin-Dresden inter-city service. The Rostock 01s had earlier worked to Berlin and also the Rostock-Schwerin-Magdeburg route before these fell to the Wittenberge 01.5s. Berlin's two 01s transferred from Jüterbog; 2029 and 2065, together with 2165 and some coal-burning 01.5s, were occupied after the dieselisation of the Dresden route for a summer on trains to Szczecin (Stettin) and one to Gdansk (Danzig) in Poland, the 01 working to the border only.

Berlin Ost Pacific 01.2065-9 tears through Böhla with a Berlin-Dresden D-Zug, 23 August 1974. (Richard Spoors)

The last two 01s in service were 01.2114 and 01.2137 at Magdeburg, working semi-fast services to Halberstadt in 1979, until an oil crisis saw 01.2114, 2118 and the heritage 01.2204 resurrected at Saalfeld to relieve some of the remaining oil-burning 01.5s on the Saalfeld-Leipzig services in 1980-1. 01.2137 arrived also, but the oil crisis was over by the time it was ready for traffic and it was retained for a few special services along with 01.2204.

Dresden 01.2118-6 drifts at speed with a Berlin-Dresden D-Zug near Böhla, 23 August 1974. (Richard Spoors)

01.2118-6 at Berlin Ostbahnhof with D924, from Dresden, 18 April 1976. (Alastair Wood)

01.2114-5 at Dresden Neustadt after arrival with D671 from Berlin, 18 April 1976.
(Alastair Wood)

01.2118-6 charges through the woods near Weinböhla with D924, Dresden to Rostock, which the 01 will take as far as Berlin Ost Hbf, 20 April 1976.
(Joachim Bügel/Eisenbahnstiftung Collection)

01.2066-7 at Dresden Hbf at the head of a D-Zug for the Polish border at Görlitz, c1978. (MLS Collection)

01.2114-5 at Berlin on the *Pannonia Express* D56, 19 April 1969. (Ulrich Budde)

Berlin Ost's 01.2069-1 heads D378 *Istropolitan* (Bratislava-Berlin) near Böhla, 9 March 1977. (Peter Schiffer/Eisenbahnstiftung Collection)

A quiet scene at Berlin Ost Station with 01.2050 awaiting its next turn to Dresden, 9 August 1975. (George Bambery)

01.2050-1 passing Doberlug-Kirchhain with a Berlin-Dresden D-Zug, 29 January 1977. (George Bambery)

01.2050-1 passing Weinböhla with the *Pannonia Express* D371, 6 October 1975. (Helmut Dahlhaus)

01.2069-1 on a Berlin-Dresden-Budapest D-Zug, 9 August 1975.
(George Bambery)

01.2204-4 at Berlin Ostkreuz with the D924 Dresden-Berlin express, 17 April 1976.
(Helmut Dahlhaus)

01.2114-5 leaving Saalfeld with E800 for Gera and Leipzig, during a period when the DR was short of fuel oil and reverted to coal-burning Pacifics on this route, May 1980. (Robert Kingsford-Smith)

01.2204-4 leaving Saalfeld for Gera and Leipzig with a morning Eilzug, May 1980. (Malcolm Holdsworth)

01.2204-4 tackles E800 (the early morning Saalfeld-Leipzig E-Zug) during the steam 'reprieve' following the oil shortage in the early 1980s, seen near Neunhofen on the climb to the summit at Triptis, 3 September 1980. (Wolfgang Bügel)

01.089, withdrawn
and used as a stationary
boiler and cannabilised
for spare parts, at Stendal
Bw, winter 1969.
(RAW Stendal/Robin Garn
Collection)

Preserved 01 Pacifics

Thirteen 01s have been saved for posterity, ten as originally built, or at least with the standard 01 boiler as designed in 1925, and three with the all-welded boiler and combustion chamber. Eight of the preserved engines are in what was the former West Germany and three in the east, with two privately preserved in Switzerland. Five of the standard design 01s are as withdrawn from the East German *Reichsbahn* at the end of the 1970s.

01.005

01.005, built by Borsig in 1926, was still in traffic in East Germany in the 1970s as 01.2005-5, After withdrawal it was restored by Meiningen Works in 1977 for display only at the Dresden Transport Museum. It is currently at Stassfurt's heritage railway depot as part of the Dresden Museum Collection.

01.008

001.008-2, the second 01 to be completed in January 1926 and the 12,000th locomotive built by Borsig, was one of the final DB 01s still in operation at Hof in 1973. On withdrawal it was obtained by the Deutsche Gesellschaft für Eisenbahngeschichte (DGEG), and is exhibited at Bochum Dahlhausen in Nordrhein Westfalen.

DB Standard 01 Pacific 01.008 at Gelsenkirchen-Bismarck, 7 December 1973, being made ready for a 'last' steam special in the area. This locomotive was one of the last survivors of the class on the DB, being withdrawn from Hof at the end of 1973. It is currently displayed at the Deutsche Gesellschaft für Eisenbahngeschichte, Bochum Dahlhausen (Nordrhein Westfalen). (Wolfgang Bügel/Eisenbahnstiftung)

01.024

Built in 1927, 01.024 became on withdrawal a stationary boiler at Stassfurt, and then stored at the Bavarian Railway Museum at Nördlingen (near Munich) and cannibalised for spare parts for other preserved locomotives.

01.066

01.2066-7, built as 01.066 by BMAG Schwartzkopff in 1928, remained after the war in East Germany and ran on the Berlin-Dresden route. On withdrawal it became a stationary boiler at Nauen and was later restored to operational condition at the Bayrische Eisenbahn Museum (Bavarian Railway Museum – BEM),

Restored DR Pacific 01.2137-6, with a special train rumbles over the Elbe Bridge at Dresden, 25 August 1983.
(Graham Stacey)

Nördlingen (for photo see pages xxx and xxx) .

01.111

001.111-4 built as 01.111 by BMAG in 1934, survived to 1973 at Hof and was restored for display at the Deutsche Dampflok Museum (DDM) at Neuenmarkt-Wirsberg, Bavaria (for photo see pages xxx and xxx).

01.118

01.2118-6, built as 01.118 by Krupp in 1934, remained operational on the East German DR until 1981 and was then bought by the Historische Eisenbahn, Frankfurt-am-Main, and operated on the Frankfurt

Eastern Harbour Railway and used on main-line steam trips out of Frankfurt (for photo see page xxx).

01.137

01.2137-6, built as 01.137 by Henschel in 1935, was one of the DR 01s based at Dresden in the 1970s, and was withdrawn from Magdeburg in 1981 and restored for operational use for many years, being a 'star' in the *Plandampfs* of the 1990s before display at the Deutsche Bahn Museum, Dresden Altstadt.

01.150

001.150-2, built as 01.150 by Henschel in 1935, was withdrawn from Hof in 1973 and was restored for operation

001.150-2, in the last year before withdrawal and preservation, heads a special enthusiasts' train, including *Rheingold* Pullman coaches, out of Cologne Hbf, 1 April 1972.
(Peter Schiffer/Eisenbahnstiftung Collection)

001.164-3, with all-welded boiler and combustion chamber, at Hof Depot, 23 June 1969.
(Graham Stacey)

by the Deutsche Bahn Museum, Nuremberg. Unfortunately it was badly damaged by the Nuremberg Depot fire in October 2005, was repaired at Meiningen, including a new boiler, and was returned to operational status in May 2013.

01.164
001.164-3 was built by Henschel as 01.164 in 1936, was rebuilt with the modernised all-welded boiler and was stationed at Brunswick before its withdrawal in 1971 – the only DB 01 at that time not based at Hof. It was purchased privately by Norbert Heidrich and is kept at Lichtenfels.

01.173
001.173-4, built as 01.173 by Henschel in 1936, is owned by the Deutsches Technik Museum, Berlin, but is currently at Heilbronn, base of the South German Railway Museum, undergoing restoration.

01.180
001.180-9 was built by Henschel in 1937 and was rebuilt with an all-welded modernised boiler. It was one of the last 01 survivors at Hof and, after withdrawal in 1973, was purchased privately and kept at Bowil in Switzerland. It returned to Germany in 2011 and was at the Bavarian Railway Museum in Nördlingen, and is now back on main-line steam specials.

01.202
001.202-1, built as 01.202 in 1936, was one of the last survivors at Hof Depot in 1973 and was subsequently purchased privately and restored in Lyss, Switzerland, where it ran many special

001.202-1 at Bamberg after arrival with the 08.29 from Hof, January 1973.
(Alastair Wood)

enthusiasts' trains, with occasional forays into Southern Germany.

01.204

01.204 was built by Henschel in 1936. After the war, it was in the Soviet Zone and became a property of the East German DR. In 1970 it was renumbered 01.2204-4 and allocated to Dresden and was one of the standard 01s operating on the Berlin-Dresden '*Magistrale*' expresses in the 1970s that were dieselised at the end of the summer 1977 timetable. It was then repaired as a DR 'heritage' locomotive and, after one or two railtour excursions, was reinstated in traffic in 1980 at Saalfeld during the two-year oil crisis. After a farewell tour, it was stored on 8 May 1982 until purchased by a group in West Germany

Dresden 01.2204-4 bursts through Böhla with a Berlin-Dresden D-Zug, 25 August 1974. (Richard Spoors)

and displayed at the Eisenbahn Museum in Hermeskeil (in the Rheinland-Pfalz area).

01.220

01.220 was one of the last series of 01s built in 1937. It was rebuilt with a modernised high-performance all-welded boiler in August 1959, renumbered 001.220-3 in 1968, but withdrawn that year. In July 1969, it was restored as first rebuilt, as 01.220 with silver bands round the boiler, as were the first twenty 01s rebuilt with high-performance boilers. It was taken by road to Treuchtlingen, a depot that had 01s for many years for Munich-Würzburg and Munich-Nuremberg services, the latter before electrification and loaned to the city on the occasion of the railway station's centenary. It is displayed there on a plinth in the Altmühltherme Park, in the open air, being last renovated in 1989.

01.2204-4 on arrival at Dresden Neustadt with the D311 *Pannonia Express* from Berlin, 10 April 1976. (Alastair Wood)

Chapter 9

THE DR 02 4-CYLINDER COMPOUND PACIFIC

Design & Construction

Most of the former State railway express passenger fleet of locomotives were four-cylinder compounds, apart from the Saxon Pacifics and the Prussian S10.2 4-6-0s. It was therefore not surprising when discussions were taking place between 1921 and 1924 over the form that the new standard *Reichsbahn* express locomotives should take, that there was strong support for a development of the Saxon 2-8-2 four-cylinder compound or a new four-cylinder compound Pacific. As described in Chapter 8, the decision was taken, driven by Richard Wagner, to build a two-cylinder simple 4-6-2, but ten similar outline four-cylinder compound Pacifics were built for comparative purposes. 02.001-008 were constructed in 1925-6 by the firm Henschel, who had been very involved in their design, and 02.009 and 02.010, by the Munich firm, Maffei, which had a long tradition of building successful four-cylinder compounds and had also produced a design too late in the day for

serious consideration. 02.001 was exhibited in October 1925 at the Munich Transport Exhibition, alongside fellow compound Pacifics, a Baden IV h and a Bavarian S3/6.

The dimensions of the 02s were – apart from the cylinder/compound arrangement – very similar to the prototype 01s. The coupled wheels were 6ft 7in in diameter, boiler 227lbpsi, grate area 47.4sqft, heating surface 2,554sqft, and superheater 1,075sqft. The inside high-pressure cylinders were 18.1in x 26in, outside low-pressure cylinders 28.4in 26in. Minimum axle-load was 20.2 tons, locomotive weight 113.5 tons and with a 7,000 gallon water capacity and 10-ton coal tender, the total weight was 185 tons. Theoretical indicated horsepower of 2,300 was just 100hp less than the two-cylinder 01. The maximum authorised speed was 81mph, 6 mph faster than the initial allowed speed of the 01, because of the presumed smoother ride and reduced hammer blow from a four-cylinder engine.

During the latter stages of the design process, Wagner personally

proposed a longer boiler barrel, at 22ft 4in, some 3ft 3in longer than the earlier-designed boiler. Wagner gave five reasons: increase in the heating surface; increase in the water-holding capacity and therefore reserve; a better weight distribution through shortening the smokebox; higher superheat; and a smaller blastpipe. The prototype long boiler was fitted to the last 02, 02.010 built by Maffei.

In the comparative tests, described in Chapter 8, the 02 rode well and was, for that reason, popular with crews. It was at its best when worked hard over heavy gradients, a characteristic of the Württemberg and Bavarian Pacifics in the South German hills. However, the slight theoretical economic advantage when worked hard was more than offset by the increased costs of construction, heavy overhaul, shed maintenance, and working in traffic on easier grades and lighter work. It was therefore decided in 1937, to rebuild the ten compounds as two-cylinder simple 01s, and they were all converted in Meiningen Works between then and 1942, being

4-cylinder compound Pacific 02.008, brand new and allocated to Bw Hof at the end of 1925, seen here early in 1926.
(RVM Berlin/Hermann Maey/Eisenbahnstiftung Collection)

02.001, the first German 'standard' Pacific, four-cylinder compound version of the 1926 Standard 01 Pacific, built by Maffei in 1926, and rebuilt as a standard two-cylinder 01 in September 1937 and renumbered 01.011, the number originally reserved for the high-pressure Pacific that was numbered H002.1001.
(Werner Hubert/ Eisenbahnstiftung Collection)

02.009, DRG four-cylinder compound version of the 1925 Standard 01 Pacific, built by Maffei in 1926 and rebuilt as a standard two-cylinder 01 in July 1940, becoming 01.238, c1930.
(MLS Collection/Carl Bellingrodt/EK-Verlag)

02.010, equipped by Wagner experimentally with a lengthened boiler and tube area, on a test run shortly after its delivery, 1926.
(Dr Kallmünzer/Robin Garn Collection)

renumbered 01.011 (02.001) and 01.233-241.

The last survivor in 01 form was 01.234 (001.234-4), formerly 02.003 which was one of the group of 01s working between Hof and Bamberg until dieselisation in 1973.

Also given an 02 number was the experimental high-pressure Pacific, built by Schwartzkopf in 1931, H02.1001, a four-cylinder compound locomotive with a very high boiler pressure of 1,707lbpsi using the Schwartzkopf-Löffler patent.

Operation

The 02s on test were found to be of greater economy compared to the two-cylinder 01s on routes with significant gradients and therefore after initial allocation to Erfurt, Hof and Hamm for detailed comparative working, they were concentrated at Hof for working the Regensburg-Hof-Leipzig, Munich-Berlin and Hof-Dresden-Warsaw routes. Even after rebuilding as 01s, they remained at Hof; 001.234-4 was among the last surviving 01s at that location, the last at which the 01s found regular traffic use.

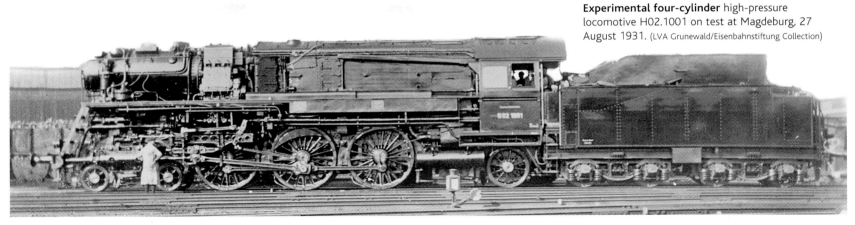

Experimental four-cylinder high-pressure locomotive H02.1001 on test at Magdeburg, 27 August 1931. (LVA Grunewald/Eisenbahnstiftung Collection)

Four-cylinder compound 02.001 heads D118 at Grobau between Hof and Plauen in 1935, two years before rebuilding as 01.011. (Carl Bellingrodt/R.Garn Collection)

001.234-4, formerly four-cylinder 02.003, rebuilt September 1938 as a two-cylinder standard 01 Pacific, was one of the remaining Hof allocated engines allocated to Bamberg for the Hof-Bamberg-Nuremberg line until dieselisation in 1973. (MLS Collection)

01.234-4, 02.003, rebuilt as a standard 01 in 1938, and retained at Hof Depot, at Lichtenfels on a DGEG Oberfranken enthusiasts' special train, 21 April 1968. (Dieter Junker/Eisenbahnstiftung Collection)

Chapter 10

THE DR (EAST GERMAN) 01.5

Design & Construction

The East German *Deutsche Reichsbahn* started to build higher superheat reconstructed boilers in 1957 and used them on the 03 and 03.10 Pacifics, and the class 39 and 41 2-8-2s, the Prussian 39s receiving a more thorough rebuilding and were given a new class 22 identification. At one stage, it was proposed to build a new three-cylinder 4-6-2 with pulverised fuel and mechanical firing, after experiments with S10 17.1055 and two French engines obtained during the war, 07.1001 (ex-SNCF 231E 18) and Est 4-8-2 08.1001 (241A 4). However, this proposal was abandoned in favour of increasing the haulage and performance capacity of the 01s. Although some diesels were built at the end of the 1950s (the V 180s – later 118), their maximum power output was only 1,800hp, insufficient for heavy inter-city expresses, the 01s in service already being theoretically capable of producing 2,240hp. Electrification of the main routes in the German Democratic Republic (GDR) was not yet possible – the Russians had removed the electric poles and wires from DRG electrified track in the Soviet Zone as war reparation,

as well as singling the former main line from Berlin to Nuremberg and Munich, now terminated at Probstzella, south of Saalfeld.

The average age of the 01s was already more than twenty years and a number had boilers that were due for replacement. A decision was, therefore, taken in 1959 to not only re-boiler, but to use the opportunity to improve the performance overall by a more radical rebuilding. A new boiler with raised performance could increase the power output to 2,400hp, about 7 per cent improvement and was of the same order as a projected new V240 diesel locomotive. Train loads for new engines running at 75mph maximum could be raised from 500 to 550 tons, ie by an extra coach. A large grate area – 52.5sqft – with heating surface of 2,356sqft and an enlarged superheater surface of 1,052.4sqft was designed, and the boiler diameter in the area of the combustion chamber was enlarged from 6ft 5in to 6ft 9in to give a better reserve as coal supplies were still poor and many DR engines had to steam on inferior quality 'brown coal'. The boiler was fully welded, but the maximum pressure remained at 227lbpsi.

A decision to retain two rather than three cylinders was taken as the additional cost was unnecessary for performance – the only advantage would be on ride quality. It was decided to test the Giesl ejector system on one of the early prototypes and the boiler height was raised to the maximum in the frames to enable mechanical coal or oil-firing to be installed at a later date if deemed necessary. It was also decided to semi-streamline the engine or at least clean up its outline with a running steel plate from smokebox to cab on top of the boiler, a front sloping deck for the running plate, a conical 'bullet nose' smokebox door and large 'witte' smoke deflectors in the standard position as on the DB. After an early experiment with the first engine, 01.501, whose 'witte' deflectors rose to enclose the top of the smokebox and surround the chimney which looked overpowering, elephantine, and frankly, hideous – it got the nickname *Fledermausohren* – bat-ears!

The first new locomotive, 01.501, rebuilt from 01.174, which had been damaged in an accident at Bitterfeld in the autumn of 1961, appeared in April 1962. It weighed 111 tons and with a tender with 7,500-gallons water capacity, ten tons of coal and equipped with roller bearings on all axles, a full 183.8 tons. The maximum axle-load was 20.2 tons. Maximum authorised speed was 81mph. The decision was made only to rebuild the more recent series of 01s (from 01.102 onwards) as the earlier older engines would require a more radical reconstruction. Initially, it was planned to rebuild fifteen 01s in 1962, but in the end only seven, some of those in Works for L2 an L3 repairs (light/intermediate, such as 01.118 and 01.204) being outshopped in original condition and lasting until 1978 or beyond.

Six more reconstructed 01s appeared from Meiningen Works in 1962, 01.502-507. 01.502 , rebuilt from 01.157, was the first to receive welded steel cylinders. The third reconstruction was of 01.142 which had been badly damaged in May 1962 when working a freight between Eisenach and Gotha, becoming 01.503. The fourth reconstruction was of 01.224, which became 01.504, the first to receive the ordered Boxpok wheels and Giesl ejector. This locomotive was sent to Halle Research Centre for tests at the Centre and on the road between Halle and Lückenwalde and in the north near Greifswald. The conclusions from the tests – which had had a number of problems on the road giving the engine sufficient time and mileage to work at maximum capacity – were:

at 30mph – 1,800 edhp achieved
at 50mph – 1,780 edhp achieved
at 60mph – 1,725 edhp achieved.

At 50mph, the highest recorded indicated horsepower at the drawbar of 1,780 exceeded that of the standard 01 by 130hp. The boiler performance was first-class. When boiler pressure was raised to 256lbpsi, the power output was raised by 150 hp and steam and coal consumption fell by 7 per cent. The Giesl ejector was calculated to achieve a 5 per cent reduction in need for steam to achieve the same performance in the middle ranges of power output. At the highest power output, the advantage disappeared and the higher temperature at the outside of the boiler caused overheating of the bearings and axle-boxes. However, many of the readings were within the normal margins of error. Although the Erfurt shedmaster claimed a 4 per cent coal consumption saving over a longer period, the authorities decided not to equip any more, although 01.504 retained its Giesl ejector to the end of its life.

All the initial rebuilt 01s were allocated to Erfurt, long the main depot for the 01 class. After experience, it was decided that a few modifications were necessary, and the first seven engines were seen as prototypes and a few changes put in hand, delaying the rebuilding of the next 01 as 01.508. There were some problems with the firebox dampers and crews complained that the 01.5s were not as good as the original 01s, expectations being unfulfilled. There were also problems with the lubrication, the higher superheat being blamed. Some cab design details were criticised and, most important, there were many complaints of rough riding over 60mph. Some thought this was the fault of the Boxpok wheels.

Eleven 01s were rebuilt at Meiningen Works in 1963 - the first production run, 01.508-518. Seven of these – 01.508-13 and 517, 518 – received Boxpok wheels and, like the earlier prototypes, were coal-fired. The earlier engines received the agreed modifications in November 1962. 01.504 received a broad band strip along its running plate, 8in wide, and a white strip for photo/publicity purposes.

The following are the conversions that took place from standard 01s to coal-burning 01.5s:

01.501 from 01.174
01.510 from 01.139
01.502 from 01.157
01.511 from 01.218
01.503 from 01.142
01.512 from 01.175
01.504 from 01 224
01.513 from 01 152
01.505 from 01.121
01.514 from 01.208
01.506 from 01.127
01.515 from 01,160
01.507 from 01.136
01.516 from 01.117
01.508 from 01.153
01.517 from 01.107
01.509 from 01.143
01.518 from 01.185

October 1964 was an important date for the DR. An agreement with the Russian authorities to supply oil to East Germany, via a 'Friendship Pipeline' to Schwedt on the Oder River, made it possible to consider oil-firing for the DR's key locomotive classes. A decision to use oil fuel if possible had been taken in 1959 and tests with a three-cylinder 2-10-0, 44.195, had been undertaken at Halle. The decision for oil-firing was taken not for performance reasons, but to reduce the heavy workload of the firemen and give them more time to assist the drivers in general observation. There were economic advantages also – the non-use of fuel when standing between work and the ability to diagram longer runs without engine change for fuel purposes. Therefore the rebuilding programme for 1964 planned for the next series of 01.5s to be oil-burning. The first was 01.186, converted as 01.519, in February 1964, which was also the fiftieth anniversary of Meiningen Locomotive Works. The production run then flowed with 01.519-533 being completed that year and the last two, 01.534 and 535, being completed early in 1965. All had strengthened spoked wheel centres instead of Boxpok wheels which were abandoned for various

reasons – including the complaints of rough-riding from crews and the tendency for the wheels to become loose on the axles. Some engines exchanged their Boxpok wheels for spoked wheels from withdrawn 01s. The last to exchange its wheel centres was 01.0503 of Pasewalk in 1976. Some of the earlier 01.5s were converted to oil-firing also and in the end, only 01.506, 511, 512, 514, 515, 516 and 518 remained coal-burning. The oil-burning engines had boilers of similar dimensions to the coal burners. All the reconstructed boilers included feedwater heaters. The oil-burning locomotive tenders held 3,000 gallons of fuel oil and the locomotive's total weight was 190.1 tons. The theoretical indicated horsepower of the oil-burning engines was slightly higher at 2,500hp.

The oil-burning series 01.519 – 535 were converted from the following 01s:

01.519 from 01.186
01.528 from 01.119
01.520 from 01.162
01.529 from 01.205
01.521 from 01.144
01.530 from 01.221
01.522 from 01.184
01.531 from 01.158
01.523 from 01.191
01.532 from 01.135
01.524 from 01.129
01.533 from 01.116
01.525 from 01.219
01.534 from 01.203
01.526 from 01.163
01.535 from 01.156
01.527 from 01.225

In traffic, the boiler performed excellently and there was some

01.509, as converted from standard DR Pacific 01.143, at Bebra, 21 March 1965. It has conical smokebox door, Boxpok wheels and is coal-burning – this engine was later converted to oil-burning as were most of the 01.5s. Just seven remained coal-burning, all based at Berlin Ostbahnhof in later years. (MLS Collection)

01.504 , converted from 01.224, at Magdeburg on a snowy day, January 1968. It has the original conical 'bullet nose' smokebox door, Boxpok wheels and is the only member of the class fitted with a Giesl ejector. (MLS Collection)

discussion of raising the maximum pressure to 256lbpsi or even 284lbpsi, but it was decided not to take the risk. There were weaknesses, however; the Boxpok wheel centres already mentioned and problems with the dampers. The crews compared the riding of these locomotives unfavourably with the unaltered 01s, possibly due to the higher positioning of the boiler, but more likely an impression given by the noise and reverberation of the steel cab and fittings, a problem experienced by other DR standard post-war

classes like the class 23 (later designated class 35) 2-6-2 mixed traffic locomotive. The reason for not rebuilding the rest of the 01s in the 01.102 series onwards was not, however, these weaknesses, but the arrival in numbers of the V 240 2,400hp diesel locomotive, causing a restriction on investment in the steam locomotive. Sometime in the 1970s, a distinctive element of their external appearance changed on all but four of these engines (01.505, 513, 516, and 517) – the conical 'bullet nose' smokebox door was replaced by the standard DR

door which the East German 01s had retained from the time of their building, although reconverted coal-burning 01.1531 received such a smokebox door after preservation.

The first 01.5 to be withdrawn was the coal-burning 01.516 (01.1516-2) which suffered a catastrophic boiler explosion at Bitterfeld in November 1977 killing eight, including the Leipzig crew who had failed their 03.20 on the forward trip and were inexperienced with the 01.5 class. At the end of steam express passenger working on the DR system in 1979-

01.0503-1, formerly 01.142, at Hamburg backing on to a train for Berlin, 2 September 1972. This locomotive has Boxpok wheels and is oil-burning. (MLS Collection)

80, the coal-burning engines were at Berlin Ost (closed in May 1979), with the oil-burners split between Pasewalk and the majority at Saalfeld, where the last diagrams for the oil-burning 01.5s held out. The oil crisis in 1980-1 meant that for a few months Saalfeld employed a few coal-burners of both 01 and 01.5 classes, but this was very short-lived and the class was extinct in service by 1981. However, as instanced later in this chapter, several 01.5s have been preserved, some in operational state.

01.0532-0 was one of the 01.5s stationed at Erfurt for working the through trains from Frankfurt to Erfurt and Dresden, eastwards from Bebra. It is oil-burning and has standard spoked wheel centres, c1978. (MLS Collection)

01.0525-4 at Göschwitz with local train P3003 from Halle to Saalfeld, 10 April 1979. (Alastair Wood)

Operation

Initially, the 01.5s were allocated to Erfurt, the depot that had maintained the largest number of 01 Pacifics for many years. However, a group soon moved to Wittenberge to take over the Berlin-Hamburg international corridor trains. They also worked the north/south trunk route from Rostock to Magdeburg through Wittenberge. A group of oil-burning 01.5s at Erfurt took regular responsibility for the other main international connection with West Germany via the Erfurt-Bebra-Frankfurt route, as far as Bebra, where they would hand over to DB 01.10 three-cylinder oil-burning Pacifics, V200 diesels or later electric E10s or E103s. In April 1976 Alastair Wood timed one of the last daytime steam-hauled services between Berlin and Wittenberge on D530 to Schwerin:

Coal-burning 01.1514-7 at Berlin Karlshorst at the head of D1654 from Halle, 13 April 1976. (Alastair Wood)

01.0527-0 at Hamburg Hauptbahnhof with D405 for Berlin, 23 August 1972.
(Alastair Wood)

Berlin-Wittenberge-(Schwerin)
D530, 06.49 Berlin-Schwerin, 12.4.76
01.0513-0 (oil-fired) Bw Wittenberge
11 chs, 362/380t

Berlin-Lichtenberg	00.00	mph (slipping)	T	0 miles
Friedrichsfelde Ost	04.27	30/pws 5*		
km 35	-	38		
Bk Wf	13.48	57½		
Ringbahn	-	74		
Schönfliess	22.33	72/78		
Hennigsdorf Nord	28.07	70/ sigs 10* via platform road		
Schönwalde	33.27	68/63½		
km 32	-	71		
Falkenhagen	38.25	sigs 5*		
Brieselang	42.00	50/65		
<u>Nauen</u>	<u>48.12</u>		8L	41.05
	00.00		3½ L	0
Berger Damm	06.01	68		
Paulinenaue	09.34	74		
Vietnitz	13.32	79		
Friesack	15.40	80/82		
km 70	-	79/76		
<u>Neustadt</u>	<u>23.02</u>		2½ L	24.9
	00.00		2½ L	0
Zernitz	06.26	65		
Studenitz	09.21	72		
Breddin	10.56	74/72		
Glöwen	15.44	79		
Bad Wilsnack	20.51	82/79/82		
Kuhblank	24.13	79		
Wittenberge Süd	26.51	70		
<u>Wittenberge</u>	<u>28.28</u>		1L	31.75

Nauen-Neustadt averaged 64.8mph start-stop, and Neustadt-Wittenberge an excellent 67mph. At Wittenberge, 01.0513-0 was relieved by another Wittenberge 01, 01.0524-7, for the onward journey. D530 was the only westbound daytime steam express on this route at that time and from Brieselang, just south of Nauen to Wittenberge, was single track, a main line congested with freights. It took excellent operating to give D530 a clear path, of which 01.0513 took full advantage.

The Berlin-based coal-burning 01.5s shared the Berlin-Dresden fast *Magistrale* inter-city trains with the Dresden 01s and also a couple of semi-fast services to Szczecin (Stettin). Alastair Wood has again given me permission to publish a couple of his logs with these engines on the Dresden route, coincidentally with the same locomotive on successive days, although 01.1511, 1512, 1514, 1515 and 1518 were all active on this route at this time.

Both trains had two extra coaches above the scheduled formation and were crammed full of standing passengers. After slow starts, both trains averaged over 64mph start-stop between Doberlug and Berlin. Weather on both runs was cold and dark with sleet and snow.

Once the Wittenberge Depot lost its Hamburg and Rostock-Magdeburg turns to diesel traction in the early 1970s, their fleet was dispersed to Saalfeld and Pasewalk, where they shared the Berlin-Stralsund expresses with Stralsund's three-cylinder oil-burning 03.10s (for the author's experiences and logs on these services, see Chapter 18).

Eventually the majority, deprived of their border work to both Hamburg and Bebra, finished at Saalfeld where they had a four-engine diagram on D- and E-Zügen to Leipzig and Halle, and another four-engine diagram on stopping services to Leipzig, Gera and Jena. They also covered a couple of engine diagrams, subshedded at Göschwitz (near Jena), working locals to Saalfeld and cross-country to Gera, although Saalfeld often substituted a class 41 2-8-2 or 44 2-10-0 if they were short of Pacifics. The writing was on the wall by 1979. Some of the Wittenberge machines were obviously absent by this time and were either stored or already withdrawn – 01.0502, 0523, 0527, 0528, 0532. The Pasewalk engines, 01.0503, 0504, 0507, 0526, 0530 and 0535, lost their Stralsund-Berlin turns at the end of the summer timetable. At Saalfeld in April 1979, there were a couple of 01.5s already stored dead out of service and rumoured withdrawn,

Dresden-Berlin, D678
20.20 Dresden-Berlin

	10.4.77			11.4.77			
	01.1506 - 3 (coal-fired) Bw Berlin			**01.1506-3 (coal-fired) Bw Berlin-Ostbhf**			
	11 chs, 350/400t			**11 chs, 359/415t**			
Dresden Neustadt	00.00	mph	T	00.00	mph	1L	0 miles
Radebeul Ost	07.13	50		07.06	51½		
Neucoswig	12.38	56/52		12.16	61/57		
Weinböhla	15.35	54		15.10	52		
km 22	-	52		-	48		
Böhla	21.15	75		21.05	76		
Grossenhain	25.37		4½ L	25.23		5½ L	21.4
	00.00		4½ L	00.00		6L	0
Frauenhain	08.50	59		08.23	63		
km 48	-	72		-	71		
Elsterwerda	14.13		3½ L	14.06		5L	11.65
	00.00		3L	00.00		4L	0
Hohenleipisch	08.12	33½		07.00	44		
Rückersdorf-Oppelhain	13.13	65		11.34	70		
Doberlug-Kirchhain	17.03		4L	15.30		3½ L	12.4
	00.00		3½ L	00.00		3L	0
Brenitz-Sonnewalde	08.05	62		07.45	64		
Walddrehna	12.41	64/60		12.29	65/59		
Gehren	15.21	69		15.01	72		
Uckro	17.55	76		17.33	77		
Dabendorf	21.42	70/78		21.23	74		
Golssen	25.00	76		24.56	69/72		
Klasdorf	27.50	74		27.56	70		
Baruth	30.08	70		30.15	71		
Neuhof	34.50	75		35.01	76		
Wunsdorf	36.25	68		36.31	70		
Dahrendorf	40.47	73/69		40.45	77/71		
Dahlewitz	46.27	61/63		46.03	70/64		
Blankenfelde	47.10	62		46.50	68		
Ringbahn	-	58		-	61/sigs 39*		
Berlin-Schönefeld	53.36		4L	54.14		4½ L	57.85

01.0524 and 0533 (the latter subsequently being preserved and restored). Others like 0513, one of two still retaining its conical bullet smokebox door, were on shed acting merely as standby or on the breakdown train. In April 1979, 01.0510-6, 0521-3, 0525-4 and just ex-works 0529-6 were on the D504 Saalfeld-Leipzig and various E-Zug services, and 01.0501-5, 0505-6 (still with conical smokebox door), 0509-8 and 0520-5 were working the four-engine local diagram. 01.0534-6 and a three-cylinder 2-10-0, 44.0601-3, were outbased at Göschwitz (for the author's personal experiences of the 01.5s at Saalfeld, see Chapter 18).

In 1980, with a temporary shortage of fuel oil, a few of the Berlin coal-burners appeared on the Saalfeld D-/E- diagrams including 01.1511, 1512, 1514 and 1518, but this was short-lived and the Romanian-built class 119 diesels soon flooded the area, taking over the class 95 2-10-2T turns to Probtszella, Sonnenberg and Meiningen, as well as the

01.502 (Bw Wittenberge) at speed with a Hamburg-Berlin D-Zug through the 'west corridor', August 1970. (Jorp Schlüter/Eisenbahnstiftung Collection)

01.0502-3 with a train for Berlin at Hamburg Hbf, c1972. (MLS Collection)

Pacific turns, leaving just four class 41 2-8-2s to soldier on with local services for another three or four years. 01.1514 remained for a further year as reserve locomotive at Saalfeld, and 01.1511/12 moved to Halberstadt and Magdeburg where they worked D641, D643 and D646 trains to and from Berlin for the duration of a timetable in 1982. More ambitious plans mooted in 1980 to repair and reinstate further 01s, 03s and rebuild the Saalfeld 01.5s as coal-burners finally came to naught. A number of 01.5s eked out a year or two more as stationary boilers before final scrapping in the mid to late 1980s.

01.0525-4 arriving at Hamburg Altona with D406 from Berlin, 1 September 1972.
(MLS Collection)

01.0524-7 at Magdeburg with a train for Wittenberge alongside a DR E11 (211) electric locomotive, c1972.
(MLS Collection)

Oil-burning 01.0508
with D1332 Berlin
Friedrichstrasse-
Wittenberge-Hamburg
express near Nikolassee,
19 April 1976.
(Helmut Dahlhaus)

Oil-burning 01.533
climbing to Hönebach
Tunnel through
Ronshausen with a cross-
border train from West
Germany to Erfurt, 16
September 1968.
(Richard Spoors)

01.0507, still with 'Boxpok' wheels and 01.0533 double-head D217, Paris-Berlin D-Zug, at Hönebach, 29 April 1973. (Helmut Dahlhaus)

01.0528 and 01.0501 at speed with the D1100 Stralsund-Bebra, 30 July 1972. (Helmut Dahlhaus)

The East German Pacifics worked heavy fast freights also. Here 01.532 nears the summit just past Hönebach Station with a freight from Erfurt for the DB transfer at Bebra, 26 July 1969. (Helmut Dahlhaus)

01.0533 with the very late-running D198 Frankfurt (Oder)-Bebra shortly after leaving Hönebach Tunnel, 28 April 1973. (Helmut Dahlhaus)

Coal-burning 01.1518, said by Alastair Wood to be one of the best performing Pacifics on the Berlin – Dresden expresses, here at the head of D379 Istropolitan Berlin-Dresden-Bratislava, on the Berlin Ring, 31 March 1975. (Helmut Dahlhaus)

01.0530-4 climbs to Hönebach Tunnel with D207 through a spectacular winter landscape, 21 December 1972.
(W Sieberg/Eisenbahnstiftung Collection)

Coal-burning 01.1511 nearing the end of its journey passing Warschauer Strasse, a Berlin metro train in the background, with a Budapest-Dresden-Berlin D-Zug, 9 August 1975. (George Bambery)

Oil-burning 01.0520-5 backing down into a train at Saalfeld is passed by three-cylinder 2-10-0 44.0553-6, c1978. (MLS Collection)

One of Saalfeld's four-engine top-link Pacifics, 01.0522, leaving the busy town with D504 to Leipzig and Berlin via Jena, 10 December 1977. (Robert Kingsford-Smith)

01.0533, a top-link Saalfeld Pacific, leaving the town with D504 to Leipzig and Berlin via Jena, 8 December 1977. (Robert Kingsford-Smith)

Saalfeld's 01.0521-3 at Unterwellenborn on E800 Saalfeld-Leipzig via Gera, 8 July 1979. (Graham Stacey)

Coal-burning 01.1512, drafted into Saalfeld during the 1980-1 oil crisis, climbs up the Saale Valley past Weisenberg Castle, near Uhlstadt, with a Leipzig via Jena to Saalfeld train, 10 May 1980.
(Robert Kingsford-Smith)

Coal-burning 01.1512 hurries a local stopping train up the Saale Valley en route to Jena and Camburg, May 1980.
(Malcolm Holdsworth)

Coal-burning 01.1518 departs Saalfeld with the early morning E800 for Gera and Leipzig, 10 May 1980.
(George Bambery)

01.0521-3 and 01 0519-7 on the bufferstops at Leipzig Hbf after morning arrivals from Saalfeld on E- and P-trains respectively, September 1978. (Roger Johnson/Eisenbahnstiftung Collection)

Pasewalk's 01.0503 off D717 from Stralsund, 03.2002 off P3516 from Halle and Lutherstadt-Wittenberg and on the left, Berlin Ost's 01.1515 preparing to leave for E314 Gydania for Gdansk in Poland, at Berlin-Lichtenberg depot, 4 November 1978. (Robin Garn)

Preserved 01.5 Pacifics

01.509

01.143 was rebuilt as 01.509 in 1963 at Meiningen Works, later converted to oil-burning and, after early operations on the Berlin-Hamburg corridor, was renumbered 01.0509-8 in 1970 and finished at Saalfeld, being withdrawn in 1982. It was saved by the Ulmer Eisenbahn Freunde (UEF) at Heilbronn and maintained in operational status (see photos on pages 159 and 356).

01.514

01.208 was rebuilt as 01.514 in 1963 and retained as a coal-burner, being renumbered 01.1514-7. In the 1970s, it was based at Berlin Ostbhf, and was used on services from Berlin to the Polish border and to Dresden. During the oil crisis in 1980-1, it was stationed for a short time at Saalfeld before being withdrawn in 1983 and preserved at the Technikmuseum, Speyer, in the Rhineland (Palatinate) (see photo on page 162).

01.519

01.186 was the first of the new tranche of 01.5s built as oil-burners in February 1964. It was numbered 01.519 and renumbered 01.0519-7 in 1970, and completed its DR

Oil-burning 01.531, in pre-preservation days, climbing to Hönebach Tunnel through Ronshausen with an express from Frankfurt to Erfurt and East Germany, 16 September 1968. (Richard Spoors)

career at Saalfeld in 1983. It was acquired by the Eisenbahnfreunde Zollernbahn (EFZ), Tübingen (Baden-Württemberg), restored for active service as a coal-burner and renumbered 01.1519-6 in accordance with DR practice. It ran until 2005 and was expected to run agian in 2016 (see photo on page 176).

01.531

01.158 was rebuilt in 1964 as an oil-burner as 01.531 and renumbered 01.0531 in 1970, and based at Erfurt

for services to the West German border at Bebra, finishing its DR career at Saalfeld. It was converted back to coal-firing in 1984 after withdrawal and renumbered 01.1531-1, and placed with the Deutsche Bahn Museum, now BSW Group, at the Historisches Bw (engine shed) at Arnstadt. It was active in the 1990s on the DR *Plandampf* events.

01.533

01.116 was rebuilt as oil-burner

01.533 in 1964, and was based at Erfurt for services between Leipzig, Dresden and the border at Bebra. Renumbered 01.0533-8 in 1970, it was based at Saalfeld until withdrawal in 1984 when it was acquired by the Ősterreichische Gesellschaft für Eisenbahn Geschichte (Austrian Society for Railway History), Ampflwang, Austria , converted to coal-burning, renumbered 01.1533-7 and maintained for special train service in both Austria and Germany.

01.1531-1 at Meiningen during the 1994 *Plandampf* between Meiningen and Arnstadt on N6840 to Erfurt, 4 May 1994. (David Maidment)

Chapter 11

THE *DEUTSCHE REICHSBAHN* 01.10

DRG 1939 STREAMLINED LOCOMOTIVES
Design, Construction & Operation

In the 1930s the German Railways Board were becoming concerned at the growing strength of road and air traffic, and looked to accelerate their trains over key routes, aiming for 60mph average speeds. Despite DRG publicity making the best of it, there was some disappointment that there had been little advance in the development of the standard 01 and 03 Pacifics, which were fine when compared with the State railway Pacifics and 4-6-0s that they'd partially replaced, but were not comparable to the latest designs in America, France or Britain. The E04 and E17 passenger electric locomotives were capable of hauling 570 tons at 81mph (130km/hr), and at 69mph (110km/hr) could haul a train the weight of which was double that of the maximum of an 01. In 1935, the E18 electric was introduced, authorised to run at 94mph (150km/hr). But on non-electrified lines, both standard Pacifics were limited by the capacity of their boilers and struggled to produce steam at the rate developed elsewhere. In 1933, the two car high-speed railcars were introduced on some routes (eg the *Flying Hamburger*), but their passenger capacity was limited and the engineering authorities still sought to equip a suitable steam fleet for higher-speed services on the main city routes. To that end, there were a number of experiments with streamlining involving a couple of 03s, 03.154 and 193, the high-pressure 04 Pacific and the 05 4-6-4s. There were boiler problems with the 04 and the 05s were too heavy and long for widespread use. An 06 4-8-4 was in the development stage, but it took three years from 1936 to 1939 to come to fruition and the same length limitation would apply. The bogie wheels of the 01 and 03 classes were increased in diameter, and from 01.102 and 03.123 onwards, their maximum speed was raised from 75 to 81mph. 03s on very lightweight FD trains from Hamburg Altona were permitted to reach 87½mph on certain routes.

Despite all the developments elsewhere, Wagner and his colleagues stuck to the basic 01 design, but modified it to use three cylinders to improve the ride at higher speeds and to use the streamlining developed on the two 03s and 05s, which was calculated to give an extra 200 horsepower above 75mph. By 1938, with the extension of the German Reich to Austria and the Sudetenland, more main-line higher speed locomotives were urgently needed and, therefore in 1938, the *Reichsbahn* Board ordered five three-cylinder streamlined express locomotives, the first of which was completed and delivered in March 1939. According to a conversation reported between Adolf Wolf, chief of the construction office of Borsig, and Richard Wagner about the proposed three-cylinder variant of the 01, under Wagner's influence 200 of the new locomotives were ordered without waiting for the tests of the prototype to be completed. Although interest had been expressed in Chapelon's developments in France, especially with the rebuilt 4700 class of 4-8-0s, the die had been cast and it was too late to incorporate any of that learning without delaying the introduction of the urgently-needed new fleet. Although the Kylchap double exhaust had been shown to be particularly effective, the 01.10s appeared with a conventional single blastpipe. In July 1939, the construction plan for the new 01.10s was increased to 400 locomotives to be built between 1939 and 1943. The performance specification – to be capable of hauling 500 tons on the level at 75mph – was, however, less ambitious than the actual performance of the 06 4-8-4, which was completed about the same time.

The first locomotive, the prototype 01.1001, was delivered in August 1939. The dimensions of the new locomotive included 6ft 7in coupled wheels, three cylinders of 19.7in x 26in, grate area of 46.4sqft, heating surface of 2,657sqft, and superheater 925sqft. Boiler pressure was still 227lbpsi, the same as the 01, axle-weight 20.2 tons, engine weight 114.3 tons, 192 tons with ten-wheel 8,360 gallons water capacity and ten tons of coal. Tractive effort was 34,920lb and the planned horsepower, 2,350, almost identical to the 01. Maximum speed was set at 94mph, the main improvement envisaged. The cost of the three-cylinder 01 was 8,000 Reichmarks more than the two-cylinder version.

01.1001 went immediately to the test centre at Grunewald in August 1939, and ran up 4,000 miles in tests between then and March 1940. A few minor changes in the production runs were agreed as a result of the test experience, but the trials were halted after damage was encountered at speeds higher than 87mph, and the priority was the

development of the freight class 50 2-10-0 to meet the war and military priorities. Coal consumption was better than the standard 01s only over 60mph – about 3.5 per cent when running at 75mph.

The final planned building programme for 1940/41 included the following:

01.1001 (Prototype)
Schwartzkopf (BMAG)

01.1002 – 01.1051
Krupp

01.1052 - 01.1105
Schwartzkopf (BMAG)

01.1106 – 01.1130
Borsig

01.1131 – 01.1155
Henschel

01.1156 – 01.1180
Krauss-Maffei

01.1181 – 01.1205
Schwartzkopf (BMAG)

However, only the prototype and the first order from Schwartzkopf were delivered, before the engineering firms' construction capacity was required for freight locomotives, munitions and other war supplies. 01.1001 and 01.1052-1100 received a glossy black livery whilst 1101-1105 appeared in grey – 1102-3 in a lighter shade, the grey engines retaining this livery until de-streamlined. The last five locomotives were also fitted with roller bearings. In February 1941, by order of the Reich Transport Minister, the maximum speed of both the 01.10 and 03.10 locomotives was reduced to 87½mph. Apart from the effect of the streamlining, which was really only effective over 75mph, the 01.10 was really no advance

over the 1925-built class 01. And, of course, the continuation of the war and consequent deteriorating condition of locomotives and track meant that regular high-speed passenger work became irrelevant. There was continuing criticism that German development of express steam locomotives had not progressed since 1925 and when the building of express engines was stopped to concentrate on the wartime Austerity class 42 and 52 2-10-0s, Wagner retired.

The first production locomotives emerged in traffic at the end of a very harsh winter in February 1940, and their introduction was immediately complicated by the heavy snow swirling in the streamlining and cab. In April 1940, the manager of the Halle Test Centre delivered a list of twenty-eight defects experienced with the first locomotives and, in May 1940, a further list of weaknesses was provided by the Hamburg motive power division to the Brunswick Works. As a result, the streamlining was removed from the motion and cylinder areas, commencing in the autumn of 1941. The early years, however, were plagued with continuing problems of overheating, and shortage of spare parts for essential maintenance and casual repairs, causing some 01.10s based at Bebra to be put to store in April 1941. However, the maximum speed reduction in early 1941 was more because of rolling stock limitations than the faults of the locomotives.

Many of the defects were attributed to problems caused by or exacerbated by the streamlining

Streamlined 01.1089, built in 1940, being prepared at Halle Depot, 9 June 1942.
(RVM Halle /Eisenbahnstiftung Collection)

01.1062 at Breslau in 1943, showing the external effect of wartime conditions and shortage of staff for non-essential work.
(Werner Hubert/Wenzel Collection/EK-Verlag)

and various parts were removed during the 1942-44 period, especially as the war had ended the opportunity for high-speed running. The locomotives' initial rapid introduction meant that they soon appeared on the northern plains for which they were primarily designed, based at Hamburg and Hanover operating in the Ruhr industrial area, and on the prestige main lines from Berlin to Leipzig, Dresden, Frankfurt, Nuremberg and Munich, to the east to Breslau, and from Munich to Linz and Vienna. The highest monthly mileage accumulated by any of the 01.10s during the war was the 10,437 miles by 01.1082 of Bebra in October 1940, with an average train weight of 672 tons (including the weight of the locomotive), but high coal consumption of 17.4 tons per 1,000 kilometres. Most of the locomotives were accumulating between 8,750 and 10,000 miles per month, with coal consumption ranging between 11 and 17.5 tons per 1,000kms. This availability and utilisation reduced rapidly as the war progressed, although 01.1093 ran 9,600 miles in July 1943 from Kattowitz and 01.1079 was recorded as running 9,925 miles with an availability of thirty days in August 1944 from Brunswick Depot.

However, because of the many early teething problems and the increasing impact of the war, their planned dominance of high-speed services throughout the Reich was not realised. In fact, they appear to have been a major disappointment – at least conceded privately – and it was not until after the war and

01.1053 (Bw Leipzig) at the Anhalter Station in Berlin at the head of D24 Berlin-Munich, Summer 1940.
(Eisenbahnstiftung Collection)

their de-streamlining and boiler modernisation that they achieved any success. In hindsight, it is clear that they were introduced too hastily before proper development had been completed absorbing the lessons from elsewhere, and the foreshortened trial period and onset of the war prevented correction of the many faults and problems encountered.

01.1064 at Berlin Anhalter Bhf with D240 Berlin-Munich, August 1940.
(Collection Gerhard Gress/ EK-Verlag)

Partially de-streamlined 01.1052 on D90 near Wernfeld in 1949.
(Carl Bellingrodt/Eisenbahnstiftung Collection)

Preserved 01.10 Streamlined Pacific

01.1102

01.1102, built in 1940, de-streamlined in 1950, reboilered in 1954, oil-fired in 1957 and renumbered 012.102-0 in 1968, was withdrawn in April 1973 and preserved, being re-streamlined to its original external condition (but with the streamlining clear of the motion and cylinders), and painted steel blue. It ran a few rail enthusiast excursions in the 1990s under the auspices of Trans Europe, Giessen (Hessen), and was at Meiningen from 2004 and subsequently at the South German Railway Museum in Heilbronn (see photo page 219).

DB DE-STREAMLINED 01.10 PACIFICS
Design, Construction & Rebuilding

The 01.10 locomotives fared better than the 01s during the war and all but one of the fifty-five survived, 01.1067 being severely damaged in a collision in the Eschwege West area in 1946, rather than a direct consequence of war. Most had had their streamlining removed below the running plate to give access to the valve gear and bearings which had had overheating problems, as described earlier. All had been retrieved from the Soviet Zone and were available to the new *Bundesbahn*. Passenger services requiring the use of large Pacific locomotives were not running until 1947 in the American and British Zones, and nearly all the former pre-1920 State passenger engines had been stored unserviceable and

were withdrawn between 1947 and 1950 without entering traffic again. The exceptions in West Germany were most of the Bavarian S3/6 design built after 1920 and a few of the Württemberg class 'C's, all in the southern part of the country in the French and American Zones. The standard 01 and 03s were the priorities for heavy repair, but a few part de-streamlined 01.10s were operating from Göttingen, Kassel and Bebra on the North-South trunk route. Sixteen of the fifty-five locomotives were in use, thirteen in the American Zone and three in the British.

A decision was taken in December 1947 to repair and restore to traffic a further twenty-five three-cylinder 01.10s, and the remaining streamlining was removed and the smaller defects remedied. The summer service of 1949 required more locomotives. However, the boilers soon started showing serious flaws. As the DB could not afford to be without these locomotives, it was decided to provide new boilers and expensive overhauls were undertaken. Many of the failings identified in the 1940-1 experiences were addressed. These locomotives were the first DB locomotives to receive the small 'witte' smoke deflectors, and the top of the smokebox had a low lying feedwater heater, giving the locomotives a novel and rather strange appearance. The weight, without the streamlining, was slightly lower and the maximum axle weight dropped to approximately 19.8 tons for most of the restored engines.

A couple of the locomotives received new liveries, 01.1087 being

distinctive; boiler, cab, cylinder covers and tender were painted blue. Various shades of blue were applied in 1949-50 to match some new FD train liveries, but the final appearance in 1950 in a shade of green/blue with silver boiler bands, red wheels and black smokebox must have been striking. Earlier in April 1950, the Henschel Company were instructed to paint three 03.10s blue during their overhaul for use on the new prestige FD trains. Although there were complaints that it was difficult to keep clean, 01.1087 retained a blue livery until rebuilt with a new boiler in 1954.

Despite the heavy overhauls, many boilers were developing dangerous faults in the postwar situation and this included the 01.10s. In the autumn of 1952, there was severe concern about the safety of further use of these locomotives and in January 1953, a three-year programme of building all-welded boilers with combustion chambers was authorised, to include all the 01.10s. Henschel delivered sixteen new boilers in 1953. On test, the new boiler was able to produce 10 per cent more steam, despite changes in dimensions including a reduction in grate area to 42.6sqft, heating surface to 2,220sqft, but a big increase in the superheater area to 1,034sqft.

The first locomotive rebuilt with the new boiler was 01.1060 in December 1953. Boiler pressure and cylinder dimensions and axle-load were unchanged, and the engine weight was reduced slightly to 110.8 tons. Maximum speed was still 87½mph (140km/hr) and tractive effort remained at 34,920lb. 01.1105 and 01.1072 were completed the same month. As when first built, there were initially a lot of teething problems and defects to be corrected, some of which were caused by assembly faults at the Brunswick Works. However, it was nearly a year before there were rigorous trials with a test vehicle, with newly rebuilt 01.1092 going to Minden in September 1954. One problem encountered was the propensity of the Pacific to slip at speed, a problem unknown with the standard 01s. However, the locomotive was able to exert 1,850 horsepower at the drawbar at 75mph, a significant improvement. In a thirty-two minute long test, 01.1092 produced 2,145 hp at the drawbar at just over 56mph. In the four previous years of the 01.10s with the old boilers, they were in service on average 249 days a year in which they travelled 378 miles a day and 94,257 miles in the year. Availability was 68 per cent. With the new boilers, availability rose to 281 days (77 per cent), and annual distance to 116,329 miles. However, cost of maintenance rose by a third, and even taking the additional daily distances run, costs were 12 per cent up per kilometre run. On the other hand, coal consumption reduced by 5 per cent, 14.1 tons per 1,000 kilometres instead of 14.9. More boilers were built using the experience gained and the final fitting was made in 1958.

The aim had been to produce a locomotive capable of developing 2,650 hp, but this was considered to be at the limit for manual firing. The two class 10 new-build Pacific locomotives and a number of Bebra

01.1089 de-streamlined and reboilered after the war, at Düsseldorf Station, 2 April 1953. (A E Durrant/Eisenbahnstiftung Collection)

01.1095, the only 01.10 equipped with an 01 boiler and never given an all-welded boiler, in Frankfurt-am-Main, 30 July 1960. (J. Claus/Eisenbahnstiftung Collection)

Coal-burning 01.1053 (later class 011) at Emden West, 21 August 1967. (MLS Collection)

class 44 2-10-0s had been converted to oil-firing in 1955-6. The price of oil had dropped dramatically at this time and in the autumn of 1955, a decision was made to convert an 01.10 to oil-firing. In March 1956, 01.1100 was the 'guinea-pig' and, after successful trials in the summer of 1956, a further thirty-three engines were rebuilt as oil-fired machines, leaving twenty as coal-burners. It was heavier overall at 196.5 tons with axle-weight maximum of 20.8 tons and the ten-wheel tender held 3,000 gallons

of fuel oil. Although tractive effort remained the same as the coal-burners, the theoretical horsepower performance was raised slightly to 2,470. The last 01.10 to be converted to oil-firing was 01.1063 in June 1958.

In 1968, under the DB renumbering scheme, the coal-burning locomotives became class 011, and the oil-burners, class 012. As electrification and dieselisation spread in the 1960s, the work of

Coal-burning 01.1065 at Rheine Bw, 19 August 1967. 01.1065 has the earlier oval stovepipe chimney that was replaced by the wide, but very short chimney that became standard on the large-boilered 01s and coal-burning 01.10s. (MLS Collection)

Coal-burning 01.1090 at Brunswick, 24 August 1967. The oval stovepipe chimney is very visible in this photograph. (MLS Collection)

the 011s and 012s shrank, and the first withdrawals took place around 1967. When the 012s lost their work on the Cologne-Osnabrück-Hamburg 'Rollbahn' in 1967-8, they took over work between Hamburg and Westerland and Münster, Rheine, Emden and Norddeich, where the last members of the class were withdrawn in May 1975. The coal-burners had finished, also at Rheine, in 1973. Several members of both coal and oil-burning examples have been preserved, including some oil-burners in working order.

When 18.319, one of the three Baden 18.3 Pacifics at Minden Research Centre, was withdrawn, coal-burning 01.1090 was selected and acted as a counter-pressure brake test locomotive for a period in the 1960s. Here is 01.1090 at Minden, 1968.
(Johannes Glöckner/ Eisenbahnstiftung Collection)

Coal-burning 011.062-7 at Rotterdamm on railtour duty, 11 September 1971.
(MLS Collection/J. Davenport)

Oil-burning 01.1101 (later 012.101-2) at Hamburg Hbf , 20 June 1967.
(MLS Collection/J. Davenport)

01.1077 arrives at Osnabrück with a Hamburg-Cologne D-Zug, April 1968. It is in the period during the renumbering of DB locomotives to computerised numbers and before the fitting of the new numberplates.
(MLS Collection/J. Davenport)

012.054-3 departing from Rheine towards Lingen and Emden, 18 October 1969. (Graham Stacey)

012.057-6 departs from Rheine with an express for Emden and Norddeich, 19 October 1969. (Graham Stacey)

Coal-fired 011.072-2 stands at Rheine Depot, 19 October 1969. (Graham Stacey)

01.1061 at Kassel Station with a parcels train, 28 January 1967. (Helmut Dahlhaus)

012.102-0 at Hamburg Altona after arriving with D533 from Westerland and Niebüll, 21 August 1972. (Alastair Wood)

Oil-burning 012.075-8 (01.1075) awaiting the arrival of the late-running D1334 from Münster which it will take over for the run to Norddeich, July 1973. It picked up eight minutes of an eighteen-minute late start, touching a maximum (and unauthorised) 85mph.
(David Maidment)

012.082-4 after withdrawal and storage in the open at Rheine Bw, awaiting removal for scrap, together with a class 44 2-10-0, January 1975.
(David Maidment)

Operation of the De-streamlined Locomotives

The performance of the streamlined 01.10s in the few months of their main-line availability before war conditions interrupted was, as stated earlier, disappointing and, if anything, weaker than that of the standard two-cylinder 01s. They were never properly tested above 75mph, at which speed the advantages of streamlining should have shown its worth – in fact, some idea of its capabilities in this form were only tested after the restoration in streamlined form of the preserved 01.1102 in the 1990s.

The stored 01.10s were de-streamlined and repaired between 1949 and 1951, and worked on the north-south trunk route between Hamburg and Frankfurt/Würzburg, the Hamburg-Cologne route and in the Ruhr, but continuing problems, especially weaknesses of their boilers, caused them to be reboiled between 1953 and 1958, and the majority converted to oil-firing between 1956 and 1958.

After the war, train loading and scheduled speeds were lower than in 1940-41, and it was not until 1952 that any locomotive monthly utilisation reached 12,500 miles, albeit at a maximum speed of 75mph. The highest mileages were achieved by the Bebra-based locomotives on the Frankfurt/Würzburg-Hanover/Hamburg route, which in the period 1953-55 were regularly working around 12,500-13,000 miles per month, the highest recorded being 01.1082 (again) with 13,676 miles in June 1954, with an average load of 511 tons at a coal consumption of 12.8 tons per 1,000kms. None of the locomotives still fitted with the old boilers based at the other locations – Hagen-Eckersey, Offenburg and Kassel – achieved as much as 12,500 miles in a single month.

One of the diagrams for the few working 01.10s between 1949 and 1951 was a 267 mile run from Brunswick to Aachen, with a Hagen-based locomotive. From 1951, most of the longer-distance diagrams were planned for 01.10s, on average between 125 and 250 miles a day, seldom over 300. From 1952, they took over the running of the *Blauer Enzian* (F55/56) between Bebra and Munich, (289 miles), D511 from Frankfurt to Lübeck, (348 miles), and F11/12 between Hamburg and Aachen, (327 miles). Planned speeds gradually increased and in the summer of 1952, F44 *Roland* was scheduled at 62.8mph average over the 76 miles between Bremen and Hanover. However, in comparison with other European railways, runs on the DB network steam-hauled at over 60mph were few. From 1957, most of the fastest and longer distance diagrams were planned for the oil-burners.

After rebuilding with the modernised all-welded boilers, the performance of the 01.10s increased significantly, with some Bebra engines reaching as much as 15,625 miles a month. The highest ever recorded monthly mileage of a DB locomotive was achieved by 01.1052 in July 1956, when just over 18,000 miles were recorded, an average of over 600 miles a day. Offenburg had a few 01.10s in 1956, but they had gone by the following year. After sufficient locomotives had been converted to oil-firing in the summer of 1957, Bebra Depot had diagrams of over 1,000kms (625 miles) a day as far as Hamburg in one direction and Treuchtlingen in the other. Planned trains included D84/D87/D89 Würzburg-Hamburg, and D276 Hamburg-Frankfurt. The last DB steam diagram over 300 miles for a single run was D89 in the summer of 1962, which planned a Bebra oil-burning 01.10 to work through from the electrified route at Ingolstadt to Hamburg Altona, a distance of 427 miles. It was not until 1963-4 that a DB train was timed at over 60mph over a long distance, the pair of express trains D195/196, between Osnabrück and Hamburg which included an intermediate stop at Bremen. The fastest steam-hauled train of all was a four-coach flyer, D832, Flensburg-Hamburg, between Kiel and Neumünster as late as 1971, which was scheduled to run the 19.4 miles in 17 minutes, start to stop, an average of 68.4mph. On these light-weight trains, the 01.10s were worked at 25 per cent cut-off and half-regulator, and reached speeds of 94mph. However, the Hamburg-Cologne services were much more demanding with consistently heavy trains of 550-600 tons, which could rise at peak periods to 700 tons.

Comparison of annual maintenance costs between the thirty-four oil-burners and the twenty coal-burners showed that the oil-burners were around 12 per cent more expensive over the period between main overhauls in the late 1950s, but on average they ran 8-10 per cent more miles per year and with heavier and faster trains.

Between 1958 and 1961, the planned utilisation and performance of the oil-burners was increased by 25 per cent.

From 1961, the locomotives at Osnabrück reached the pinnacle of operations, especially after sections of the north-south route had been electrified between 1962 and 1963. Some trains were booked to run at sustained speeds of 84mph between Hamburg and Cologne with an engine change midway at Osnabrück. Initial diagrams on this route required thirteen oil-burning 01.10s to run on average 552 miles a day and 4.2 million miles a year (over 200,000 miles per locomotive). The Ruhr section from Cologne to Hagen via Wuppertal was electrified by the summer timetable of 1964 and eliminated the last DB steam diagrams over 250 miles

Oil-burning 01.1052 at Osnabrück on the *Holland-Skandinavien Express*, April 1968. (MLS Collection /J. Davenport)

for a single run. The last timetable before electrification of the rest of the route in the summer of 1968 required twenty-one oil-burners to run around 81-87,500 miles each in the year. D497, a ten-coach train between Osnabrück and Hamburg-Harburg, with an intermediate stop at Bremen, was scheduled to average 64mph. However, this intensive use took its toll on the mechanical condition of the locomotives and there were increasing experiences of cracked frames, valve gear and motion failures and breakages, especially of the inside motion. In performance on the road, however, the Osnabrück oil-burners went down with 'all flags flying'.

After the 01.10s were displaced from Osnabrück, Hamburg-based oil-fired locomotives were diagrammed to the Hamburg-Westerland route

with accelerations that pushed planned schedules over 60mph. D836 was scheduled to run the 148 miles in 142 minutes at an average of 62.5mph. There were also some fast Monday morning services timed non-stop at this speed, returning coast weekenders to the city. However, these were light, five-six coach trains. The last daytime heavier expresses on this route in 1972 were very fast, requiring an indicated horsepower of 2,600, and a drawbar horsepower of 2,100. My friend, Alastair Wood, logged a number of excellent runs on this route at that time and I show three fast lightweight expresses as well as a number of heavily-loaded trains, all recorded during an August holiday week in 1972 when traffic was at its peak (see table opposite).

012.082 ran from Heide to Husum in 23 minutes 51 seconds for

(Westerland) - Niebüll – Hamburg Altona

	D1223, 18.8.1972 16.30 Westerland-H-Altona 012.077-4 Bw Altona 8 chs, 273/295t				D1223, 21.8.1972 16.30 Westerland-H-Altona 012.082-4 Bw Altona 6 chs, 217/230t		D1223, 22.8.1972 16.30 Westerland-H-Altona 012.071-7 Bw Altona 6 chs, 217/230t	
Niebüll	00.00	mph	3½ L	0 miles	00.00	mph ½ E	00.00	mph 2½ L
Lindholm	03.19//10.29	Defective brakes			04.13	48/65	04.06	49/66
Stedesand	17.20	58			06.15	73	06.10	72
Langenhorn	21.04	62	Brakes dragging		09.15	75/73	09.02	83
km 144	-	50½			11.14	65	10.48	81/71 1 in 147R
Bredstedt	26.04	55			16.03	75	15.28	71½
Struckum	29.17//33.01	To release brakes			17.58	77½ /70½	17.34	76/70½
km 134	-	52			-	58	-	62
Hallstedt	38.40	62/65			19.36	65	19.15	68 ½
Husum	44.59		20½ L	25	26.06	2½ E	25.38	T
	00.00		18L		00.00	½ E	00.00	½ L
Friedrichstadt	07.55	71½ /53			08.03	70½ /54	08.07	70/55
Lunden	11.54	65/62			12.13	62/60	12.06	62/60
Wittenruth	15.44	74			16.06	71½	16.05	69
Weddingstedt	18.12	68/73/55			18.39	60½/60	18.43	59/60½
Heide	21.40		17L	21	22.18	1E	22.31	T
	00.00		16½ L	0	00.00	½ E	00.00	T
Hemmingstedt	04.07	63½			04.13	65½	04.21	60
Meldorf	07.51	76½			07.54	78	08.07	76½
Windbergen	10.25	80			10.30	77½	10.41	78
St Michaelisdonn	13.18	79/81			13.30	78/73	13.46	74/69
Burg	18.25	76½ /43* SL			19.35	36* SL	19.30	30* SL
Kiel Canal	-	42½			-	42½	-	43½
Vaale	24.03	83			25.31	80	25.26	78
km 42	-	88			-	82	-	81
Wilster	28.14	65			30.00	58	30.01	57
Bekdorf	29.57	63			31.51	56	32.04	51
Itzehoe	34.32//35.08	sig stand			36.03	34* sigs	36.14	40*
Kremperheide	40.20	70			40.25	66	40.22	62½
Krempe	43.06	72/60* sigs			43.26	67//60	43.20	61½
Glückstadt	46.48	72/64½			47.40	63/62	47.20	66/62
Herzhorn	48.58	72/74			49.58	66	49.41	68
Siethwende	51.52	71			53.05	69	52.46	70
Elmshorn	56.38	34*			57.51	32*	57.32	30*
Tomerch	61.25	72/78			63.03	67/65	62.45	71½
Prisdorf	63.14	83			65.01	75	64.41	75
Pinneberg	64.44	80/85			66.45	73/75	66.24	76½
Halstenbek	66.28	84			68.44	73	68.23	73/74½
Eidelstedt	69.20	84/64			72.18	70/50	72.01	70/45
	-	pws 23*			-	pws 20*	-	slow
Hamburg Altona	75.24		9L	76.6	79.05	4½ E	78.47	4E

(net time 72 mins)

Hamburg –Heide – (Niebüll - Westerland)

	D533, 16.8.1972 08.17 Cologne-Westerland 012.082-4 Bw Altona 14 chs, 516/535t				D533, 18.8.1972 012.105-3 Bw Altona 14 chs, 516/540t			D533, 19.8.1972 012.102-0 Bw Altona 14 chs, 519/545t		
Hamburg Altona	00.00	mph	T	0 miles	00.00	mph	T	00.00	mph	3½ L
Eidelstedt	-	47			06.21	45		06.32	47½	
Halstenbek	10.10	71½	T	6.9	10.13	65	½ L	10.24	69	4L
Pinneberg	12.10	75			12.20	69		12.27	71	
Prisdorf	13.50	73/75			14.10	71½		14.14	73	
Tomerch	15.46	79/73	2E		16.16	69		16.17	72	
Elmshorn	21.04	75/15* sigs	1E	18.5	21.29	18* sigs	T	20.37	40*	2L
Siethwende	27.25	59	½ L		27.16	61	½ L	25.51	63	
Herzhorn	30.44	66			30.39	63		29.03	67	
km 14	32.40//34.33 emergency stop									
Glückstadt	37.14	35*	4½ L	28.9	33.09	54	½ L	31.30	53½	2L
Krempe	42.14	64			37.30	61		35.41	65	
Kremperheide	45.08	68½			40.33	65		38.36	68½	
Itzehoe	48.46	42*	5L	39.75	44.13	40*	½ L	42.24	48*	2L
Bekdorf	53.21	64	5½ L		48.41	62	1L	46.27	64	2L
Vaale	60.04	70/64	4L		55.43	65/60	T	53.24	66/62	1L
km 50 (1:150R)	-	51			-	55		-	52	
Kiel Canal	-	34½			-	34½		-	32	
Burg	66.45	67	6L		62.16	60	1½ L	60.17	59	3L
St Michaelisdonn	71.38	78	5½ L	62.2	67.23	74/78	1½ L	65.16	75/78	2½ L
Windbergen	74.37	79½			70.30	72/75		68.17	80/77	
Meldorf	77.08	78½	5L		73.06	76½	1L	70.42	78	2L
Hemmingstedt	80.45	72	5L		76.51	70/66		74.15	79½ /73	
Heide	84.32		3½ L	76.6	80.26		½ E	78.21		1L

the 21 miles, running steadily in the upper 60s mph with a maximum of 72 at Lunden, and then ran the 25 miles to Niebüll in 27 minutes 13 seconds with maintained running at 73-75mph, arriving just half a minute late. 012.105 dropped half a minute to Husum with nothing over 66mph and with a steady 70-73mph thereafter, reached Niebüll one minute late. 012.102, with the heaviest 545-ton-load reached Husum on time in 23 minutes 46 seconds with very similar speeds to 012.082, and then raced away for the final timed section-covering

the 25 mile stretch in just over 27 minutes, sustaining 77-80mph and arriving at Niebüll a minute and a half early.

All the 012s had to be pushed hard with these loads, the first two being in reasonable condition, 012.071 leaking steam around the cylinders.

The Hamburg-Westerland fast services were dieselised in 1972, and the remaining 011 coal-burners (011.062 and 011.072) and oil-burners were based at Rheine for the services to Emden and the North Sea resorts reached from

Norddeich. 011.072 was withdrawn in 1972, 011.062 in February of the following year. Thirteen 012s were active on the line in the summer of 1973, when the line speed was raised from 69 to 75mph. The schedules between 1973 and 1975 required some very fast running between stops, D714 being scheduled over the 88 miles to Emden from Rheine in 87 minutes with four intermediate stops and a load of seven coaches, around 275 tons. The evening D730 Norddeich-Munich sleeper, also seven coaches, was booked to cover the 52.4 miles

Hamburg-Heide-(Westerland)

D820, 17.8.1972
07.56 Hamburg Altona-Westerland
012.001-4 Bw Altona
13 chs, 461/480t

D820, 18.8.1972
012.082-4 Bw Altona
14 chs, 488/515t

D820, 19.8.1972
012.071-7 Bw Altona
14 chs, 501/530t

Station	time	mph	note	miles	time	mph	note	time	mph	note
Hamburg Altona	00.00	mph	T	0	00.00	mph	2L	00.00	mph	1L
Eidelstedt	06.25	48			06.36	45		05.57	52	
Halstenbek	10.16	72	T		10.18	63	2L	09.45	66	½ L
Pinneberg	12.18	76½			12.38	72		11.53	70	
Prisdorf	13.57	73/75			14.22	67/69		13.41	67	
Tomerch	15.55	77½/74			16.30	70/66/69		15.57	62* sigs/65	
Elmshorn	20.42		1½ E	18.5	21.38		1½ L	21.10		T
	00.00		½ E	0	00.00		1½ L	00.00		T
Siethwende	06.44	63			07.00	61½		06.57	61½	
Herzhorn	10.00	68 ½			10.19	66		10.16	65	
Glückstadt	13.00		½ L	10.4	13.19		3L	13.29		1½ L
	00.00		½ L	0	00.00		2½ L	00.00		1½ L
Krempe	06.37	63			06.34	60½		07.11	58½	
Kremperheide	09.33	69½			09.46	68½		10.19	65½	
Alsen	-	57			-	62		13.23//13.58 sig stand		
Itzehoe	14.00		2E	10.85	14.10		½ L	17.38		3L
	00.00		½ E	0	00.00		½ L	00.00		2 ½ L
Heiligenstedten	04.19	55			04.21	56		04.18	55½	
Bekdorf	06.15	63			06.11	62		06.13	61½	
Wilster	08.00	67			07.56	65		08.18	45* sigs	
Vaale	12.53	72			12.57	69½		14.31	58	
Burg	19.23	39/66			19.36	35/60		21.15	60	
km 60	-	77½			-	78		-	75	
St Michaelisdon	25.05		½ L	22.45	25.01		1½ L	27.01		5½ L
	00.00		½ L	0	00.00		1½ L	00.00		6L
Windbergen	05.57	66			05.57	64/66		06.11	63/66	
Meldorf	09.36		T	7.05	09.26		1L	09.52		6L
	00.00		T	0	00.00		1L	00.00		5½ L
Hemmingstedt	06.30	63			06.38	59		06.51	62	
Heide	10.19		3E	7 .4	10.18		1½ E	10.45		3L

from Leer to Lingen in 50 minutes, but frequently did it in 43-45 minutes at average speeds start to stop of around 70mph. The D1337/D1371 ten-coach 400-ton trains from Rheine in the morning, which were non-stop to Leer, 72 miles, were scheduled 68 minutes and on a couple of runs, logs of a net even hour were recorded, another 70mph run with allegedly 75mph line maximum speed (though there were undoubtedly some very loose observances of this).

In the last year of steam express services in West Germany, 1975, D714, after being dieselised on weekdays in 1974, surprisingly returned to steam and the very last steam-hauled D-Zug on the DB in regular service was the D714 of 31 May 1975, hauled by 012.081-6 and the last steam passenger service was the late-evening Eilzug from Norddeich Mole to Rheine with 012.100-4. Eight 012s had survived until 1975, 012.061, 063, 066, 081 and 100 bowing out on the last day. Two three-cylinder coal-burning Pacifics exceeded two million miles

01.1054 at Vehrte with a Hamburg-Cologne D-Zug, 20 August 1967. (MLS Collection)

in the locomotives' lifetime (01.1097 and 011.062) and twenty-four of the oil-burners, with eight exceeding 2.5m miles, with 012.081 achieving

2.7m miles and 012.082, the highest of all at 2.76m miles.

For logs of my own personal runs behind oil-burning 01.10s

between Hamburg and Cologne, and between Rheine and Norddeich, see Chapter 18, pages 314–5 and 319–21.

01.1060 entering Osnabrück Station where it will change engines with another locally based 01.10 on the *Arlberg Express*, 14 April 1968. This was during the period of DB locomotive renumbering to the computerised system. (MLS Collection/J.Davenport)

01.1068 (about to be renumbered 012.068-3) roars through Diepholz with a Cologne-Hamburg D-Zug, September 1968. (MLS Collection)

Oil-burner 01.1085 restarts a D-Zug on the '*Rollbahn*' after an engine change at Osnabrück, 20 August 1967.
(MLS Collection)

Coal-burning 01.1094 attaching an extra coach during the engine change of a D-Zug at Bremen Station, 21 June 1967. (MLS Collection)

Coal-burner 01.1097 leaving Osnabrück with a D-Zug on the '*Rollbahn*' where a substantial proportion of the three-cylinder coal and oil-burning 01.10s were stationed until the electrification of the route in the winter timetable 1968, April 1968. Note the woman photographer on the platform – she appears in several photos around this time. (MLS Collection)

Sandblasting the chimney at speed was a common occurrence with the oil-burning 01.10s. Here 012.058-4 shows how it's done at an unknown location, c1970. (MLS Collection)

Coal-burning 01.1098 at Kassel with D846 night train to Cologne, August 1967. (Helmut Dalhaus)

012.071-7 arrives in Husum with D532 Westerland-Hamburg Altona, passing 012.081-6 waiting to depart with D820 Cologne-Westerland, 14 July 1971. (Joachim Schmidt/Eisenbahnstiftung Collection)

012.105-3 departing Hamburg Altona with an express for Westerland on the North Sea island of Sylt, May 1971. (K D Hensel/Eisenbahnstiftung Collection)

Sandblasting of firebox, tubes and blastpipe taking place on the Hindenburgdamm as 012.077-4 hauls E2109 Westerland-Hamburg Altona, 28 September 1972. Sandblasting was often carried out at this location avoiding the nuisance of operation in built-up areas, although being a favourite location for photographers it was sometimes activated by arrangement. (Ulrich Budde)

012.077 speeds D533, 8.17am Cologne-Westerland, through Bullendorf, just before dieselisation of the Hamburg-Westerland route and the transfer of its 012s, including 012.077, to Rheine, 29 September 1972.
(Helmut Dahlhaus)

012.077-4 on the Rendsberger Hochbrücke with D532 Westerland-Hamburg Altona, 27 September 1972.
(Wolfgang Bügel/ Eisenbahnstiftung Collection)

012.077-4 high over the Nord-Ostseekanal on the Hochdonnerbrücke with D533 Cologne-Westerland, 25 June 1972. (Peter Schiffer/Eisenbahnstiftung Collection)

012.077-4 with D1223 Westerland-Hamburg Altona on the Hindenburgdamm, 15 July 1972. (Peter Schiffer/Eisenbahnstiftung Collection)

012.102-0 on the Hindenburgdamm, crossing the Wattenmeer to Sylt with D533 Cologne-Westerland, 14 July 1972.
(Peter Schiffer/Eisenbahnstiftung Collection)

012.102-0 at Niebüll Station with D533 Cologne -Westerland, where car passengers will transfer to the car shuttle to Sylt, 14 July 1972.
(Peter Schiffer/Eisenbahnstiftung Collection)

Oil-burner 01.1063 (later 012.063-4 and one of the last survivors of the class) entering Emden Hbf with a Norddeich Mole-Cologne D-Zug which it will haul as far as Rheine, September 1970. (MLS Collection/J. Davenport)

Oil-burning 012.075-8 roars through Lathen with a Norddeich-Rheine (Cologne) D-Zug, September 1972. (Richard Spoors)

Oil-burning 012.063-4 hurries through Lathen with D1734 Cologne-Norddeich Mole, 10 August 1974.
(Dr Willi Hager/ Eisenbahnstiftung Collection)

The Norddeich-Munich sleeper train, D730, attains 120km/hr (75mph) behind Rheine's 012.080-8 between Leer and Ihrhove, 18 July 1974. (Udo Paulitz)

012.055-0 climbs the short bank to cross the Leda Canal Bridge after leaving the Leer stop with the afternoon semi-fast, E2730, from Emden to Rheine and Münster, 18 July 1974. (Udo Paulitz)

An 012 (012.080) speeds past Steenfelde on E2738 at sunset around 8.30pm, 23 July 1974. (Udo Paulitz)

012.075-8 ready for departure from Emden Hbf with D1737 to Norddeich Mole, 9 August 1974. (Udo Paulitz)

012.080-8 roars through Lingen with a D-Zug on the Rheine-Emden line, on a crisp December day in the last timetable worked by express steam locomotives in West Germany, December 1974. (Malcolm Holdsworth)

012.066-7 powers through Lathen with D1334, the afternoon express from Norddeich to Cologne, 23 June 1973. (Helmut Dahlhaus)

The outline of an oil-burning 012 Pacific on the Rheine-Emden line in the setting sun, 1975. (Malcolm Holdsworth)

012.081-6 departs from Lathen after stopping there with E1806 from Norddeich to Münster, 15 September 1973. (Helmut Dahlhaus)

012.075-8 accelerates hard out of Lathen with an afternoon Eilzug from Rheine to Emden, May 1975. (Malcolm Holdsworth)

012.063 accelerates hard out of Meppen with the sharply-timed D714 4.55pm Rheine-Norddeich, 10 April 1975. (George Bambery)

A peaceful evening scene as 012.066 drifts over a waterway near Neermoor, between Leer and Emden, with the evening E3265 from Rheine to Emden, 10 May 1975. (Helmut Dahlhaus)

012.075-8 departs Lingen with the evening E3265 Rheine-Emden, 10 May 1975. (George Bambery)

The last steam-hauled D-Zug in West Germany, D714, near Meppen, hauled between Rheine and Norddeich by 012.081-6, 31 May 1975. The service was fully dieselised in the summer timetable which commenced the following day. (Ulrich Budde)

011.062-7 on one of the railtour specials in the Netherlands near Amsterdam, 12 September 1971. (MLS Collection/J.Davenport)

Preserved 01.10 Coal-burning Pacific

01.1056

01.1056 was built in 1940, was de-streamlined in 1949 and, after rebuilding with an all-welded modernised boiler in 1954, remained as a coal-burner, being withdrawn from Rheine in July 1971 having run 1.9m miles in traffic. It was 'plinthed' at Rheine, in 1975, and is now at the Deutsches Museum Eisenbahn, Darmstadt Kranichstein.

Preserved 01.10 Oil-burning Pacifics

01.1061

01.1061 was built in 1940, de-streamlined in 1949, reboilered in January 1954 and equipped for oil-burning in October 1957. It was renumbered 012.061-8 in 1968 and was one of the last survivors at Rheine, being withdrawn in June 1975, after running virtually 2.5m miles. It was restored in working order and is currently displayed as a static exhibit at the Deutsches Dampflok Museum, Neuenmarkt-Wirsberg (see page 191).

01.1063

01.1063 was built in 1940, de-streamlined in 1949, reboilered in July 1954 and was the last 01.10 to be converted to oil-burning in June 1958. It was renumbered 012.063-4 in 1968 and was based at Rheine in the 1970s. It was withdrawn in June 1975 at the end of DB's steam passenger train working, having run 2.56m miles. It is preserved and displayed in the car park outside Brunswick Hauptbahnhof (see pages 208–9 and 214).

01.1066

01.1066 was built in 1940, de-streamlined in 1949, reboilered in February 1954 and converted to oil-burning in November 1957. It was renumbered 012.066-7 in 1968 and was the last 012 to be given a heavy overhaul at the end of 1973, and was withdrawn from Rheine in June 1975. It had run 2,498,592 miles before preservation. It was restored in operating condition and is currently based with the Ulmer Eisenbahn Freunde (Ulm Locomotive Enthusiasts' Club) at Heilbronn,

although its mainline 'ticket' expired in 2016 (see page 212).

01.1075

01.1075 was built in 1940, de-streamlined in 1949, reboilered in June 1954 and equipped for oil-burning in September 1957. It was renumbered 012.075-8 in 1968 and was withdrawn from Rheine in June 1975, after running 2.4m miles in traffic. It was preserved in running order and reconverted to burn coal, renumbered again as 01.1075 and has operated enthusiasts' specials out of Holland, being based with Stoom Stichting Nederland, at Rotterdamm Noord. It has also worked specials in Germany, Belgium and Luxembourg (see pages 191–2, 208, 211,216, 215).

01.1081

01.1081 was built in 1940, de-streamlined in 1949, reboilered in December 1955 and converted to oil-firing in June 1957. It was renumbered 012.081-6 in 1968 and was based at Rheine, hauling the last D-Zug on the DB in May 1975, being withdrawn in June that year. It completed 2.7m miles in traffic, the second highest mileage of an 01.10. It was initially displayed at Bad Münster am Stein, subsequently owned by the Ulmer Eisenbahn Freunde, Heilbronn, and is currently exhibited in Augsburg Railway Park (see pages 203, 213, 215).

01.1082

01.1082 was built in 1940, de-streamlined in 1949, reboilered in October 1956 and converted to oil-burning less than a year later. It figured as one of the Bebra engines achieving very high monthly mileages in the late 1950s and was renumbered 012.082-4 in 1968. It finished its days in 1974 at Rheine and when withdrawn, had the highest mileage of any 01.10 (2.76m miles). In 1961 it ran 159,000 miles, (an average of 435 miles a

Preserved 01.1075 at the Hook of Holland on a Locomotive Club of Great Britain (LCGB) railtour, 30 August 1995. 01.1075 was a star performer on the 'Rollbahn' (Cologne-Hamburg) in the 1950s and early 1960s, then was based at Rheine, a star performer there also, being withdrawn at the end of steam-hauled passenger services there in 1975. It is seen here as a coal-burner, but retains the large chimney that was fitted to the oil-burners. (MLS Collection)

Preserved 01.1100 (DB 012.100-4) at Altenbeken on arrival with the railtour from Osnabrück, 11 May 1995.
(David Maidment)

day if utilised every single day!) the highest annual mileage ever believed to have been achieved by a European steam locomotive. It is currently preserved in the national collection at the Deutsches Technik Museum, Berlin (see page 192).

01.1100

01.1100 was built in 1940, de-streamlined in 1949, was reboilered and equipped for oil-firing at the same time in June 1956 – the pilot for the oil-burning programme of express locomotives. Renumbered 012.100-4 in 1968, it worked the last passenger steam

train in regular service on the DB, was withdrawn in June 1975 from Rheine Depot and preserved in running order, and has operated many enthusiast specials since then. It ran 2.36m miles before preservation. It is based at the Deutsches Bahn Museum, outbased at Neumünster in the care of the Rendsburger Eisenbahnfreunde. It had major repairs to firebox and boiler in 2005, but has not worked on the main line since then.

01.1102

01.1102 was built in 1940, was the last to be de-streamlined in

September 1950, was reboilered and converted to oil-firing in May 1957. It was withdrawn in December 1972 from Hamburg after running just over four million kilometres (2.5m miles) and preserved, being restored externally to its 1940 fully-streamlined condition in the 1990s in a dark blue livery. It ran a few railtours in this condition in the late 1990s when based in the city of Bebra but is now displayed by the Ulmer Eisenbahn Freunde at Heilbronn.

01.1104

01.1104 was built in 1940, the

01.1100 moves off for servicing after hauling a railtour to Altenbeken, 1996. The detail of the oil-burning ten-wheel tender is evident in this photograph.
(David Maidment)

penultimate of the fifty-five Schwartzkopf-constructed locomotives delivered over a six-month period. It was de-streamlined in March 1950, and reboilered in March 1954, converted to oil-firing in May 1957 and was withdrawn from Rheine Depot in March 1974, after running 2.62m miles, the third highest after 012.081 and 082. It was purchased, restored and brought to the UK in the 1970s, and kept at Carnforth Depot, but its size and gauge prohibited it from running outside the Carnforth sidings in Britain, and it returned to Germany to the UEF at Heilbronn, and was initially at Crailsheim Depot from whence it has gone to Krefeld for overhaul.

Preserved 01.1102, restreamlined and seen at Kreuzberg (Ahrtal), October, 1999. (Richard Spoors)

012.104-6 at Rheine a year before withdrawal and preservation, 30 October 1972. (Graham Stacey)

Now deprived of its taller wide-diameter chimney, 012.104-6 stands at Carnforth prior to being repatriated to the Museum at Heilbronn. 012.104-6 stands in front of another engine rescued from foreign soil, DB shunter 80.014. 9 May 1976. (MLS Collection)

Chapter 12

THE *DEUTSCHE REICHSBAHN* 03

Design & Construction

I n 1926, the Board of the DRG was considering the need for a smaller standard locomotive for light fast trains that would be more economic than the heavy 01s, and a proposal for a 4-6-0 with a 20-ton axleweight was made, but soon discarded as the cost of its development would not be offset by sufficient savings in traffic. However, intentions to upgrade the track with heavier rail to take locomotives with 20-ton axleloads were restricted by the financial collapse and subsequent Depression, and the need for a standard engine with an 18-ton maximum axleload was recognised. Indeed, many secondary main lines, including most in the south and east, were only capable of using locomotives with a 17-ton axle-load. Initially the need was met by building a further forty S3/6s of the Bavarian four-cylinder compound design, 18.509-548.

In 1929, a number of designs were prepared by Henschel-Maffei, BMAG (Schwartzkopf) and the DRG's own central design office under Richard Paul Wagner, all Pacifics, with four-cylinder compound propulsion or four or two-cylinder simples. All the designs proposed a locomotive with a 17.5-6-ton axleload, 227lbpsi boiler, 43sqft grate, 2,150sqft heating surface, bar frames and driving wheels of 6ft 7in diameter. The main weight gains were made through adoption of a smaller boiler, thinner and lighter frames and wheels. Wagner and his colleagues chose their own design, preferring a two-cylinder simple engine rather than a compound, considering the extra potential efficiency of the compound would not counter the initial cost at a time of extreme financial stringency.

Thus in 1930, 03.001 was built by Borsig, a 17.7-ton axle-load version of the 01 with smaller boiler and cylinders and lighter bar frames. Some dimensions were common to the 01s – 6ft 7in coupled wheels, 227lbpsi boiler pressure – but it had a smaller grate at 42.7sqft, heating surface 2,172sqft and superheater area of 752.5sqft. The two cylinders measured 22.5in x 26in and the locomotive weight was 100.3 tons. It was initially fitted with a 6,600 gallon water capacity tender, holding 10 tons of coal, but some were subsequently fitted with 7,000-gallon or 7,500-gallon water tenders. Total weight in service varied from 168.1 to 175.8 tons depending on the size of tender. Tractive effort was 30,247lb and available horsepower 1,980. The series was built between 1930 and 1937 and eventually numbered 298 locomotives, built by Borsig, Schwartzkopf, Henschel and Krupp. From 03.123, the diameter of the front bogie wheels was raised from 2ft 9in to 3ft 3in. The cost of the new locomotives was around 199,000 RMs with a variation of plus or minus 5 per cent.

03.001 was exhibited at Tempelhof, Berlin, in June 1930 and later, in 1935, appeared on a German postage stamp to commemorate the centenary of railways in Germany. On test, the new 03 demonstrated its capability of hauling 790 tons on the level at 62mph and maintaining 37½mph up a 1 in 100 gradient with 380 tons. Initially the maximum speed was 75mph but after modifications to the running gear and brakes, this was raised to 81mph. All locomotives from 03.162 (1935) onwards were built with this authorised maximum speed. As

03.001, as originally built, on a railtour special at Königstein in Saxony in the 1990s.
(MLS Collection)

pressure increased to accelerate services in the mid-1930s, a group of Hamburg Altona 03s (03.032-038, 073, 108, 139 and 171) were authorised to travel at 87½mph between Hamburg and Berlin only.

A number of experiments were made to increase the speed potential of the 03s. 03.175 and 03.207 were equipped with Lentz valve gear, and in 1934 03.154 was partially streamlined as tests for the later 01.10s and 03.10s. Over a nine-month period in 1934, it ran over 72,500 miles and coal consumption was 12.3 tonnes per 1,000kms, but there were problems with the valve

gear and motion hidden under the streamlining, and this was partly removed below the footplating in 1936. A further locomotive, 03.193, was built in 1936, fully streamlined on the same pattern as the high-speed 4-6-4 05s, and was tested at Grunewald. At 50mph wind resistance was reduced and extra power released of 8 per cent; at 75mph a 26 per cent advantage was gained over non-streamlined engines and at 87½mph, 48 per cent. 03.193 often acted as a standby engine for the high speed Berlin-Hamburg services in the late 1930s and on one occasion, with 275 tons, ran the 178

miles in 149 minutes (139 net), only one minute more than the *Flying Hamburger*'s schedule. The highest speed reached was 93mph.

The partially-streamlined 03.154 achieved about half of these gains. 03.193 also had a five-axle streamlined tender identical that of the 05s and the engine was nearly 7 tons heavier than the standard 03s with a maximum axleweight of 19 tons. The experiments influenced the design of both the 01.10 and 03.10 three-cylinder engines introduced in 1939. The streamlining on both 03 locomotives was removed after the war. There were some tests with the Lentz valve gear 03s, but these were inconclusive – indeed many of the records have been lost – and the two engines were rebuilt with the standard Heusinger gear in 1944; 03.175 was retained in Poland, subsequently. By November 1939, 81 per cent of the class had been fitted with Indusi signal-warning systems and the large smoke deflectors were replaced by smaller 'witte' deflectors between 1948 and 1958.

After the war, the extant 03s not still in the USSR were split roughly equally between East and West Germany. Some 03s in West Germany were equipped with new fireboxes in the 1950s and it was

originally intended to rebuild forty or fifty with all-welded modernised boilers as part of the programme for 01.10s, 01s and 03.10s, but the 03

boilers did not give as much trouble as those on the larger engines and in 1957, it was decided that it was unnecessary for this class.

03 003 at Osnabrück, 11 August 1930. (DLA Darmstadt/Maey/ Eisenbahnstiftung Collection)

The brand-new 03.033 built by Henschel in Kassel, August 1931, before delivery to Hamburg Altona Depot. (Helmut Bürger/ Eisenbahnstiftung Collection)

The unique semi-streamlined two-cylinder 03.154, after removal of the valances covering the driving wheels and motion, 1936. (Hans-Jürgen Wenzel Collection)

The only fully- streamlined two-cylinder 03, No.03.193, running with the valances covering the wheels closed, at Ludwigslust, 23 May 1937. The locomotive did not experience in this form the troubles of overheating that the streamlined three-cylinder engines suffered. (Johannes Glöckner/ Eisenbahnstiftung Collection)

The new boilers were fitted to a number of class 41 2-8-2s instead, many becoming oil-burners later as class 042. In East Germany, new all-welded boilers (given the classification 39E) were supplied for the former Prussian P10 (class 39) which were renumbered as class 22, but many of these were stored and withdrawn by 1965, and half of the eighty-five-strong class by 1968. A decision was made to use these relatively new boilers for the 03s, and between 1969 and 1975 some fifty-two East German 03s were rebuilt with these 39E 'Reko' boilers. Between 1961 and 1966, nearly all the DR 03s were also equipped

with very visible feedwater heaters placed over the smokebox in front of the chimney.

The DB locomotives were renumbered with computer numbers plus check digit (class 003) in January 1968 and the DR engines were renumbered as 03.2001, etc. as coal-burners. The last DB examples were 003.088-2 and 003.131-0, withdrawn from Ulm in 1973, and the last active DR engines were seven examples (03.2002, 2058, 2153, 2155, 2176, 2243 and 2254) made redundant at Lutherstadt-Wittenberg when the line between Berlin and Leipzig was electrified in June 1979, and a couple which lingered on until 1980, though little work was available after 1979. A few remained for a few months on stationary-boiler duties, including 03.2002, the shell of which was preserved and restored as a streamlined 03 in the guise of 03.193. Examples of both East and West German versions are preserved (see later in this chapter).

The 'face' of 03.028, with the flat smokebox door of DR engines in the early post-war period, at Berlin-Rummelsburg Depot, ex-works 4 July 1953.
(ZBDR/Robin Garn Collection)

03.247, stored after the war in original condition, at Hanover, 7 April 1946.
(MLS Collection)

DB 03.284, just before the DB renumbering scheme, at Herzongenrath, on the line from Aachen to Mönchengladbach, April 1968.
(MLS Collection/J. Davenport)

East German 03.2105-9 (formerly 03.105), rebuilt with new boiler and feedwater heater atop the smokebox, c1978.
(MLS Collection)

Operations before 1945

In the 1930s, the 03 Pacifics were mainly allocated to the northern plains of Germany, leaving the various State railway compound Pacifics to continue to reign supreme in the more hilly routes of the south. The first locomotives were allocated to Osnabrück in the Münster motive power division and replaced the S3/6 18.5 Pacifics built by Maffei and Henschel between 1926 and 1930, which were despatched south. By 1938, the Osnabrück allocation had risen to a massive thirty engines at the home depot and a further six at Rheine. They were used extensively on the route to Hamburg and on the various routes through the Ruhr to Cologne.

138 locomotives had been built by 1933, with the main allocations at Schneidemühl (now Pila in Poland), Hanover East, Frankfurt (Oder), Breslau (now Wroclaw in Poland), Königsburg (Kaliningrad) and Hamburg Altona, from which depot they dominated services to the north, to Flensburg, Westerland, Stralsund, Lübeck, Kiel and the Ostbahn to East Prussia. At this stage, they were mainly replacing the Prussian S10 classes. The only depots to which they were allocated outside the former

Münster-based 03.059 is power for the Hamburg Altona-Cologne D94, seen here near Wuppertal-Elberfeld. Coal has disappeared from sight in the engine's tender after the long journey, and former Prussian suburban 2-6-0T 74.463 departs on a local train on parallel lines, c1933.
(Carl Bellingrodt /Eisenbahnstiftung Collection)

Hamburg Altona's
03.245 and three standby coaches deputise for a diesel high-speed railcar on the Berlin-Hamburg BFD express, seen here passing Hamburg-Dammtor, 1938.
(Carl Bellingrodt/A.Gottwaldt Collection)

Prussian State railway network were at Ludwigshafen, Wiesbaden, Nuremberg, and Würzburg. The complete class of 298 locomotives was finished by 1938 with the largest number, ninety-two, in the Ruhr area – Cologne, Hanover, Wuppertal and Essen. Thirty were in Berlin, twenty-eight at Halle, nineteen at Hamburg, thirty-five at Osnabrück and Rheine, and thirty-nine in the east at Breslau, Danzig, Stettin and Schneidemühl.

The 03s were active between Hamburg and Berlin, including lightweight high-speed services FD 23 and 24, which loaded to 275-300 tons and averaged around 63mph over the 183 miles, with stops at Hamburg Dammtor and Hauptbahnhof. Speed over the 179-mile non-stop section averaged 68½-70mph and was just sixteen minutes slower than the two-car express diesel railcar – if the *Flying*

Hamburger unit was out of action, an 03 Pacific had to substitute. On a run with 03.073, one of the Hamburg 03s authorised for higher maximum speeds, on FD 24 on 1 June 1933, with a load of 240 tons, with one p-way slack near Nauen, arrival in Hamburg Hbf was a minute early (179 miles in 162 minutes, 157 net), with a maximum speed of 75-78mph sustained for 40 miles between Grabow and Schwanheide. On 3 July 1933, 03.073 (again) on FD 2, the *Flying Hamburger* replacement, with 172 tons, took 150½ minutes (143¼ net) for the 179 miles between Berlin Lehrte and Hamburg, touching 87mph before Ludwigslust, at Strohkirchen and before Brahlstorf. A couple of days earlier, 03.038, with 177 tons, had covered the same route on the same train in 152½ minutes (146¼ net) with a maximum of 86½mph sustained

over two miles between Hagenow and Brahlstorf. The schedule of the *Flying Hamburger* diesel unit was 148 minutes. 03s on FD 23/24 were replaced by the streamlined 05s in 1936, with streamlined 03.193 acting as standby. Because of failures of the 05s, the 03 accumulated the same mileage on these runs as the two 05s did over 1936-37. By 1939 there were ten pairs of fast services between the two cities, three pairs with the express railcar, one pair booked for the 05s, a pair with 01s, and five with 03s.

Berlin-allocated 03s worked the pair of luxury trains L11/12 from Paris to Warsaw and D23/24 Paris-Warsaw-Russia between Berlin and Hanover, and Berlin and the Silesian border, as parts of the Berlin city railway were forbidden to 20-ton axleload engines. Because of extreme curvature, these trains on the city railway were restricted to 37½mph. Three FD trains were worked non-stop over the 159 miles between Hanover and Berlin by 03s with an authorised maximum speed of 81mph at an average speed of 62mph. However, the vast majority of their work was on D- and E-trains formerly worked by the Prussian S10 4-6-0s.

Another important route on which the 03s performed was the north-south trunk line from Hamburg to Munich. In 1933, the DRG authorities wished to accelerate trains on this route and tests were conducted on a 1 in 40 gradient with 01.023 of Erfurt, S3/6 18.511 of Nuremberg and 03.075 of Leipzig West. At a steady and sustained speed of 34½mph, the 03 and the S3/6 could haul 200 tons, and the 01, 250 tons. Between

Saalfeld and Lichtenfels on FD 79/80, the 03 managed to cut ten minutes from the eighty-five-minute schedule of which three minutes was doing without a banker over the steepest section. In the summer timetable of 1936, the Halle 03s had two Berlin-Nuremberg runs of 298 miles, two Berlin-Kassel diagrams of 268 miles and two Halle-Breslau turns of 241 miles.

In March 1939 a boiler explosion wrecked Stralsund's 03.174, which was not repaired. During the war years, there were many 03 reallocations with twenty/thirty a year in 1940-42, over fifty in 1943 and sixty-two exchanges in 1944, over 20 per cent of the total number. A large number moved east into former Polish territories, but then in 1944 moved back towards the west, away from the advancing Red Army. In August 1944, Berlin was home to forty of the class, and Danzig, Königsberg and further east had eighty-seven 03s between them. Because of war conditions and damage, maximum speed was restricted to 62mph (100km/hr) in 1942 and further on many lines in 1943 to 53mph (85km/hr).

At the end of the war eight were stored withdrawn from service, 144 were in the jurisdiction of the West German *Bundesbahn*, 78 were in the East German DR, 36 with the Polish Railways and 29 in the Soviet Union. Most were stored damaged pending overhaul.

Operations - *Deutsche Bundesbahn* 1945-1973

In November 1945, an assessment of locomotives standing damaged was undertaken, and 128 03 Pacifics were stored in the British

and American Zones, the majority in the Hanover and Hamburg divisions. Some 148 were in the West in total, but four had been withdrawn, 03.174 after the 1939 boiler explosion, and 03.033, 165 and 217 from war damage. Few of these were undamaged and a further three – 03.103, 231 and 279 – were condemned. Thirty-four 03s were recovered from the east. The situation in the southern French Zone was critical and fifteen 03s were sent from the other Zones to the Mainz motive power division. Overhauls took place between 1947 and 1949 and 112 locomotives were back in traffic after overhaul by August 1949. By February 1951, the whole West German fleet of 144 locomotives was available for operations. By

December 1951, the express fleet of the *Deutsche Bundesbahn* stood at 502 locomotives – 165 01s, 144 03s, 80 three-cylinder Pacifics and 110 former State four-cylinder Pacifics, mainly the Bavarian S3/6s. Such was the amount of work for these locomotives that daily mileages were necessarily high and there were twenty-six 03 diagrams requiring 429 miles a day.

In 1955, there were forty-six locomotives of class 03 which were achieving more than 10,000 miles a month, engines based at Cologne, Osnabrück, Hanover, Bremen and Hamburg Altona. The highest mileages were by engines at Cologne-Deutzerfeld and Osnabrück which were reaching nearly 12,500 miles a month. In July 1956, 03.296 of Osnabrück ran

The still part-streamlined two-cylinder 03.193 hauls D3 Cologne-Hamm-Brunswick through Wuppertal-Barmen, 17 April 1949. (Carl Bellingrodt/ Eisenbahnstiftung Collection)

An 03 at Hamburg Hbf awaiting departure with a postal and parcels train, 1968.
(MLS Collection/J. Davenport)

nearly 14,000 miles at an average of 450 miles a day.

As electrification spread rapidly in the late 1950s, older locomotives of classes 18.5, 38.10 (P8) and 39 (P10) were replaced by standard 01s and 03s redundant elsewhere, and the DB engines were allocated fairly generally throughout the system from Flensburg in the north to Stuttgart and Ulm in the south. The first post-war withdrawal was of 03.048 after an accident in 1959, and more went gradually until 1965, when twenty-five were withdrawn. Between that year and 1968, the remaining seventy-six locomotives fell to thirty. The number of diagrams in the north dropped rapidly from sixty-one in 1964 to just fourteen in 1967, mainly at Mönchengladbach, plus some seasonal trains in the Hamburg division. In the west and south, Trier had nine good diagrams and Ulm seven for 03s in 1964, however the Trier engines were replaced by 01s, though at Ulm the diagrams increased to replace the rebuilt S3/6 18.6s.

03.127 on an Eilzug at Osnabrück, June 1967. (MLS Collection/J.Davenport)

From 1965, no more L3 overhauls were to be undertaken for 03s and from 1968, no further Works repairs were to be made. After 1970, the remaining ten engines were all at Ulm, the last three going in 1972. They worked from Friedrichshafen to Ulm on through train services from Lindau to Ulm and further north. Two of the Ulm 03s, 003.131 and 003.188, were preserved (see later in the chapter).

For logs and accounts of my own personal experience behind 03s between Kiel and Hamburg, and Aachen and Cologne, see Chapter 18, pages 326–7.

03.283 with a train of '*Silberlinge*' coaches on an Eilzug at Bielefeld, 22 August 1967. (MLS Collection)

03.079 of Hamburg brings a D-Zug from Westerland over the Hindenburgdamm towards Hamburg, 16 July 1952. (DB/Robin Garn Collection)

03.074 stands at Flensburg in the pouring rain with the post-war *Skandinavien Express*, 26 August 1948. The 03s were widely used in north Germany, and replaced the Prussian S10s in Mecklenburg and East Prussia. (W Hollnagel/Eisenbahnstiftung Collection)

03.268 with a D-Zug at the Belgian/German border at Aachen, which it will take as far as Cologne, c1967. (MLS Collection/J.Davenport)

03.268 of
Mönchengladbach hauls a
P-Zug to Cologne-Deutz
over the Hohenzollern
Bridge in Cologne, 2
March 1968.
(Helmut Dahlhaus)

Operations - *Deutsche Reichsbahn*, 1945-1979

After the war, ninety-five 03s and three-cylinder 03.10s remained in the Soviet Zone of Germany, of which thirty-two were serviceable, thirty-three were damaged, awaiting Works repair, four were damaged and stored in the Works, ten were damaged on shed and another thirteen locomotives, although undamaged, were not fit for traffic until they'd received major repairs. Eighty of these were two-cylinder 03 Pacifics, although two – 03.023 and 03.216 - were so badly damaged that they were withdrawn before being repaired. The Soviet military authorities sequestered a number of those in best condition for movement of Red Army troops and equipment, and kept them until 1950.

One of the 03s still
operating in the immediate
post-war period, Halle's
03.119, at Berlin-Zoo,
September 1945.
(ADN/Robin Garn's Collection)

Between 1950 and 1955, the 03s were put through Works, although progress was slow because of a shortage of material and spare parts. An edict from the transport authorities concentrated different classes in specific motive power divisions to limit the location of spares for maintenance and, up to 1955, all the 03s were allocated to the Halle Division, based at Halle, Leipzig Süd and Leipzig West depots. Then, twenty-six were reallocated to Berlin. By 1961, there were five at Dresden and five in the Schwerin Division in the north, followed by a larger contingent in 1962 and 1964. In 1961, many of the Berlin engines were reallocated to Magdeburg, and worked some of the cross-border services at Helmstedt and Oebisfelde.

Berlin Rummelsburg and Berlin Ostbahnhof used their 03s for express and semi-fast services to Frankfurt (Oder), Dresden, Leipzig, Magdeburg, and the longest runs to Warnemünde and Rügen on the North Sea coast (179 and 166 miles respectively), and from the late 1950s to Hamburg via the corridor to the West. They hauled the *Pannonia Express* non-stop over the 118 miles to Dresden, although at an average speed of 34mph it hardly warranted the title! Postwar track repairs and line speed restrictions were still rife. In 1954, E316 from Warnemünde to Berlin via Rostock and Neubrandenburg managed to take nearly seven hours for the 177 miles at an average of 25.6mph! Most express Berlin turns were handed over to 01 Pacifics in 1961. By 1970, most of their work at Berlin was on stopping services, apart from a pair of express trains

Dresden - Berlin
D1274 Metropol, 19.7.1974
22.05 Budapest-Rostock
03.2081-2 Bw BerlinOst
12chs, 455/500t

		mph		
Dresden Hbf	00.00		T	0 miles
Dresden Mitte	04.14	29		
Dresden Neustadt	06.40		½ E	2.4
	00.00		T	0
Radebeul Ost	08.16	45		
Neucoswig	13.50	56½ / 49		
Weinböhla	17.26	43/41		
km 23 (summit)	-	39		
Böhla	24.24	64		
Grossenhain	28.40	72		
Zabelitz	31.51	65/69		
Frauenhain	34.05	70		
km 50	-	73		
Elsterwerda	39.26		1½ E	33.05
	00.00		T	0
Km 116	08.30	38½		
Rückersdorf-Oppelheim	13.15	62		
Doberlug-Kirchheim	17.34		½ E	12.4
	00.00		½ L	0
Brenitz-Sonnewalde	08.50	54		
Walddrehna	14.17	48/51		
km 84 (summit)	-	50		
Gehren	17.45	62		
Uckro	20.26	75		16.7
km 72	-	78		
Drahnsdorf	24.11	77		
Golssen	27.36	74		
Klasdorf	30.40	70		
Baruth	33.06	71½		
km 48 (summit)	-	65		
Neuhof	38.11	70/pws 35*		
Wunsdorf	40.56	45		
Zossen	45.14	64		
km 21	52.26//53.03 sig stand			
Dahlewitz	54.34	15*		
Blankenfelde	56.12	40/pws 16*/37		
Berlin Schönefeld	68.17		10L	58 (arrived Berlin Ost 4L)

to the Polish border (D310/311 and D314/315) which were taken over by 01.5s in 1975. Other 03s based at

Cottbus also worked to the Polish border at Görlitz. Frankfurt (Oder) 03s had a regular working, E992 north from Cottbus to Frankfurt and on to Angermunde. Görlitz had several 03s which shared with diesels all classes of trains from the Polish border westwards on the scenic but slow route to Dresden and local trains to Spremberg and Cottbus. 03 work in this area lasted until 1977, when they were replaced by class 118 diesel hydraulic locomotives.

The Dresden Depot received 03s first in 1956 and had further engines in 1959 to replace the Saxon 18.0 Pacifics on express workings to Berlin. The exchange of 03 engines frequently between depots was a common practice in the 1950s and '60s, and Dresden had eighteen different engines between 1959 and 1969, though never more than nine in any one year. Their longest turn was the 286 miles run on the D51/56 pair from Dresden to Rostock. By the 1970s, it was unusual to see an 03 on an express on the Berlin-Dresden route, but Alastair Wood recorded a run with the heavily-loaded D1274 *Metropol* in July 1974 (see table on left).

Alastair also recorded a couple of 03 runs on the Stendal route as late as 1975-6 (see table on the right).

The 1976 train was two coaches over booked load (strengthened for Easter) with 03.2098 being worked vigorously after slow starts and the pws checks. At Stendal, 03.2098 continued with E548, now classified as a stopping train, N9450, 20.52 to the East/West German border at Oebisfelde. The 1975 run was the normal load, but the engine was pushed hard to recover time lost earlier in the journey, achieving better than even time start-to-stop to Rathenow and virtually

Berlin-Stendal, 16.4.1976
03.2098-6 Bw Oebisfelde
E548, 18.48 Berlin-Stendal
10 chs, 290/300t

Wustermark-Stendal, 31.8.1975
03.2242-0 Bw Oebisfelde
E540, 08.13 Berlin-Stendal
7 chs, 202/210t

Station	Time	mph	L	miles	Time	mph	L
Berlin Schöneweide	00.00	mph	T	0 miles			
Grunauer Kreuz	07.10	40/45					
Berlin Schönefeld	12.12		T	6.05			
	00.00		T	0			
Diedersdorf	08.50	56/66					
Genshagener Heide	13.16	70					
Saarmund	-	pws 28*					
Bergholz	26.00	54/50/pws 45*					
Potsdam	32.23		2½ L	23.25			
	00.00		1½ L	0			
Golm	06.33	40/ pws 32*					
Marquardt	10.10	60					
Satzkom	11.15	70					
Priort	14.03	32* s igs					
Elstal	17.00	45					
Wustermark	21.08		5½ L	15			
	00.00		4½ L	0	00.00		18L
Neugarten	05.23	55			04.52	55	
Gross Behnitz	10.05	70/75			09.25	77	
Buschow	14.40	75			13.50	79	
Km 56	-	70			-	74	
Nennhausen	18.50	74/71½			17.46	75/72	
Km 66	-	75			-	79	
Rathenow	25.07		5½ L	25.1	23.35		16½ L
	00.00		4½ L	0	00.00		15½ L
Km 76	-	62			-	63	
Grosswudicke	07.12	64/61½			06.30	65/64	
Schönhauser Damm	11.00	72/74			10.15	69/77	
Schönhauser	14.59		5½ L	13.3	13.08	75	
	00.00		5L		-	pws 20*	
Elbe Bridge	-	39/pws 22*			-	sigs 30*	
Hämerten	06.45	49			18.13	40/63	
Km 102	-	62			-	60	
Stendal	12.45		4L	7.9	24.04		14L

achieving even time in just thirteen miles from the departure from that station. Alastair commented on the rough riding of the train on the single-track secondary route, which had just three Eilzüge in each direction diagrammed for two Oebisfelde 03s at that time.

A few 03s went to Stralsund in the Greifswald division in 1955, but their work there was shortlived as it was decided to concentrate the three-cylinder 03.10s at that depot. A few remained as reserves to the 03.10s and then moved to Pasewalk, where ten remained until 1970, the last three there being condemned in 1975.

As stated earlier, the Halle division had the largest allocation – in fact all of them during the immediate post-war repair period – forty-six being based at Halle itself and thirty-one at Leipzig West. The last one to be restored was 03.2176, which incidentally was one of the last withdrawn in 1979. After 1955, when the 03s were redistributed over the whole DR system, the Halle allocation dropped to ten-twelve engines in the 1960s, although the Leipzig allocation held up, with over twenty allocated throughout the 1960s. The Halle engines

East German reboilered 03.162 with the 13.03 Hamburg Altona-Berlin leaving Hamburg Hbf, June 1967.
(MLS Collection/J.Davenport)

worked from Erfurt to Berlin, and Halle to Nordhausen, Halberstadt and Cottbus. The Leipzig engines covered services to Magdeburg, Dresden, Karl-Marx-Stadt, and Saalfeld via both Jena and Gera. The main Leipzig-Berlin services were dieselised in 1967 although a couple of D-Züge (D562/567, later D660/563) remained as a pocket of 03 activity well-known by enthusiasts until the 1979 summer timetable. 03.2058 of Lutherstadt–Wittenberg operated the last D660 and 03.2155 the last D563 in May 1979.

The pioneer 03.001 was withdrawn in December 1966 after running two million miles and was designated for a museum, being

stored at Meissen for many years. The first withdrawals for other than accident or war damage reasons were in 1967, although some stored engines were taken back into traffic and rebuilt with the 39E boilers from condemned class 22 2-8-2s. In 1972, seventy-two 03s still existed, in the following motive power divisions:

Berlin:	21
Cottbus:	14
Dresden:	2
Grunewald:	3
Halle:	16
Magdeburg:	16

By 1978, there were just twenty left and at the end of May 1979,

the remaining seven Lutherstadt-Wittenberg engines were withdrawn or reallocated for their last few months to Halberstadt and Oebisfelde in the Magdeburg division. Güsten still had a three-day stopping (P-Zug) diagram in the summer of 1978, and 03.2117

and 03.2235 finished there in February 1979, although 03.2002 and 03.2117 were brought back to celebrate '*Fifty years of 03s*' in September 1980, running between Magdeburg and Oebisfelde. Some finished their last days as stationary boilers at Leipzig Süd

and West deports and Engelsdorf. The last official withdrawals were of 03.2128 and 03.2243 in April 1981.

For a log of my own personal experience behind 03.2058 on D563 between Berlin and Leipzig, see Chapter 18, pages 328.

DR 03.254, on the 08.57 Hamburg Altona-Berlin, awaiting departure, 20 June 1967.
(MLS Collection/J. Davenport)

03.2154 (the former semi-streamlined 03 – see page 224) leaving Berlin with a DR express, 19 April 1969. (Ulrich Budde)

03.2250 passes Warschauer Street near Berlin Ost with a Berlin-Warsaw-Moscow express made up of Russian rolling stock, 9 August 1975. (George Bambery)

03.2081-2 arriving at Berlin-Schöneweide with stock of D653 for Leipzig, 14 April 1976. (Alastair Wood)

DR 03.2256-0 on an international D-Zug from Magdeburg to Stendal, which the 03 would work to Oebisfelde, 16 August 1973. (Richard Spoors)

03.2028 at Wuhlheide with D241, *Ost-West Express,* Paris-Moscow via Berlin and Frankfurt (Oder), including two Russian through coaches, 30 March 1975. (Helmut Dahlhaus)

DR 03.2180-2 with a Berlin-Stendal D-Zug near Stendal, 2 September 1974. (Roger Bastin)

03.2117-4, with a semi-fast Berlin-Dresden train, passes Böhla, 24 August 1974. (Richard Spoors)

03.2058-0 enters Jüterbog with D567, Berlin-Leipzig, 30 March 1978. (Alastair Wood)

03.2243-8 arrives at Berlin-Schönefeld with D567, Berlin-Leipzig, 6 September 1977. (Alastair Wood)

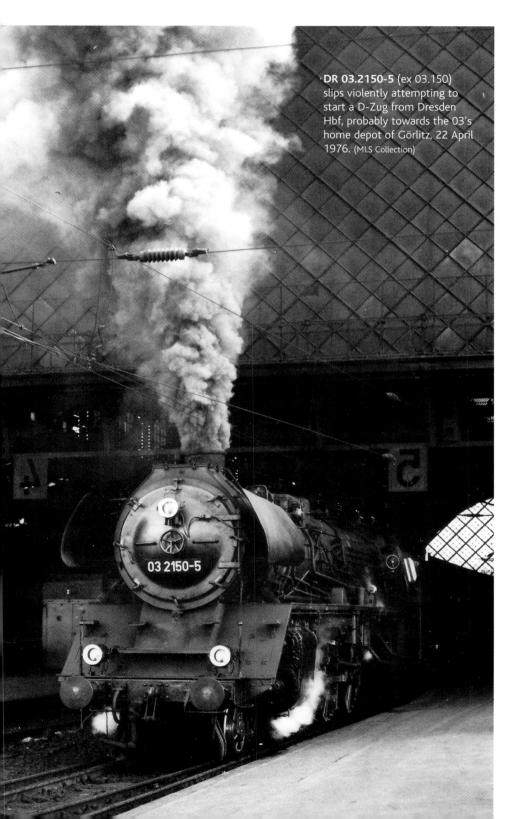

DR 03.2150-5 (ex 03.150) slips violently attempting to start a D-Zug from Dresden Hbf, probably towards the 03's home depot of Görlitz, 22 April 1976. (MLS Collection)

03s in Austria, USSR and Poland

03.113 was moved from Schneidemühl to Landeck in Austria in 1945, and spent short periods in operation at Innsbruck, Landeck and Bregenz in 1945 and 1946, before going to store at Linz between 1947 and 1952 when it returned to West Germany, was overhauled at Brunswick and allocated to Wiesbaden Depot.

Twenty-nine 03s were stored in Lithuania, part of the USSR, after the war, and by 1950 had been repaired and become part of Russian Railways' stock, renumbered TC-07 to TC-290, retaining their class identification number (ie 03.007 became TC-07). Eight then went to Belaruss and there were proposals to regauge them to the Russian 5ft gauge, but all were withdrawn between 1950 and 1952, which suggests that there were problems or that they were not converted – all records have been lost. The other twenty-one remained in Lithuania on standard gauge, and were withdrawn between 1955 and 1957.

The largest contingent remained in Poland (the former East Prussia) in the former German Danzig, Königsberg and Oppeln motive power divisions. Eighteen 17-ton axle-load locomotives with 2ft 9in-diameter bogie wheels were renumbered Pm2-1 to 18, three more with 18-ton axleloads were renumbered Pm2 -19 to 21, and the remaining 18 ton axleload engines with 3ft 3in-diameter bogie wheels were renumbered Pm2-22 to 35. In Poland, they retained their large smoke deflectors, had flat smokebox doors, and were black with a red

Polish Railways Pm2-34 (former DRG 03.273) at speed with the *Pomorzanin* from Lodz-Kutno-Torun (Thorn)-Gdansk (Danzig)-Gdynia departing northwards from Torun, four years before its withdrawal and retention as a preserved locomotive, 9 September 1973. (Helmut Dahlhaus)

strip along the running plate and wheel centres, white wheel rims, and yellow buffer-beams. They had 7,500-gallon water capacity tenders, were allowed 15 per cent heavier loads in traffic than their German equivalents and were restricted to 75mph, although most main lines only allowed 55-60mph maximum. Twenty-three were initially in the Gdansk (Danzig) area and a few at Poznan (Posen), but by 1968 they were nearly all at Bydgoszcz (Bromberg) with a few at Olsztyn (Allenstein). The latter had been displaced by electrification in 1973, and then all remained at Bydgoszcz until the late 1970s, working to Katowice, Poznan and Pila (former Schneidemühl). The last diagrams for the Pm2s were in August 1977, and the last four, Pm2-8 (03.069), Pm2-13 (03.052), Pm2-21 (03.152) and Pm2-34 (03.273), were withdrawn in November 1978, the latter engine being preserved in the Warsaw Railway Museum.

Preserved Locomotives
03.001

03.001 was withdrawn in 1966 after running two million miles and retained for preservation. Stored until 1971, it was finally restored to operating condition in 1978 at Meiningen Works and renumbered

Preserved 03.001 on a railtour at Decin, 16 May 1981. (Graham Stacey)

Preserved 03.2001-0 at Arnstadt with E4400 09.06 Saalfeld-Erfurt during the 1994 *Plandampf*, 5 May 1994.
(David Maidment)

03.2001-0 as would have been the case had it remained in DR service after 1970. It operated out of the Deutsches Bahn Museum, Dresden Altstadt, in either pre- or post-1970 garb in active service for twenty years before being displayed at the Dresden Altstadt Museum from 2005.

03.002
03.002, built by Borsig in 1930, remained in East Germany after the war, was renumbered 03.2002-8 and was one of the last survivors of the class at Lutherstadt-Wittenberg when withdrawn in May 1979. It then acted as a stationary boiler until the frame and boiler of the locomotive was rescued and restored externally in 2001 as a streamlined replica of 03.193, although retaining the number 03.002. It is displayed in a red livery at the Technikmuseum, Prora on the island of Rügen.

03.098
03.098 was built by Borsig in 1933 and remained in East Germany after the war, rebuilt with a '*Reko*' boiler and renumbered 03.2098-6 in 1970. After withdrawal, after many delays it was acquired in 1981 by the Historical Railway Society of Frankfurt-am-Main, preserved and

displayed at the Technikmuseum, Speyer (Rhineland Palatinate).

03.131
03.131 was built by Henschel in 1933 and was one of the last two 03 survivors at Ulm, numbered 003.131-0 after 1968, being withdrawn at the end of 1972. It

03.2098 with E544 Berlin Schöneweide-Stendal at Berlin-Marzahn, 16 June 1974.
(Helmut Dahlhaus)

03.131 at Bad Harzburg about to work an Eilzug to Brunswick, August 1967.
(Reiner Moritz/ Eisenbahnstiftung Collection)

appeared at a number of exhibitions until in 1975 it was acquired and displayed by the Deutsches Dampflok Museum, Neuenmarkt-Wirsberg.

03.155

03.155 was built in 1934 by Borsig, remained in East Germany after the war, was rebuilt with a 39E '*Reko*' boiler, renumbered 03.2155-4 in 1970, and was one of the last DR 03 survivors at Lutherstadt-Wittenberg, withdrawn in 1979. In 1984, it was purchased by the railway museum based in the West German locomotive depot at Dieringhausen run by the Eisenbahnfreunde Flugelrad Oberberg (Nordrhein-Westfalen) and partially restored to exhibition standard. In 2004, one of the Society's members attempted a restoration to active operation, but the project was put on hold in 2006. Eventually, the restoration succeeded and the locomotive took part in the 01 steam tour of Germany in 2015 (see photo on page 357).

03.188

03.188 was built by BMAG (Schwartzkopf) in 1935 and renumbered 003.188-0 in 1968. It was withdrawn from Ulm Depot in 1969 and purchased for display outside the Max-Eyth-Technical School in Kirchheim (Teck). After thirty-five years in the open, its condition had deteriorated badly, but the present owners, the Esslingen City Council, decided to restore it in its current situation, the work being completed in 2006.

03.204

03.204 was built by Borsig in 1936 and was based at Cottbus until 1945, and then from 1972 until its withdrawal in 1976. It was renumbered 03.2204-0 in 1970. Initially, it was retained as a static monument in Cottbus, and by 1991 was the possession of the Lausitzer Dampflok Club, Cottbus, which restored the locomotive to active operation in 1992-3. 03.204 has been active for many years in *Plandampf* and other special train operation.

03.243

03.243 was built in 1936 by Borsig, and remained in East Germany after the war, where it was rebuilt with a 39E 'Reko' boiler, renumbered 03.2243-8 in 1970 and was one of the last 03 survivors at Lutherstadt-Wittenberg. After withdrawal in 1979, it was used for spare parts, but in 1983, efforts were made to bring it back into operation. However, this proved to be impossible to finance and the remains were brought to Meiningen Works to act as spares for other preserved locomotives being overhauled there.

03.273

03.273 was built by BMAG (Schwartzkopf) in 1937 (see photo page 242) and although stored at Saarbrücken in 1944, it was one of the locomotives that was acquired by the Polish State Railways (PKP) where it was renumbered Pm2-34. It remained in active service there until 1978, when it was one of the last five survivors in that country and, after withdrawal, was taken for display in various locations in Poland, based at its former depot of Bydogszcz (Bromberg), becoming an exhibit in the Warsaw Railway Museum in 1995, where it is see in its PKP livery of jade green, including its large smoke deflectors, with red stripe running plate.

03.295

03.295 was one of the last 03 Pacifics built in 1937 by Borsig and it remained in East Germany after the war, received a 39E 'Reko' boiler, was renumbered 03.2295-8 in 1970 and was withdrawn from Leipzig Süd in 1978. It acted for a number of years as a source of spare parts for other preserved locomotives, and was purchased in 1992 by the Bavarian Railway Museum at Nördlingen. After scouring Europe for the missing parts, the locomotive was brought back into operation in 1996. The Museum's own workshop overhauled the locomotive in 2005.

Preserved 03.2204-0 on arrival at Dresden Hbf with D456 Warsaw-Dresden, during a *Plandampf* event, 30 April 1994. (David Maidment)

Chapter 13

THE *DEUTSCHE REICHSBAHN* 03.10

DR 1939 streamlined locos
Design & Construction

At the start of the Second World War, just eighteen streamlined locomotives existed on the *Deutsche Reichsbahn*, only the two experimental 03s, the three 05s, two 06 4-8-4s, the first 01.10 and a few tank engine 'oddities' plus the high-speed Henschel-Wegmann Zug. As a result of the success of the diesel railcar *Flying Hamburger*-type sets, the steam competitor was designed, a streamlined 4-6-4T and four lightweight close-coupled streamlined coaches. It ran two return trips daily from June 1936 to August 1939 between Berlin and Dresden, at 100mph in scheduled service, but authorised to 110mph and achieving 115.5mph on one test occasion, although excessive juddering from the two-cylinder engine, 61.001, was experienced. A three-cylinder engine of similar design, 61.002, was built in 1939. After the war, the coaches of the Henschel-Wegmann train were formed into a conventional express, the *Blaue Enzian* (Blue Gentian),

running from Hamburg to Munich behind conventional Pacifics. 61.001 was involved in an accident at Münster in 1951, withdrawn and later scrapped, but 61.002 was converted to a high-speed Pacific for test purposes (see Chapter 16).

The 01.10s had a heavy axleload and a high-speed locomotive with an axleload of 18 tons or under was needed for many routes. As a further development of the 03 Pacific, in similar vein to the progression from 01 to 01.10, a series of 140 three-cylinder 03.10s was planned, completely streamlined as with the 1939-built 01.10s. 03.1001 appeared in December 1939, built by Borsig, but by 1941 when the war restricted further construction, only sixty had been completed, 03.1001-22, 03.1043-60 and 03.1073-92, with the firms of Krupp and Krauss-Maffei sharing the order with Borsig.

Key dimensions included coupled wheels of 6ft 7in diameter, 227lbpsi boiler pressure, three cylinders measuring 18.5in x 26in, grate area of 41.8sqft, heating surface of 2,184sqft and superheater of 776sqft. The axle-load maximum was 18.4 tons and the engine weight 103.2

tons, and with a 7,500-gallon water capacity streamlined tender holding 10 tons of coal, 178.4 tons in full service order. Tractive effort was 30,864lb and horsepower calculated as 1,870. Maximum authorised speed was 87½mph. The locomotives were designed to haul 540 tons on the level at 75mph or 315 tons at 87½mph. The additional cost of the three-cylinder engine compared with the two-cylinder 03 was 7,500 RMs.

Although the streamlining gave a modern image, and it was in the vogue in the late 1930s in the USA, France and Great Britain also, the full streamlining to near rail level created many access problems for efficient maintenance and drivers found difficulty in oiling the machines, especially the middle cylinder with crosshead, valve gear and especially the big end of the connecting rod on the first axle. Of course, as the war progressed the opportunity and need for high-speed travel reduced, maximum line speeds over main lines were reduced, and the streamlining lost any value it had and became a considerable nuisance, and by 1941 it was decided to remove the

A rare colour photo of the newly-built streamlined 03.1081 at Bw Amstetten in the Lower Danube Valley, 20 September 1940. (RVM Berlin/Eisenbahnstiftung Collection)

February 1941 the maximum speed for all streamlined locomotives was reduced from 94 to 87½mph. The number of depots holding 03.10s was reduced to ten. In 1944, it was decided to concentrate all the 03.10s in just two home depots in the east – Posen (Poznan) having twenty-five examples and Breslau (Wroclaw) thirty-one engines. One locomotive, 03.1092, was stored after receiving severe bomb damage.

As the Red Army advanced through Poland and into Germany's eastern borders, the DR tried to withdraw their 03.10s further west and, in May 1945, sixteen were in the British Zone, six in the American, twenty-six in the Soviet Zone and ten still in Poland. After the Yalta Conference, a redistribution of Zonal territory meant that twenty-six stayed in the west while nineteen remained in East Germany, nine in Poland and five were moved to the Soviet Zone. The class suffered just the one casualty during the war, fifty-nine surviving, the locomotives in West Germany and East Germany, as follows:

streamlining from the coupled wheel area to give improved access to the motion.

Operations until 1945

The first two machines were allocated to Berlin Grunewald for testing, but after that 03.1003-07 went to Saarbrücken, 03.1008-10 to Berlin Grunewald Depot, 03.1011-12 to Breslau and 03.1013-15 to Schneidemühle. Others went to Stargard, Rostock, Cologne, Hagen, Heidelberg, Nuremberg whilst the last batch of thirteen followed the German expansion into Austria. From January 1940 a reduced timetable was published and in

The streamlined three-cylinder light axle-load 03.1020 as built in 1940. This locomotive survived the war in the Eastern Zone, and was reboilered and oil-fired to become DR's 03.0020 , which was withdrawn c1978. In this photo, the 1941 decision to remove the streamlining from the coupled wheel area has already been implemented. (MLS Collection/C.Bellingrodt/EK-Verlag)

An unidentified 03.10, still with full streamlining, between Salzburg and Vienna, 1940. (A. Hofbauer / Eisenbahnstuiftung Collection)

DB examples:

03.1001	03.1045
03.1004	03.1049
03.1008	03.1050
03.1009	03.1051
03.1011	03.1054
03.1012	03.1055
03.1013	03.1056
03.1014	03.1060
03.1016	03.1073
03.1017	03.1076
03.1021	03.1081
03.1022	03.1082
03.1043	03.1084

DR examples:

03.1010	03.1075
03.1019	03.1077
03.1020	03.1078
03.1046	03.1080
03.1048	03.1085
03.1057	03.1087
03.1058	03.1088
03.1059	03.1089
03.1074	03.1090

03.1081, delivered in 1941 with streamlining removed from the coupled wheel motion, in service before the neglect of the war years took their toll, c1941, on the *Westbahn* between Munich and Salzburg. 03.1081 was retained in West Germany after the war, destreamlined and reboilered, and withdrawn from Hagen Depot in 1966. (MLS Collection/C.Bellingrodt/EK-Verlag)

Nine locomotives were retained by the Polish Railways as the PKP Pm3 class, and were numbered Pm3-1 to Pm3-9. Five were retained by the Soviet Union, although 03.1006 and 03.1018, originally there, were returned to Poland and became Pm3-6 and 8. The Polish locomotives included in addition 03.1047 which was not repaired after the war and was cannibalised in 1956 to keep the others running, 03.1092 which was damaged in a raid on Poznan in 1944 and was scrapped in 1948, and the last survivor, Pm3-5 (either 03.1005 or 03.1015), withdrawn in May 1968, and retained for the Warsaw Railway Museum.

03.1008 among a row of stored damaged 03.10 Pacifics at Wolfenbüttel in 1947 awaiting decisions re overhaul. Also stored there were 03.1009, 1017 and 1054. They were hauled in 1945 from Breslau to Frellstedt, near Helmstedt, to 'rescue' them from the Soviet Zone and planned for restoration at the nearby Brunswick Works, but it was five years later before they were given L4 heavy overhauls at the Henschel Company and 03.1008 was allocated to Dortmund, 1947. (RAW/Eisenbahnstiftung Collection)

DB rebuilt with all-welded boiler Design, Construction & Operation

At the end of the war, all the locomotives had most of their streamlining part-destroyed or in parlous condition and were de-streamlined during the first major repairs in both countries. March 1947 found just three of the class active in the west – 03.1060 and 03.1081 at Bebra in the Kassel District, and 03.1055 at Mühldorf in the Munich area. There were no express services requiring the use of such locomotives at that time, but by 1949 there was a shortage of motive power, and a decision was made to repair and de-streamline

A damaged 03.10 stored in former East Prussia that became part of Poland after the war, c1945. The unidentified locomotive was one of nine 03.10s reclassified PKP class Pm3, and overhauled for operation. The last, Pm3-5, was withdrawn in 1968 and is now in the Warsaw Railway Museum collection. (MLS Collection)

all the 03.10s and they were rebuilt by Henschel at their factory in Kassel, at a cost between 105,000 and 138,000 Deutschmark (DM) during 1950. 03.1013 was the first of this programme to be returned to service, in March 1950. Three of the locomotives were finished in steel-blue livery – 03.1014, 1022 and 1043 – for use on some of the reintroduced international trains and all these locomotives had a high profile over the following five years with many of their diagrams demanding a high daily mileage – including the 1953 439-mile run from Hamburg to Frankfurt-am-Main via Cologne. Average daily mileages for the Dortmund-based 03.10s ranged from 507 miles in 1953 to 658 miles in 1955 – later, only the first V200 diesel hydraulics and the oil-burning 01.10s of Bebra and Osnabrück exceeded these daily figures. A group of Offenburg 03.10s were replaced by 01.10s in 1952 and were transferred to Paderborn, where they worked to Aachen, Altenbeken, Bebra, Düsseldorf, Hamm and Münster.

In 1954, Hamburg Altona received six 03.10s, which worked between Hamburg and Dortmund, Flensburg, Hamm, Hanover and Cologne. Eight Ludwigshafen engines were used in the Rhine Valley to Heidelberg, Mainz, Mannheim, Cologne and Saarbrücken until 1958, and the electrification as far as Koblenz. In May 1954, the dispersion of the 03.10s was as follows:

Dortmund: 03.1013, 1014, 1021, 1022, 1043, 1054, 1055, 1056, 1073, 1081, 1082, 1084

Hamburg Altona: 03.1008, 1011, 1012, 1017, 1049, 1050
Ludwigshafen: 03.1001, 1004, 1009, 1016, 1045, 1051, 1060, 1076

On 24 October 1956, K.B. Stone recorded a run on the *Lorelei Express* from Mannheim to Cologne behind 03.1001 with 382 tons. The forty-six miles from Mannheim to Mainz took the scheduled 63 minutes including a long p-way slack, maximum 66mph, and the fifty-seven miles onto Koblenz, 75 minutes, three minutes less than scheduled with a maximum of 68mph. The thirty-seven miles to Bonn took 49 minutes, a minute under schedule with nothing over 60mph, but with a signal stop outside Cologne Hbf, arrival there was 1½ minute late. Typical of the early post-war years, the 03.10s were performing long runs at moderate speeds while the German main line network was being restored to pre-war speed capability.

The locomotives were capable free-runners, but the boilers were showing signs of their age and were prone to needing frequent maintenance. Other locomotives with similar boilers were suffering significant failures and in 1955, a class 41 2-8-2 experienced a boiler explosion. Between 1956 and 1958, the West German locomotives were refitted with the high-performance all-welded boilers with combustion chambers, built and fitted at the Brunswick Works. The front skirt was also removed, giving easy access to the cylinders and motion, although hardly improving their appearance. The wide flat chimney as fitted to the reboilered 01s and

the coal-burning 01.10s was also fitted to the 03.10s. The 7,500-gallon water capacity tender was also provided with a coal cover and coal pusher. The rebuilding was costly, ranging from 159,000 DM to 175,000 DM, which rose to over 250,000 DM when normal overhaul costs were added (the currency exchange rate at the time was roughly four DMs to the pound).

The new boilers were not without their problems. Ludwigshafen had a mixture of old and new-boilered engines and between May and August 1957, the five new-boilered locomotives suffered sixteen failures requiring another locomotive's help or replacement, and twenty-six reports of serious delays caused by problems with the steam regulator. The regulator would stick in either the open or shut position. There was damage in the cylinders and many of the problems were ascribed to the crews' inexperience on these engines. Coal consumption was improved, but the engines gained a dubious reputation. In October 1962, 03.1013 was involved in a serious incident from this cause. The violent effort to open the regulator jerked the train and broke the coupling between the first and second vehicles, and while the crew got down to deal with this, the engine ran away, as it was later ascertained that the driver had failed to close the regulator fully. It ran into Hamm Station at 47mph and was diverted by the signalman to avoid a collision, but it derailed, causing considerable damage.

In order to familiarise the crews with the rebuilt locomotives, all were allocated to Hagen-Eckesey in the Ruhr from the 1958-9 winter timetable. With hand-picked crews, and good coal, and the engine in good condition, their performance on the road was excellent and they ran up some high mileages. Between February 1941 and August 1965, 03.1017 accumulated 1,875,000 miles. However, electrification of the Cologne-Wuppertal-Hagen-Hamm main line through the Ruhr in May 1964 and the Hagen-Siegen-Giessen line in May 1965 removed much of their work.

The first to be withdrawn was 03.1022 in April 1965 and four more – 03.1016, 1051, 1055 and 1082 – were also taken out of service that year. Efforts were made to offer the redundant locomotives to other

03.1081 after destreamlining after the Second World War, but before reboilering, c1953. (Herbert Schambach)

Destreamlined 03.1008 of Dortmund hurries E113 along the Rhine Valley near Oberwesel, 10 September 1950. (Carl Bellingrodt/Eisenbahnstiftung)

03.1014, repaired and de-streamlined, and in steel-blue livery after the Second World War, c1950. (MLS Collection/C.Bellingrodt/EK-Verlag)

motive power districts, specifically Hamburg, Hanover, Cologne and Münster, but there were no takers, the simplicity of the two-cylinder 01s and 03s being preferred. There was an edict in June 1965 that no members of the class were to receive L2 or L3 repairs and the remaining examples were all withdrawn at the end of 1966. The last turns in September 1966 were on the Kassel-Bestwig-Paderborn route, and the final day's working on 24 September 1966 saw 03.1050 on D80652 from Kassel, 03.1076 with E682 also from Kassel and finally, just before midnight, 03.1011 running light

03.1014 at Kassel, with all-welded boiler and combustion chamber, and nearing the end of its short life in this rebuilt form, 13 April 1965. (MLS Collection)

engine from Hamm off D424 from Hanover. Despite efforts to find them alternative work, nothing suitable had been found and they were prematurely scrapped. The DB found itself with a number of modern boilers from both the 03.10 and 18.6 classes, and many were utilised for several years as stationary boilers. The boiler of 03.1051 was used for 2-8-2 042.105, an oil-burner. 03.1001 stood for a number of months awaiting possible purchase for display by the city of Hagen, but the price asked was too high and the engine was scrapped.

For a log of my own run behind 03.1013 between Cologne and Aachen, see Chapter 18, page 327.

03.1055 at Hagen Hbf, May 1965. (Helmut Dahlhaus)

03.1073 on shed at Wuppertal Langerfeld with 2-10-0 50.1840, 9 April 1961. (Herbert Schambach)

A trailing view of 03.1084 displaying its covered tender, entering Wuppertal Oberbarmen, 12 June 1963.
(Herbert Schambach)

03.1017 leaves Cologne with a D-Zug for the Ruhr, c1965. All the DB-reboilered 03.10s were concentrated at Hagen Depot in the late 1950s until their mass withdrawal in 1966, after electrification of the Ruhr area in which they operated. Attempts to find alternative work for these modern coal-fired Pacifics were unsuccessful, and they were all cut up, although their East German contemporaries survived for a further thirteen or fourteen years.
(MLS Collection)

03.1008 at Schwerte Ost with E682 for Hagen and Dortmund, 20 March 1966. (Helmut Dahlhaus)

03.1014 hauls dead electric loco E.10.131 at Wuppertal-Oberbarmen, 25 September 1960. (Herbert Schambach)

03.1082 at Bestwig on a freezing morning (-18C) in the harsh winter of 1962-3, 24 February 1963. (Herbert Schambach)

03.1076 on the very last day of the Hagen 03.10s before their mass withdrawal, here at Warburg ready to take E682 to Dortmund as far as Hagen where it will drop its fire for the final time, 25 September 1966. (Helmut Dahlhaus)

East German 03.10s Design, Construction & Operation

At the end of the war twenty-four 03.10s were in the Soviet Zone of Germany and were distributed as follows:

Cottbus: 03.1002, 1019
Leipzig: 03.1010, 1046, 1088
Hadmersleben: 03.1012, 1021, 1045, 1050
Pasewalk: 03.1020
Berlin: 03.1048, 1085, 1089
Stendal: 03.1057
Güsten: 03.1058, 1059, 1075
Zwickau: 03.1074
Halle: 03.1077, 1079, 1087
Döbeln: 03.1078
Salzwedel: 03.1080
Neubrandenburg: 03.1090

With the adjustment of the Zone boundaries after the Yalta conference, the four 03.10s stored at Hadmersleben were appropriated by the West and 03.1002 was also acquired from Cottbus, leaving nineteen for the East German *Deutsche Reichsbahn*. By the end of 1946, seven of these had been repaired and returned to traffic, although by the end of the year this had dropped to five: 03.1059 and 1075 in Magdeburg; 03.1079 at Halle; 03.1085 at Berlin Grunewald; and 03.1088 at Leipzig. However, very few of the trains running were for the civil population, just twenty-three pairs of services, twelve of which were in the Halle / Leipzig area, which included the 03.10 diagrams. Some 03.10s, after repair, were used purely for Soviet military traffic movements. 03.1079 was dismantled to provide spare parts to keep other 03.10s running. At the end of 1951, the DR had just four active 03.10s, 03 1057, 1075, 1080 and 1088, all working from Leipzig West Depot. They all retained only remnants of their former streamlining, the running motion being clear for access.

One of the immediate problems for the railways in East Germany was access to reasonable steam coal, for the suitable coalfields lay in the Ruhr and in the province of Silesia which was now within the revised Polish post-war boundary. The coalfields in the east of the country produced only low-quality 'brown coal', for which the grate areas and fireboxes of the locomotives were unsuited. Ash content was high and there was an absence of sufficient air to allow proper combustion with the result that locomotives struggled to maintain steam. For example, one of the 03.10s that was active early in 1946 was 03.1046 which began operating from Halle, and in a six-month period burned five tons of coal for every 100 kilometres travelled, and 03.1010 in March 1949 as much as 5.3 tons per 100 kilometres, compared with the normal consumption of 1.5 tons per 100 kilometres with suitable steam coal. The brown coal very quickly turned to clinker.

Between 1952 and 1954, all eighteen remaining intact 03.10s had been given a 'general' overhaul, the first, 03.1087, leaving the Chemnitz Works in April 1952 and allocated to Berlin Rummelsburg. This engine was equipped to burn pulverised fuel following successful experiments with the Prussian 4-6-0 17.1119. However, there were many problems and the engine was stored in February 1953, before moving to Halle and finally Dresden in 1958, where the maintenance costs were said to be two and a half times greater than with the other 03.10s. In the meantime, the other 03.10s were repaired and the partial streamlined casing was removed, and some boiler exchanges were made. Seven of them, 03.1019, 1046, 1048, 1058, 1059, 1087 and 1090, received large 'Wagner' smoke deflectors and externally were indistinguishable from the two-cylinder 03s, apart from the piston from the inside cylinder visibly protruding through the centre of the running plate front skirt. From 1954, they were being widely used and high daily mileages were being achieved, with Leipzig's 03.1090 running on average 321 miles a day in July 1954, and most of the others between 250 and 300 miles. By 1957, thirteen of the class were stationed at Stralsund, running expresses from Berlin to the Baltic Coast resorts. In July 1954, 240 special Trade Union and Communist Party holiday expresses were run in addition to the normal timetabled

DR coal-burning
03.1087 *Erwin Kramer*, the only East German named locomotive. Erwin Kramer was East Germany's first Minister of Transport. 03.1087 was one of the guinea-pigs for burning pulverised fuel, experiments carried out at the Halle Research Centre in the 1950s when the supply of steam coal for the DR was difficult to obtain. 03.1087 was one of two DR 03.10s not converted to oil-burning and was withdrawn in 1971, 03.1087 is seen here during the pulverised fuel tests in Wünsdorf , c1952.
ZBDR/Hans-Jürgen Wenzel Collection)

services. From August 1958, the whole class – apart from 03.1010 which was at the Halle Test Centre – was allocated to Stralsund.

The East German 03.10s – like their West German sisters – were in need of new boilers. In fact, 03.1046 suffered a boiler explosion in October 1958 when working D78, Berlin-Prague-Vienna, and all the 03.10s apart from 03.1077 and 03.1088 were taken out of traffic (those two did not have their original boilers). The DR equipped their fleet with improved '*reko*' (reconstructed) boilers, with feedwater heaters obvious above the smokebox as was also the case for the DR two-cylinder 03s. The 03.10 that was used at Halle Test Plant equipped with counter-

East German reboilered three-cylinder 03.10 Pacific, 03.0077-2 at Stralsund with a relief D-Zug, D10513, for Berlin Lichtenberg, 12 April 1979. (Alastair Wood)

03.0048-3 stands at Berlin Ostbahnhof ready for departure with D270 Meridian Budapest-Sassnitz/ Malmö express, April 1979. (Alastair Wood)

03.0058-2 at Stralsund with D613 for Berlin Lichtenburg, 14 April 1979. (Alastair Wood)

Whilst still in DR regular traffic as an oil-burner, 03.0010-3 is on Stralsund Depot, April 1979. (Tim/Robin Morton)

pressure brakes, 03.1010, had a surface-type feedwater heater with the drum visible on the smoke box (as did 03.1074) and so presented a different front-end impression. 03.1010 was the first to emerge from Meiningen Works with the reconstructed all-welded boiler with combustion chamber in February 1959, and fifteen more by the end of 1959, with 03.1077 and 03.1088 not receiving new boilers until 1966. Although no technical trials or tests were made, the rebuilt engines had an additional 300 horsepower, giving a total power output of 2,100hp.

When the DR were able to realise their intention of equipping their most modern fleet of locomotives as oil-burners after the oil pipeline Soviet agreement was completed, all bar two of the East German 03.10s were equipped as oil-burners, thirteen between 1965 and 1967, the other three in 1970 (03.1080) and 1972 (03.1020 and 1048). After conversion they were numbered in the 03.00XX series with computerised check number, eg 03.1010 became 03.0010-3. The two remaining coal-burners, 03.1057 and 03.1087 (the latter now converted to conventional coal use), retained those numbers plus a check digit, and 03.1087 was used for various tests and became the only named German locomotive of modern times, *Erwin Kramer*, after the DDR Transport Minister who oversaw the recovery of the DR after the war.

03.1010 left Halle in 1974 and moved to Stralsund with the other members of the class that had been domiciled there for more than ten years, continuing to dominate the services north of Berlin towards the North Sea Coast for a further six or seven years. They hauled the heavy expresses between Berlin and Cottbus, Rostock, Putbus, Stralsund and Sassnitz, including the *Sassnitz Express* (Munich-Berlin-Stockholm), the *Berlinaren* (Berlin-Malmö) and the *Meridian* (Belgrade-Budapest-Prague-Berlin-Malmö). They were expected to move 500-ton trains at up to 75mph and recover lost time against the schedule with such heavy trains. Some of these trains over certain sections were the fastest on the DR, with D126 in 1971 averaging 65.6mph start-to-stop between Fürstenberg and Oranienburg. In comparison with the 01s and 01.5s on the fast Berlin-Dresden trains which had just one or two intermediate stops, the three-cylinder engines of Stralsund had at least six stops on their tightly-timed trains between Berlin and the North Sea Coast resorts. The oil-burning Pacifics could be up to seventeen hours a day in traffic and were reaching 653 miles a day in the 1969-70 timetable.

The first diesels of both 132 and the more powerful 142 class began to appear on some Stralsund turns in 1977, although the *Berlinaren* and *Meridian* remained steam-hauled

03.0085-5 at Neubrandenburg, 12 July 1979. (Graham Stacey)

03.0074, with feedwater heater drum on top of the smokebox (as for 03.0010 and 0074 only), at Berlin Ost having arrived from Sassnitz with the D271 *Meridian* to Prague and Budapest, 16 June 1974. (Helmut Dahlhaus)

03.0046-7 stands on the right awaiting departure from Neubrandenburg with D270 *Meridian* Budapest-Sassnitz and Malmö international express, while 03.0077-2 arrives with D613, Stralsund-Berlin Lichtenburg train, 13 April 1979. (Alastair Wood)

until 1979. The two coal-burning engines were withdrawn first, as early as 1971, but withdrawals of the oil-burning 03.10s did not start until 1977 (03.0089). 03.0078 was destroyed in a catastrophic head-on collision in June 1977 with a diesel-hauled freight whilst working the night D1918 Zittau-Stralsund. 03.0010, 0046, 0048, 0058, 0059, 0075, 0077, 0080, 0085 and 0090 lasted until the end of the 1979 summer timetable. Although most of the remaining Berlin-Stralsund expresses were dieselised with the summer timetable 1979, the express pair D1918/1919 Cottbus-Stralsund

03.0077 leaving Berlin and crossing the Landwehrkanal with D316 Berlinaren, 3 July 1976. (Helmut Dahlhaus)

03.0075-6 at Demmin on D610 Berlin Lichtenburg-Stralsund, 25 March 1978. (Alastair Wood)

remained diagrammed for the Stralsund 03.10s until the end of August. Six 03.10s lasted until the end of the year, 03.0075 and 03.0085 being withdrawn in February 1980, 03.0059 in March, 03.0080 in April and 03.0058 in May. The last steam-hauled Stralsund diagram finished on 31 May 1980 with 03.0010-3, which had been Stralsund's specially decorated engine for a number of years, and was then preserved as a heritage engine and reverted to coal-burning as 03.1010-2. 03.0090 has also been preserved.

For logs of my own runs between Berlin and Stralsund, see Chapter 18, pages 332–5.

03.0090 with D316 *Berlinaren* near Berlin Bellevue, 9 August 1975. (George Bambery)

03.0077, with D512 Berlin Schöneweide-Stralsund via Pasewalk, passes a Berlin metro on the northern Ring line, 17 April 1976. (Helmut Dahlhaus)

Oil-burning 03.0010-3 near Blankensee with a Stralsund-Berlin express, 5 May 1980. (Robert Kingsford-Smith)

03.0010-3 near Düsterförde with D814 Berlin Stralsund express (return working of the *Berlinaren*), May 1980. (George Bambery)

03.0010-3 gathers speed after a stop at Neustrelitz with the 9.17 Stralsund-Berlin, 5 May 1980. (George Bambery)

03.0046-7 on a seasonal express to the North Sea coast, D1919, at Schönfliess, a single-line section near Frankfurt/Oder that was the sight of a head-on collision between sister engine 03.0078 and a goods train a couple of years previously, 6 June 1979. (Wolfgang Bügel/Eisenbahnstiftung Collection)

Preserved Locomotives
03.1010

03.1010 was built in November 1940 by Borsig as a streamlined three-cylinder coal-burning Pacific. During the war years, it was allocated to Berlin Grunewald, Stargard and Breslau, and in 1945 was stored with other locomotives at Cottbus. It was then repaired and taken to Leipzig West in 1947, and was in operation there until 1952. At that time, it retained some of its streamlining. It was completely rebuilt in 1953, de-streamlined and allocated to the Halle Research and Test Centre until October 1974. During that period it received a reconstructed boiler in 1959 (the first 03.10 on the DR). It was converted to oil-firing in 1967 and in 1971 received a Giesl ejector. It joined its sister 03.10s at Stralsund in November 1974, working fast expresses to Berlin. Its counter-pressure brakes were removed in 1975 and Giesl ejector replaced by a conventional chimney in 1976.

It was the last Stralsund 03.10 to be withdrawn in June 1980, and was stored there until December 1981. In January 1982, it was rebuilt again as a coal-burner, changing its computerised number from 03.0010-3 to 03.1010-2, and, based at Halle once more, became an active 'heritage' locomotive, being used on many excursions. It took part in many *Plandampf* events in the 1990s and was given a thorough overhaul at Meiningen in 2011, allowing it to continue to operate special trains, with a maximum authorised speed of 87½mph. It has run over 164,000 miles in railtour special train work since 1982.

03.1015

After the Second World War, some 03.10s were retained in Poland becoming class Pm3. One numbered Pm3-3 (although in reality it ran as Pm3-5 on the PKP) has been preserved in partially restored streamlining and is displayed outside Warsaw's Railway Museum. Its original identity is uncertain, though believed to be 03.1015. It is painted in the PKP livery of jade green with a red horizontal stripe along the boiler streamlining. The red painted wheels and green cylinder covers are exposed.

03.1090

03.1090 was built in October 1940 and was one of eight allocated initially to Linz in Austria. In 1945 it was located at Neubrandenburg in the Soviet Zone and thus became a DR engine. It received a general repair, along with the other DR 03.10s, between 1952 and 1954 after which it came to Leipzig West. From 1957 it was stationed with a dozen other 03.10s at Stralsund. It was converted to oil-burning by 1967 and renumbered 03.0090-5 in June 1970. It was stored out of action at Stralsund in June 1979, withdrawn officially in November 1979, and saved from cutting up by the intervention of some Stralsund railwaymen, then purchased by someone in West Germany. It was cosmetically restored in 1985 and given a new lease of life in 1992 being acquired by the Deutsche Bahn Museum, with the ultimate intention of restoring it to working order, however currently (2016) it is outbased and displayed at Schwerin.

Preserved **03.1010** at Meiningen after overhaul, 1999. (Richard Spoors)

Chapter 14

THE *DEUTSCHE REICHSBAHN* 04

Design & Construction

In the early 1930s, the German Railways Headquarters officers were seeking to upgrade their express passenger services and set the designers of the main engineering companies a target of producing a steam locomotive with good acceleration and at least 80 tons of adhesion weight, to achieve and maintain 75mph on the level, or 37½mph on a 1 in 100 gradient, with heavy trains of 650 tons. A maximum speed of 85mph would also be the target. A number of experiments were developed, including 'Baltic' 4-6-4, 2-8-2 and 4-8-4 wheel arrangements, but there were some Pacific wheel arrangement experiments also with turbine propulsion (see Chapter 16 for a description of all these experimental engines built in the mid to late 1930s).

However, in 1932 the firm Krupp produced for the DRG what looked like a standard 01, but was a four-cylinder compound with a high pressure boiler of 330lbpsi, and the two prototypes built were classified '04'. Coupled driving wheels were a standard 6ft 7in, grate area 44sqft, a heating surface of 2,223sqft and superheater surface of 909.5sqft. The high-pressure inside cylinders were 13.8in x 26in and outside cylinders of 20.5in x 26in. The maximum axle load was just 18.9 tons and the engine weight was 106.3 tons plus a 7,000-gallon water capacity tender. They were the last four-cylinder compound locomotives built by the

04.001 was one of two high-pressure four-cylinder compound experimental locomotives built by Krupp in 1932.
(MLS Collection/Carl Bellingrodt/EK-Verlag)

02.102 (formerly 04.002). Both class 04 locomotives suffered severe failures and damage, and their boiler pressure was lowered to the standard, the engines now being nearly identical to the 02s, and were renumbered 02.101 and 102. It is seen here c1936, decorated with the Nazi 1936 Olympic insignia. Its sister engine's boiler exploded in April 1939, and both were scrapped by 1940. (DLA Darmstadt/Eisenbahnstiftung Collection)

German Railways after a tradition that went back to the nineteenth century and had its highpoint in the Maffei pacifics for the Bavarian and Baden State Railways in the first quarter of the twentieth.

Just the two locomotives were built, but they very quickly developed serious problems, especially around the firebox. After a number of repairs and reconstruction, the management was still dissatisfied, and in 1935 the boiler pressure was reduced to the standard 227lbpsi and the two engines were given numbers in the 02 series and numbered 02.101 and 02.102, as they now closely resembled those four-cylinder compounds. They were not rebuilt to conform with the 01 class, as were the 02s, and in April 1939 02.101's boiler exploded south of Weiden, near Rothenstadt (Oberpfalz). The crew were killed. 02.102 was taken out of traffic shortly afterwards and scrapped in 1940.

Chapter 15

THE *DEUTSCHE BUNDESBAHN* CLASS 10

Design & Construction

The *Deutsche Bundesbahn*, as part of its programme for a modernised steam locomotive fleet in the 1950s, included the design of a three-cylinder express passenger locomotive to replace the standard 01 Pacific and eventually the three-cylinder 01.10s as well. However, the design really came too late and only two of the new locomotives were built by Krupp in 1956 before it became obvious that further electrification supplemented by the V200 and V200.1 diesel engines was the way forward.

The new locomotives, 10.001 and 10.002, were semi-streamlined handsome machines and had some

The brand-new 'standard' post-war Pacific, 10.001, at the Krupp Essen Works after completion, coal-burning before conversion to oil fuel, 21 March 1957. (Eisenbahnstiftung Collection)

dimensions in common with the 01.10s. The coupled wheels were the standard 6ft 7in diameter, the three cylinders measured 18.9in x 28.3in, and the boiler was developed from the 01.10 boiler, with pressure raised to 256lbpsi. The heating surface was 2,326sqft, but the superheater was large with 1,136.3sqft heating surface. The axle weight was a heavy 22.4 tons and the engine weight in service was 118.9 tons, with an eight-wheel bogie tender with water capacity of 8,800 gallons. Theoretical horsepower of 2,500 was calculated and the authorised maximum speed was 87½mph.

10.001 was built as a coal-burner and was converted to oil in January 1958, before completing its tests at Minden Research Centre. 10.002 was built as an oil-burner. These locomotives should have been able to raise running performance

The second DB Pacific 10.002, built as an oil-burner, seen here ex-works at an unknown date. (Author's Collection)

10.001, the prototype 1956-built standard postwar Pacific, at Bebra with a train from Frankfurt-am-Main, c1965.
(MLS Collection/Photomatic)

DB Standard Pacific
10.002 at Kassel, 13 April
1965. The oil-burning
equipment on the
double-bogie tender is
very evident.
(MLS Collection)

10.001 shortly
before withdrawal
and preservation at
Braunschweig (Brunswick)
Works, 24 August 1967.
(MLS Collection)

to a new level, but because there were only two of them, it was not possible to change any main route timetables to exploit their potential and the 01.10s retained their monopoly of the 'Rollbahn' (Cologne-Hamburg) where the speed potential of the new engines might have had most impact.

The post-war Pacifics unfortunately suffered a number of failures causing major cylinder damage and both locomotives were withdrawn after a very short life in 1967-8.

Operation

After tests at Minden between March 1957 and March 1958, 10.001 was allocated to Bebra, before being reallocated to Kassel in September 1962. 10.002 was allocated to Bebra from its entry into service in April 1958, and both engines operated from Kassel until 10.002 was withdrawn in January 1967 and 10.001 in January 1968. They spent their entire ten-year life working heavy D-and E-Zug services on the Frankfurt-am-Main–Bebra-Hanover route. The 1961 timetable had two Bebra diagrams for the two locomotives – the first started with an overnight train from Bebra to Hanover, returning at 11.03am from Hanover back to Bebra, a three and half hour run, then the 6.15pm Bebra to Frankfurt. The second leg started from Frankfurt at 11.43pm with D75 to Kassel at 2.50am, then the 4.47am D476 back to Frankfurt, D283 10.28 Frankfurt-Kassel, D197 2.08pm Kassel-Bebra, D373 6.13pm Bebra-Kassel and finally 10.33pm D388 Kassel back to Bebra again.

I have not come across logs of

Kassel-Giessen
6.18am Wilhelmshafen-Basle, D184, 16.9.1966
10.001, 3 cyl oil-burning 4-6-2
11 chs, 416/455t

		mph		miles	
Kassel	00.00			0.0	2L
Kassel-Wilhelmshöhe	05.02	39		2.3	
Kassel-Oberzweren	08.22	61/58		5.2	
Rengershausen	10.05	50*		6.7	
Guntershausen	12.27	36*		8.6	
Grifte	14.52	55		10.4	
Wolfershausen	16.59	60½		12.5	
Altenbrunslar	19.10	58		14.6	
Gensungen-Felsberg	21.25	67½		17.1	
Wabern	24.59	67/69½		21.1	
Singlis	28.01	68½		24.6	
Borken	29.58	63½		26.7	
Zimmersrode	34.07	sigs 15*/45 ½ /SLW 35*		30.7	
Schlierbach	41.22	30* SLW ends		34.0	
Treysa	47.49	53/59		38.7	1 in 122 R
Wiera	51.11	57½		41.8	
Neustadt (Hessen)	53.41	55½		44.2	summit of 1 in 122
KM 77	59.33	33*/ SLW / 31*		47.9	
Stadt Allendorf	63.08	67 fast recovery		51.0	
Kirchhain	67.22	57*		55.5	
Anzefahr	70.20	69		58.6	
Bürgeln	71.58	72		60.5	
Cölbe	73.32	68		62.3	
Marburg	76.33	(67¾ mins net)		64.9	2½ L
	00.00			0.0	1¾ L
Marburg Süd	04.01	52		2.2	
Niederweimar	06.45	66		4.9	
Niederwalgern	08.40	58*		6.8	
Fronhausen	10.47	65½		9.0	
Friedelhausen	13.08	64		11.5	
Lollar	14.54	64		13.4	
Giessen	21.16			18.4	2L

maximum power output of either of the two locomotives, but have found just two runs recorded in 1966-7, months before their withdrawal, when the steam leg was restricted to the stretch between Kassel and Giessen, as the route further south onto Frankfurt had by then been electrified. The

log above is printed by courtesy of my friend Mike Hedderley who had extensive experience of locomotive performance recording on the continent.

The line follows river valleys and the speed restrictions indicated are for curvature. The best work was the climb of over 5 miles of 1 in 122

10.001, still coal-burning, working from Bebra Depot on a D-Zug between Frankfurt and Kassel, 12 April 1958.
(Eisenbahnstiftung Collection)

10.001, now converted to oil-burning, at Bad Sassendorf with E687 Kassel-Münster, 1 July 1967. (Helmut Dahlhaus)

to Neustadt and the fast recovery from the second bout of single-line working shortly afterwards.

The second run, timed by B. Harrison on 21 September 1967, was a short snippet between Soest and Münster on the 300-ton 06.59 Bebra -Rheine. It maintained a steady 66-67mph over much of the Soest Hamm section and just touched 70mph at Drensteinfurt on the twenty-five-minute run to Münster, averaging 68mph over six miles. Coal-burning 01.1072 of Rheine replaced it there for the last part of the journey. This was one of their last duties which also involved an Eilzug turn from Kassel to Münster – for a short time before

electrification, the Pacifics worked through to Rheine and turned there. Despite their late design and intensive testing before entering service, the two locomotives were disappointments, suffering from significant maintenance problems. In fact, they were so rarely both available for the two-day diagrams that a Kassel driver joked: 'Why are they both called 10.001 and 10.002? Because 10.001 is available on 1 day in a 10-day diagram, and 10.002, 2 days!'

10.001 was preserved after withdrawal – see below – but 10.002 was stored initially at Brunswick Works, then hauled to Kaiserslautern where it was rebuilt

as a stationary boiler. It took up duties in Ludwigshafen, then stored in 1971 and was scrapped in 1972 at Offenburg.

Preserved Locomotive
10.001
10.001 (allocated the number 010.001-6, but not carried before withdrawal in late 1967) was retained and externally restored at Kassel, and was exhibited at a number of exhibitions and depot 'Open Days' throughout the 1970s. In between these displays it was a static exhibit at the Deutsches Dampflok Museum, Neuenmarkt-Wirsberg, where it still resides.

10.001 displayed at an exhibition of DB rolling stock at Kassel Station in 1973. (Helmut Dahlhaus)

Chapter 16

FURTHER DEVELOPMENTS OF THE GERMAN EXPRESS PASSENGER STEAM LOCOMOTIVE

Turbine 4-6-2 T18.1001 Design, construction and operation

In the early 1920s, as the new *Reichsbahn* engineers were developing the standard powerful, but conventional Pacifics, strenuous efforts were being made to improve the efficiency of the steam locomotive. Such research led to the building, between 1923 and 1924, of a steam-turbine engine of the Krupp-Zoelly type. The main turbine for the forward direction of travel was over the front bogie. The drive was via gears on a lower reel and from there onto the coupled wheels. A second, somewhat smaller, turbine was provided for backwards movement.

The coupled driving wheels were 5ft 5in diameter, the boiler pressure was a conventional 213lbpsi, the heating surface 1,666sqft, superheater 710sqft, the turbine revolutions at 6,800 per minute, and maximum permitted speed 69mph. The weight of the engine in service was 112.4 tons and it was attached to an eight-wheel 4,290-gallon water

The Henschel steam-turbine locomotive at Seddin, in 1924.
(RVM/Eisenbahstiftung Collection)

Steam-turbine experimental locomotive T18.1001, built by Henschel, with part of the casing along the running plate covering the turbines removed to give easier access for maintenance.
(MLS Collection/C.Bellingrodt/EK-Verlag)

capacity tender.

In test runs, significant improvements in coal consumption were noted compared with conventional locomotives. The engine was in regular passenger service based at Hamm until 1939, then later, unfortunately, it was destroyed in a bombing raid.

The Henschel steam-turbine locomotive at Cologne Hbf, with 'bullet nose' smokebox door which was later replaced by a conventional door, c1925.
(Eisenbahstiftung Collection)

The Henschel steam-turbine locomotive, T18.1001, hauling a D-Zug in Wuppertal Elberfeld, c1925. (Eisenbahnstiftung Collection)

The Henschel steam-turbine locomotive, T18.1001, at speed working D4 Berlin-Cologne near Ennepetal-Milspe, 5 August 1935. (Carl Bellingrodt/Eisenbahnstiftung Collection)

A competing turbine-Pacific locomotive built by Maffei of Munich, T18.1002.
(MLS Collection/C.Bellingrodt/EK-Verlag)

Turbine 4-6-2 T18.1002

After the Krupp steam-turbine locomotive, the Maffei Company in 1926, also produced an experimental steam-turbine engine which was in many ways similar to T18.1001, but with a Ljungstrom turbine. T18.1002, as this locomotive was identified, was also different in the way in which the condensing apparatus was designed. However, the drive was similar to that of the Krupp locomotive via gears to the coupled wheels. Performance on the road was as good as expected, but no significant improvement in fuel consumption could be identified.

The dimensions of this locomotive included coupled wheels of 5ft 8in diameter, a high-pressure boiler of 313lbpsi, heating surface of 1,717sqft, superheater 548sqft and a maximum turbine revolution of 8,800 per minute. The weight of the locomotive was 104 tons and it was attached to an eight-wheel tender with a water capacity of 5,280 gallons.

After periodic introductions to express passenger train working, the locomotive was scrapped after receiving war damage in 1944. The high-pressure boiler was recovered and utilised until

The Maffei steam-turbine locomotice, T18.1002, at its Munich-Allach Works, 1926.
(Eisenbashnstiftung Collection)

1954 at the test centre at both the Munich-Freimann Works and at the Ingolstadt Works.

Rebuilt Pacific 18.201 Design & Construction

In order to test new locomotives and rolling stock after the Second World War, the Research and Testing Centre at Halle required some high-speed locomotives to act as counter-pressure brake engines. Although they acquired former Baden IV h 4-6-2 18.314 in exchange for S3/6 18.434, which found itself isolated in the east after the war, they had the frames and wheels of the pre-war high-speed 4-6-4 streamlined tank engine, 61.002. The East German *Deutsche Reichsbahn* also had a large 2-10-2, 45.024 and parts from this, the 'Baltic' tank and a boiler from a class 22 (a reboilered former Prussian P10 2-8-2) were combined into a new high-speed locomotive that the DR numbered 18.201. The locomotive was equipped with Riggenbach counter-pressure brakes, a Giesl ejector and semi-streamlining. The rebuilding took place in 1961, and in 1967 18.201 was rebuilt further as an oil-burner. It was renumbered 02.0201-0 in 1970.

The dimensions of this unique high-speed locomotive include the 7ft 6in coupled wheels from the Baltic tank, three 20.5in x 26in cylinders, a 227lbpsi boiler, heating surface of 2,218sqft, a large superheated area of 900sqft, and it was authorised for a maximum speed of 100mph (160km/hr).

Once its research centre work was no longer required, it was retained for enthusiast and other special trains. On a trial run on 11 October 1972, it

Gloggnitz-Wien (Vienna) Meidling,
15.50 Gloggnitz-Wien Nord öBB 150th anniversary special train, 10 Oct 1987
18.201 DR 3-cylinder oil-burner
6 chs, 227/250t

		mph		miles	Gradient
Gloggnitz	00.00	mph	5¼ L	0.0	Gradient
Pottschach	04.12	84/88		3.2	1 in 124 F
Ternitz	05.25	87/91/86½ *	5½ L	5.0	
Neunkirchen	07.18	89/92		7.5	
KM 59	08.43	100		10.0	
St-Egyden	09.29	93½ */99	5¾ L	11.2	1 in 105 F
		91*/ sigs 45*/ pws			
Wiener Neustadt	14.59	41*	7¼ L	16.7	1 in 494 R
Wiener-Neustadt Nord	17.18	58½		18.4	
Theresienfeld	18.47	69½		20.0	
Felixdorf	20.25	77½	8¾ L	22.0	1 in 387 F
Sollenau	21.04	81/85		22.8	
Leobersdorf	23.18	63*	8½ L	25.6	1 in 213 F
Bad Vöslau	25.22	73/ sigs 25*	8¾ L	27.8	
Baden	29.26	52	10¾ L	30.5	1 in 672 R
Gumpoldskirchen	32.41	68 ½		33.8	
Guntramsdorf Südbahn	33.25	71/75		34.6	
Mödling	35.32	73½	11¾ L	37.2	1 in 269 R
Brunn-Maria Enzersdorf	36.44	69½	12L	38.6	
Liesing	38.35	65	11¾ L	40.7	1 in 769 F
Attgersdorf-Mauer	39.23	63/68½		41.5	
Hetzendorf	41.01	sigs 55*		43.4	
Wien Meidling	44.29	sigs 5*	12¾ L	44.43	

reached 113.3mph. In October 1987, as part of the Austrian Railways 150th anniversary, at the suggestion of two British enthusiasts, Mike Hedderley and David Sprackland, a high-speed run with steam power was arranged between Gloggnitz and Wien Meidling, a 44-mile stretch of railway authorised for 125mph running for test purposes. Special authority was given for high-speed running on this occasion with some suitable rolling stock and Mike Hedderley's record of the run is printed above.

Net time for the 44½ mile run was one minute less than the 37-minute schedule at an average start-to-stop speed of 74.1mph. In

the year 2016 it was the only steam engine in the world officially still authorised to run at 100mph.

Preserved Locomotive 18.201

18.201, renumbered 02.0201-0, was retained for special trains following its retirement at Halle Test Centre. It was purchased from German Railways AG in 2002, and was repainted red, sponsored by the model-making firm, Roco, between 2002 and 2005, and then restored to its original dark green livery and number 18.201. Operational at 'Dampf Plus', Nossen, in Saxony.

18.201 at Halle when it was utilised as a test locomotive at the Research Centre, 1961. It was rebuilt as a three- cylinder Pacific with 7ft 6in-diameter driving wheels from pre-war high-speed 4-6-4T 61.002, and is still operational as a preserved locomotive and authorised to run at 100mph.
(MLS Collection)

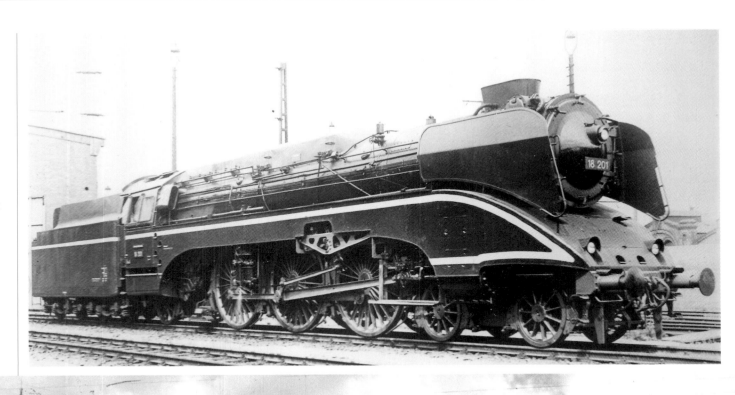

Preserved 18.201 at the North Bridge, over the Elbe, near Dresden Neustadt station.
(Roger Bastin)

18.201 on railtour duty near Unterloquitz, 8 May 1992. (Roger Bastin)

02.0201 performs a photo 'runpast' on a railtour at Orlamunde, 28 August 1983.
(Graham Stacey)

Saxon 2-8-2 19.0
Design & Construction

Despite the success of the three-cylinder simple Pacific, the Saxon Company developed a more powerful express 2-8-2 locomotive, but reverted to the traditional four-cylinder compound layout. The class was given the XX HV identification, and twenty-three locomotives were built between 1918 and 1925, numbered 19.001-023.

Dimensions of this machine included 6ft 3in coupled wheels (the same as the Pacific), 18.9in x 24.8in inside cylinders and huge 28.4in x 24.8in low-pressure outside cylinders, heating surface of 2,440sqft, superheater surface of 796sqft and 213lbpsi boiler pressure. The axle load was a light 17.2 tons maximum and the locomotive itself weighed 99.9 tons, and was coupled with an eight-wheel tender with 6,800-gallon water capacity.

The 2-8-2s performed strongly, capable of an indicated horsepower of 1,800, their maximum permitted speed was 75mph, but the valve gear and motion suffered from frequent damage and difficulty of maintenance.

Twenty of the locomotives were still in active operation in 1945, all in the eastern part of Germany, allocated to Dresden and Reichenbach. Just three examples remained in 1968, 19.017 in its original condition which was preserved for display at the Dresden Altstadt Museum, and two, 19.015 and 19.022, which received new boilers and were converted to oil burning for use at the Halle Research and Testing Centre. 19.022 was withdrawn from service at the end of 1974 and scrapped at Meiningen Works in October 1975. 19.015 was withdrawn at the same time, but was not officially condemned until October 1976.

A 19.0 2-8-2 on test on a Munich-Stuttgart train at Munich Hbf in 1922. (MLS Collection)

A **splendid** portrait of Saxon 2-8-2 19.001 nicknamed '*Sachsenstolz*' ('Pride of Saxony'), c1936.
(MLS/Carl Bellingrodt/EK-Verlag)

19.011, XX HV 2-8-2, c1935.
(MLS Collection/Carl Bellingrodt/EK-Verlag)

19.011 at Dresden Hbf on a
D-Zug for Leipzig, 1929.
(MLS Collection)

19.007 hauling D222 in
Freital-Potschappel, 31
May 1936.
(Werner Hubert/
Eisenbahnstiftung)

19.017 as displayed at Dresden Altstadt Open Day, 2 May 1997. (MLS Collection)

Preserved Locomotive 19.017

The Saxon 2-8-2, 19.017, built in 1919, was withdrawn in 1968 and restored in its original condition, and displayed at the transport museum at Dresden Altstadt.

Streamlined 2-8-2 19.10 Design & Construction

In the 1930s and early 1940s, many experiments were being made by the DR to improve the efficiency of the basic steam locomotive. One, built in 1940 and numbered 19.1001, was a unique design, influenced by the E18 electric locomotive which had drive on each axle. Henschel built this steam locomotive with a steam generator driving each main axle. Each steam motor was a two-cylinder 11.8in machine built in a V shape. The locomotive had the wheel arrangement 2-8-2 with the centre four axles independently driven, each of these wheelsets being 4ft 1in in diameter. It had a high-pressure 284lbpsi boiler, heating surface of 2,577sqft, very high superheat of 1,075sqft. The maximum axle-load was 18.7 tons and the locomotive without tender weighed 109.3 tons.

The engine was streamlined in the same style as the 01.10 and 03.10 Pacifics, had a theoretical 1,700 horsepower and a potential maximum speed of 110mph. After a number of test runs, which were not very successful at first, the locomotive was released into normal express train operation in 1943, and demonstrated excellent performance in the circumstances of the time, until it was damaged by a bomb in 1944. After the war it was

Experimental streamlined 2-8-2 individual axle-driven locomotive 19.1001, built by Henschel in 1940. (MLS Collection/Carl Bellingrodt/EK-Verlag)

19.1001, seen here at the Henschel Works in 1940. (RVM/Eisenbahnstiftung Collection)

retrieved as it stood and deported to the USA. There it was overhauled and, after being exhibited in various locations, was broken up in 1952 in the State of Virginia.

High Speed 4-6-4 05
Design & Construction

At the beginning of the 1930s, high-speed developments with electric and diesel traction were at the fore, but efforts were made to develop high-speed steam traction also. Initially a lightweight standard Pacific, 03.193, was streamlined, and when this appeared successful, Borsig built the streamlined 4-6-4s, 05.001 and 05.002, in 1935.

The locomotives had three 17.7in x 26in cylinders, coupled wheels of 7ft 6in diameter, a 284lbpsi boiler, grate area of 50.6sqft, a heating surface of 2,747sqft and a large superheated area of 968sqft. The maximum axle load was 19.4 tons and the engine weight was 129.9 tons, excluding the ten wheel tender with its 8,140-gallon water capacity. The locomotives were fully streamlined to virtually ground level, the valve gear and motion being accessible for maintenance via sliding shutters in the streamlining. The theoretical horsepower of 2,360 was calculated and a maximum speed of 110mph in normal traffic was stipulated.

On 11 May 1936, on a special test train, 05.002 achieved a world speed record for steam locomotives of 200.4km/hr (125mph). A cylinder performance indicating that 3,400 hp was reached was the high point of German steam locomotive development. The record was only just eclipsed in 1938 by the British LNER A4 streamlined Pacific, 4468 *Mallard*, which reached 126mph on the descent of Stoke Bank between Grantham and Peterborough on the East Coast main line. On special demonstration runs in 1936 during a visit to Germany by the Institute of Locomotive Engineers, 05.002 achieved a speed at 111mph between Wittenberge and Ludwigslust, albeit only with a load of four coaches (141 tons gross). On the return demonstration it ran the 70 miles from Wittenberge to a signal stop east of Nauen in 48½ minutes, with speed sustained between 90 and 102mph over 57 miles. In 1938 05.001, on a six-coach train of 275 tons gross on a Berlin-Hamburg FD train, averaged 87.8mph over the 24 miles from Nauen to Neustadt and 89mph from Ludwigslust to Hagenow

The experimental individual axle driven 2-8-2, 19.1001, on D42 operating from Bebra Depot on the Frankfurt/Main-Erfurt route, seen here at Hönebach, 9 July 1942.
(R Kreutzer/Eisenbahnstiftung Collection)

firing restored. After the war when it was urgent to repair as many locomotives as possible, small classes like the 05s looked likely to be overlooked and withdrawn. However, 05.003 was further reboilered and repaired in 1950 in conventional form, and the other two locomotives followed suit; all three were allocated in 1951 to the depot at Hamm. For a time, the three locomotives were regular performers on the longest through steam diagram in Europe, the 439-mile Hamburg-Cologne-Frankfurt-am-Main route of F3/F4 Merkur long-distance express. The locomotives remained at Hamm until prematurely withdrawn from traffic operation in February 1958, replaced by diesel traction, with little work left where the power of these engines could be adequately utilised to offset the cost of maintaining such a numerically small class. The three engines were

05.002, which achieved a world record top speed of just over 125mph on 11 May 1936, seen here at Hamburg Altona whilst undertaking various tests just prior to the world speed record attempt, April 1936. It held this record until *Mallard* achieved 126mph in 1938.
(Walter Hollnagel/ Eisenbahnstiftung Collection)

Land with a maximum speed of 93mph.

Borsig followed this success in 1937 by a third 4-6-4 of revolutionary appearance, 05.003. Although of similar engineering dimensions, the cab was built onto the front to improve the crew's vision, the smokebox was at the rear and the tender followed. The locomotive was built with a steel firebox and combustion chamber, and designed to burn pulverised fuel. The locomotive was stoker-fired. After a number of problems with the combustion, the machine was returned for modifications to the air/ coal supply mix, but problems

The record-breaking streamlined 05.002 at speed on FD 23 Hamburg-Berlin, passing the station of Anmühle between Bergedorf and Friedrichsruh, 1938.
(Carl Bellingrodt/A.Gottwaldt Collection)

continued. The locomotive was rebuilt on conventional lines and de-streamlined in 1944, and normal

05.002 on a 271-ton test train organised by the RZA (research centre) Grunewald, achieving a speed of 112½mph near Zernitz between Berlin and Hamburg, 23 July 1935. (DLA Darmstadt/Eisenbahnstiftung Collection)

officially condemned in July 1958.

Former senior railway manager Gordon Pettitt, when doing his national service in Germany in the early 1950s, recorded a number of runs behind 01s and 03s in the Hanover area, and was lucky to get a couple of short runs behind the rebuilt 05s on train F112 with through coaches from Warsaw, Berlin and Leipzig to Cologne and Paris. On 11 March 1953, 05.003 with 9 coaches (382 tons net, 410 gross) was heavily delayed by signals between Lindhorst and Stadthagen after steady running in the mid-60s over the previous ten miles, and lost four minutes on the

43-minute schedule for the 40 miles between Hanover and Minden, regaining a minute and a half on

the next ten mile section to Bad Oeynhausen. 05.001, on 15 March 1953, on a 392-ton train (425-tons

The record-breaking streamlined 4-6-4, 05.002, seen here in a state of disrepair after the Second World War. It was then repaired, reboilered and de-streamlined, and operated in that form for a few years before withdrawal, and sister locomotive 05.001 was restored in streamlined form and dark red livery at the Nuremberg Railway Museum. (MLS Collection)

The record-breaking 05.002 after reconstruction and de-streamlining in 1951, stationed with its two sister locomotives at Hamm, before withdrawal in 1958. (MLS Collection/Carl Bellingrodt/EK-Verlag)

gross) was unchecked, keeping time exactly to Minden, averaging 62mph over the 30 miles from Dedensen to Buckeburg with a top speed of 68mph, arriving at Bad Oeynhausen a minute early.

05.001, sister of the record-breaking 05.002, was restored to its pre-war splendour, streamlined and in a deep red livery, and is a prize exhibit of the German National Railway Museum in Nuremberg.

Streamlined 4-8-4 06 Design & Construction

The most powerful express locomotive of the DR was developed in 1936 although the two locomotives, 06.001 and 06.002, were only delivered in traffic in 1939 by the engineering firm of Krupp. They were 4-8-4s with standard 6ft 7in coupled wheels, three 20.5in x 28.4in cylinders, and a high-pressure boiler of 284lbpsi. Grate area was 51.8sqft, heating surface covered 3,100sqft and a

05.002, de-streamlined after the war, standing at Solingen-Ohligs with a D-Zug working towards Wuppertal, 1955. (Klaus Feller/Eisenbahnstiftung Collection)

DR streamlined 4-8-4, 06.001, an extended version of the 05 4-6-4, designed initially in 1936, but not delivered until 1939, damaged during the war, stored in 1945 in Frankfurt-am-Main and scrapped in November 1951. (RVM/Eisenbahnstiftung Collection)

DR streamlined 4-8-4, 06.001, demonstrating its extreme length which restricted its operation in the DRG network and, after bomb damage in December 1944, was stored and withdrawn immediately after the Second World War. (MLS Collection/Carl Bellingrodt/EK-Verlag)

The streamlined 4-8-4 06.001 at Hanau working the D43
Basle-Berlin between Frankfurt/Main and Erfurt, March 1939.
(Dr Joachim Feisal/Eisenbahnstiftung Collection)

large superheater of 1,424sqft was fitted. The maximum axle load was 20 tons and the engine weight was 141.8 tons exclusive of the ten-wheel 8,360-gallon water capacity tender, and a massive 224 tons when included full of water and 10 tens of coal.

The calculated tractive effort was 51,500lb, 2,800 hp, and the maximum authorised speed was 87½mph. The locomotives were streamlined in the same style as the 01.10s. Unfortunately such power was of little use at that period, as the need was met by the 01s and 01.10s, and a number of serious defects and problems with the high-pressure boiler meant that the will to spend much effort correcting these for such a small class was not worthwhile.

Both locomotives suffered damage during bombing raids towards the end of the war and as a result they were not repaired after 1945, but were withdrawn and finally scrapped in November 1951.

Chapter 17

FOREIGN PACIFICS AND OTHER EXPRESS LOCOMOTIVES ON GERMAN RAILWAYS

After the First World War, many German locomotives were taken to foreign railways as war reparations. In the course of the Second World War, after the German invasion of France, some of these were recaptured and taken back to Germany. Many other French locomotives, especially those of the former Alsace Lorraine operating area, were commandeered by the German authorities and ended up after the war in the Soviet Zone, where they remained initially under Soviet control, then later as the property of the *Deutsche Reichsbahn*. On 25 April 1949, SMAD (*Sowjetischen Militäradministration* in Deutschland) in *Befehl* (command) 43 demanded an inspection of all locos, both German and foreign, and decisions on whether to overhaul or not. 7 October 1949

was the founding date of the DDR (German Democratic Republic) and end of the Soviet occupation.

We can conclude from *Befehl* 43 that up till that time and presumably for some time afterwards, there was no comprehensive record of locos physically in the Soviet Zone. However, at the end of 1949 there was now a coherent management structure for the railways under a German administration, rather than a left-over from the days of the Third Reich under Soviet military command. They, no doubt, wanted to get a Socialist grip on what would have still been a fairly chaotic situation. The SNCF seemingly took a census of its loco stock in 1950, no doubt recognising that since the Cold War had set in by then, any locos in Eastern Europe wouldn't be coming back.

No less than 306 ex-Alsace-

Lorraine locomotives were never to be seen again in France, out of a total of more than 800 for SNCF as a whole. Of course, Alsace-Lorraine engines would have been especially useful in that they had right-hand drive and were mostly of German design anyway. A few of these were Pacifics, as noted below, extant and in the Soviet Zone of Germany in 1945.

SNCF 231A (Alsace Lorraine S12 class)

The S12 four-cylinder compound Pacifics were built at Grafenstaden for the Alsace Lorraine Company in 1909 and numbered 401-408. The eight locomotives were renumbered in 1912 as 1301-1308 and were allocated SNCF numbers 231A 1301-1308. Two locomotives were stored in the Soviet Zone of Germany at the end of the war. All the locomotives remaining in France had been withdrawn by 1950.

231A 1302: Was based at Engelsdorf and allocated CFL No.3701, but remained in East Germany until scrapped in November 1955.

231A 1304: Was based at Leipzig, allocated CFL No.3702, but remained in East Germany until scrapped in January 1956.

SNCF 231B (Alsace Lorraine S14 class)

This class of four-cylinder compound Pacifics was built in 1922 by Fives Lille as part of an order by the *État*, also owned at that time by the French Government. 1311 to 1350 were delivered to the AL in 1922 with right-hand drive. 1351 to 1370 were delivered originally to the PO, but diverted to the AL in 1929 and 1933. They retained left-hand drive. Most of the S14s in Germany were those with right-hand drive. The locomotives remaining in France after the war had all been withdrawn by 1957. All those outside France were written off by the SNCF in March 1950, although they remained on the DR as indicated below:

231B 1315: Based in 1945 at Gerstungen, and withdrawn by the DR in August 1956.
231B 1327: At Saalfeld in 1945, and withdrawn in March 1956.
231B 1328: At Zeitz in 1945, and withdrawn in December 1955.
231B 1329: At Leipzig in 1945, and withdrawn in November 1955.
231B 1333: At Zeitz in 1945, and withdrawn in December 1955.
231B 1353: At Gera in 1945, and was the class last survivor, being

withdrawn in 1958.
231B 1366: At Zeitz in 1945, and was withdrawn in January 1955.

SNCF 231C 63 (Est Region 231-063)

The Est Railway of France had twenty-three Pacifics, numbered 231-051-073, that had been PO 3500 series, rebuilt for the PO-Midi in 1934. They were renumbered in 1938 by the SNCF as 231C 51-73. 231C 63 was the sole member of this class found after the war in the Soviet Zone, stored at Engelsdorf, but it was severely war damaged and was scrapped without being repaired sometime after 1945.

SNCF 241D 44 (PLM 4-8-2)

145 4-8-2 express passenger locomotives were built by the PLM Railway between 1925 and 1931, and 48 of them were modernised by André Chapelon in 1932, becoming 241D in 1938. 241D 44 was in the Soviet Zone of East Germany after the war, stored at Naumburg in 1945. It was reported as operating from Erfurt Depot in 1952, and was withdrawn and scrapped in 1956.

The original 241A class were 4-cylinder compounds, with 5ft 11in coupled wheels, 227lbpsi boiler, grate area of 54sqft and 2,752sqft heating surface. Its maximum speed on the SNCF was 69mph.

07.1001 (Ex-SNCF Nord Region 231E 18)

This Pacific locomotive was constructed in 1912 as Paris-Orleans Railway 3580 as part of a batch built 1909 to 1914. It was rebuilt by André Chapelon in the 1930s and was transferred to the

Nord Railway with a number of new-build Chapelon four-cylinder compound Pacifics, becoming 3.1188 and later 231 E18 with SNCF. They operated out of the Gare du Nord from La Chapelle Depot to Calais and the Belgian border and this example was taken by the German authorities after the fall of France in 1940. After the war, it remained in the Soviet Zone at Stralsund and was experimentally converted to burn pulverised fuel, using a built-up standard DR tender. This was at a time when only very inferior coal was available in the DDR for transport use, and experiments were made using both 'brown coal' and pulverised fuel. It was of particular interest to the DR for the pulverised coal experiments because of its long grate. It was rebuilt by the DR works in Stendal, converted to right-hand drive and handed over to the DR for service on 6 July 1952. While it first worked out of Bw Berlin Ost, it was transferred to Bw Dresden Altstadt in 1954 to work D trains between Berlin and Dresden. As a one-off and with its complex inside motion, it wasn't liked by either the operating or maintenance staff and was withdrawn on 4 February 1958. However, its SNCF high-capacity tender was retained and attached to former Saxon 'Mikado' 19.017, which was the last example in unrebuilt form and was subsequently preserved, but with an original Saxon tender.

The Chapelon 231E Pacifics on the Nord Region remained in service on the Calais-Amiens section until the mid-1960s when they were replaced by ex-PLM

Ex-SNCF **Chapelon** pacific 231E18, retained in East Germany after the Second World War, converted experimentally to burn pulverised fuel and renumbered 07.1001, c1955. (MLS Collection)

Ex-SNCF 241A 4, retained by the DR after the war , renumbered 08.1001 and used for experiments with pulverised fuel. It worked expresses between Berlin and Dresden in the 1950s, and was withdrawn in 1957. (MLS Collection)

231G and 231K Pacifics. 231E 22 has been preserved as 3.1192 in Nord Railway chocolate-brown livery at the SNCF national railway museum at Mulhouse and 231E 41 has also been privately preserved in SNCF dark-green livery.

08.1001 (Ex-SNCF Est Region 241A 4)

Although not a Pacific, this 4-8-2 locomotive has its place in the development of DR express passenger locomotives in similar fashion to 07.1001. It was built by the Est Railway in their works in Épernay in 1925 as 41004, and used with other members of its class on the main routes from Paris Gare de l'Est to Strasbourg and Basle, and in 1938 became SNCF 241A 4. It was of particular interest to the DR for pulverised coal experiments

because its boiler had a combustion chamber. It was converted by the DR works in Zwickau , rebuilt with right-hand drive, and handed over to the DR for service on 30 June 1952, initially based at Stralsund. It was the only SNCF loco appropriated by the DR to retain its original smoke deflectors and cab. The chimney extension provided was similar to that on 01.10s. On emerging from Zwickau works in 1953 after conversion to RH drive, replacement of ACFI water heater by a Knorr model, round buffers instead of squared ones, electric lighting, extended chimney, new tender for pulverised coal and modified ashpan, it was sent first to Halle Testing Centre then allocated to Berlin-Ostbahnhof before being transferred to Dresden-Altstadt in 1954. It was withdrawn on 4

February 1958 because of cylinder defects. However, it could still be seen stored at Altstadt Depot awaiting scrapping as late as 1963.

The last SNCF examples remained at work on heavy *rapides* between Paris and Mulhouse (about forty miles short of Basle), based at Chaumont midway on the line until the early 1960s. The prototype, 41001, later 241A 1, was withdrawn in 1959 and is now displayed in the 'City of the Train' Museum at Mulhouse in Eastern France. One further example, 241A 65, was purchased privately and is preserved in operating condition in Switzerland, making a few rare outings for railway enthusiast special trains.

18.601 (PKP Pm36)

Two Pacific locomotives were ordered by the Polish Ministry of Transport in 1936, the first, Pm36-1, was streamlined and the second, Pm36-2, in conventional form. Both locomotives were absorbed by the DRG during the war after the invasion of Poland, and renumbered 18.601 and 602. The streamlined locomotive was

08.1001, stored out of use with a number of Saxon 18.0 Pacifics, at Dresden Altstadt in 1960. (Eisenbahnstiftung Collection)

destroyed in Germany by enemy action around 1942 and scrapped; the remaining locomotive at Berlin Grunewald, renumbered 18.601, was moved after 1944 to storage in Austria and from there was returned to the PKP in 1947, as Pm36-1. It was withdrawn in 1970, restored to special service in 1995 in its original identity, Pm36-2, and named *Piekna Helena* (*Beautiful Helena*). It was said to be a difficult engine to fire, partly because of the distance between the tender and the firehole door, and had a very healthy appetite for coal. It completed its boiler certificate for operation in 2012 and now is stabled at the Warsaw Railway Museum.

Another photo of 18.601 (ex-PKP Pm36-2) at Berlin Grunewald, 1944.
(Robin Garn's Collection)

A rare and illicit photograph of the unstreamlined 18.601 (former Pm36-2) at Berlin Grunewald Depot, 1944.
(Robin Garn's Collection)

Chapter 18

PERSONAL EXPERIENCES OF GERMAN PACIFICS, 1958 – 1979

The Bavarian S3/6 18.4-5 & rebuilt 18.6

I was a German language and literature student at London University, and my studies required me to register at a German university for the summer vacation of my second year in 1959. I chose Munich, despite my knowledge that it was at the heart of the *Deutsche Bundesbahn* electrified network. However, after a twenty-four-hour journey and a second sleepless night on Munich's Hauptbahnhof (all the hotels I could afford were fully booked), I thought I was hallucinating when I was confronted at the bufferstops early the next morning by the bullet nose, huge outside cylinders and flared chimney of a steam locomotive. This 'apparition' was so unlike my earlier experiences of German steam engines further north.

It was, of course, as I soon realised, one of the former Bavarian State Railways S3/6 four-cylinder compound Pacifics, rebuilt in the 1950s with a high-performance all-welded boiler. Thirty of the 1926-30 DRG-built engines, constructed to fill the gap before the light axle-weight 03 Pacifics were ready, had been transformed and nearly all of them were based at Lindau on the edge of Lake Constance ('*Bodensee*') on the German/Austrian/Swiss border. After a belated registration for my course, I made my way back to the city's main station to explore further and discover the key trains likely to be worked by these unique locomotives. As well as the three or four daily international trains to Zurich or Geneva, which these class 18.6 engines worked as far as Lindau, I discovered a useful late-afternoon Eilzug to Memmingen (E826) which I could just about afford to take to its first stop – Munich-Pasing, only some ten minutes away, but passing the main Munich electric and steam locomotive sheds en route.

Within a week I was escaping from my study of Thomas Mann's novels to learn the language at the station and made my first trip out behind 18.606, rebuilt from the Henschel 1930-constructed 18.535. The trip was not long enough to get more than 45mph, but the compensation was a good view of the sheds and a return trip behind a P8 4-6-0 hauling tender-first a long train of suburban six-wheelers. I soon became addicted to this habit, and lined up trips behind 18.603, 606 (again), 609, 611, 612 (twice), 618 (twice) and 630 (twice). As the course continued and I economised by avoiding other student temptations – the Munich beer halls – I was confident to splash out on tickets to Buchloe, some forty miles distant, though usually eschewing the D-Zug services for which a two-mark supplement was payable.

In the last couple of weeks of my course, I calculated that I could be more ambitious, and cut my day's serial lecture on *Death in Venice* and arose early to catch the first Eilzug for Freiburg behind 18.617 which

The author's first run behind a rebuilt Bavarian S3/6 compound, 18.606 (formerly 18.535) at Munich Hbf with E826, 16.35 Munich-Memmingen, July 1959. (David Maidment)

18.481 stands at Buchloe (on the right) with an evening Augsburg-Oberstdorf Eilzug, waiting to follow 18.611 on the D98 Munich-Geneva D-Zug, August 1959. (David Maidment)

ran energetically and was early at all points, although the line speed to Buchloe was only 62mph. On one of my earlier trips to Buchloe, I had discovered the existence of an evening Eilzug from Augsburg to the Bavarian Alps resort of Oberstdorf, which had steamed into the station behind an original unrebuilt S3/6, 18.481 (Maffei 1923), for which I had hastily bought a ticket to Kaufbeuren, some fifteen miles distant. I subsequently repeated this, getting 18.516 and 18.528 (Krauss-Maffei 1927-28), connecting off the 18.6-hauled E826 from Munich. I therefore set off on an early-morning train, E766 07.30 Munich-Freiburg with 18.617 (ex-18.548 Henschel 1930) and planned to change to a morning Augsburg-Oberstdorf Eilzug in the hope of another 18.4/5 (a driver had told me that the last seven unrebuilt Maffei Pacifics were all based at Augsburg). However, to my surprise the heavy train was hauled by a former Prussian Railways-designed three-cylinder P10 2-8-2, 39.227, whose staccato roar as we climbed the fir-tree-lined cuttings to the summit at Günzach was stirring to hear. At Kempten's dead-end station (the former Hauptbahnhof), 18.626 backed on to take the train forward to Immenstadt where it would split, the coaches for the holiday resort being detached by a class 64 2-6-2T or an 86 2-8-2T, whilst the S3/6 would continue with the remaining four coaches to Lindau.

I caught the next Eilzug back from Kempten with another P10, 39.184 (one of two now preserved), and alighted at Buchloe to try my luck on a stopping service to

18.626 (Henschel built 18.546 in 1930) stands at Kempten (Allgäu) station, having backed onto E689 Augsburg-Oberstdorf, which had been brought from Augsburg by Prussian P10 2-8-2 39.227, August 1959. 18.626 will take the full train to Immenstadt where the Oberstdorf portion will be removed by a class 86 2-8-2T or 64 2-6-2T, the remaining four coaches being hauled by 18.626 to Lindau. 18.626 will return to Munich that evening with the last D-Zug of the day from Lindau. (David Maidment)

Augsburg which sported 18.618 (yet again). However, at Augsburg, a smart 1923-built 18.483 backed onto the same five coaches and we trotted back to Buchloe, just stopping at Schwabmünchen without exceeding 50-55mph – but on time (see photo page 59). I finished a very satisfactory (but expensive) day on the last evening D-Zug (D195 from Zurich) back to Munich, having rejected a heavy Eilzug doubled-headed by 18.616 and 18.625. The D-Zug appeared behind 18.626 (ex-18.546, Henschel 1930), which I'd seen heading in the other direction at Kempten, and a punctual run was made to the Bavarian State capital, non-stop from Kaufering, covering the 35 miles in fifteen seconds less than the 44-minute schedule.

With just a week to go, I attended enough lectures to get my certificate for attending the course and decided to gather my final coins together for a last trip to Buchloe, determined to go out in style on the evening D-Zug. However, my first effort was aborted when a Munich-based P8 backed onto the six lightweight Swiss coaches, presumably after the failure of a Lindau 18.6. I tried again the next day, my last chance before my homeward journey, and got the last one, 18.630 (the rebuilt 18.543), which reached Buchloe comfortably in a few seconds under the scheduled fifty-four minutes without exceeding 62mph. I returned punctually with 18.621 (ex-18.526 Maffei 1928) on an Eilzug from Lindau and made my farewells, determining to return this way again when I could better afford it.

I got my chance to return two years later. I had joined British Railways and had been accepted as a Management Trainee after a year's clerical work, and had qualified for my first continental free passes. I just had a week's leave owing, so it was a brief but action-packed visit. I travelled through France by steam most of the way (an *Etat* Pacific from Dieppe to Paris, ex-PLM Pacifics from Paris to Troyes and Troyes to Mulhouse) and, after a V200 through the Black Forest, and a class 50 2-10-0 and a Baden 2-6-2T along the north bank of Lake Constance, I spied 18.620 at Friedrichshafen and tumbled into its train (an Eilzug from Ulm) for the last leg into Lindau. I was met there with the sight of 18.629 on a D-Zug for Munich and 18.607 on D75 for Kiel, which the rebuilt S3/6 would take just as far as Friedrichshafen where an 03 would take over for the run onto Ulm (photo, see page 93). After this second mini-trip on the latter,

Kaufbeuren-Kempten, 1961

13.48 München-Lindau [Geneva] D96 *Rhône-Isar*
18.8.61
18.610 Lindau [18.523 built Maffei 1927]
9 chs, 352/395t

		mph		
Kaufbeuren	00.00		T	0
Biessenhofen	05.57	49		
Ruderatshofen	08.59	56		
Aitrang	12.09	51		
Günzach	20.05	pw 28*		
Wilpoldsried	26.40	83/56*		
Betzigau	28.37	65		
Kempten-Hegge arr	35.16		5E	27

08.39 Lindau/Oberstdorf-München E689
18.8.61
18.602 Lindau [18.547 built Henschel 1931]
11 chs, 426/445t

miles			mph	
Kempten Allgäu	00.00			½ L
Betzigau	08.22	42		
Wilpoldsried	10.39	53		
Günzach	19.39	42/69		
Aitrang	28.19	44*/53		
Ruderatshofen	31.39	62/25*		
Biessenhofen	36.39			T
	00.00			
Kaufbeuren arr	07.09			T

18.610 (formerly 18.523) at Munich Hbf with D96 *Rhône-Isar* which it will haul to Lindau, August 1961. The author travelled to Kempten Hegge on this journey, recording his highest speed behind an 18.6 of 83mph descending from Günzach – the class was officially restricted to 75mph. After withdrawal in 1962, 18.610 was retained as a stationary boiler in Lindau until being selected for trials with central automatic coupling and tests at the Minden Research Centre from 1967. The front-end and wheel-set has been preserved, and is in the Deutsches Dampflok Museum in Neuenmarkt-Wirsberg. The remainder of the engine was scrapped in 1976.
(David Maidment)

I checked into the Hotel Helvetia on the harbour front and quickly discovered the Lindau Shed just behind the Station, the roundhouse full of rebuilt Maffei Pacifics, whilst the water of the lake lapped the pathway by the engine shed low wall.

The next morning, I watched a number of Pacifics being prepared and turned whilst I dipped my feet into the water on a glorious August day. I had just time to take a return trip right through to Munich before my schedule needed me to start my return journey. 18.613 (the former 18.536) came off shed for the first up Eilzug (E689) for Augsburg, which would be a four-coach load to Immenstadt where it would pick up a number of through coaches from Oberstdorf. The Pacific made light of the gradients in the Bavarian Alp foothills (47mph minimum on the steepest gradient) and then accelerated its eleven-coach 440-tons gross load after Immendstadt to a full 75mph, recovering a three minute late departure before the reversal in Kempten Hauptbahnhof. 18.602 (formerly 18.547, Henschel

Lindau to Immenstadt, 1962

16.28 Lindau-Munich D95, 14.7.1962 — 18.602, Bw Lindau — 6 chs, 219/240t

09.33 Lindau-Munich D91, 15.7.1962 — 18.614 Bw Lindau — 7 chs, 272/285t

16.28 Lindau-Munich D95, 16.7.1962 — 18.622 Bw Lindau — 6 chs, 214/225t

Station	Time	mph	L	Time	mph	L	Time	mph	L	miles
Lindau Hbf	00.00	mph	12L	00.00	mph	5¾ L	00.00	mph	2¼ L	miles
Aeschach	03.18	33/24		03.05	29		02.58	32		
Oberreitnau	12.18	37		11.13	38		10.08	40		
Rehlings	16.15	37½		14.55	41		13.32	43		
Schlachters	18.07	43/45		16.43	40/51		15.15	45/52		
Hergensweiler	20.56	51/47		19.24	53		17.53	55/51		
Hergatz	25.01	56½		23.16	60		21.42	60		14½
Wohmbrechts	26.42	48		24.55	45		23.23	47		
Heimenkirch	33.45	43/pw 37*		32.07	38/pw 28*/37		30.23	42/pw 37*/39		
Röthenbach	38.35		12L	37.30		5¼ L	35.43		½ E	
	00.00			00.00		5½ L	00.00		¼ L	
Harbatshofen	07.10	37pw 29*		07.35	34/pw 27*		07.24	35/pw 27*		
	-	50		-	49		-	48		
Oberstaufen	14.14		13¼ L	14.43		7L	14.48		2L	
	00.00			00.00		7½ L	00.00		2L	
Thalkirchdorf	04.07	55/68		04.34	53/65		04.39	49/65		
Ratholz	08.24	sigs 14*		07.37	57*		07.49	55*		
Bühl	12.13	60		-	62		11.09	61		
Immenstadt	14.12		12L	12.32		5L	13.04		T	45

The four-cylinder Bavarian compound Pacifics were extremely economical especially in the heavily-graded lines of the Bavarian Alps, the summit of this section being at Oberstaufen. The Pacifics would work throughout to Munich (138 miles) via Kempten Hegge, which obviated the need to reverse in Kempten Hbf.

1931) backed on for the run to Augsburg. It ran noisily up the gradients to Günzach and I baled out at Kaufbeuren to join the 09.33 D91 Lindau-Munich which had left Geneva in the early hours. 18.615 (ex-18.529, Krauss-Maffei 1930) arrived punctually and made light work of the D-Zug's six Swiss coaches, touching 74mph through Kaufering and 69 at Geltendorf, although line speed restrictions thereafter meant no higher speed than 65½mph. The 43 miles from Buchloe were covered in just under forty-seven minutes and arrival at Munich Hbf was a minute early.

I'd intended to hang around for a while in Munich and visit some of my old haunts, but the sight of 18.610 (formerly 18.523 built by Krauss-Maffei in 1927) standing ready at the head of D96 *Rhône-Isar* was too much and I took it right through to Immenstadt (it was routed via Kempten-Hegge, thus avoiding reversal in the Hauptbahnhof). I was rewarded with an excellent run and my highest speed behind an S3/6, which hurled us down the gradient from Günzach at an estimated (illegal) 83mph. After that it was an anti-climax to complete the run to Lindau with just four coaches of an Augsburg-Oberstdorf/Lindau Eilzug behind 18.604. I left Lindau the next morning on

a train for Singen behind a pair of P8s, but I determined to return the following year and use my full leave entitlement with a round tour of Germany over a full two weeks. I give, on the previous page, extracts of the logs of the runs from Lindau to Munich and back that August day.

I persuaded my colleague from University College London, Alastair Wood, to join me the following year – I benefitted not only from his company, but also from his more professional and accurate train-logging skills. We again travelled through France with steam – Chapelon Pacific 231E 38 from Calais to Amiens, and a

Lindau to München, 1962

09.33 Lindau-München Hbf
(00.55 Geneva), D91, 17.7.62
18.614 Lindau (18.532 built Henschel 1930)
6 chs 228/240t

		mph		miles
Lindau Hbf	00.00		T	0
L-Aeschach	03.15	30		
Oberreitnau	10.54	31/40		
Rehlings	14.28	38/43		
Schlachters	16.13	50		
Hergensweiler	18.56	56/53		
Hergatz	22.42	63		14½
Wohmbrechts	24.16	51		
Heimenkirch	31.07	46/ pw 27*		
Röthenbach	36.44		1¾ L	
	00.00		¾ L	
Harbatshofen	07.40	32/ pw 24*/51		
Oberstaufen	14.47		2½ L	
	00.00		3 L	
Ratholz	07.47	60/50*		
Bühl	11.12	60		
Immenstadt	13.11		2 L	45
	00.00		½ L	
Seifen	05.14	44*/62		
Oberdorf	08.11	47*/59½		
Waltenhofen	11.31	49*		
Kempten-Hegge	14.15		¼ E	
	00.00		T	55 ½
Betzigau	09.22	44/ pw 19*		
Wilpoldsried	11.25	62		
Günzach	19.00	50/39		
Aitrang	26.10	61/43*		
Ruderatshofen	28.27	59 ½		
Biessenhofen	31.40	66/53*		
Kaufbeuren	35.58		T	82
	00.00		T	
Leinau	05.05	55		
Pforzen	06.56	64		
Beckstetten	10.05	60/52*		
Buchloe	15.43		¾ L	
	00.00		1½ L	95
Igling	06.36	63		
Kaufering	09.15	pw 29*		
Schwabhausen	16.48	66		
Geltendorf	19.20	59 ½		
Grafrath	25.25	55/60		
Fürstenfeldbruck	31.28	56		
Puchheim	35.57	64		
Aubing	38.47	59½		
Pasing	41.02	62		133
Mü-Laim	43.00			
München Hbf	47.16		1 ½ E	137

241P 4-8-2 and an Est 241A from Paris to Mulhouse and, avoiding the V200s on the Black Forest railway, took a P8-headed Eilzug from Basle via Schaffhausen in Switzerland through to the shores of Lake Constance. Looking out at Friedrichshafen, after spying 18.620 there the previous year, I was surprised and very pleased to catch a sight of what seemed to be an unrebuilt S3/6 backing on to a train from Ulm which was reversing at Friedrichshafen. I persuaded Alastair to alight and we watched as 18.508, the Seddin 1924 exhibition engine 3709, made a brake test and prepared for departure. We both enjoyed the trip behind this famous engine round the shores of the lake at a steady 60mph. We loitered at Lindau to watch the locomotive back out of the Station and run to the Shed. A chat with the driver gave a more realistic view of the condition of the engine which externally looked fine. Apparently the engine was known by local crews as the 'Saunalok' as it had a propensity to fill the cab with steam whilst running! In fact, it only had weeks to go before it was withdrawn, leaving just 18.528 as the last representative of the original S3/6s, and that would be gone before autumn was over.

The afternoon was spent watching the movements in the Lindau Roundhouse, reassuringly still inhabited by a flush of 18.6s and a couple of P8s, without a diesel in sight. We took a quick evening trip out to Immenstadt behind 18.602 and returned with P10 2-8-2 39.122. We stayed in the area for a couple more days and included some mountain walks after a visit to Oberstdorf and repeated our evening trips to Immenstadt and back, giving us some more 18.6 runs over the most scenic and interesting part of the route. We returned to Lindau on the two days with 18.605 on the Lindau four coaches of E690 (Augsburg-Oberstdorf/Lindau) and 18.614 on D98 Munich-Geneva. The main interest was the climb from the east to Oberstaufen on which the P10 (also with just four coaches on E690) made the fastest start, but it was recovering a seven-minute late departure from Immenstadt, whereas the two S3/6s were running on time. The speeds at the summit were 45mph (39.122), 46mph (18.605) and 43mph (18.614 with 6 coaches). The P10 was allowed to run up to 65mph on the descent, braking frequently for the curves, and ran into Lindau on time. The other two took it more easily without exceeding 62mph, and both arrived early.

After another night at the splendid Hotel Helvetia, our plan was to go through to Munich on D91, reaching there in time to catch D673, the *Tirol Express*, which had been an 01 throughout from Munich to Würzburg back in 1959. 18.614 backed on to the D-Zug of

Swiss and German coaches which had been brought in from Bregenz by an ancient Austrian electric locomotive, and we took our places for the run right through to Munich, timed by Alastair – see the log on the opposite page.

After our punctual arrival and a quick bite at one of the Hauptbahnhof's cafeteria, we joined the *Tirol Express,* whose route had now been electrified. Our motive power was an old Bavarian electric, E16.06, and we were to be

18.508, the 1924 exhibition locomotive, and the last built to the Bavarian Railway order before the DRG contracted the building of a final forty locomotives for work in central and north Germany, seen here running to shed at Lindau after hauling D76 from Kiel on its last leg round Lake Constance (*Bodensee*) from Friedrichshafen, July 1962. This engine was nicknamed the '*Saunalok*' by its drivers because of its propensity to fill the cab with steam. It was withdrawn a month later in September 1962.
(David Maidment)

18.614 has charge of the morning 09.33 D-Zug from Lindau, D91 Geneva-Munich, seen from the train as it climbs the Bavarian Alps foothills towards Oberstaufen, 17 July 1962. (David Maidment)

disappointed that our steed from Treuchtlingen was not one of that depot's 01s that I had promised Alastair, but V200.008 which dawdled through the countryside (a diesel locomotive that has since been preserved, as has V200.033 which was my locomotive through the Black Forest the previous year). However, enough for now – that run behind 18.614 was my last run (and sight) of a German four-cylinder compound, and we both lingered at the bufferstops in the grand hall of Munich Hauptbahnhof, taking a good hard look at the imposing and

distinctive front end of the engine simmering quietly after its punctual and efficient run. This was, I was to find out later, the last summer that the D-Züge from Switzerland were steam-hauled, a few V200s from Kempten depot took over the express services in the winter of 1962-3, while the 18.6s continued for two or three more years on the semi-fast and stopping services to Kempten and Munich.

DB 01, DR 01 & 01.5

In 1958, I was in my second year of my German language and literature course, and that April the department year group was introduced to German art and literature culture at a centre in Bad Harzburg, in the Harz mountains very close to the Brocken and the East German State border. The students had a special coach on the *Holland-Skandinavien Express* to Osnabrück hauled by a Rheine 03 from the Dutch border at Bentheim. We changed into another special coach attached to a P-Zug that trotted across to Löhne during the late evening behind a P8, and then sat in the yard until D119 Cologne-Berlin rushed in, a train onto which we were shunted by a class 50 2-10-0. I caught sight of the locomotive of the D-Zug in the darkness and, from the light from the corridor, I just made out a front numberplate with a jumble of 0s and 1s. I wrote 01.010 in my notebook, and alighted quickly at Hanover where we had to change and dashed along the length of the seventeen-coach train to confirm, but it had already disappeared into the night and I found 01.1087 backing on for the trip to the

East German border. I assumed that I had misread the number and that it had probably been an 01.10, one of 01.1001, 1100 or 1101, but I later discovered that D119 was diagrammed for a Hanover 01, not an 01.10, and that 01.010 was actually based at Hanover at that time, so my quick note was probably correct.

After trips to and from Bad Harzburg behind 03s and a cultural visit to Goslar, where most of the students visited the castle and I stayed by a level crossing photographing P8s, class 50 2-10-0s and 01.017 on a Brunswick-Hanover train, we returned the way we had come, with another overnight Hanover-Löhne journey on the equivalent D-Zug from Berlin. This time I know it was an 01, for I have a photograph to prove it – albeit a very blurred one in the darkness. I stood beside 01.161 as it waited for the arriving D-Zug. However, my photo is of insufficient standard to be reproduced here, so the photo of 01.161 at Bremen taken a few years later will have to suffice.

My next encounter with an 01 Pacific was in the summer of 1959 on my way to the course at Munich University referred to earlier. My journey from Ostend was mostly behind electric traction with short interludes of steam haulage. A Belgian 'American' S160 2-8-0 took us from Liège to Aachen and an 03 then to Cologne. Electric and diesel traction down the Rhine Valley to Wiesbaden and a reversal there produced 01.171 for the short run to Frankfurt-am-Rhein before another reversal produced electric traction all the way to Munich (behind prewar 2-D-2s of class E18).

Most of my time in Munich was spent enjoying the presence of the rebuilt Bavarian compound Pacifics, but I did note the odd 01 Pacific arriving with expresses from Nuremberg via Treuchtlingen and Ingolstadt. After admiring 01.037 at the Munich main station, I ventured out as far as Dachau (not realising the significance then of that notorious location, now a peaceful country village) behind a P8 and got another of Treuchtlingen's well-kept Pacifics, 01.102, the first of the later series of 01s with larger diameter bogie wheels and higher-authorised maximum speed. The train was an Eilzug and made no great demands on the power of the locomotive, but during my hour or

so at Dachau, I'd been impressed by 01.052 roaring through at full throttle with the lunchtime *Tirol Express* for Würzburg, Cologne and eventually Ostend. I made a decision there and then that I would catch that train back to Ostend at the end of my course.

The *Tirol Express* at the end of August appeared a few minutes late behind electric locomotive E04.018 and I was surprised to see two steam locomotives backing down with a bogie parcels vehicle onto the seven-coach passenger accommodation. The power was clearly not for the load, but presumably to get the Würzburg P8, 38.3346, back to its home depot. It was marshalled inside what was obviously the

diagrammed Würzburg Pacific, 01.046, one of the five 01s rebuilt in 1950 with a feedwater heater positioned rather clumsily above the engine's smokebox. In contrast to the obvious energy and speed of 01.052 a few weeks earlier, our progress seemed laboured and at around the steady 55-60mph, a strong fore-and-aft motion was obvious in the first coach, presumably from the P8 rather than the 01. We left late, just maintained the somewhat easy schedule, gained a few minutes during the station stops, but lost them again because of a long p-way slack and arrived a disappointing seven minutes late at Würzburg after the 173-mile run. I give an outline of the run below, but it was far from

01.161 of Bw Hanover leaves Bremen with a E-Zug for Hamburg composed of DB 1950s rolling stock, June 1967. 01.161 hauled the author's train overnight from Hanover to Löhne, during the UCL German Department visit to Bad Harzburg in April 1958. (MLS Collection/J. Davenport)

Munich-Würzburg, 1959
D273 *Tirol Express* 13.30 Munich (01.44 Bologna), 30.8.1959
01.046 Bw Würzburg (1928 Henschel)
38.3346 Bw Würzburg (1921 Breslau)

8 chs, 305/325t		mph		miles
Munich Hbf		00.00 (late departure shunting postal/parcels vehicle to train) 7L		0.0
Mü-Allach		09.51	50	6.2
Dachau		14.12	63	11.2
Walpertshofen		-	59½	
Röhrmoos		20.24	57	16.9
Esterhofen		22.31	61	19.0
Petershausen		26.10	62	22.7
Paindorf		28.45	55	25.1
Reichertshausen		31.01	59	27.4
Pfaffenhofen		34.33	64	31.0
Walkersbach		38.05	65½	34.64
Wolnzach		40.59	70	37.6
Hög		-	66	
Reichertshofen		48.39	61	45.3
Oberstimm		51.51	51	48.2
Ingolstadt	arr	55.20		5½ L 50.6
	dep	00.00		6 L 0.0
Ingolstadt Hord		04.13	40	2.1
Gaimersheim		08.27	49	5.6
Eitensheim		11.38	47	8.3
Tauberfeld		14.23	45	10.3
Adelschlag		18.31	61/ pw 5*	13.7
Eichstätt		23.15	22	16.7
Obereichstätt		26.45/27.25 (Special stop)		18.8
Dollnstein		33.47	61	23.1
Solnhofen		38.23	70½ / 50* curvature	27.6
Pappenheim		42.18	49*	30.8
Treuchtlingen	arr	48.00	(42 net)	11 L 34.9
	dep	00.00		9 L 0.0
Wettelsheim		-	50	
Markt Berolzheim		07.20	59	5.0
Ehlheim		09.21	62	7.1
Windsfeld-Dittenheim		11.41	63	9.5
Gunzenhausen		17.12	57	14.8
Altenmuhr		21.25	60	18.6
Triesdorf		25.10	pw 25*	22.3
Winterschneidbach		31.02	46	26.4
Ansbach		37.18	62/30*	32.1
Lehrberg		43.37	57	37.3
Rosenbach		46.40	56	40.1
Oberdochstetten		51.10	56	44.3
Burgbergheim		57.16	61	49.9

Steinach		59.25	50*			51.9
Ermetzhofen		64.42	59½			56.1
Uffenheim		68.48	60			60.1
Herrnberchtheim		73.02	53			64.1
Gnötzheim		75.42	57 / pw 25*			66.4
Obernbreit		79.41	67			70.0
Marktbreit		80.33	69			70.9
Ochsenfurt		84.05	63			74.4
Gossmannsdorf		-	59			
Winterhausen		88.50	55			78.9
Rottenbauer		90.31	56			
Randersacker		94.45	pw 12*			82.8
Würzburg-Heidingsfeld		96.04	49½			83.7
Würzburg-Sud		99.05	45			86.0
Würzburg Hbf	arr	102.32	(97 net)		7½ L	87.6

Both engines blew off steam on occasions, but speed was limited by the official authorised speed of the P8 at 62mph. Both locos shut off steam on downhill sections, the P8 working hard on rising gradients with much black smoke. Strong fore-and-aft oscillation felt in the train.

the best run I had behind an 01.

After the disappointment of a V200 instead of an 01 Pacific from Treuchtlingen to Würzburg during my 1962 round-Germany trip with Alastair Wood, we waited in vain for steam northwards, though with the help of the platform train formation diagrams we identified a D-Zug from Fulda to Bebra with an 01.10 on a train for East Germany, and then from Göttingen we picked up a D-Zug from Frankfurt for Hanover and Hamburg which ran in behind a grubby, down-at-heel 01.064. Progress was sluggish and by this time I was not really forming a good opinion of the standard 01 class. We lost fifteen minutes waiting for a late-running connection at Kreiensen, which we

failed to regain thereafter.

After overnighting in Hanover, Alastair and I turned up in hope next morning to see what was running to Hamburg, our next port of call on our planned itinerary.

D81, the *Alpen Express*, a heavy fifteen-coach train weighing 630 tons gross, rolled in doubled-headed by an 01.10 and P8 which were replaced by two standard Pacifics, 01.111 leading 01.043, and

01.046 of Würzburg, with feedwater heater and 'defrocked' front running plate, at Munich Hbf, double-heading P8 38.3346 on D673 *Tirol Express* to Ostend, which the pair will work as far as Würzburg via Ingolstadt and Treuchtlingen, 30 August 1959. (David Maidment)

Göttingen-Hanover, 1962
D73 Basle-Hamburg, 18.7.1962
01.064   Bw Hanover
11 chs, 418/460t

		mph			miles
Göttingen		00.00		5¾ L	0.0
Bovenden		-			
Nörten-Hardenberg		09.05	57/66		6.4
Südheim		12.22	64/66½		10.1
Northeim	arr	14.54		5L	12.2
	dep	00.00		4L	0.0
Edesheim		06.32	59		3.8
Salzderhelden		10.15	48		7.4
Kreiensen	arr	16.40		1½ L	12.4
	dep	00.00 (wtg connection)	12L		0.0
Freden		09.18	61/65		6.3
Alfeld		14.50	66/pw 25*		11.9
Brüggen		20.38	60/63		16.6
Banteln		22.35	62/66		18.6
Elze	arr	26.43		14¾ L	22.4
	dep	00.00		13½ L	0.0
Poppenburg		04.27	48		2.0
Barnten		09.15	63		6.3
Sarstedt		12.00	68/65		9.1
Rethen		15.25	70		13.1
Grasdorf		-	pw 28*		
Hanover-Wülfel		19.03	54		16.3
Hanover-Bismarckstrasse		21.55			18.6
Hanover Est		24.50/26.00 sig stand			
Hanover Hbf	arr	28.50 (26 net)		15½ L	20.6

A heavy packed train, but the 01 was sluggish from rest and struggled to maintain net time against schedule, seemed to lose its way after the Kreiensen delay.

the two of them rollicked away with the heavy load, sustaining 75mph-plus over the flat landscape through Celle and Lüneberg Heath to arrive virtually on time in Hamburg. The run timed by me with Alastair's assistance is logged on the page opposite.

We saw few 01s during the rest of our trip round north Germany, 03s to Kiel and back, 01.10s to Cologne, then southwards behind P10 39.232 and DB post-war 23.023 to Frankfurt. After more wanderings, we arrived at Crailsheim and picked up a Nuremberg-Stuttgart D-Zug, D232, in the morning behind an 01 with the all-welded boiler and combustion chamber, 01.182. However, our load was only four coaches, so we were unable still to really assess its capability. We stopped at Ellwangen, Aalen, Schwäbisch Gmünd and Schorndorf, and arrived on time without exceeding 65mph anywhere. The rest of our tour of Germany that year was made behind a succession of P8 4-6-0s before returning once more from Basle with SNCF steam power

01.043 arrives at Hamburg Hbf with a D-Zug from Hanover, June 1967. This locomotive, coupled with 01.111, brought the heavy overnight *Alpen Express* from Hanover to Hamburg in scintillating fashion during the author's circular tour round the DB network in July 1962.
(MLS Collection/J. Davenport)

Hanover-Hamburg, 1962
D 81 08.23 Hanover *Alpen-Express*
01.043 & 01.111 (leading) , both Bw Hanover

14 chs, 598/630t		mph			miles
Hanover Hbf	00.00		9¼ L		0.0
Anderten-Misberg	08.56	59/63			5.3
Lehrte	14.53	pw 26*			10.2
Aligse	16.43	52			12.1
Burgdorf	20.09	66			15.4
Otze	22.38	70½			18.3
Ehlershausen	24.43	75			20.6
Celle	31.23	pw 22*			27.7
Garssen	36.53	59			30.0
Eschede	43.36	66/61			36.8
Unterlüss	50.23	66			44.0
Suderburg	56.53	75			51.6
Klein-Süstedt	59.13	77			54.6
Uelzen	62.20	75/65*			58.5
Emmendorf	65.45	71			62.4
Bevensen	69.06	66/76			66.4
Bienenbüttel	73.50	72			72.3
Deutsch Evern	77.47	68*/70			76.9
Lüneburg	80.50	60*			80.4
Bardowick	84.22	66			84.1
Winsen	91.56	63			92.3
Ashausen	94.35	63			95.6
Stelle	96.33	59			97.1
Maschen	99.05	59			99.7
Meckelfeld	100.39	60			101.2
Hamburg-Harburg	105.53/107.18		sig stand		104.1
Veddel	-	16*	v. slow entry		108.9
Hamburg Hbf	122.50	(112 minutes net)		3L	111.6

A cheerful 'runaway' effort with little apparent effort from the two standard 01s, one of which, 01.111, was one of the last survivors at Hof over ten years later.

---

from Mulhouse in the shape of another 241A, the same class as East German 08.1001, commandeered by the German Army during the war.

The rest of the 1960s was spent experiencing the last steam expresses in Britain and France, and it was 1972 before I ventured to Germany again with a Locomotive Club of Great Britain (LCGB) tour in the Friesland and Ruhr areas behind various classes - 011, 012, 044, 050 and 055 – but no 01. By this time, the only 01s remaining were working from Hof and responsibilities for a new young family restricted my availability for long periods overseas. I did take a few short breaks between 1973 and 1975 on the Emden line, where the last 012 oil-burning three-cylinder Pacifics were working out their days in

exhilarating form. It was not until 1979 and my first visit to the DR in East Germany that I encountered an 01 again, and it was in the form of the reconstructed 01.5s, rather than the standard 01s which I'd unfortunately missed on their Dresden-Berlin swansong, though Alastair Wood had tried to entice me there before it was too late.

I did make one trip to East Germany before all the worthwhile main line steam activity came to an end. It was April 1979; the winter had been harsh in North Germany and I was fortunate that trains had started running again to Stralsund on the Baltic Coast, as until the week before most of the steam turns north of Berlin were cancelled while repairs were carried out on the ravaged track which had been blocked by snow for several weeks. The most memorable performances were by the three-cylinder 03.10s of which more later, but my first trip north had landed me in Stralsund just in time to catch D717 back to Berlin. An ex-works oil-burning 01.0530-4, still with gleaming red paintwork and unsullied black, stood at the head of a train of eleven standard DR lightweight coaches. Alastair Wood had warned me not to expect anything energetic on this train, but the 01.5 surprised me from the start by accelerating the train up to 78mph within a dozen miles of Stralsund. Apparently, much of the route in the south through Greifswald had only just been doubled and line speed raised from 62 to 75mph. The train stopped every twenty miles or so and the 01.5 made very sharp start to stop times as far as Pasewalk, where the engine took water and

Stralsund-Berlin, 1979

14.57 Stralsund Hbf-Pasewalk (Berlin Lichtenberg) D717

		18.4.79			22.4.79				
		01.0530-4 Pasewalk			**01.0535-3 Pasewalk**				
		12 chs, 383/410t			11 chs, 354/380t				
Stralsund Hbf		00.00	mph	T	00.00	mph		T	0 miles
Wüstenfelde		09.04	59		08.39	56/65			
Miltzow		12.19	64		11.46	61			
Jeeser		15.21	67/75		14.51	68			
Mesekenhagen		17.21	78		17.13	63			
Greifswald	arr	21.30			22.07				19.4
	dep	00.00			00.00	01.58/03.15 sigs stand			
Greifswald Süd		02.55	54		05.45	48			
Gross Kiesow		08.51	69		12.42	70			
Züssow	arr	13.00			15.46				30.6
	dep	00.00			00.00				
Klein Bünzow		06.12	69		05.37	72			
Anklam	arr	12.10			11.10				41.3
	dep	00.00			00.00				
Ducherow		08.50	65		-	60/63			
Borckenfriede		12.10	75/60*		12.22	70/44*			
Ferdinandshof		16.32	65		17.02	60			
Jatznick		20.50	66		21.17	67/60			
Sandförde		23.38	67		24.14	64			
Pasewalk	arr	28.08		2E	28.26			1E	67.5
	dep	00.00		T	00.00			T	
Nechlin		09.13	65/61		09.29	54/59			
Dauer		12.27	73		13.07	60			
Prenzlau	arr	17.34			18.48				
	dep	00.00			00.00				
Seehausen		08.58	68		09.15	60/68			
Warnitz		11.55	70/65		12.18	61			
Wilmersdorf		16.52	59/63		17.21	54/67			
Greffenberg		-	74		-	75/72			
Angermünde	arr	24.58			25.29				
	dep	00.00			00.00				
Herzsprung		05.13	54/58		04.59	55/57			
Chorin		10.21	66		10.20	61			
Britz		14.20	75		14.29	71/66			
Eberswalde	arr	17.42			17.49				
	dep	00.00			00.00				
Melchow		09.21	50/55		09.22	50			
Biesenthal		10.55	66		11.02	66			
Rüdnitz		13.56	66½		14.08	64			
Bernau	arr	17.44			18.42				
	dep	00.00			00.00				
Zepernick		04.41	58		04.14	69			

Berlin-Buch	-	63		06.42	72	
Karow	-	sigs 3*/ 60		09.17	sigs 15*	
Springfühl	19.05	63		16.52	70/ 50*	
Friedrichsfelde Ost	21.03			18.40		
Berlin-Lichtenberg arr	24.32		2L	21.35		T

01.0530 ex-works, and driven unusually hard for this train and route. 01.0535 was driven hard from rest, but then eased when 60-70mph was reached.

the crews changed. Afterwards, progress was more normal and we arrived in Berlin Lichtenberg a few minutes late. A few days later, I repeated the experience and got the alternating 01.5 on this two-day diagram, 01.0535-3, which performed very competently and punctually without the fireworks of the previous day. Later in the trip, I returned to the north and nearly chose to ride behind another of Pasewalk's 01.5s, 01.0507, but the opportunity was on a packed overnight train from Berlin to Stralsund, and I was already shattered from some long days' activities and chose my tourist hotel, the Berolina, which the Communist authorities had allocated to me instead. I did have a go one evening at the Eilzug (E314 *Gydania*) for Szczecin (Stettin) and Gdansk (Danzig) as far as Angermünde where the line for Pasewalk and Stralsund turned off, and got Berlin Ost's coal-burning 01.1518-8 in external excellent condition, embellished with white paint in a few places. I'd been hoping for Berlin Ost's last standard Pacific, 01.2065, but every time I saw this train that week it had a coal-burning 01.5. Alastair had told me 01.1518 was the pick of the Berlin Pacifics, but despite the presence of a German railway enthusiast who had tried

to energise the driver to make his tape-recordings worthwhile, the running with a comparatively light load was lacklustre and not a patch on the 03.10 running over the same stretch with much heavier loads.

After a week in the north I made my way south from Berlin to spend a couple of days with Lutherstadt-Wittenberg's 03.2s and a week at Saalfeld, experiencing the last area where the oil-burning 01.5s were present in numbers, plus a day on the scenic line to Probstzella, Lausche and Sonnenberg with the former Prussian T20 class 95 2-10-2Ts. After a very rough ride in the buffet car on a class 132 diesel-hauled train from Berlin to Leipzig and Saalfeld, I alighted at Camburg when I saw a local (P3003 07.28 Halle-Saalfeld) made up of double-deck coaches hauled by an obviously ex-works 01.0529-6. The train stopped at all stations, a run of about an hour, but acceleration from each stop up to about 56-60mph was brisk. I alighted at Rüdolstadt in the sunshine to pick up the northbound D504 for Leipzig and Berlin scheduled, I knew, for a Saalfeld 01.5, and in due course 01.0510-6 drew in with a thirteen-coach, 430-tonnes gross train. Performance was unremarkable, the engine working noisily, but it seemed sluggish and exerted violent fore-and-aft movement on the train. We eventually roused the echoes through

the industrial suburbs of Leipzig just exceeding 70mph, but there were a lot of p-way checks on the line at the time and most trains ran late.

Saalfeld was a very steamy place and there were periods during the day when two or three 01.5-hauled train were in the station plus one or two 2-10-2 tanks heading stopping trains to Oppurg, Rüdolstadt or the border route to Sonnenberg through the Thüringerwald. I quickly ascertained which 01.5s were in the four-engine top link working the solitary steam D-Zug and the heavy Eilzüge, and which four had dropped down to the stopping passenger train link to Jena, Gera and through to Leipzig, and managed to get runs during the week behind all the top-link engines – 01.0510, 0521,

DR rebuild of Standard 01, 01.0535-3, at Stralsund with D717, 14.30 Stralsund – Berlin Lichtenberg, April 1979. (David Maidment)

Saalfeld 01.5s, Saalfeld-Leipzig
D504 10.39 Saalfeld-Berlin, via Jena, 20.4.1979
01.0510-6 Bw Saalfeld
13 chs, 402/430t

Rudolstadt		00.00	mph	3½ L
Kirchhasel		05.40	pw 19*/44/ sig stand 10.45/ 15.08	
Uhlstädt		17.45	15*	
Zeutsch		22.42	31*/42	
Orlamünde		27.10	15*	
Kahla		31.53	52	
Rothenstein		36.48	pw 15*	
Göschwitz		39.56	50	
Jena Paradies		43.30	56	
Jena (Saale)	arr	45.38		13L
	dep	00.00		
Porstendorf		05.59	52/ pw 19*	
Dornburg		12.08	pw 10*/47	
Camburg		20.18	pw 15*	
Grossheringen		29.40	pw 15*	
Saaleck		32.50	54	
Bad Kösen		35.10	66	
Naumburg	arr	41.20		17L
	dep	00.00		
Leissling		07.21	50/54	
Uicheritz		-	pw 28*	
Weissenfels	arr	13.51		16L
	dep	00.00		
Grosskorbetha		07.06	53/48/22*	
Bad Dürrenberg		12.35	51/ pw 5*	
Kötschau		19.19	14*	
Grosslehna		22.39	56	
Markranstädt		25.37	44*	
Mililitz		28.00	66	
Rückmarsdorf		29.32	68	
Leipzig-Leutsch		31.09	70/59*	
Leipzig-Möckern		33.05	56	
Leipzig-Gohlis		34.30		
Leipzig Hbf	arr	37.47		21L

How the 01.5 (or anything else) was expected to keep time with all these p-way slacks was unfathomable. However, this 01 struggled, making a lot of noise and creating heavy fore-and-aft movement, only just reaching 70mph on the outskirts of Leipzig.

0525 and 0529 – and three out of the four P-Zug link – 01.0505, 0509, and 0520. I had an opportunity to ride behind the fourth, 0501, on an early-morning stopping train to Oppurg on the Gera line, but chose to ride to Rüdolstadt and back behind 95.0043 instead. I had several runs on the D504 again and on the heavy evening Eilzug from Leipzig that was the return working of the locomotive off D504, and seemed blighted to get 01.0510 several times which seemed the weakest (or roughest riding) of the

E800 07.03 Saalfeld-Leipzig via Gera, 25.4.1979
01.0521-3, Bw Saalfeld
12 chs, 356/385t

E800, 26.4.1979
01.0529-6, Bw Saalfeld
12 chs, 356/390t

Station		time	mph	L	time	mph	L
Saalfeld		00.00	mph	1½ L	00.00	mph	½ L
Unterwellenborn		08.27	31/15*'/27		07.35	31/15*	
Könitz		-	pw 22*		14.13	pw 15*	
Krölpa-Ranis		19.42	15*/pw 22*		19.15	43/15*/41	
Pössneck	arr	25.04		2½ L	23.45		¼ L
	dep	00.00		2½ L	00.00		¼ L
Oppurg		04.54	52/58		04.46	53/56	
Neunhofen		08.47	48/44		09.13	45/39	
Neustadt (Orla)	arr	12.25		2L	12.50		T
	dep	00.00		2L	00.00		½ L
Traun		05.47	41		-	37 (summit)	
Triptis	arr	09.44		½ L	10.16		¼ E
	dep	00.00		1¼ L	00.00		½ L
Niederpöllnitz		07.09	60 coasting		11.47	pw 41*/56	
Weida	arr	14.33	sigs 15*	1¾ L	14.07		¾ L
	dep	00.00		1¾ L	00.00		½ L
		-	pw 10*		-	pw 15*	
Gera-Röppisch		06.42	53		06.04	55	
Gera-Zwötzen		08.55	50		08.49	sigs 15*	
Gera-Süd		10.45	40*		11.04	30*	
Gera-Hbf	arr	13.32		2¼ L	13.59		1½ L
					00.00		T
Gera-Langenberg					05.13	sigs 15*/43/28*	
Bad Köstritz					07.53/14.40	sigs (Xing E403)	
Krossen					20.58	50/pw 15*	
Wetterzeube					25.58	62	
Haynsburg					28.55	56/pw 20*	
Zeitz	arr				35.09		1¼ L
	dep				00.00		¼ L
Bornitz					05.10	60/ sigs 5*	
Reuden					08.33/08.49	sig stand (Diesel 120 freight ahead)	
Profen					13.12	pw 15*/62	
Pegau					16.46	66	
Gross Dalzig					19.29	58/66	
Knautnarendorf					22.22	60/62/60	
Leipzig-Grossschocher					26.43	65 easy	
Leipzig-Plagwitz					28.27	60	
Industriegelände-West					30.22	30*	
Leipzig-Leutsch					31.55	55/57	
Leipzig-Möchen					33.55	60	
Leipzig-Gohlis					35.05	43*	
Leipzig-Hbf	arr				38.07		1½ L

The Saalfeld – Leipzig route via Gera seemed as slack-infested as via Jena. However, the schedules seemed to allow for this. There is a steady steep gradient out of Saalfeld to the summit at Triptis and a similar gradient then down to Gera (gradient not shown, but estimated at 1 in 100). Both 01.0521 and 01.0529 were part of the four-engine top-link team and were in external excellent condition, 01.0529 being just ex-works.

Gera to Triptis Summit

E807 17.51 Leipzig-Saalfeld, 24.4.1979   **E807, 25.4.1979**
01.0510-6, Bw Saalfeld   **01.0525-4, Bw Saalfeld**
13 chs, 393/410t   **13 chs, 393/405t**

Gera		00.00	mph	¾ L	00.00	mph		T
Gera Süd		03.10	28*		03.17			
		05.25/06.10	sigs		03.30/10.52 (door open)			
Gera-Zwötzen		-	44/50		-	48/50		
Gera-Röppisch		-	46/43		15.37	48/45		
Weida	arr	17.04		5L	21.20			8¼ L
	dep	00.00		6L	00.00			8L
Niederpöllnitz		10.30	35/53		10.11	37/54		
Triptis	arr	17.30		6½ L	16.37			7¾ L

After the unexpected stops at the foot of the gradient to Triptis, both engines worked hard, but 01.0510 was worked harder and seemed more harsh, 01.0525 having the distinct edge and not hammered quite so much, with a lovely even beat.

---

four. Tabulated above and on the previous page are a number of runs, the best with 01.0525-4, on the evening Eilzug ex-Leipzig. All of the Saalfeld engines looked in excellent external condition, and the Depot clearly took great pride in their top-link fleet as both 0521,

and 0525 were liberally 'decorated' and 0529 was too by the end of the week. I managed to note nearly every Saalfeld 01.5 active that week, though 0534 was outbased at Göschwitz for trains on the Jena-Gera cross-country route, 0513 was on standby on the breakdown train

the whole week, 0519, 0522 and 0531 flitted in and out of the depot. 0524 and 0533 were present, though out of use, either awaiting repair, Works overhaul or withdrawal. The only Saalfeld 01.5 that made no appearance was 0508.

At the end of the fortnight, just before returning from Magdeburg to West Germany and home, I sought out one of the two remaining standard DR 01s still active. There was a 16.00 Eilzug from Magdeburg to Halberstadt booked for either 01.2114 or 01.2137, and despite nearly missing it by taking a chance on a quick trip out to Rothensee with a class 50.35 2-10-0, I made it with a couple of minutes to spare. 01.2137-6 was the train engine that day, decorated with the workers' '*May Day*' flags on the smokebox. The load was only four double-deck coaches, but I enjoyed the sound and sight from the upper deck of the first coach with the 01 making rapid acceleration up to around 65mph between stops. Arrival was hopelessly late, however, as a mile-long p-way check to walking pace

01.0510-6 at Leipzig waiting to depart with E807 to Saalfeld, 24 April 1979. (David Maidment)

Magdeburg-Halberstadt
E-Zug 16.03 Magdeburg-Halberstadt, 26.4.1979
01.2137-6, Bw Halberstadt
4 double-deck chs

Magdeburg Hbf		00.00	mph
Magdeburg-Buchan		04.33	22*
Magdeburg-Thälmannwerk		06.08	50/54
Wolfsfelde		08.25	22*
Beyendorf		09.49	56
Dodendorf		11.02	62/26*
Osterweddingen		12.58	63
Langenweddingen		14.53	30*/57
Blumemberg		18.37	63/26*/50
Hadmersleben		26.06	58/22*/68
Oschersleben	arr	31.41	
	dep	00.00	
		-	pw 5* (long)
Hordorf		09.08	55
Krottorf		11.22	56
Nienhagen		13.10	66/ 26*
Gross Querstadt		17.10	26*/63
		-	pw 3* (very long right into station)
Halberstadt	arr	27.32	

01.2137 filthy but blowing off steam regularly and accelerating hard between slacks. The p-way slack before Halberstadt had been in place for over a year and every train was losing approximately ten minutes in consequence.

occurred just before Halberstadt and I was told no train had arrived at that city on time as a result for over a year! My return journey after a couple more 50.35s and a quick trip to Drei Annen Hohne on the *Harzquerbahn* from Wernigerode was even worse when a 132 diesel on another four-coach semi-fast managed to lose forty-five minutes and arrived back in Magdeburg well after midnight.

DB 01.10 (011/012)
After my first trip to Germany in 1958, I began to read more about German railways and therefore first became acquainted with the 01.10 three-cylinder Pacifics

through the written word. I had seen the back of the tender of one at about 5am at Hanover when I was seeking the number of the 01 that had hauled me from Löhne, but the sight in the darkness of 01.1087 protruding from the end of the platform meant nothing to me at the time. Then I read about the oil-firing of 01.1100 and 01.1101 in a paragraph and small photo in a British magazine, but my first real meeting was at Cologne Station, again in the middle of the night, in December 1961. My best friend at college, Gordon Fielden, was marrying a German girl, Walburg, who, with her mother, had fled from East Germany and now lived in Plön, north of Lübeck, and he

had invited me to be a witness at the civil ceremony and then give a running translation to his parents of the informal marriage service. I made my own way out via Ostend and, after electric and diesel traction through Belgium, met steam at Aachen with Hagen-based three-cylinder 03.1011, but at Cologne 01.1075 backed on and although it was now the early hours of the morning, I remember being very impressed with the way our heavy train swept out of Cologne Station and the rapid acceleration before I tried to get some sleep. I was aware of a long halt at Osnabrück and in the early dawn went to investigate, and found that we were changing engines, with another three-cylinder Pacific, 01.1059, being coupled up. It looked different somehow, and apart from the 'witte' smoke deflectors being adorned with Christmas greetings, I realised that the chimney was almost invisible. In fact, although an oil-burner, it ran for a while without the built-up chimney that was the style for all the oil-burners. In the darkness and being new to the route, I did not attempt to time the trains, but remember being impressed with the speed (and the noise!).

My return journey was a bit of an anti-climax. Instead of an 01.10 as I now expected, only an 03 was turned out for the heavy train and it laboured badly, losing over half an hour to Osnabrück. It was by then daylight and I was pleased to see the exchange for an 01.10, but it was coal-burning 01.1078 and it did no more than hold scheduled times without regaining any of the lost minutes. The *coup de grâce* was an appalling ferry crossing over mountainous seas in a howling gale and feeling seasick for just the second time in my life.

My next experience of the 01.10s was definitely planned. The itinerary that Alastair and I had drawn up for our July 1962 tour of Germany deliberately included areas where we knew the 01.10s operated, ie on the Frankfurt/Würzburg-Hanover and Hamburg trunk line, and the Hamburg-Osnabruck-Cologne 'Rollbahn'. After arriving at Würzburg we waited a long time for a northbound steam-hauled express, but a succession of trains were V200 hauled. Then we discovered the platform train formation boards, which very helpfully showed the outline of a V200 or 01.10 at the head of the rake of coaches, and discovered that nearly all the daytime trains were diesel-hauled and the 01.10s seemed to be night owls. One express set off with a P8 cut inside the V200 and we were tempted, but in the end we went forward to Fulda to try again. There we found an indicator showing a Frankfurt-Leipzig train booked for steam haulage to the border at Bebra and it ran in with 01.1082, which we accepted gratefully. The load was moderate, eight coaches, 340 tonnes gross, and we made noisy progress without any significant speeds over the short forty-five-minutes run. Then we alighted to try again, settling for another V200 that was banked by 50.1883 up the seven-and-a-half-miles 1 in 75 from Bebra to Cornberg, before detraining at Göttingen to see if we had any better luck.

As already recounted, our further journey north was made

Hamburg to Köln, 1962 (Oil-burning 012 Pacifics)

08.26 Hamburg Hbf-Köln, D94
20.7.62
01.1079 Osnabrück (to Osnabrück)
01.1068 Osnabrück (from Osnabrück)
12 chs, 409/445t
11 chs, 375/410t from Hamm

		mph		miles
Hamburg Hbf	00.00		2L	0
Veddel	05.46	45		
Hamburg-Wilhelmsburg	07.52	52		
Hamburg-Harburg arr	14.02	sigs 10*		7.5
	00.00		T	0
Bk. Glüsingen	-	pw 15*		
Hittfeld	11.39	45		
Klecken	15.50	49		
Buchholz	19.44	65		
Sprötze	22.22	69/75		
Tostedt	25.50	66/73		
Königsmoor	29.16	76		
Lauenbrück	32.58	75		
Scheessel	35.56	73/75		
Rotenburg	arr	41.23	2L	37.8
		00.00	1L	0
Sottrum	07.49	66		
Ottersberg	12.03	72		
Sagehorn	15.53	74		
Bremen-Oberneuland	18.57	75		
Bremen	arr	27.13	1E	26.7
		00.00	Sigs.	9½ L	0
Bremen-Hemelingen	06.17	61		
Dreye	09.10	68		
Kirchweyhe	11.27	67		
Barrien	13.54	65		
Syke	16.00	62		
Bramstedt	19.30	55 minimum up 1 in 200		
Bassum	21.52	72/66		
Twistringen	26.40	69/65		
Drentwede	30.23	76		
Barnstorf	33.15	80		
Drebber	36.37	75		
Diepholz	arr	41.10	8½ L	43.3
		00.00	Slipping	9L	0
Lembruch	08.02	64		
Lemförde	12.06	69/64		
Bohmte	18.27	73		
Ostercappeln	22.49	59		
Vehrte	27.01	51 minimum up 1 in 200		
Belm	-	69		
Osnabrück	arr	34.59	8L	32.6	(01.1079 off)
		00.00	8¾ L	0	(01.1068 on)
Hasbergen	07.48	64		

Natrup-Hagen		10.41	66 / 65		
Lengerich		13.38	75 / pw 51*		
Kattenvenne		18.05	75		
Brock-Ostbevern		21.03	76		
Westbevern		22.10	76		
Sudmühle		26.39	75		
Münster	arr	31.10		7L	31.3
		00.00		6½ L	0
Hiltrup		06.31	66		
Steiner See		07.52	72		
Rinkerwald		10.23	75		
Drensteinfurt		13.22	75		
Bockum-Hövel		19.33	66 / 72		
Hamm Hbf	arr	23.33		5L	22.05
		00.00		4½ L	0
Wiescherhöfen		05.10	65		
Bönen		08.05	74 / 65		
Unna		12.46	pw 28* / 48		12.8
Holzwickede		18.56	31* / 60		
Schwerte	arr	27.00		4½ L	21.8
		00.00	Sigs.	7½ L	0
Bk. Steinhausen		-	pw 25* / 41		
Westhofen		05.12	pw 44*		
Hohensyburg		07.32	64		
Hagen	arr	13.22		10L	8.2
		00.00		9L	0
Hagen-Haspe		05.38	35 / 44		
Gevelsberg		10.03	45 working very hard		
Ennepetal-Milspe		11.54	44		
Bk Martfeld		14.03	45 ½ / 56 summit of 1 in 101		
Schwelm		15.21	70		
Wuppertal-Oberbarmen		18.49		6¾ L	16.8
		00.00		6¾ L	0
Wuppertal Barmen		02.42	38		
Wuppertal-Unterbarmen		04.08	50		
Wuppertal-Elberfeld		06.07		7L	
		00.00		6L	
Wuppertal Steinbeck		02.00	29		
W-Zool-Garten		04.25	55		
W-Sonnborn		04.55	58		
W-Vohwinkel		06.15	64		
Grüten		10.05	sigs 28*		
Haan		12.10	66		
Solingen-Ohligs	arr	14.31		5½ L	10.3
		00.00		5½ L	0
Solingen-Landwehr		03.27	66		
Leichlingen		05.05	75 / sigs 15*		
Opladen		09.30	53 / 68		
Leverkusen-Schleebusch		11.50	71		
Köln-Mühlheim		-	50*		
Köln-Deutzerfeld		21.45 / / 22.33 sigs stand			
Köln Hbf	arr	26.18		6½ L	17.5

Two good typical runs with oil-burning 3-cyl 01.10 (012) Pacifics on the '*Rollbahn*' - the Hamburg-Köln run regularly worked by these locos until taken over by V200 diesels in the mid-60s. There were several sections at or near even time - Rotenburg to Bremen, 26.7 miles in 27mins 13secs (59mph average); Bremen-Diepholz, 43.3 miles in 41mins 10secs (63mph average); and Osnabrück to Münster, 31.3 miles in 31mins 10secs (60mph average).

---

by two-cylinder 01s rather than the three-cylinder variety and we saw no more 01.10s until we'd spent a night in Hamburg and got up in time to catch the D94 08.26 Hamburg-Cologne, which was headed by 01.1079 with a twelve-coach load of 445 tons gross. We were now treated to a very noisy and, I suspect, typical run over this main trunk route which was dominated in the early and mid-1960s by Osnabrück oil-burning 01.10s until eventually the line was dieselised, then electrified. The oil-burning Pacifics had diagrams and utilisation that could match any diesel, and it was said by crews that an 01.10 could be ready for the road within forty-five minutes of starting from cold. We were held ten minutes at Bremen awaiting a connection and ran hard afterwards, the noise level increasing by several decibels, and the replacement oil-burning 01.1068 from Osnabrück continued with equal energy gradually recouping our lost time, and would even have been slightly early, but for a signal check at Deutzerfeld just outside Cologne Hauptbahnhof.

My logs of 01.1079 and 01.1068, authenticated by Alastair Wood, are given on the left.

I was absent from Germany then for ten years, until finally I was tempted by a railway society advertised tour in April 1972. The LCGB railtour was unusual in

01.1079 at speed near Vehrte with a Hamburg-Cologne D-Zug, 20 August 1967. The author travelled behind this locomotive on this route in July 1962 during his circular tour of Germany with college friend Alastair Wood. (MLS Collection)

that it involved using a Parkeston Quay-Emden ferry as a base and overnight hotel, and our first afternoon on the Rheine-Emden line at a small country station just south of Emden, Ihrhove, had been chosen to photograph the oil-burning 01.10s, by then categorised as 012s, together with double-headed oil-burning three-cylinder 2-10-0s (043 class) on heavy iron-ore hopper trains. Typically,

it poured with rain throughout, though I did manage to photograph 012.064 drifting through on a light Eilzug and an impressive 012.101-2 accelerating hard from Emden with an Eilzug for Rheine. We then had a tour round north Friesland via Oldenburg behind an oil-burning 042 2-8-2, followed by a Kabin-tender 050 2-10-0, still in a grey mist and rain.

The following day saw some sun

as, after breakfast on our floating hotel, we joined our eleven-coach special of 450 tonnes gross, headed by one of the only two remaining 011s (the coal-burning 01.10). 011.062 and 011.072 (formerly 01.1062 and 1072) were the last survivors, and 011.062-7 was to take our special non-stop to Lingen for a visit round the Works – it was the last week before its closure and 001.111-4 was under repair as

012.101-2, on the afternoon Eilzug from Norddeich to Rheine, speeds past Ihrhove in pouring rain, the occasion of an LCGB railtour to Germany and photoshoot, 29 April 1972. (David Maidment)

well as a few 2-10-0s. The Pacific ran punctually, but without any spectacular effort at a steady 65-70mph (I learned later that the route speed restriction was only raised from 69 to 75mph the following year). At Rheine, 011.062 was replaced by an ex-works oil-burning 012.092-3 (former 01.1092) now with thirteen coaches, 550 tons (as from Lingen), and we were treated to a noisy display, heard well down the train, to Münster and Hagen, where we exchanged the Pacifics for freight engines (two- and three-cylinder 2-10-0s, and a Prussian G8 0-8-0) for the rest of the tour.

This taster whet my appetite and I got 'leave passes' from my wife

The last coal-burning 01.10 Pacific in service, 011.062-7 (formerly 01.1062), at Emden Hbf with the Locomotive Club of Great Britain special railtour in Friesland, North Germany, 30 April 1972. The engine will work the eleven-coach train to Rheine with a pause for enthusiasts to visit the Works at Lingen, before handing the train over to an oil-burning 012 for the run on to Münster and Hagen. (David Maidment)

Ex-works oil-burning 012.092-3 takes over the LCGB special train at Rheine for the run onto Hagen, 30 April 1972. (David Maidment)

and family to spend some time on the Rheine-Emden-Norddeich line in the summers of 1973 and 1974, and the winter of 1975, just before final dieselisation and the end of steam on main line passenger work in West Germany. In 1973 the 012 turns on the Hamburg-Westerland route had been dieselised and all the 012s still fit for further work were now based at Rheine, all thirteen of them – 012.055, 061, 063, 066, 068, 075, 077, 080-082, 100, 101 and 104. Astonishingly, in just ten days there, I managed to get runs behind all thirteen locomotives, which says something for their maintenance and availability. Both 011s and 012.092 had been withdrawn by then and their hulks were rusting on Rheine Depot.

The first run behind 012.063-4 on the mid-morning D735, non-stop to Emden, 88 miles, was scheduled at a better than mile-a-minute eighty-four minutes and I was disappointed that we lost seven minutes attributed to just a couple of signal checks (exactly 84 minutes net). This run was atypical, as I soon discovered. The crews seemed to find the relaxation

of the line speed an incentive to show off and there were many very fast performances, especially on the 16.55 Rheine-Norddeich D714, which had incredibly tight start-to-stop schedules between the intermediate stations before Emden at Lingen, Meppen, Papenburg and Leer, and the evening D730 sleeper from Norddeich to Munich which was only allowed 50 minutes for the 52.4 miles between Leer and Lingen, and on which runs with 012. 077, 101 and 104 beat the demanding schedule, with net times of around 44-45 minutes (average start-to-stop speed of 70-72mph).

The outstanding run of the week was with my star from the 1961 Cologne-Osnabrück night run, 012.075-8, which left Rheine eighteen minutes late and was driven flat-out, making the most astounding noise, and reaching an unauthorised 85mph between Lingen and Meppen. On another day, I had three consecutive runs with 012.077-4 which managed a combined average of over 60mph for its day's turns.

In 1974, things were mainly unchanged, though the fast D714

was diesel weekdays but steam at weekends. 012.066-7, which was obviously due for overhaul in 1973, after a major overhaul was one of the most regular steeds. 012.082-4, which was the only engine in 1973 that really seemed to struggle, had also received an intermediate repair as had 012.081-6, the latter engine in 1974 and 1975, with 012.075-8 and 012.066-7 being the stars of the bunch. 012.068-3, which had seemed in poor condition, but which was pushed hard in 1973, had been withdrawn as well as 012.104-6, and 012.055-0, which performed well in 1973, had, by 1974, got its valve settings in a bit of a mess and sounded really syncopated, one beat almost missing, another crashing out as it struggled to accelerate a moderately-loaded Eilzug over the windy heaths of the Friesland. The two most memorable runs were with 012.100-4 (01.1100) and 012.081-6, the former on a Sunday morning 7.07am Rheine departure (E3251 6.30am Münster-Norddeich) booked for five coaches and very tightly timed, but on my run had eight, three extra coaches being taken to strengthen the southbound E2738, and made so much noise that I had to retreat to the third coach to avoid the distortion on my tape-recorder experienced in the first coach. Why a virtually empty Sunday morning train was so tightly timed seemed curious, but our driver did his best, finally winding the engine over the last stretch from Leer to Emden when we were flailing away into a fierce cross wind. 012.081-6 starred on D730, the evening sleeper, and I have a superb tape recording of it leaving Leer with fierce even

Rheine-Emden-Norddeich, 1973-75

	08.41 Münster-Norddeich, D1337				08.41 Münster-Norddeich, D1731				
	23.7.73				13.7.74				
	012.075-8 Rheine	(3 cyl oil-burning 4-6-2)			012.066-7 Rheine				
	10 chs, 397/415t				10 chs, 375/400t				
Rheine	00.00	mph		18L	00.00	mph		1L	0 miles
Deves	05.52	56			05.47	50			
Salzbergen	07.25	65			07.11	66			
Leschede	12.10	76			11.50	76			
Elbergen	15.29	65*/67			15.06	65*			
Lingen	19.49	76			19.23	74			19.2
Holthausen	22.15	75			21.48	75			
Geeste	24.15	80			23.53	75			
Meppen	29.31	80/73*			29.38	75/62*			31.8
Hemsen	32.08	71/74			32.32	sigs 43*			
Haren	35.03	79			35.57	68			
Lathen	39.03	83/81			40.13	80			
Kluse	42.39	85			43.43	82/79			
Dörpen	44.39	70*/75			46.28	75/65*			
Aschendorf	49.27	77			51.27	75			
Papenburg	52.52	sigs 26*			54.09	71*			60.4
Steenfelde	57.27	62			57.28	74			
Ihrhove	59.15	71/62*			58.55	75/60*			
Leer arr	64.01	[60.5 mins net]	14L		63.46	[62.5 mins net]		3E	71.0
dep	00.00		12½ L		00.00			½ L	0
Neermoor	06.49	66/69			06.12	66			
Oldersum	-	74			10.27	75			
Petkum	-	75			-	75			
Emden Bw	-	easy			15.48//19.15	sigs stands (brake problems)			
Emden Hbf arr	18.25		12L		23.20			4L	16.75

Both trains had a schedule of 68 minutes for the 71 miles, which both completed in 63-64 minutes (ave. speed 67-68mph) although net times of 60½-62½ mins = 69-71mph average start to stop. 012.075, running late, was pushed very hard and well exceeded the line limit of 75mph. 012.066, overhauled in 1973, was a fixture on D1731 in 1974, was in good condition and ran hard, but not thrashed like the previous run. However, it suffered a brake problem on the canal bridge approaching Emden, slipped violently and roared to 40mph past the loco shed.

acceleration, sounding like an automatic machine-gun, 0-75mph in just over six minutes! On my last trip in January 1975, 012.081-6 was still game, as was 012.066-7. and 012.055-0 had recovered. 012.082-4, 012.077-4 and 012.101-2 had been withdrawn, and the condition of the remaining engines had clearly gone downhill, at least externally, but they were still pushed hard, especially on D714 which, surprisingly, had reverted to steam still tightly timed as ever. My swansong on this last trip was a fine run behind 012.081-6, which was becoming my favourite, on D714, which included a storming exit from Meppen racing a sports car on an adjacent road which we ultimately outran!

I include a selection of logs from my three years, shown above and on the next page, although there is no room to print all those of interest. Depite this only being a secondary main line, at least the 012s went out flying the 'steam' flag with vigour, as, I understand, the Hof 01s did in 1973.

19.04 Norddeich-München, D730
20.7.73
012.104-6 Rheine
7 chs, 273/285t

19.04 Norddeich-München, D730
22.7.73
012.077-4 Rheine
7 chs, 273/290t

19.07 Norddeich-München, D730
14.7.74
12.081-6 Rheine
7 chs 272/285t

	time	mph		time	mph		time	mph		miles
Leer	00.00	mph	2½ L	00.00	mph	5L	00.00	mph	8L	0 miles
Ihrhove	05.39	75		06.06	73		05.44	73		
Steenfelde	-	76		07.41	78		07.19	75		
Papenburg	10.53	sigs 26*		11.06	sigs 41*		10.42	pw 37*		10.6
Aschendorf	14.29	67		14.51	68		14.05	75		
Dörpen	19.38	65*/74		19.59	65*/73		19.06	65*/73		
Kluse	21.53	75		22.16	77		21.18	77		
Lathen	25.53	77		26.05	78/79		25.17	78/72		
Haren	30.10	75		30.18	76		29.42	69/75		
Hemsen	32.48	78		32.53	80		32.24	77		
Meppen	35.22	62*		35.26	65*		35.02	62*		39.4
Geeste	41.29	71		41.26	75		40.40	76½		
Holthausen	43.45	72		43.33	76		42.46	78		
Lingen arr	47.00	[44.5 mins net]	½ E	46.29	[44.5 mins net]	1½ L	45.51	[43.5 mins net]	3¾ L	52.5

This very sharply-timed sleeper train (52.5 miles in 50 minutes) was consistently achieving net times around 44-45 minutes (average around 70-72mph). 012.081 achieved a start to stop average of 68.6mph actual including the moderate p-way slack at Papenburg. 012.104 was withdrawn shortly afterwards and was exhibited for several years at Carnforth; 012.077 had achieved three runs averaging over 60mph consecutively on the same day; and 012.081 was recently given a light overhaul and was in excellent nick, beat very even.

Oil-burning 012.081-6 arrives on time at Meppen with the 16.55 Rheine D714 which will maintain 60mph start-to-stop times over very short distances on its journey to Papenburg, Leer and Emden, 22 July 1973. (David Maidment)

D714 16.55 Rheine-Norddeich — 20.7.73 — 012.055-0 Rheine — 7chs, 259/275t

07.07 (Suns) Rheine-Norddeich — E3251, 14.7.74 — 012.100-4 Rheine — 8 chs, 293/300t

D714 16.50 Rheine-Norddeich — 23.1.75 — 012.081-6 Rheine — 6 chs, 220/245t

Station	time	mph	L	time	mph	L	time	mph	L	miles
Rheine	00.00		4L	00.00		4L				0
Deves	05.08	63		05.07	61					
Salzbergen Box	-	68		06.30//08.21 sig stand						
Salzbergen	06.33	75		11.02		9L				
				00.00		9L				
Leschede	11.18	80		05.53	65/76					
Elbergen	14.22	65*/74		09.22	60*/67					
Lingen	18.57		5L	14.30		8½ L				
	00.00		4¼ L	00.00		7L				19.4
Holthausen	04.19	70		04.17	68					
Geeste	06.35	79		06.34	71½					
Meppen	13.02		4¼ L	14.11		8L				
	00.00		4½ L	00.00		8L	00.00		5½ L	32.5
Hemsen	04.38	66		04.25	72		-	71		
Haren	07.39	76		08.10			06.12	75		
				00.00						
Bk 274	-	76		-	65/72		-	74		
Lathen	11.53	77		07.01			10.40	75		
				00.00			-	73/75		
Kluse	-	75		06.05	68		14.52	75		
Dörpen	17.58	65*/72		08.34	70/60*/65		17.04	60*/76		
Aschendorf	22.58	75		14.32		9L	22.14	68*		
				00.00		9L	-	pw 41*		
Papenburg	26.46		3½ L	05.28	56	9½ L	26.47		4L	
	00.00		4L	00.00		9½ L	00.00		4½ L	61.3
Steenfelde	-	66		05.11	61		04.23	75		
Ihrhove	06.29	78		07.02	63/60*		05.55	77/60*		
Leer	11.07		4L	12.23		12L	10.42		4¼ L	
	00.00		1½ L	00.00		9L				71.9
Neermoor	06.07	68		08.23	49					
				00.00						
Bk Rorichum	-	72		-	56					
Oldersum	10.03	76		07.40						
				00.00						
Petkum	12.33	77		05.16	55					
Emden Hbf	17.01		1½ L	11.09		13½ L				88.1

These were three hard-running services with 012s thrashed to their limit. D714 was a 'mile a minute' schedule between all stops and on the standard 7-coach load, the 012s could just about maintain schedule provided there were no out-of-course delays, but there was little in hand. By 1974, this service was steam only on Saturdays. The 07.07 Sunday-only semi-fast train to Norddeich was an incredible train - booked for 5 coaches and with mile-a-minute schedules over very short distances, 012.100 was three (empty!) coaches overload and was worked flat out from Rheine to Papenburg. After that, the boiler was beaten and the crew had to ease to allow steam pressure to recover. 012.081, in the last few months of steam, was still up to the 16.55 Rheine schedule which surprisingly had reverted to steam in 1975.

Oil-burner 012.063-4 (01.1063) leaving Rheine with the E1631, 8.10am Eilzug to Emden and Norddeich, July 1973. (David Maidment)

012.077-4 at Rheine on the 08.10 Eilzug to Emden, 21 July 1973. This engine achieved three consecutive even-time (60mph) runs in one day, culminating in a time of 44 minutes net for the 50 miles between Leer and Lingen, an average of 72mph. (David Maidment)

012.100-4 , later preserved as 01.1100, accelerates the heavy mid-morning D735 to Norddeich over the Papenburg Swing Bridge, 23 July 1973. This photo was used on the cover of the magazine, *European Railways*, edition No.163. (David Maidment)

012.066-7, regular engine for D1731, the morning Cologne-Norddeich D-Zug, waiting in pouring rain at Rheine for its train to arrive behind a DB electric locomotive from Münster, 13 July 1974. (David Maidment)

012.080-8 standing at Emden ready to depart with the early-afternoon D1334 to Rheine and Cologne, 23 July 1973. (David Maidment)

DB 03 & 03.10, DR 03 & 03.10

My very first encounter with a German locomotive was with an 03 at nearly midnight on the Dutch/German border at Bentheim in April 1958, during the student trip to Bad Harzburg. Surprisingly I had done little research on what I was to expect, having assumed most continental railway systems were largely electrified. I was curious therefore when the Dutch electric disappeared into the night and the tender of a steam engine loomed out of the darkness with the number 03 091 highlighted – a number which at that time meant nothing to me. The Rheine Pacific took the *Holland-Skandinavien Express* through to Osnabrück where we changed and I presume (but don't know) that the 03 exchanged for an Osnabrück 01.10. At 6am the following morning,

012.055-0 accelerates away from Emden with a harsh syncopated exhaust past the depot roundhouse with D1734 Norddeich Mole-Cologne, 13 July 1974. (David Maidment)

012.081-6 on my last day of regular 012 working to the North Sea coast, waiting at Leer to take over E3112 from Oldenburg to Norddeich, 24 January 1975. (David Maidment)

03.131 at Hanover Hbf with the 06.00 Eilzug to Bad Harzburg on the occasion of the University College London German Department visit, April 1958. 03.131, built in 1933, was the penultimate 03 Pacific in traffic in West Germany, being withdrawn from Ulm in 1973. It is now displayed at the Deutsches Dampflok Museum, Neuenmarkt-Wirsberg. (David Maidment)

I came across my second 03 in daylight, as our Eilzug from Hanover to Bad Harzburg was in the charge of 03.131, which was eventually the penultimate survivor of the class and is now preserved at Neuenmarkt-Wirsberg. A week later, our Eilzug back to Hanover was hauled by 03.086 and, after an 01 and P8 back to Osnabrück, had Rheine's 03.169, still with large 'Wagner' smoke deflectors, back to the Dutch border.

I had no contact with any 03s during my 1959 summer in Munich, but I came across a three-cylinder 03.10 at Aachen en route to a friend's wedding in North Germany at Christmas 1961 – however, at the time the number 03.1011 meant little to me and I just assumed it was a variant of the two-cylinder 03s I had met before. During an unsatisfactory run back from my

03.086 at Saarbrücken, 4 October 1964. The author's first experience of a German locomotive was in April 1958 when on a London University German Department study visit to Bad Harzburg, 03.091 backed onto the *Holland-Skandinavien Express* at the Dutch/ German border at Bentheim. 03.086 was the first locomotive to haul the party on their return journey from Bad Harzburg to Hanover. (MLS Collection)

Kiel to Hamburg, 1962
15.01 Eilzug Kiel-Hamburg Altona, 19.7.1962
03.062 Bw Hamburg Altona
8 chs, 276/300t

			mph	
Kiel Hbf		00.00		3¾ L
Meimersdorf		06.26	50/60	
Flintbek		09.40	66	
Bordesholm		14.40	70/65	
Einfeld		17.50	72	
Neumünster	arr	22.23		3L
	dep	00.00		3½ L
Arpsdorf		07.38	63	
Brokstedt		10.30	69	
Wrist	arr	16.03		2½ L
	dep	00.00		3¾ L
Dauenhof		08.17	62	
Horst		11.15	58	
Elmshorn	arr	16.13		3¾ L
	dep	00.00		3¾ L
Tornesch		07.49	56	
Prisdorf		10.02	68	
Pinneberg		11.45	71	
Halstenbek		13.54	68	
Elbgaustrasse		16.43	70	
Eidelstedt		17.25	50	
Hamburg Altona	arr	23.09		2¾ L

friend's wedding in Plön, 03.078 had charge of a night sleeper from Hamburg to Ostend as far as Osnabrück, presumably substituting for an 01.10, and was grossly overloaded, barely making 60mph at any point and showing clear signs of shortage of steam. We lost over thirty minutes on the relatively easy night schedule. In my earlier summer 1961 trip to Munich and back, having taken a brief trip from Lindau out to Friedrichshafen behind an S3/6 on D75 to Kiel, I went as far as Aulendorf with 03.132 which would take the train as far as Ulm, and returned to Friedrichshafen with 03.108, when the last leg back to Lindau was P8-hauled. By this time, the 03s had

displaced the 18.6s from that section which had been a regular route for the 18.4/5s and later 18.6s.

In July 1962, we had an encounter with an 03 in the far north, when we made a brief side-trip from Hamburg to Kiel. A filthy Hamburg Altona 03.062 had backed on to the Eilzug, but just before departure a V100 centre-cab diesel attached itself as pilot, much to our disappointment. After a walk around the city and a quick bite to eat, we found our return Eilzug for Hamburg was again 03.062, fortunately this time without the diesel pilot, and Alastair was able to time it properly.

We did, however, have one splendid short trip with one of Hagen's three-cylinder 03.10s. As mentioned earlier, I had had 03.1011

03.1013, rebuilt with all-welded boiler, at Cologne on a thirteen-coach train for Ostend which it will take as far as the Belgian border at Aachen, July 1962.
(David Maidment)

Cologne to Aachen, 1962

D 467 22.20 Rijeka-Ostend
18.55 Köln-Aachen, 20.7.62
03.1013 Hagen-Eckersey (reboilered 03.10)
13 chs, 517/550t

	mph		miles	
Köln Hbf	00.00		7L	0
Köln-Ehrenfeld	05.29	51		
Köln-Stadion	08.09	52½		
Lövenich	09.49	53/56		
Grosskönigsdorf		12.42	55	
Horrein	15.51	72		
Sindorf	17.39	75		
Buir	21.57	64		
Bk Merzenich	-	63		
Düren	27.27	56*/65		24.4
Langerwehe	33.27	62/69		
Nothberg	36.34	pw 37*		
Eschweiler	39.04	pw 34*		
Stolberg	42.25	48/62		
Aachen-Rothe Erde	47.48	pw 12*		
Aachen Hbf arr	51.24	(46 mins net)	3L	43.75

The 03.10 (coal-burning loco) was a case of 'all-out' with this load - the noise was deafening.

---

once between Aachen and Cologne, but hadn't timed it or noticed anything out of the ordinary, but our run from Cologne to Aachen in July 1962 with 03.1013 on a heavy thirteen-coach 550-ton train was far from routine. It was a boat train to connect with the Ostend cross-Channel ferry and despite the fact that all the West German 03.10s were coal-burning, the driver had no mercy on his fireman with the sparks flying high as the locomotive roared out of Cologne, accelerating to 75mph at Sindorf before easing for the curve at Düren. As the engine was to be relieved at Aachen, the driver presumably had no concern about tearing the fire apart. Whilst the 03.10's performance was first-rate, I have

no hesitation in saying that in their rebuilt form with all-welded boiler and no skirt to the front end above the bogie and cylinders, 03.1013 was, unlike its sisters in the German Democratic Republic, quite one of the ugliest express steam engines I have ever seen.

We returned from Aachen with a curious little run. Two-cylinder 03.179 of Cologne-Deutzerfeld was waiting at Aachen with a lightweight five-coach relief to the *Skandinavien*, the 20.45 Aachen-Copenhagen. The start was terrible with much 'waffling' and we didn't touch 60mph until we'd been going twenty minutes – although 03.1001 had left just six minutes ahead with the heavy D52 Ostend-Vienna, so our driver may have been holding

back. Then after a slight p-way slowing to about 30mph the driver let fly, and we held speed between 72 and 75mph for another twenty minutes, arriving three minutes late at Cologne's main station.

There were no 03s in the Rheine area when I was there between 1972 and 1975, so the next opportunity I had to see and ride behind an 03 was in East Germany in 1979. Many of the 03s there had been rebuilt with *reko* boilers with feedwater heater and a few were still based at Lutherstadt-Wittenberg, running stopping services between Berlin and that city until electrification of the route at the beginning of June 1979 would render them redundant. They also had one heavy express between Berlin and Leipzig, D563, on which apparently they often struggled to keep time – I was told its timekeeping was notorious, although that may have been because of the numerous electrification works rather than the locomotive performance. This was belied by my own experience – I saw 03.2155-4, which looked the smartest of the bunch, arrive punctually at Leipzig when I was based at Saalfeld, but travelling to Leipzig behind 01.5s; my final run in East Germany in April 1979 was on D563 and a massive fourteen-coach packed train with grimy Pacific 03.2058-0, which thundered along, covering the countryside in a black smokescreen, achieving 75mph downhill from Radis and passing Bitterfeld six minutes early before being brought to a stand by signals intervening at Delitzsch. After a five-minute stop, 03.2058 found it hard to really get going again and our arrival was

Berlin-Leipzig, 1979
07.25 Berlin Schöneweide-Leipzig, D563
28.4.79
03.2058-0 Lutherstadt-Wittenberg
14 chs, 452/505t

		mph		miles
Berlin Schönefeld	00.00		½ L	0
Via Spiral	-	50 / pw 10*		
Genshagener Heide	16.58	56		
Birkengrund Süd	18.09	62		
Ludwigsfelde	19.21	65		
Thyrow	22.41	70		
Trebbin	25.02	69		
Woltersdorf	33.39	pw 20* /60		
Luckenwalde	36.09	56*/ 60		
Forst Zinna	39.58	pw 25* [long]		
Grünna Klein Zinna	44.22	41		
Jüterbog	47.51	56/58		37.5
Niedergörsdorf	52.09	60/54 min		
Blönsdorf	56.03	59		
Klebitz	58.50	66		
Zahna	61.23	72		
Bülzig	63.15	68		
Zönigall	64.28	65		
Lutherstadt-Wittenberg	67.55	40*		57.5
Pratau	70.53	56		
Bergwitz	74.50	62/55		
Radis	79.53	52 min		
Gräfenhainichen	82.43	65		
Burgheunitz	85.50	71		
Muldenstein	88.27	75		
Bitterfeld	91.47	60*		80.6
Petersroda	97.15	sigs 22* /50		
Delitzsch	104.00//109.45	sigs stand		
Zschortau	116.10	44		
Rachnitz	120.02	50		
Neuwiederitzsch	123.36	56		
Leipzig Hbf arr	132.05	[111 mins net]	11L	101.9

Two-cylinder coal-burning 03.2058 was filthy and was driven hard with this very heavy load. The train was packed and would have arrived punctually, but for the dead stand at Delitzsch and laboured recovery. This was the only daily steam-hauled express between Berlin and Leipzig, which finished in June when the electrification was switched on. The p-way slacks between Woltersdorf and Forst Zinna were in connection with electrification.

eleven minutes late. The 03s on the Berlin Schöneweide-Lutherstadt-Wittenberg P-Züge had little opportunity to show their paces, with 48-50mph between stops being normal with the standard set of seven DR lightweight coaches, though the constant 'barking' starts away from stations gave good tape-recording, occasionally spoilt by the squeals from the ill-maintained rolling-stock. It was on one of these runs that I befriended Fireman Werner Schmager and his driver Alfons Liehs, and nearly had a footplate run with them on 03.2155-4, but the presence of a security policeman at the last moment deterred us, unfortunately. This was also the sprightliest of the local train runs, the train chirruping merrily along at 65mph around the Berlin ring railway, passing a whole series of diesel-hauled expresses at a standstill in the other direction. At this time there were just seven 03s left at the depot – 03.2002, 2058, 2153, 2155, 2176, 2243 and 2254, and I rode behind four of them, 03.2058, 2155, 2176 and 2243. 03.2153 was also active though I didn't see the other two, but I was only there a couple of days. With their withdrawal, the two-cylinder 03 class became virtually extinct, although 03.2002 and 03.2155 from that group survived into preservation.

One of the key objectives of my 1979 East German visit was to obtain runs behind the oil-burning three-cylinder East German version of the 03s, which were working north of Berlin to Stralsund and the island of Rügen via both Neubrandenburg and Pasewalk. I nearly missed out. The winter of 1979 had been particularly

One of Lutherstadt-Wittenberg's two-cylinder 03s, 03.2243-8, at Luckenwalde on a Berlin Schöneweide– L-Wittenberg P-Zug, April 1979. They were withdrawn the following month on completion of the next stage of electrification of the Berlin-Leipzig main line. (David Maidment)

and Malmö. 03.0046-7 had backed down and we were on our way before I discovered that this was one of the rerouted trains via Pasewalk, so I purchased an excess ticket from the bemused on-board female ticket collector and travelled right through to Bergen. My next surprise was the energy that the driver and engine put into this run. Admittedly the train was late, very late, not uncommon on a train that had already been travelling for many hours. However, the scheduled Berlin station time was excessive and we set off only nine minutes late. Alastair had warned me not to expect much from the 03.10s, yet here was I experiencing an actual mile-a-minute run over the sixty-eight miles between Bernau and Pasewalk with a thirteen-coach 485-ton train. We arrived apparently sixteen minutes early by the revised schedule, took water at Pasewalk and set off again on time, still with tremendous energy, although I still had no knowledge of the revised schedule

Leipzig West's 03.2058-0 at speed passing through Wetterzeube Station on D1000 Gera to Berlin, 12 May 1978. The following year 03.2058 was one of the L-Wittenberg 03s active on the Berlin P-Zügen and on D563 from Berlin Schöneweide-Leipzig, on which train the author had an excellent run with this engine, though in much filthier condition. (Wolfgang Bügel/ Eisenbahnstiftung Collection)

severe in the north, and much of the track had been snow and ice damaged, and train services had been suspended in March and early April to enable repairs and only commenced again the week I arrived. Even then the Neubrandenburg route was closed between Demmin and Grimmen for part of the day and night, with some trains being diverted to the Pasewalk route and others terminated at Demmin for road transport further north. On my very first day behind the Iron Curtain, I had bought a ticket from Berlin Ostbahnhof to Neustrelitz (the station before Neubrandenburg) to sample an 03.10 on D270 *Meridian*, an international express with through MAV blue coaches from Hungary to Sweden via the train ferry from Sassnitz to Trelleborg

for the rerouted train. I only know that we arrived, after a signal check at Stralsund Rügendamm, just two minutes early! To my surprise, 03.0046-7 hooked off at this juncture and another oil-burning 03.10, 03.0090-5, took over for the short run through Rügen to Sassnitz and the Swedish ferry. I went with it just in case I didn't see 03.0090 again (I did – several times).

After the run back with an 01.5, I copied the habits of the East Germans, and rose early and walked past the statue of Lenin to the S-bahn to catch the 06.10 D610 Berlin Lichtenberg-Stralsund via Neubrandenburg. After a few scares with a number of early-morning D-Züge emerging from the carriage sheds behind 132-type diesels, 03.0077-2 appeared with twelve lightweight DR coaches, and again we displayed energy when the signalman and the track repair staff let us. North of Neubrandenburg, the delays got heavier as we were clearly becoming involved in emergency single-line working, and it was no real surprise when the train terminated at Demmin and we were all turned out to waiting buses. As the return D-Zug was obviously going to restart from Demmin with the same set of coaches, I spent a couple of hours sight-seeing in this strange and remote town, feeling very conspicuous, before rejoining D613 with 03.0090-5 simmering at the front end. We had a long wait before the buses arrived with hordes of passenger spilling out, and set off twenty-five minutes late, which had soon become forty-five after the single-line working before Neubrandenburg. I went through to Oranienburg and was actually glad

of the lateness to reduce the time I had to spend at this draughty station which totally lacked any eating facilities – not even a chocolate bar or crisp machine. I was waiting for D814, the lunchtime express from Berlin which I was intending to take right through to Stralsund as I was advised that the route was now open in the afternoon. 03.0085-5 was the train engine – it had worked south on the early-morning ferry-connecting service from Sassnitz, normerly the turn of Stralsund's 'pet' 03.0010-3 (later to become the famous preserved coal-burning 03.1010-2). We ran energetically enough to Neubrandenburg, then the delays began; after Demmin as we roared, braked and roared again through the desolate landscape it was becoming obvious that I would not only miss my planned return to Berlin by steam, but the next diesel service as well. I spent a couple of hours in the attractive city of Stralsund at dusk, found some food and got the last D-Zug back to Berlin behind one of the half-dozen class 142 more powerful diesels which were never multiplied – by that time the DR had developed a significant seven-year electrification plan. The next day, I took an even later D270 *Meridian*, with 03.0085-5 again, and virtually replicated 03.0046's times. In the meantime, I came across 03.0058-2, one of the most common 03.10s, which settled down alternating with 03.0090 on the early-morning D-Zug via Neubrandenburg as far as the Demmin bus stop.

At the end of the time I'd allocated for this stretch of line, I had still not had a run with 03.0010, but I saw it arrive that morning with the early

Swedish ferry train and made up my mind to catch it that lunchtime. In the meantime, I had gone to Neutrelitz to await D613, planning to alight at Oranienburg on the return run as before. However, the single line was clearly even more congested on this occasion, and the southbound service turned up eventually – 89 minutes late – behind 03.0058, so I decided not to risk the ninety-minute connection at Oranienburg and alighted at Fürstenberg thirty minutes earlier to enjoy a wander around the attractive lake-surrounded town until I nearly walked by accident into a Russian military camp, whereupon I fled back to the station and ate my sandwiches there. 03.0010, much decorated, including a brass ring round the chimney, ran very efficiently to Neubrandenburg before the single-line working delays, so I did not go through to Stralsund and risk missing the evening D317 *Berlinaren*, the connection with the day ferry, but returned to Neubrandenburg to stroll round the historic city in the afternoon sunshine and get a decent meal for once. My ploy was successful, for the *Berlinaren*, although 32 minutes late, turned up behind 03.0085-5 (again) but tore away with its seven-coach train in an effort to recoup the lost time. We actually touched 80mph twice before and after a signal check from a diesel-hauled parcels train that had preceded us, and had averaged over 66mph before a series of bad signal checks from a queue of trains waiting to enter Berlin put us back to square one to the frustration of the driver. I had so enjoyed this that I returned to Berlin on the last day of my stay in East Germany and caught the afternoon D-Zug with a packed twelve-coach train weighing 430 tons (it was the May Day Festival Holiday) with 03.0058-2, having turned down 03.0077 on the eight-coach relief which couldn't physically accommodate any more passengers. Again, despite the unpropitious circumstances, we ran well with much noise and 75mph maxima, and I was hoping to return on the relief to the Pasewalk regular 01.5 turn. The main train duly passed us with 01.0507, but when the relief turned up with a class 118 diesel, I took a local cross-country to Neubrandenburg to sample the *Berlinaren* again. Once more, it was 03.0085-5, but a more normal run was experienced this time, efficient enough, but no fireworks. It was back to my hotel for another short night and that last trip on D563 with 03.2058 and then home.

Oil-burning three-cylinder DR Pacific 03.0046-7 at Berlin Ostbahnhof on D270 *Meridian* from Budapest to Stralsund and connecting ferry to Sweden, April 1979. The *Meridian* was diverted via Pasewalk instead of its usual route via Neubrandenburg because of heavy snow, and covered the 68 miles from Bernau to Pasewalk in 'even time' (60mph average start-to-stop) with thirteen coaches, 485 tons.
(David Maidment)

Oil-burning 03.0058-2 hurries D613, Stralsund-Berlin, between Neustrelitz and Fürstenberg, through the heavy snows of the winter of 1979. The line was blocked north of Demmin and buses conveyed passengers from Stralsund to Demmin where D613 started its journey throughout March and April, 2 March 1979.
(Wolfgang Bügel/Eisenbahnstiftung Collection)

Berlin-Stralsund, 1979
07.10 Beograd-Berlin Ostbhf-Stralsund-Sassnitz, D270 *Meridian* **(09.22 Berlin Ostbhf diverted via Pasewalk)**

		18.4.79			22.4.79			
		03.0046-7 Stralsund (3 cyl oil-burning 4-6-2)			**03.0085-5 Stralsund**			
		11 chs, 439/475t			**11 chs, 439/485t**			
			mph			mph		miles
Berlin Ostbahnhof		00.00		9L	00.00		34L	0
Warschauerbrücke		03.20			02.59			
Rummelsburg		07.03	49		06.42	48		
Wühlheide		11.08	35*		-	30*		
Springpfühl		13.19	50		12.42	50		
		-	55		17.05//17.29	sig stand		
Karow		20.54	60		24.45	50		
Berlin-Buch		22.35	65		26.25	62		
Röntgental		-	65		27.45	63		
Zepernick		-	easy		28.57	69		
Bernau	arr	28.11			32.05			
	dep	00.00			00.00			27 5
Rüdnitz		05.43	65		05.39	63		
Biesenthal		08.34	70		08.33	71		
Melchow		-	72		-	73		
Eberswalde		14.52	65/59*		15.10	61*		41.3
Britz		17.23	68		18.04	60		
Chorin Kloster		20.08	70		21.00	63		
Chorin		-	74		22.40	70		
Herzsprung		26.05	75		27.11	74		
Angermünde		28.47	60*		30.00	60*/70		57.5
Greffenberg		34.21	65		35.45	68/ sigs 54*		
Wilmersdorf		36.27	75		38.33	75		
Warnitz		40.43	72		43.03	73		
Seehausen		43.31	67		45.53	66/75		
Prenzlau		51.55	pw 15*		52.05	60*		80.6
Dauer		56.58	76		56.56	70		
Nechlin		59.46	78		59.57	73		
		-	pw 26*/ 50		-	pw 26*/51		
Pasewalk	arr	68.03	[water] 16E		68.11	[water]	13L	95.6
	dep	00.00		T	00.00		12L	
Sandförde		06.25	51		05.57	57		
Jatznick		08.44	65		09.02	62		
Ferdinandshof		13.00	65		13.27	65		
Borckenfriede		16.53	67		17.32	67		
Ducherow		20.13	72 / sigs 22*		20.57	67/69		
Anklam		30.27	51/25*/41		28.19	25*		121.9
Klein Bünzow		38.50	56		36.49	pw 41*		
Züssow		43.42	62/45*		41.51	62/45*		132.5
Gross Kiesow		48.06	71		45.56	68		
Greifswald Süd		53.18	68/72		-	70		

Greifswald	54.32	72		52.09	73			143.8
Mesekenhagen	57.13	71		-	70			
Jeeser	-	68		57.49	68			
Miltzow	62.54	60		61.09	60			
Wüstenfelde	66.14			·64.18				
	73.09//74.38	sig stand		70.53//73.40	sig stand			
Stralsund Rügendamm 77.35			2E	76.31			9L	163.1

21.40 Neubrandenburg (Malmö/Sassnitz)-Berlin Ostbahnhof *Berlinaren*
23.4.79
03.0085-5 Stralsund
7 chs, 282/290t

Neubrandenburg	00.00	mph	32L	0 miles
Burg Stargard	07.33	55		
Cammin	12.43	71		
Blankensee	15.01	79/65*		
Neustrelitz	23.23	72/63*		21.9
Strelitz Alt	-	70		
Düsterfelde	30.33	75		
Fürstenberg	34.18	75/67*		35.0
Drögen	37.23	71		
Dannenwalde	40.56	82		
Altlüdersdorf	43.20	80		
Gransee	45.58//51.43	sigs stand		48.1
Buberow	56.23	50/ sigs 41*		
Guten Germendorf	58.03	62		
Löwenberg	62.15	sigs 22*		
Grüneberg	64.53	75		
Nassenheide	68.02	82		
Fichtengrund	69.46	80		
Sachsenhausen	-	75		
Oranienburg	72.26	sigs 2*		66.3
Lehnitz	74.30	56		
Borgsdorf	76.48	62		
Birkenwerder	78.52	60/55*		
Hohen Neuendorf	80.31	65		
Bergfelde	82.51	40*		
Schönfliess	84.06	72 / sigs 25*		
Springfühl	98.51	75/ 40*		
Wühlheide	100.36	30*/65		
Rummelsburg	104.31	70		
Warschauerbrücke	106.15//113.53	sigs stand		
Berlin Ostbahnhof arr	117.24	[net 88 minutes]	43L	106.3

03.0085 was driven hard from every slack in an attempt to regain time on a sharp schedule. It followed a parcels train from Gransee to Löwenberg and joined a queue of trains awaiting a platform at Berlin Ostbhf. The net time gives an average start to stop speed of 72mph. This was my fastest DR run, with two maxima of 82mph.

Oranienburg-Fürstenberg-Neubrandenburg (from Berlin-Stralsund D-Zügen)

D610 06.10 Berlin Lichtenberg-Stralsund, 21.4.1979　　**D814 13.44 Berlin Lichtenberg-Stralsund, 23.4.1979**
03.0077-2 Bw Stralsund　　　　　　　　　　　　　　　　**03.0010-3 Bw Stralsund**
12 chs, 372/390t　　　　　　　　　　　　　　　　　　　**8 chs, 258/275t**

			mph	T		mph	
Oranienburg		00.00					
Sachsenhausen		02.57	47				
Fichtengrund		04.25	52				
Nassenheide		06.38	66				
Grüneberg		10.38	60				
Löwenberg		13.07	pw 5*				
Guten Germendorf		18.11	54/61				
Buberow		19.19	72/66				
Grausee		21.45	73				
Altlüdersdorf		-	73½				
Dannenwalde		26.33	69/71				
Drögen		30.43	65/70				
Fürstenberg	arr	34.13		2¼ L			
	dep	00.00	pw 10*		00.00	pw 15*	T
Düsterförde		07.25	53/66		06.50	58/68	
Strelitz Alt		13.03	65/73		12.22	75/55*	
Neustrelitz	arr	16.33		3E	16.01		5E
		00.00	38/51	½ E	00.00	48/65	T
Blankensee		12.24	65		12.02	65	
Cammin		14.51	63		14.40	60/65	
Burg Stargard		20.38	pw 10*/56		20.25	sigs 5*/62	
Neubrandenburg	arr	27.34		3E	28.14		3E

There were then bad delays with single-line working between Neubrandenburg and Demmin because of single-line working to restore the track after the snow and frost damage. Both engines in excellent condition, with 03.0010 (later heritage locomotive 03.1010) decorated as the 'pride' of the Stralsund fleet.

03.0010-3 departing from Demmin on D814 13.44 Berlin Lichtenberg-Stralsund a week after the author travelled on this train, 29 April 1979. The train continued through snow-ravaged countryside to Stralsund, but the author abandoned further travel north in order to connect with the southbound *Berlinaren* from Sassnitz and Sweden. 03.0010 was preserved, returned to coal-burning and now stars as 03.1010-2, authorised for maximum speed of 87½mph. (Wolfgang Bügel/ Eisenbahnstiftung Collection)

Berlin-Pasewalk
D514, 16.11 Berlin Lichtenberg-Stralsund, 27.4.1979
03.0058-2 Bw Stralsund
12 chs, 372/430t

Berlin Lichtenberg		00.00	mph
Springfühl		06.06	60
Karow		14.03	55*
Berlin-Buch		15.50	60
Röntgental		17.03	60
Zepernick		18.10	63
Bernau	arr	21.10	(4 mins overtime loading passengers into packed train)
	dep	00.00	
Rüdnitz		05.57	56/60
Biesenthal		09.02	68
Melchow		10.27	75
Eberswalde	arr	15.53	
	dep	00.00	
Britz		05.20	48
		07.30/08.38	sigs stand
Chorin Kloster		12.23	51
Chorin		14.27	56/62
Herzsprung		19.28	70
Angermünde	arr	22.42	
	dep	00.00	
Greiffenberg		07.31	63 working very hard
Wilmersdorf		10.08	65/73
Warnitz		14.19	78
Quast		15.51	74/76/69
Seehausen		16.51	75
Prenzlau	arr	24.11	
	dep	00.00	
Dauer		10.30	60/74
Nechlin		-	75/ pw 26*/50
Pasewalk	arr	19.03	

This was the Friday evening before the May Day holiday, and all trains were crammed full and a relief (with 03.0077) was running ahead of E514. 03.0058 was pushed hard and the exhaust could be heard clearly from around the seventh and eighth coach.

03.0058-2 departs Demmin with D613, the foreshortened Stralsund-Berlin Lichtenberg express formed of the terminated D610, which 03.0085-5 (seen in the small shed) had brought from Berlin. Buses operated between Demmin and Stralsund at this time during repairs to the track after the severe snows of the winter, 29 April 1979. (Wolfgang Bügel/Eisenbahnstiftung Collection)

03.0085-5 roars through Teschenhagen, a small station on the island of Rügen, with D270 *Meridian* formed with some MAV coaches, 1 May 1979. It will connect with the train ferry at Sassnitz for the Swedish port of Trelleborg and onward journey to Malmö. The former train ferry station at Sassnitz Harbour is now closed and replaced by a new freight and road ferry harbour a few miles south of Sassnitz.
(Wolfgang Bügel/ Eisenbahnstiftung Collection)

03.0085-5 leads D270 *Meridian* Budapest-Sassnitz across the Rügendamm with the spires of Stralsund in the background, 30 April 1979.
(Wolfgang Bügel/Eisenbahnstiftung Collection)

Chapter 19

THE 'PLANDAMPF' EXPERIENCE

Railway enthusiasts in Germany, aided and abetted by some overseas enthusiasts, particularly from Great Britain, have encouraged the German railways to mount an occasional event called in German a 'Plandampf' – literally 'Planned steam'. It is an event when some scheduled passenger and freight diagrams, normally scheduled for diesel (or electric) operation, are covered for two or three days by a group of preserved steam locomotives, for the benefit of railway buffs who wish to ride behind, or photograph, or just observe what seems in many ways a return to a time when steam was the regular traction power. Because the passenger services selected are open to the general public buying their tickets in a normal way, it is quite interesting sometimes to watch the reaction of those caught unawares.

The first privately-sponsored D-Zug runs took place in September 1990 between Dresden and Görlitz with DR 03.2001, with a 3-day event a month later with three preserved locomotives running thirty-six passenger and goods trains on the Saalfeld-Camburg-Weimar route. The word *Plandampf* was coined then to describe the financing of such runs in advance. Between then and 1995, when DBAG disallowed further express passenger *Plandampf* events because of lack of carriage heating facilities and PR concerns (a decision luckily overturned in later years), some 339 regular express passenger trains were operated with preserved steam traction, the peak year being 1994, when

Restored 01.137 departs Görlitz with a special train for Dresden, part of a *Plandampf* event on 5 September 1993.
(Roger Bastin)

01.137 and preserved Saxon 2-8-2 19.017 on display at Freital Hainsberg, 26 August 1983. (Graham Stacey)

A special train double-headed by 03.1010-2 and the unique Pacific rebuild 02.0201-0 (also identified as 18.201) at Riestedt, passed by a coal train hauled by a class 232 diesel locomotive, 27 August 1983. (Graham Stacey)

The *Viva* Magistrale (a *Plandampf* event) with the photo of 01.1531-1 hauling D1643 at speed towards Berlin taken from the footplate of 03.1010-2, travelling at 80mph on D642 westbound to Magdeburg and Halberstadt, at Gerwisch Station, October 1991. (Robin Garn)

The *Metropol* took place between 2 and 4 April 1994, with steam (including a Russian troop train) between Berlin and Magdeburg. 03.2204-0 approaches with the empty stock of D2242 from Berlin to Amsterdam-Schipol, taken from the sleeping car of D243 Paris-Berlin, behind 01.1531-1 as they pass each other (on time) at Berlin-Ostkreuz, 4 April 1994. (Robin Garn)

101 fast trains were steam-hauled. There were a couple of final efforts in 1997-8, with five further steam-hauled D-Züge recorded. Roger Bastin and Graham Stacey enjoyed some early railtours and heritage events, and some of the photos they took are displayed here, together with photos that Robin Garn took of an ambitious *Plandampf* between Magdeburg and Berlin on heavy overnight international expresses in April 1994.

I enjoyed two *Plandampf* events in 1993 and 1994, both of which I was able to add to legitmate business commitments when I was going

01.1531-1 on arrival at Berlin (Zoo) with the heavy overnight D243 from Paris, which it took over at Magdeburg eight minutes late, arriving at Berlin a couple of minutes early as seen in this photo, 4 April 1994. (Robin Garn)

to be nearby on the continent at the right time. The conference was always held in May, and in 1993 it concluded on the Saturday morning of the weekend that the DR was holding a *Plandampf* on the Bebra-Erfurt main line, near enough to Frankfurt to join the event, and enjoy the planned services on the Saturday afternoon and evening, and the whole of the Sunday.

The event publicised the presence of three Pacifics working D-, E-, and P-Züge over the main line section and three 'lesser' locomotives (a P8, a class 50 2-10-0 and a class 62 4-6-4T) working stopping services from Eisenach towards Meiningen. In great expectation, therefore, I joined D2756 Frankfurt (Main) to Leipzig at lunchtime on the Saturday behind a DB 103 electric locomotive and duly found 01.1531-1 waiting to take us forward, just as in the

1970s. Half the population of Bebra seemed to be enjoying the spectacle on a sunny Saturday afternoon, fathers bringing their children to see the fun. Unfortunately, there was a lot of engineering work on the section chosen, with some long p-way slacks and one short stretch of single-line working, so it is surprising in the circumstances that the DR authorities permitted the *Plandampf* at all. However, most of the drivers made valiant attemts to keep time with steam, and I noted, if anything, that the steam-hauled expresses were as punctual, if not more punctual, than their diesel-hauled counterparts. The hardest trains for the steam locomotives to time were actually the tightly-timed stopping services, usually four or five coaches and diagrammed for DR class 132 diesels. The Pacifics could just about hold their own on

these, but had no margin to cope with the engineering slacks.

The three Pacifics sharing the main line turns were 01.1531-1, now coal-burning, formerly oil-burner 01.531, two-cylinder standard Pacific 01.2137-6, formerly 01.137 of Dresden, and 03.1010-2, that had been a test loco with 03.1074 at Halle Research Centre in the 1960s, and then Stralsund's oil-burning 03.0010-3 that seemed to be the Depot's mascot and was always kept in superb condition. The two 01s were limited to 75mph, but 03.1010 was authorised to run at 87½mph, though unfortunately the line speed of this route did not allow this. I alighted from D2756 at Gotha and returned to Eisenach behind 01.2137-6 on the eight-coach D2752 Cottbus-Eisenach, before completing the trio on the six-coach D2659 starting from Eisenach and destined for Cottbus, which 03.1010-2 and I would both take as far as Erfurt where I'd booked a hotel for the night.

The heavy sleeping car train to Saratov and Voronezh platformed at Berlin (Zoo) before departure of the 12 coach 691-tonnes train, D1249, to be hauled to the East German /Polish border by two-cylinder DR restored Pacific 03.2204-0, 2 April 1994. Part of a log of this train between Hangelsberg and Frankfurt/Oder, recorded by Alastair Wood, is found on page 352. (Robin Garn)

My only full day during this *Plandampf* event was Sunday, 9 May, so I had to take full advantage of it. I had received details in advance of the trains booked for steam haulage and the diagrams planned for the three Pacifics, and had worked out the following somewhat hectic roster for my own tour of duty:

5.58am N8554 Erfurt-Eisenach (3 coach + 2 vans stopping service) - 01.1531-1

7.09am D2653 Eisenach-Gotha (7 coaches) - 01.2137-6

8.15am D2758 Gotha-Bebra (9 coaches) - 03.1010-2

10.19am D2753 Bebra-Gotha (9 coaches) – 01.1531-1

12.15pm D2754 Gotha-Eisenach (7 coaches) – 01.2137-6

This intensive 'see-saw' would then be followed by a trip from Eisenach past the Wartburg on the single line to Meiningen, allowing me to watch various train movements around Eisenach, and then hope to pick up a couple out of the Prussian Railways P8 4-6-0, the Baltic tank class 62, or the DR 50.35 that were operating shorter-distance trains. After a turnround at Wasungen, a small country station, I would be back in Eisenach by 4.30pm, in time to pick up again on the main line schedule of:

5.09pm D2755 Eisenach-Gotha (8 coaches) – 01.2137-6 (D-Zug from Frankfurt/Main to Frankfurt/Oder)

6.15pm D2752 Gotha-Bebra (10 coaches) – 03.1010-2

9.15pm N8569 Bebra-Erfurt (5 coaches) – 03.1010-2

What were the highlights? Firstly, astonishment that everything worked to plan, no failures, no late running so extreme that any connections were missed. Secondly, another glorious May day with warm sunshine throughout that made you glad to be alive. Thirdly, locomotive running performance of the highest order, with no time loss debited to the steam locomotive, although the large number of track slowings caused some late running.

I got to Erfurt Station at dawn to find a typical DR local train, three coaches and a couple of vans, with super power 01.1531-1 and oozing steam between each vehicle as the steam heating awakened the creaking coaches. We stopped at every single station en route to Eisenach – a one-hour journey, with rarely more than five minutes between stops and speed accelerating to around 50-55mph between stations, needed to keep time. As mentioned earlier, I concluded that these local trains, presumably booked for a 132 diesel normally, were much harder to time with steam than the expresses, and we had dropped seven minutes to Gotha, admittedly with a couple of minutes station overtime and one 10mph signal check. We cut station time at Gotha and departed one minute late, and just about held point-to-point times to Eisenach, a two-minute loss accounted for by another temporary speed restriction. This sort of train was ideal for those more intent on tape-recording than performance logging.

01.2137-6 on the 7.09am from Eisenach back to Gotha performed efficiently enough, losing three

minutes on the twenty-two minute schedule for the 18.1 miles because of the 20mph single-line slack, top speed 63mph. I was looking forward to the next leg, when 03.1010-2 would have a good run with a more substantial load – nine coaches, 322 tons tare/340 tons gross. The train was one of the regular Cottbus-Frankfurt (Main) interval expresses and was well filled – indeed, most enthusiasts filled the corridors while I took an empty corridor side-corner seat in a compartment occupied by three nuns. They were clearly enjoying themselves and as we roared through the beautiful countryside, one of them suddenly wound down the main half-window and they drank in the ear-splitting sounds of the Pacific as it excelled itself, running the eighteen miles to Eisenach in 20 minutes 45 seconds (18 minutes net – even time) with a top speed of 76mph. Leaving Eisenach on time, we reached 75mph, by Herleshausen, less than ten minutes out and despite more single-line working, including a dead stand, were just over a minute early into Bebra. I shall not forget in a hurry the sight of the three elderly nuns trying with one hand to hold on to their wimples which were attempting to fly off in the fierce draught while running at 75mph, and balancing their totties of something medicinal (?) in their other hand! And laughing like schoolgirls at the same time!

After this shock to the system, I calmed down by watching 44.1486 shunting in the sidings at Bebra while 03.1010 retreated among the electrics on the depot, and 01.1531-1 appeared and stood ready for the next Frankfurt/Main-Frankfurt/ Oder Schnellzug. The train was a heavy nine-coach train, 358 tons tare, a very full 385 tons gross, and heads were hanging out of every window in the front three coaches. An initial 42mph past Ronshausen fell to 35mph before Hönebach Tunnel, and then four bouts of single line working for engineering work and a 12mph signal check made us twelve minutes late into Eisenach. Although we recovered five minutes of lost time at Eisenach, we did labour after the long slowing past Wutha and failed to get above 58mph, before arriving thirteen minutes late at Gotha. This was probably the poorest performance of the event, although there was no net time loss.

Midday at Gotha and the platforms were crowded with weekenders going back to Frankfurt and points west, 'normal' passengers far outweighing the enthusiast fraternity. It was therefore a joy to watch the incredulity of the awaiting hordes as 01.2137-6 swept into the platform virtually on time, with D2754 (Cottbus-Frankfurt/Main). The seven-coach train was full and standing, and despite a special unscheduled stop at Fröttstadt, we only dropped three minutes on the twenty-minute schedule (net time seventeen minutes well under even time) by dint of sustained high speed running between 77 and 79mph for over five minutes.

It was now time to use the interval available to visit the Eisenach Mitropa, although there was so much to see. 50.3688 had arrived on a local from Meiningen and 44.1486 arrived from Bebra,

and, after shunting out a heavy freight, departed thunderously for Bebra again. Next 03.1010 ran in smoothly with a Bebra-Erfurt stopping train. In the meantime, ex-Prussian P8, 38.1182-5, sidled down to the four coaches that had just arrived from Meiningen in order to form my next trip – the 2.04pm N7729 local from Eisenach to Meiningen via Bad Salzungen. I returned behind Baltic Tank 62.015 arriving back in Eisenach nine minutes late.

A half-an-hour wait and it was another sprint from Eisenach to Gotha, D2755 connecting Frankfurt (Main) with Frankfurt (Oder), with 01.2137-6 yet again. The eight-coach 340-ton gross load was enough to tax the 01 with the usual long p-way slack and we dropped three minutes on the twenty-two-minute schedule without exceeding 62mph. Now for the last round trip – to Bebra and back to Erfurt, both with my favourite 03.1010-2. The train was the heavy ten-coach D2752, from Cottbus to Frankfurt (Main), packed tight that Sunday evening and weighing a full 440 tons gross. It was a good omen that it arrived only two minutes behind schedule and it was obvious from the start that we were in for something exceptional. The ten-minute sprint to the first stop, Fröttstadt, was completed on schedule and then we winged it for Eisenach with sustained high-speed running at 80-82½mph from Mechtenstadt-Sättelstadt to Schönau before the obligatory slowing onto the single line at Wutha. The eighteen miles had taken only twenty-five minutes, including the Fröttstadt stop and I reckoned it was another

net seventeen minutes start to stop. Departing five minutes late, we thundered out of Eisenach, reaching 50mph in just under three minutes, and then ran at a steady 75mph until the temporary speed restriction to 37mph before Gerstungen, after which we had to climb steadily to Hönebach Tunnel from the east. We settled to a sustained 48mph, plunged into the tunnel at 45mph and freewheeled down the other side of the bank at 70mph. Despite a slow entry to the west side of the station, we had regained a minute and were just four minutes late when we handed over to the DB 103 electric at Bebra.

I now had time for a leisurely evening meal, watched 03.1010 being coaled, watered and turned, and waited for it to gracefully couple up with the five-coach all-stations local to Erfurt (N8569) – the parting shot of this *Plandampf*. Darkness fell as we departed and it was a joy to open the window wide to the mellow air, few enthusiasts or genuine passengers paying attention to this stopping service. Merry noises were heard as the Pacific blasted away to overcome the tight timings and the effects of the p-way slacks, and we were a couple of minutes late at Gerstungen where we waited to catch our breath, leaving on time. An immediate mile-long 20mph speed restriction and four minutes station overtime at Hörschel put us nearly ten minutes late into Eisenach, and after that it was a real struggle, flailing away in the darkness, unable to see kilometreposts, losing time steadily as the speed restrictions took further toll. By Fröttstadt

The Frankfurt-am-Main-Leipzig D2756 with 01.1531-1 seen from the train as it departs from Bebra and climbs to Hönebach Tunnel with the first steam-hauled *Plandampf* service of the 1993 event, 8 May 1993. 01.1531 was converted from oil-burning 01.0531 to coal-burning on preservation. (David Maidment)

01.1531-1 departs from Gotha for Erfurt and Frankfurt (Oder) with D2753 as part of the *Plandampf* event, 9 May 1993. (David Maidment)

our lateness had grown to sixteen minutes, but then we got, second wind, and raced away between stops to 65mph and more, with an estimated 70mph just before Gotha. We finally wended our way into Erfurt just before midnight, with me virtually the only passenger, and I spent a few minutes in the dim lighting of the station absorbing the hiss of steam, the oily smell, the pant of the air brake – a scene so 'ordinary' in many ways that it did not seem like a special day, but a time warp back to the 1960s and 1970s.

The following year, 1994, I had a further opportunity to sample the *Plandampf* experience. It was going to be a complex week though, with sleep opportunities even fewer than usual. I had a meeting at the Paris HQ of the *Union International de Chemins de Fer* (UIC) on Monday 2 and Tuesday, 3 May, and found that these coincided with another DR-based *Plandampf* event. Before my UIC meeting, I could savour two days of booked steam services on the Dresden-Görlitz and Dresden-Zittau main lines, and after the meetings I could catch up on the last two days of a similar event in

the Thüringerwald, based around the Erfurt-Arnstadt-Saalfeld-Meiningen routes.

On Friday, 29 April, a punctual Lufthansa flight deposited me in Frankfurt (Main) in a central European heatwave in good time to catch the sleeper from there to Warsaw and Moscow, D451, 11.58pm ex-Frankfurt. I awoke on the Saturday morning to a misty sunrise over a flat landscape near

Preserved coal-burning three-cylinder 03.1010-2 (formerly oil-burning 03.0010-3), runs into Eisenach with a three-coach P-Zug from Bebra to Erfurt, 9 May 1993. (David Maidment)

coach nearer the front of the train, now apparently thirteen coaches, 524 tons tare / 550 tons gross, and spied a wisp of steam in the distance. Reassured, I watched DR standard Pacific 01.2137-6 back down onto this international express and couple up, observed by a small band of fellow participants and a larger gaggle of genuine passengers, and bystanders who wondered what on earth was going on. At the back, a bleached red 232.533-0 attached itself to provide electric heating and some initial banking up the steep grades for the first dozen miles – after that it just applied enough power to provide no drag on the train engine as 550 tons was quite enough for a single 01 to time an international express without the weight of the heavy 232 diesel as well.

We departed Dresden Neustadt right on time at 07.27

01.2137-6 running into Gotha with a Sunday afternoon D2754 Cottbus-Frankfurt-am-Main express during the May 1993 *Plandampf* between Bebra and Erfurt, 9 May 1993. (David Maidment)

Riesa, and by 7am we were snaking our way round the western leg of the triangle avoiding Dresden Hauptbahnhof across the Elbe

Bridge into Neustadt station just five minutes late. I humped my case and camera bag out of the sleeper along the platform to a

and hammered out through the industrial suburbs into wooded hills at a steady 38mph, reaching a maximum of 56mph at Arnsdorf before a couple of p-way speed restrictions and single-line working before Bischofswerda. Then the 01 opened up to reach 70mph, and the sun broke through the mist as we negotiated the long curve into Bautzen Station, arriving a full six minutes early. We waited time, then negotiated yet another temporary single-line 20mph slowing with a maximum of 56mph, arriving at Löbau on time. The line speed for most of this route was only 62mph, with a small section at 75mph between Bischofswerda and Bautzen. At Löbau, the end of the platform beyond the perspiring 01 jutted onto a viaduct and swarms of black flies were hovering round the bushes in the heat. After photographing the departing train and listening to its exhaust beats echoing back from the wooded hill ahead, most of us found a small snack bar outside in the cobbled station yard and ate a bockwurst as breakfast in the heathaze – 9am and the temperature already in the upper seventies Fahrenheit.

A twenty-minute wait saw us back in the station to pick up D456 Warsaw-Dresden, which drifted in on time behind a two-cylinder 03.2 hauling a lightweight international express of only three coaches; apparently a defect on the booked rolling stock had reduced the formation, including the loss of the buffet. The *Plandampf* crowd crammed into the already overfull train and blocked the corridors, all windows lowered to the maximum! Preserved 03.2204, based at Cottbus,

whirled its featherweight 125-tons load up to 64mph before the first station – Breitendorf – but then a long speed restriction to 25mph past Kubshütz made us five minutes late into Bautzen and station over time, whilst further crowds tried to pack themselves into the reduced formation made us seven minutes late away. For some reason, we then made a special additional stop at Bischofswerda and despite yet more single-line working for engineering work, with a last-minute dash past Arnsdorf at 65mph, we were only nine minutes late on arrival in the cavernous Dresden Hbf.

The DR seemed to be undertaking very extensive engineering work at this time, investing a significant sum to bring the former DR up to DB standards. I had seen this the previous year during the Bebra-Erfurt *Plandampf* and the Dresden-Bautzen section in particular had two sections of single line working and a further 25mph speed restriction – all long. Not only were delays encountered because of these restrictions, but late running meant delays often waiting access to the single line sections. In the circumstances, I'm very surprised the DR authorities had agreed to the *Plandampf*, although the steam locos seemed to be as successful at reducing the delays to a minimum as the diesel-hauled services. I discovered that because of the limited track capacity, some locals between Dresden and Bautzen had been cancelled, hence the additional stops inserted to some expresses.

Dresden Hbf on this Saturday morning was a very steamy place. 03.2204-0 stood proudly at the buffer stops in the lower-level

train shed. Baltic tank 62.1015-7 was belching sulphurous smoke just inside the overall roof at the head of a local to Arnsdorf. Three-cylinder 03.1010-2 was taking water at a column just outside the main shed, prior to backing on to four coaches forming a D-Zug to Görlitz standing on the upper level platforms. Bone fide passengers looked bemused as though they had dropped into a time warp.

I joined D1853, 11.42am Dresden Hbf-Görlitz, with 03.1010-2 and four coaches, 175 tons gross. We left the Hauptbahnhof and Neustadt on time, and showed energy whenever we could with a slightly over the top 71mph before Arnsdorf and 65mph after all the engineering work just before Bautzen. We took 50 minutes 30 seconds start to stop for the thirty-five miles from Neustadt, a loss of nearly five minutes on a section with a low line speed as well as all the engineering restrictions. We ran the fourteen miles on to Löbau in 19 minutes 59 seconds, with a top speed of 71mph and yet another 25mph single-line section, lost another minute in station overtime and then hot-footed it for Görlitz, the final fifteen miles taking 20 minutes 30 seconds, top speed 69mph, but with a 30mph restriction through Reichenbach and a 10mph signal check approaching the terminus. We arrived six minutes late.

The three-cylinder Pacific turned and was now standing at the head of the same four coaches forming D1854, 2.47pm Görlitz-Dresden. We left on time and completed the fifteen miles to Löbau in 18 minutes 27 seconds, with a top speed of 65mph and 35mph slowing through Reichenbach. There we waited for nearly ten minutes for the arrival of 03.2204 off the single-line section, and then covered the fourteen miles to Bautzen in 16 minutes 45 seconds, maximum speed 70mph. The 03.10 was in beautiful condition, with a perfectly even roar, heard to great effect on these two runs in the constant accelerations to permitted line speed.

The old part of the town was undergoing much restoration (like the railway), and the square round the cathedral and the main castle was resplendent. Bautzen seemed to be a very attractive city, deserted apart from kids playing in a fountain on this sunny afternoon. I got back in good time to see D1852 (4.57pm Görlitz-Dresden) run in on time behind 03.2204-0.

The run to Dresden hardly permitted the 03 to demonstrate its capabilities, although the many additional stops allowed it to show off its starting prowess and throw its exhaust, echoing off numerous station buildings. We departed just over one minute late, touched 68mph by the first station, Seitschen, but then substituted for a cancelled local train by stopping at Bischofswerda, Weikersdorf, Grossharthau and Arnsdorf. We then roared away, accelerating our four-coach train to 70mph down the grade to Dresden, arriving at Neustadt nine minutes late.

I woke, prompted by my alarm, at 5.30am on May Day, a Sunday. Breakfast was served in the Tourist Centre opposite at 6am precisely – not a second earlier despite the queue of the *Plandampf* crowd, bleary-eyed and hopeful, standing

a few minutes earlier before a resolutely shut door. I joined the first local to Arnsdorf that was shuffling in to the upper level on a very bleak morning – the temperature must have dropped twenty degrees overnight after a violent thunderstorm – behind the 4-6-4T, 62.1015-7. We departed at 6.49am on the dot at a brisk pace, stopping briefly at Dresden Mitte and arriving at Neustadt Station a minute early. This place now became very steamy as 03.2204 was blowing off steam furiously on the 7.15 Eilzug to Zittau, and 03.1010-2 ran in light engine from Altstadt Depot and passed through the Station positioning itself to take over D451 for Görlitz and points east to Warsaw and Moscow, which the engine would work as far as the Polish border. The sleeping car express from Frankfurt drew in punctually behind a 143 electric and, as soon as the train came to

a stand, a 232 diesel buffered up to the rear to provide heating and a bit more assistance than had been given to the 01 the previous day. The train was eleven coaches, weighing 448 tons tare, 470 tons gross and departure was on time, the climb out past the industrial district being achieved at a steady 45mph, and a full 75mph being reached after Bischofswerda and the succession of engineering slowings. Bautzen was reached a triumphant eight minutes early and the run onto Löbau was made punctually without any further fireworks. The 03.10 was worked very hard and emitted its usual satisfying roar, but assistance from the rear diesel was more apparent, especially in recovering from the single-line engineering slowings.

01.2137-6 swept into Löbau Station with the four-coach D456, Warsaw-Dresden. We kept time to Bautzen, with a maximum speed

Preserved 01.2137-6 takes over from a 143 DR electric locomotive at Dresden Neustadt at the head of the thirteen-coach sleeping car express D451 from Frankfurt (Main) to Moscow during the *Plandampf* between Dresden and the Polish border at Görlitz, 30 April 1994. (David Maidment)

View from D451, the Frankfurt (Main)-Moscow sleeping car train, with 01.2137-6 accelerating from Dresden Neustadt, where it took over from an electric locomotive, nearing Bischofswerda, 30 April 1994.
(David Maidment)

Reichsbahn Standard 01 Pacific 01.2137-6 on D451 23.58 Frankfurt (Main) Warsaw-Moscow sleeping car express at Löbau in the former East Germany between Dresden and Görlitz, during the *Plandampf* of April/May, 30 April 1994.
(David Maidment)

03.1010-2 at Dresden Hbf (high level) with D1853 Dresden-Görlitz during the 1994 '*Plandampf*', 30 April 1994. (David Maidment)

of 70mph, then a special stop at Bischofswerda and the usual engineering slowings made our arrival at Dresden Neustadt seven minutes late. I baled out here this time as I had promised myself a run as far as Bischofswerda on the Zittau semi-fast. This was formed of five newly-liveried Interregio coaches and a resplendent 03.2001-0, adorned with large smoke deflectors and burnished boiler bands. The train was E4487, 11.15am Dresden-Zittau, and it ran crisply, stopping at Arnsdorf with maxima of 61 and 64mph before and after this stop. Arrival in Bischofswerda was on time.

The Zittau-Dresden Neustadt train, E4486, arrived punctually

03.2204-0 rushes into Löbau with the three-coach D456 Warsaw-Dresden, 30 April 1994. (David Maidment)

Preserved 03.2001-0 (03.001), the prototype 03, restored to its original condition, but carrying its later DR number, at the head of E4487 to Zittau at Dresden Neustadt, 1 May 1994. (David Maidment)

behind 03.2204-0, but was held for ten minutes awaiting a diesel-hauled train off the temporary single-line section to Arnsdorf. There were no additional stops this time, and the 03 and its light four-coach train lost no further time despite the single-line working and a signal check outside Neustadt Station.

I was going to have to terminate my involvement in this part of the *Plandampf* as I had to catch the 4.45pm Intercity express to Frankfurt and an overnight sleeper service from there to Paris to be ready for my UIC meeting on Monday morning, and to look forward to the next day when the meeting would finish at lunchtime, enabling me to return to Frankfurt and Erfurt, ready for another couple of days' *Plandampf* on the scenic and heavily-graded Erfurt-Arnstadt-Meiningen route.

On Tuesday 3 May 1994, I finished my UIC meeting at 12.30, and went back via Strasbourg, Karlsruhe, Mannheim and Frankfurt, connecting to D451 sleeper back to Erfurt (the same Dresden-Warsaw-Moscow sleeper caught the previous Friday night that was then scheduled for steam haulage between Dresden Neustadt and Görlitz). I made my way to the now-familiar PKP sleeping car on D451 waiting alongside the post office activity on platform 1. I alighted with some difficulty at Erfurt as the Polish sleeping car attendant was sure I was booked through to Leipzig, and was reluctant to release my passport and tickets.

The *Plandampf* programme was called *Der Berg ruft* ('The Mountain calls'). The initial steam elements on the line from Erfurt south to Arnstadt and Meiningen were with the class 41 2-8-2, 41.1185-2, which I covered, but my main aim was to get to Leipzig in good time to connect with the scheduled steam 12.22pm Leipzig-Arnstadt-Würzburg D2155. The vast empty concourse of Leipzig and its twenty-plus platforms glistened cathedral-like in the dusty sun rays, and I walked to the end of the platform in the hot sun and peered to see if I could see any sign of steam and, after an anxious quarter of an hour, a plume of smoke could be glimpsed behind some buildings on the horizon. A few moments later, a black tender could be seen inching its way towards the station, and the 03.2, with its original style tender and large smoke deflectors, stood poised to back on to the late-running Cottbus-Würzburg express.

The six-coach train ran in fifteen minutes late behind a 143 and 03.2001-0 backed smartly down, cylinder drain cocks hissing noisily, alerting the casual passengers to the unusual sight of a steam Pacific in the midst of electric expresses, and push-pull suburban trains rushing in and out of the station.

The 03 was coupled up so swiftly and the station work conducted so efficiently that our departure was almost on time. The staccato exhaust from the Pacific leaving the station alerted the unsuspecting casual passengers and heralded straightaway that the driver meant business. A quite exceptional run followed. The noise from the front end turned people's heads upwards from the streets below, their back gardens or from their bedroom windows and those of us in the train got a sharp reminder of the days when smuts in the eye were a common hazard! One of the pleasures of the *Plandampf* programme is watching the reaction of ordinary people going about their business suddenly confronted by a roaring, snorting beast belching black smoke over the town. Best of all are the faces of impatient motorists waiting at level crossings as they realise the nature of the thundering train bearing down on them. The young children get excited, and elderly folk stop and stare wistfully at the vision from their youth. This journey from Leipzig was a particularly rich experience of this phenomenon. In the next compartment a small boy of three or four travelling with his mother could not believe what was going on, and spent most of the time hanging out of the open

window mesmerised until the inevitable smut got lodged in his eye and the experience began to pall rather rapidly.

The train was D2155 Cottbus-Würzburg and was formed of six coaches, 224 tons tare, 245 tons gross. We had already reached 65mph by the suburbs of Leipzig-Leutsch and 70 before a 50mph restriction at Militz, then speed was piled on with a maximum of 76mph between Kotschau and Bad Dürrenberg. With a slack to 47mph through Grosskorbetha, we stopped at Weissenfels in 26 minutes 33 seconds from Leipzig Hbf. We then roared away, achieving a full 75mph in the 9-minute 40-second run to Naumburg, the thirty-four miles from Leipzig being completed in 36 minutes 13 seconds including the Weissenfels stop! Another acceleration to 75mph before the Apolda stop followed, but the next section was spoiled by a check to walking pace to pass a message from the signalman at Ossmannstedt to the driver, so that we took 30 minutes 27 seconds for the 25.5 miles, including the Apolda stop. Despite this delay, we were still running on time and on the next section to Erfurt, the driver pushed his willing steed to a steady 78mph (other timers made it a full 80mph) between Hopfgarten and Vieselbach, before our rapid entrance took Erfurt by surprise and we were stopped outside the station for half a minute. Even so, we had completed the fourteen miles in 17 minutes, 01 second, or about 15 minutes net. It had been a thrilling experience as the engine roared through the countryside at top speed, whistle shrieking, smoke swirling everywhere. We continued at a slightly more sedate pace with a maximum of 65 before a dead stand at signals at the Neudietendorf Junction, but arrival at Arnstadt, now in torrential rain, was still on time.

D2157, an express from Stralsund to Würzburg, was scheduled for steam haulage through to Meiningen each day of the *Plandampf* arrangements, and on this day, as Pacific 01.1531-1 was diagrammed with an eight coach train (325 tons gross), a banker was provided to assist to the summit of the line at Oberhof. The train ran in a couple of minutes late behind a 143 electric and while the 01.5 backed on to the head end, 2-10-0 50.3688-4 buffered up to the rear. The climb through Gehlberg to Oberhof through the dripping trees was thrilling in the extreme, with both ends of the train and their hard-working locomotives almost continuously in view on the winding and heavily-graded route. I was about three coaches from the rear, but the noise from the 01.5 at the front was deafening and I was very surprised that it kept its feet as the weather deteriorated even more as we neared the summit. The climb was completed in spectacular style, with speed sustained at 48mph on the lower reaches and 43mph near the summit, and the overall time from Arnstadt to Oberhof of 28 minutes 45 seconds turned a three-minute late departure into a four-minute early arrival. Timekeeping then fell apart as we had to wait for a late-running diesel-hauled train before we could access the single line and drift downhill to

Zella-Mehlis, Suhl and Meiningen. The line's curvature meant we did not exceed 60mph and we were seven minutes late into Meiningen.

The air was fresh and the trees glistened in the reflected sunlight after the torrential rain as I made my way through Meiningen's 'English Park' to the castle and square in the old part of the town in search of a substantial meal – luckily fulfilled. The timing was just right and an amble back through the same park, complete with folly and lake, found 01.1531-1 turned and heading the last local back to Erfurt, framed by a gaudy rainbow etched against the black sky that dominated the northern hills. Despite the light load (three coaches) and superfluity of power available, there was still plenty of opportunity for graphic

noises and volcanic exhaust on the climb to Oberhof. The departure from Suhl was especially dramatic, leaving the Station on a viaduct high above a main road junction, threatening to cause a road accident as drivers caught sight of a huge steam engine charging the steepest part of the climb to Zella-Mehlis. We had left Meiningen eight minutes late (waiting a connection), but the sustained 46mph on the steepest part of the climb meant we had regained all but two minutes by the summit. We rocketed downhill round the curves under light steam at an uncomfortable 67mph and arrived at Arnstadt just one minute late.

Next day (Thursday, 5 May) I arrived early at Arnstadt Station on a misty morning promising more rain and caught the 7.49am

Preserved prototype
03.2001-0 (formerly numbered 03.001) at Leipzig Hbf with D2155 Cottbus-Würzburg, which it worked at 'even time' speeds as far as Erfurt, as part of the 1994 *Plandampf* between Arnstadt/Erfurt and Dresden/Görlitz, 4 May 1994. (David Maidment)

Halle-Berlin
D2208, 31.3.1994
06.08 Saalfeld-Berlin
03.1010-2
5 chs, 187/200t

Halle	00.00	mph	1L	0 miles
Hohenthurm	09.17	pws 39*/66		
Landsberg	12.07	75		
Brehna	14.23	76		
Bitterfeld	20.49		2½ L	18.64
	00.00		3L	o
Wolfen	04.46	69		
Jossnitz	06.02	74		
Marke	09.15	79		
Dessau Sud	12.37	75		
Dessau	15.44		3 ½ L	15.9
	00.00		1L	0
Rosslau	05.02	55		
Mainsdorf	06.33	66/pws 46*	Line speed 100km/hr	
Theissen	11.44	65	"	
Medewitz	19.48	64/62	"	
Wiesenburg	23.01	61	"	
Borne	25.52	80/87		
km 68	-	90		
Belzig	29.55		T	29.32
	00.00		½ L	0
Boltz	05.25	85½		
Brück	08.08	75/82		
Borkheide	11.48	82		
Beelitz	14.41	84		
Seddin	17.04	73		
Michendorf	20.05	pws 30*		22.8
Ringbahn	Sigs stands (several) incl SLW			
Berlin Schönefeld	65.44		17L	44.7

Hangelsberg-Frankfurt (Oder)
D1249, 2.4.1994
15.06 Berlin-Saratov & Voronezh (Sats only)
03.2204-0
12 Russian sleeping cars, 660/680t

Hangelsberg	00.00	mph	10½ L	0 miles
Furstenwalde	09.33	54		
Berkenbrück	14.08	62		
Briesen	19.05	64/62		15.8
Jacobsdorf	22.23	53		
Pillgram	24.44	49/50		
Km 74 (summit)	27.22	42		
F-Rosengarten	29.02	49/52		
Frankfurt (Oder)	33.58	sigs 5*	8 ½ L	27.4

Magdeburg-Brandenburg, 3.4.1994
D2243 08.35 Amsterdam Schipol-Berlin
03.2204-0
8 chs, 312/330t

Magdeburg	00.00	mph	1L	0 miles
Biederitz		08.19	60	
Möser	15.44	SLW 15*		
Burg	23.40	52/pws 30*		15.1
Güsen	31.23	72		
B-Parchen	35.01	78		
Genthin	38.29	76/78		31.2
Km 88	-	79		
Kade	42.41	pws 54*		
Wusterwitz	47.02	57/47		
Kirchmöser	49.21	59		
Brandenburg	60.06		4E	49.96

03.2204 continued with D2243 to Berlin with speeds in the low seventies before Potsdam and despite a signal stand at Berlin-Charlottenburg, arrived at Berlin Ostbahnhof just one minute late.

N-Zug from Arnstadt to Saalfeld, four coaches and 01.1531-1 again. Timekeeping was fairly simple and speeds were low between the frequent stops. We were delayed two minutes at Singen by a large party of schoolchildren joining the train and ran up to the early 50s mph down the Saale Valley arriving at Saalfeld two minutes late. Our set, minus one coach that

the 01 removed, formed E4400 9.06am Saalfeld-Erfurt and 03.2001-0 dropped onto us as soon as we stopped. The three-coach train provided no obstacle as far as Rottenbach, where we were early, but after a 10mph engineering slack at Paulinzella we almost slipped to a standstill on the steep gradient and wet rails, eventually recovering amid sudden bouts of slipping to

29mph. Even so, we arrived right time at Stadtilm and then drifted downhill to Arnstadt.

The *Plandampf* continued for another day, and the motive power included the 41 and a 44 2-10-0, but no further Pacific runs. Further descriptions of the rest of the *Plandampf*, along with other accounts of overseas journeys between 1961 and 2002, can be found in my

Berlin-Halle, 4.4.1994
D2207, 15.21 Berlin-Saalfeld & Nuremberg
18.201, 3 cylinder oil-burning 4-6-2
10 chs, 379/405t

Berlin Schönefeld	00.00	mph	½ L	0 miles
Glassower Damm	07.46	60		
Genshagener Heide Box	14.49	sigs 10*		
Saarmund	25.18	47		
Michendorf	31.26	55 / /30*		21.9
Berlitz	39.03	68		
Borkheide	42.13	76		
Brück	46.07	83		
Boltz	49.03	71		
Belzig	54.36		5L	44.76
	00.00		6L	0
Bergholz	05.13	32		
Km 74 (summit)	-	48		
Wiesenburg	13.28	61	Line speed 100km/hr	
Medewitz	16.43	69/71	"	
Thiessen		25.14	53*//68	"
Meinsdorf	31.26	20*		
Dessau	37.57		10L	29.3
	00.00		9½ L	0
Ragohn	11.43	65/sigs 20*		
Bitterfeld	23.44		15½ L	15.72
	00.00		12½ L	0
Km 139	-	26*/55		
Brehna	09.50	65		
Landsberg	12.25	69		
Hohenthurm	15.12	76½		
Halle	22.52		16L	18.64

This was a heavy train for a 7ft 6in-wheeled Pacific in adverse weather conditions.

railway autobiography, *An Indian Summer of Steam*, also published by Pen and Sword.

Alastair Wood also joined a number of *Plandampf* events and recorded several enterprising performances behind a number of Pacifics at Easter 1994. The pick are shown above.

Further *Plandampf* and railtour events took place in many years subsequently, though unfortunately I had no opportunity to get involved. There is a photo of such an event attended by colleague, Richard Spoors on page 354. I was given details by the Railway Performance Society of two such in the south west of Germany at the turn of the century. In September 1999, the Eifel *Plandampf* was centred around Gerolstein on the Trier-Cologne Moselle route and a number of Regional Expresses were hauled by three-cylinder oil-burning Pacific 01.1066 (formerly 012.066-7 of Rheine) supported by a P8 4-6-0 and Prussian T18 4-6-4T 78.468 on local stopping services. However, loads were light (4-5 coaches), and line speed was only 62mph (100km/hr) on most of the route winding through the Moselle hills. North of Gerolstein in the Euskirchen area, there were brief spurts at 72-75mph. The following year there was a more ambitious *Plandampf* on the Kaiserslautern-Neustadt Weinstrasse-Ludwigshafen route with four Pacifics involved, two-cylinder 01.118 (formerly DR 01.2118 of Dresden), the DR rebuilt 01.519, light Pacific 03.2295 and 01.1066 once more. Loads were again light – no more than five coaches – but the Pacifics by and large maintained the diesel schedules (designed for the Class 215 hydraulics) with speeds reaching around 70-72mph between frequent station stops. Forty-two scheduled trains were steam-hauled over the four days of the event.

As part of a celebration of 150 years of railways in Germany, an ambitious nine-day tour round the network behind a number of locomotives, including three Pacifics, took place in 2010. Although most of the tour was on easy schedules with an emphasis on covering the network with steam, the pair of Pacifics shone when double-heading the heavy 460-ton gross train over the scenic section from Lindau on the Bodensee (Lake Constance) to the summit of the route to Munich, through the foothills of the Bavarian Alps at Oberstaufen.

In 2015 a similar celebration of the 90th anniversary of the 01 Pacific took place in early August involving no less than eight different Pacifics, numbers 01.066 (as 01.2066-7), 01.150, 01.180, 01.202,

Open Day at Meiningen Works
with three-cylinder post-war
rebuild 18.201 and S3/6 18.478
in Bavarian livery as 3673, 1999.
(Richard Spoors)

DR rebuilds 01.509 (as oil-burner 01.0509-8) and coal-fired 01.1533-7, and DB three-cylinder oil-burner 012.066-7, plus one interloper, 03.2155-4. Astonishingly, a final part of the tour from Lindau back to Augsburg was triple-headed by three Pacifics over the Alpine section – two Standard 01s, 066 and 150 with the three-cylinder 012 – hauling the eleven-coach, 455 ton train. It is perhaps fitting to finish this book with the highlights of these tours recorded once again by my friend, Alastair Wood.

These two 'snippets', shown on the right, are of interest to compare with the running of the

Lindau-Oberstaufen, August 2010
16.15 Lindau-Augsburg
01.1533-7 + 01.1066
11 chs, 429/460t

		mph	Miles	
Lindau	00.00	mph	0	3½ L
Causeway	01.24	22		
Oberreitnau	10.16.	34/45		
Schlachters	14.25	41/48		
Hergensweiler	16.57	55		
Km 132	19.29	51		
Hergatz	20.52	58		
km 120	29.16	39/42		
Rothenbach	34.41		23.86	9L
	00.00		0	7L
Harbatshofen	08.04	33/43		
km 103	-	48/ pws 15*		
Oberstaufen	14.53		8.2	pass

Lindau-Oberstaufen, 8 August 2015
14.30 Lindau-Augsburg
01.066, 01.150 + 012.066-7 (01.1066) (in that order)
11 chs, 434/455t

		mph	
	00.00	mph	16½ L
	-	30	
	09.01	42/47	
	13.40	45/50	15L
	-	60½	
	18.21	52	
	19.45	58	13L
	27.16	46/48/43	
	33.23		
	00.00		8L
	06.39	39/43	
	-	48½ / pws 5*	
	13.49		pass

03.1010 departs Hamburg Hbf alongside ICE 773 with special train 61910 to Eystrup, 5 May 2005. (Robin Garn)

01.0509-8 overtakes the preserved class 35 2-6-2 near Dresden Strehlen with a railtour, 19 April 2015.
(Roger Bastin)

Preserved DR 03.2155-4 and coal-burning 01.1533-7 at Berlin Lichtenberg with the 90th '*01 Anniversary*' train on its 08.30 Berlin-Hamburg leg, 2 August 2015. (Alastair Wood)

rebuilt Bavarian 18.6 Pacifics back in 1962 (see page 299/300) when I accompanied Alastair on his first German steam tour.

Even now as this book is being written in the summer of 2016, plans are being prepared to hold a 3-day *Plandampf* event in the Erfurt/ Eisenach-Arnstadt-Meiningen region in September 2016 and whilst most of the trains will involve freight turns using class 50 2-10-0s and a 41 2-8-2, it is planned to replicate the 1975 running in turns of Pacific 01.2066 on a local train, P7003 between Eisenach and Meiningen. The story of the German Pacific is not finished yet ...

APPENDICES – DIMENSIONS, WEIGHT DIAGRAMS & STATISTICS

Locomotive dimensions, though quoted earlier in the text of the different chapters, are included here for easy reference. Outline drawings of the different classes, also known as weight diagrams, have been included where available, with additional ones when there are significant variations within a class.

The 'statistics' sections provide data on each locomotive - build and rebuilding dates, and withdrawal details. The German railway authorities use certain symbols to indicate the status of locomotives after their useful life is completed. 'z' = 'zurückgestellt', that is 'stored out of traffic'. The dates given here are those after which the locomotive had no further operational activity before withdrawal. The symbol '+' indicates 'ausgemustert', or 'taken out of service', ie officially withdrawn. A locomotive may stand stored for some time before a decision is taken to withdraw. This occurred for many State railway Pacifics after the Second World War, when engines were stored war-damaged or so rundown that they needed major overhauls and were low priority for repairs and ultimately decisions were taken around 1948-50 to scrap rather than repair. The symbol '++' = 'zerlegt' (scrapped) and often took place several years after withdrawal. That data is only available for some classes of locomotive, but the information is given where it is available.

Württemberg Class 'C' (DRG 18.1) four-cylinder compound Pacifics

Dimensions

Coupled wheels diameter	5' 11"
High-pressure cylinders	16.5" x 24"
Low-pressure cylinders	24.4" x 24"
Valve gear	Heusinger
Boiler pressure	213lbpsi
Grate area	42.6sqft
Heating surface	2,204sqft
Superheater	585sqft
Maximum axle weight	15.9 tons
Engine weight in service	85.0 tons
Total weight in service	131.8 tons
Water capacity	4,400 gallons (from No.2025, 6,600 gallons)
Coal capacity	5.5 tons
Horsepower	1,840
Tractive Effort (85%)	17,504lb
Maximum speed	72mph (later raised to 75mph)

Weight Diagram

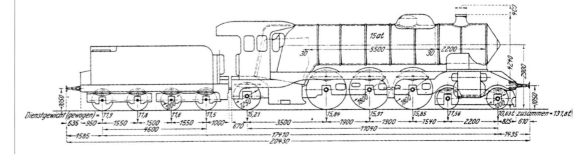

Statistics

Loco No.	Built	Stored out of traffic (z)	Withdrawn (+ 'ausgemustert')
2001 (SNCF 231.997)	1909	1934	1938 War reparation 1919
2002 (18.101)	1909	1/53	6/53
2003 (18.102)	1909	11/54	3/55
2004 (18.103)	1909	8/53	11/53
2005 (18.104)	1909	7/53	11/53
2006 (18.105)	1911	11/52	6/53
2007 (18.106)	1911	10/48	11/48
2008 (18.107)	1911	2/54	6/54
2009 (18.108)	1911	7/53	11/53
2010 (PKP Om 101-1)	1911	Unknown	War reparation 1919
2011 (18.109)	1911	8/53	11/53
2012 (18.110)	1913	12/53	3/54
2013 (18.111)	1913	1948	11/48 Not repaired after war
2014 (18.112)	1913	2/53	6/53
2015 (18.113)	1912	8/54	10/54
2016 (18.114)	1913	1948	11/48 Not repaired after war
2017 (18.115)	1913	4/54	6/54
2018 (18.116)	1913	6/45	11/45 Not repaired after war
2019 (18.117)	1913	7/53	11/53
2020 (18.118)	1913	4/54	6/54
2021 (18.119)	1914	6/48	11/48 Not repaired after war
2022 (18.120)	1914	5/52	8/52
2023 (18.121)	1914	6/48	11/48 Not repaired after war
2024 (18.122)	1914	8/54	10/54
2025 (18.123)	1915	4/53	6/53
2026 (SNCF 231.998)	1915	1934	1938 War reparation 1919
2027 (SNCF 231.999)	1915	1934	1938 War reparation 1919
2028 (18.124)	1915	1947	11/47 Not repaired after war
2029 (18.125)	1915	6/44	2/45 Bomb damage Stuttgart Hbf
2030 (18.126)	1919	10/54	10/54
2031 (18.127)	1919	1949	12/50 Not repaired after war
2032 (18.128)	1919	12/54	3/55
2033 (18.129)	1919	1948	11/48 Not repaired after war
2034 (18.130)	1919	1946	10/46 Not repaired after war
2035 (18.131)	1919	7/53	11/53
2036 (18.132)	1919	9/53	3/54
2037 (18.133)	1921	2/55	5/55
2038 (18.134)	1921	1934	1934 After accident
2039 (18.135)	1921	1948	11/48 Not repaired after war
2040 (18.136)	1921	1/55	5/55
2041 (18.137)	1921	1950	12/50 Not repaired after war

Baden four-cylinder compound Pacifics IVf (DRG 18.2)

Dimensions

Coupled wheels diameter	5' 11"
High-pressure cylinders	16.7" x 24"
Low-pressure cylinders	25.6" x 26.4"
Valve Gear	Heusinger
Boiler pressure	227lbpsi
Grate area	48.4sqft
Heating surface	2,244sqft
Superheater	537.5sqft
Axle weight	16.5 tons
Engine weight in service	88.3 tons
Total weight in service	133.9 tons
Water capacity	4,400 gallons
Coal capacity	6 tons
Horsepower	1,770
Maximum speed	62mph

Weight diagram

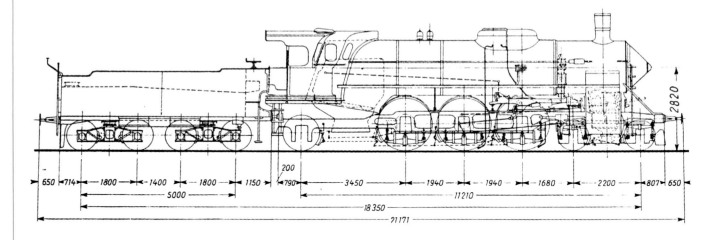

Statistics

The Baden 18.2 Pacifics were all withdrawn early and records of precise withdrawal dates have not been found. Many of the class did not receive the new numbers applied at the nationalisation of the German State railways in 1921 and are therefore assumed to have been withdrawn before that date:

Loco No.	Built	Withdrawn
751	1907	Before 1921
752	1907	Before 1921
753 (18.201)	1907	Before 1925
754 (18.211)	1909	Before 1925
755 (18.212)	1909	Before 1925

756 (18.213)	1909	Before 1925
757 (18.214)	1909	Before 1925
758	1909	Before 1921
759 (18.215)	1909	Before 1925
760	1910	Before 1921
761	1910	Before 1921
762	1910	Before 1921
763 (18.216)	1910	1927
764	1910	Before 1921
765 (18.217)	1910	Before 1925
833 (18.231)	1911	Before 1925
834 (18.232)	1912	Before 1925
835	1912	Before 1921
836 (18.233)	1912	Before 1925
837 (18.234)	1912	Before 1925
838 (18.235)	1912	Before 1925
839	1912	Before 1921
840	1912	Before 1921
841 (18.236)	1912	1927
842 (18.237)	1912	Before 1925
843	1912	Before 1921
844 (18.238)	1912	Before 1925
845 (18.251)	1913	1926
846 (18.252)	1913	Before 1925
847 (18.253)	1913	Before 1925
848 (18.254)	1913	Before 1925
849	1913	Before 1921
850 (18.255)	1913	Before 1925
851	1913	Before 1921
852 (18.256)	1913	1926

Baden four-cylinder compound Pacifics IVh (DRG 18.3)
Dimensions

Coupled wheels diameter	6' 11"
High-pressure cylinders	17.3" x 26.8"
Low-pressure cylinders	26.8" x 26.8"
Valve gear	Heusinger
Boiler pressure	213lbpsi
Grate area	53.8sqft
Heating surface	2,417sqft
Axle weight	17.8 tons
Engine weight in service	97 tons
Total weight in service	160 tons
Water capacity	6,500 gallons
Coal capacity	9 tons
Maximum speed	69mph, later 87.5mph
Horsepower	1,950

Weight diagram

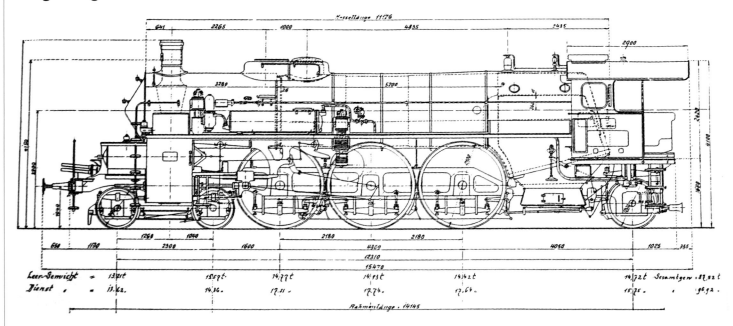

Statistics		Built	Stored (z)	Withdrawn (+)	Scrapped (++)
49	(18.301)	1918	2/45	9/48	3/52
64	(18.302)	1918	3/47	9/48	6/52
95	(18.303)	1918	2/45	9/48	3/52
1000	(18.311)	1919	2/45	9/48	3/52
1001	(18.312)	1919	1948	9/48	9/52
1002	(18.313)	1919	2/45	9/48	
1003	(18.314)	1919	To DR 4/48	3/72	Preserved
1004	(18.315)	1919	1/47	9/48	1958
1005	(18.316)	1919	1/69	7/69	Preserved
1006	(18.317)	1919	7/46	9/48	6/52
1007	(18.318)	1919	2/45	9/48	5/52
1008	(18.319)	1919	5/64	7/64	1966
1009	(18.321)	1920	2/45	9/48	6/52
1010	(18.322)	1920	2/45	9/48	3/52
1011	(18.323)	1920	10/69	12/69	Preserved
1012	(18.324)	1920	2/45	9/48	
1013	(18.325)	1920	2/47	9/48	
1014	(18.326)	1920	1944	1944 Bomb damage	6/45
1015	(18.327)	1920	1/46	9/48	
1016	(18.328)	1920	1947	9/48	3/52

Bavarian four-cylinder compound Pacifics S3/6 (DRG 18.4-5)

Dimensions

Coupled wheels	6' 1½ "
High-pressure cylinders	16.7" x 24"
Low-pressure cylinders	25.6" x 26.4"
Boiler pressure	213lbpsi
Grate area	48.7sqft
Heating surface	2,122sqft,
Superheater	797sqft
Maximum axle weight	16 tons, 17 tons (from 18.461)
Weight in service	88.3 tons
Weight with tender	143.9 tons
Water capacity	5,800 gallons or 7,150 gallons
Coal capacity	8 tons
Tractive Effort	20,017lb
Horsepower	1,660
Maximum speed	75mph

Variations for 18.441-458

As above except:

Coupled wheels diameter	6' 7"
High-pressure cylinders	16. 7" x 26.4"
Weight in service	89.5 tons
Horsepower	1,815

Variations for 18.479-508 and 18.509-548 series

High-pressure cylinders	17.3" x 25.6": 18.509-548 series only
Boiler pressure	227lbpsi
Axle weight	17.9 tons (18.479 series), 18.5 tons (18.509 series)
Total weight in service	153.2 tons (18.479 series) 165.2 tons (18.509 series)
Water capacity	6,000 gallons or 7,000 gallons
Coal capacity	8.5 tons or 10 tons
Tractive effort	21,.340lb
Horsepower	1,830

Weight diagrams

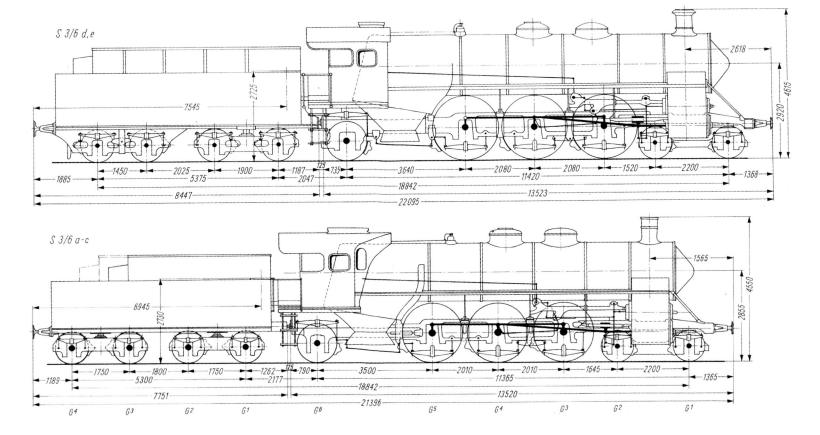

Statistics

Loco No.		Built	Stored (z)	Withdrawn (+)	Scrapped (++)
3601	(18.401)	7/08	10/48	4/49	1949
3602	(SNCF 231.981)	7/08		1946	
3603	(18.402)	10/08		4/49	
3604	(18.403)	10/08		5/46 Bomb damage	1946
3605	(SNCF 231.982)	11/08		1945	
3606	(18.404)	11/08	7/47	4/49	
3607	(18.405)	12/08	2/47	8/50	1952
3608	(18.406)	9/09	11/46	4/49	
3609	(18.407)	9/09	9/47	8/50	1951-2
3610	(18.408)	9/09	2/47	8/50	1952
3611	(18.409)	9/09	11/48	8/50	
3612	(18.410)	9/09		4/49	
3613	(18.411)	9/09		12/50	
3614	(18.412)	10/09		8/50	
3615	(18.413)	10/09		8/46 Bomb damage	
3616	(18.414)	10/09		1/46 Bomb damage	1948
3617	(18.415)	11/09	8/47	8/50	
3618	(SNCF 231.983)	9/10		1949	
3619	(18.416)	5/11		8/50	
3620	(SNCB 5920)	5/11		1923-4	
3621	(18.417)	5/11		8/50	
3622	(SNCF 231.984)	5/11		1949	
3623	(18.418)	6/11	11/46	4/49	
3624	(18.441)	3/12	1/47	8/50	1952
3625	(18.442)	3/12	3/47	4/49	
3626	(18.443)	4/12	3/47	4/49	
3627	(18.444)	4/12		8/50 Stationary boiler	1966
3628	(18.445)	4/12		8/49	
3629	(18.446)	4/12	8/48	8/49	
3630	(18.447)	5/12		8/49	
3631	(18.448)	5/12		11/51	
3632	(18.449)	5/12		12/50	
3633	(18.450)	8/12	3/47	8/50	1952
3634	(18.451)	8/12	4/52	10/54	Preserved
3635	(18.452)	8/12	12/45	8/49	
3636	(18.453)	9/12	4/45	8/50	1952
3637	(18.454)	9/12	4/48	8/50	
3638	(18.455)	10/12	2/45	8/50	1952
3639	(18.456)	10/12	6/47	4/49	7/49
3640	(18.457)	11/12	3/47	8/50	1952
3641	(18.458)	1/13	1/46	8/50	
3642	(18.419)	12/13		8/50	
3643	(18.420)	1/14	7/49	9/49	
3644	(18.421)	1/14	2/50	8/50	1952
3645	(18.422)	5/14		9/49	Frames to 18.478
3646	(SNCB 5946)	5/14		1923-4	

Loco No.		Built	Stored (z)	Withdrawn (+)	Scrapped (++)
3647	(18.423)	5/14		4/49	6/49
3648	(18.424)	5/14		8/50	1951-2
3649	(SNCB 5949)	5/14		1923-4	
341 (Pfalz) (18.425)		3/14		4/47 Accident damage	
342	(18.426)	3/14		9/48 Collision damage	
343	(18.427)	3/14		8/50	Cab & footplate preserved
344	(18.428)	3/14	2/45	12/45 Bomb damage	
345	(18.429)	3/14	3/47	4/49	1949
346	(18.430)	4/14	8/49	8/50	1951
347	(18.431)	4/14	6/45	8/50	
348	(18.432)	4/14	9/47	8/50	
349	(18.433)	4/14	9/49	8/50	1951-2
350	(18.434)	5/14	6/48	8/50 from DR	1952
3650	(18.461)	3/15	6/54	10/54	1956
3651	(18.462)	3/15	11/57	4/58	
3652	(18.463)	4/15	7/54	10/54	1957-8
3653	(18.464)	4/15	1/55	3/55	
3654	(18.465)	5/15	10/55	4/56	
3655	(18.466)	10/17	10/55	11/55	
3656	(18.467)	11/17	1/55	3/55	
3657	(18.468)	11/17		11/53	
3658	(18.469)	12/17	10/55	11/55	1956
3659	(18.470)	12/17	1/57	3/57	
3660	(18.471)	1/18		4/59	
3661	(18.472)	1/18	6/58	4/59	
3662	(18.473)	2/18	8/58	4/59	
3663	(18.474)	2/18		9/48 Bomb damage	
3664	(18.475)	3/18	1/55	3/55 Stationary boiler	1963
3665	(SNCF 231.985)	4/18		1946	
3666	(SNCF 231.986)	6/18		1946	
3667	(18.476)	6/18		5/54	
3668	(SNCF 231.987)	7/18		1945	
3669	(SNCF 231.988)	7/18		1945	
3670	(SNCF 231.989)	7/18		1949	
3671	(18.477)	7/18		5/54	
3672	(SNCF 231.990)	7/18		1945	
3673	(18.478)	7/18	4/59	7/60 Frames ex-18.422, Preserved	
3674	(SNCF 231.991)	7/18		1945	
3675	(SNCF 231.992)	8/18		1949	
3676	(SNCF 231.993	8/18		1945	
3677	(SNCF 231.994)	8/18		1946	
3678	(SNCF 231.995)	8/18		1949	
3679	(SNCF 231.996)	8/18		1949	
3680	(18.479)	11/23	6/56	11/56	
3681	(18.480)	12/23	9/55	11/55	
3682	(18.481)	10/23	6/61	8/61	1963
3683	(18.482)	11/23	4/56	8/56	1957/8

Loco No.		Built	Stored (z)	Withdrawn (+)	Scrapped (++)
3684	(18.483)	11/23	5/60	7/60	1965
3685	(18.484)	11/23	4/56	8/56	
3686	(18.485)	12/23	4/56	8/56	
3687	(18.486)	11/23	12/55	4/56	
3688	(18.487)	11/23	1/57	3/57	
3689	(18.488)	11/23	12/44	5/46 Accident damage	
3690	(18.489)	1/24	8/56	11/56	
3691	(18.490)	12/23	8/57	9/57	
3692	(18.491)	12/23	8/54	3/55	
3693	(18.492)	12/23	2/58	4/58	
3694	(18.493)	1/24	3/58	4/58	
3695	(18.494)	1/24	7/57	11/57	
3696	(18.495)	2/24	4/59	7/59	
3697	(18.496)	1/24	2/56	8/56	
3698	(18.497)	1/24	10/55	4/56	
3699	(18.498)	3/24	11/55	4/56	
3700	(18.499)	3/24	2/55	5/55	
3701	(18.500)	3/24	6/58	11/58	
3702	(18.501)	3/24	5/57	8/57	
3703	(18.502)	4/24	8/57	11/57	
3704	(18.503)	5/24		3/54	
3705	(18.504)	5/24		8/55	
3706	(18.505)	5/24	5/67	7/69	Preserved
3707	(18.506)	5/24	4/55	8/55	
3708	(18.507)	5/24	8/58	7/59	
3709	(18.508)	9/24	7/62	10/62	Preserved
18.509		10/26	12/54	Rebuilt as 18.611	
18.510		11/26	5/55	Rebuilt as 18.618	
18.511		11/26	9/55	Rebuilt as 18.622	
18.512		11/26	2/61	4/61	1962
18.513		11/26	9/57	11/57	
18.514		5/27	7/55	Rebuilt as 18.620	
18.515		5/27	6/45	9/47 Bomb damage	
18.516		12/26	4/59	4/60	
18.517		12/26	3/55	Rebuilt as 18.616	
18.518		5/27	4/54	Rebuilt as 18.608	
18.519		5/27	2/58	4/58	1960
18.520		5/27	12/54	Rebuilt as 18.612	
18.521		1/28	5/51 – 3/53	Rebuilt as 18.601	
18.522		12/27	11/53	Rebuilt as 18.604	
18.523		1/28	5/54	Rebuilt as 18.610	
18.524		1/28	3/56	Rebuilt as 18.627	
18.525		2/28	7/53	Rebuilt as 18.603	
18.526		2/28	8/55	Rebuilt as 18.621	
18.527		3/28	3/54	Rebuilt as 18.607	
18.528		3/28	10/62	11/63	Preserved
18.529		7/30	3/55	Rebuilt as 18.615	

Loco No.	Built	Stored (z)	Withdrawn (+)	Scrapped (++)
18.530	8/30	1/54	Rebuilt as 18.605	
18.531	7/30	10/55	Rebuilt as 18.623	
18.532	6/30	1/55	Rebuilt as 18.614	
18.533	7/30	12/46	3/48 Bomb damage	
18.534	7/30	6/55	Rebuilt as 18.619	
18.535	7/30	2/54	Rebuilt as 18.606	
18.536	6/30	1/55	Rebuilt as 18.613	
18.537	7/30	2/60	7/60	
18.538	7/30	5/58	11/58	
18.539	6/30	8/56	Rebuilt as 18.629	
18.540	7/30	12/55	Rebuilt as 18.625	
18.541	7/30	2/58	4/58	1960
18.542	8/30	5/54	Rebuilt as 18.609	
18.543	8/30	4/57	Rebuilt as 18.630	
18.544	8/30	3/56	Rebuilt as 18.628	
18.545	8/30	11/55	Rebuilt as 18.624	
18.546	8/30	2/56	Rebuilt as 18.626	
18.547	9/30	6/53	Rebuilt as 18.602	
18.548	11/30	2/55	Rebuilt as 18.617	

Rebuilt Bavarian four-cylinder compound Pacifics (18.6)

Dimensions

Coupled wheels diameter	6' 1½ "
Bogie wheel diameter	3' 1½ "
High-pressure cylinders	18.8" x 24"
Low-pressure cylinders	26" x 26.4"
Boiler pressure	227lbpsi
Grate area	45sqft
Heating surface	2,094sqft
Superheater	795sqft
Axle-load	18.1 tons
Weight	96.1 tons
Horsepower	1,950
Maximum speed	75mph

Weight diagram

Baureihe 18⁵

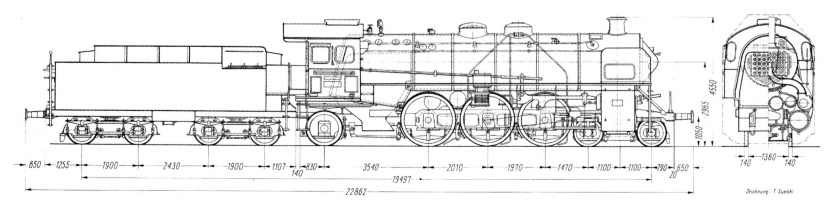

Zeichnung : T. Susicki

Statistics

Loco No.		Built	Rebuilt	Withdrawn (+)		Scrapped (++)
18.601	(18.521)	1927	3/53	10/61	6/62	
18.602	(18.547)	1930	6/53	12/63	7/64 Stationary boiler	1983
18.603	(18.525)	1928	7/53	9/64	6/66 Stationary boiler	
18.604	(18.522)	1927	11/53	9/61	12/61 Stationary boiler	1969
18.605	(18.530)	1930	1/54	11/62	5/63	
18.606	(18.535)	1930	2/54	12/61	6/62	1963
18.607	(18.527)	1928	3/54	9/63	11/63	1965
18.608	(18.518)	1927	4/54	4/63	11/63	1966
18.609	(18.542)	1930	5/54	7/62	11/62 Stationary boiler	1964
18.610	(18.523)	1927	5/54	3/62	11/62 Research Minden	1976
18.611	(18.509)	1926	12/54		7/64	1966
18.612	(18.520)	1927	12/54	2/64	7/64	Preserved
18.613	(18.536)	1930	1/55	11/63	7/64	1966
18.614	(18.532)	1930	1/55	1/65	4/65	1965
18.615	(18.529)	1930	3/55	3/64	7/64	1965
18.616	(18.517)	1926	3/55	3/64	7/64	1966
18.617	(18.548)	1930	5/55	9/64	10/64	1970
18.618	(18.510)	1926	5/55	5/61	12/61	1963
18.619	(18.534)	1930	6/55		11/63	1966
18.620	(18.514)	1926	7/55	11/64	3/65	1966
18.621	(18.526)	1928	8/55	8/61	12/61	
18.622	(18.511)	1926	9/55	9/65	1/66	1972
18.623	(18.531)	1930	10/55	11/62	11/63	1965
18.624	(18.545)	1930	11/55	3/61	12/61	1963
18.625	(18.540)	1930	12/55	1/61	5/61	1961
18.626	(18.546)	1930	2/56	12/61	6/62	1964
18.627	(18.524)	1928	3/56	10/61	6/62	1965
18.628	(18.544)	1930	3/56	5/61	5/63	1966
18.629	(18.539)	1930	8/56	5/64	7/64	1966
18.630	(18.543)	1930	4/57	4/65	1/66	1970

Saxon three-cylinder Pacifics XVIII H (DR 18.0)

Dimensions

Coupled wheels diameter	6' 3"
3 cylinders	19.7" x 24.8"
Boiler pressure	199lbpsi
Grate area	48.4sqft
Heating surface	2,320sqft
Superheater	774sqft
Axle weight	17.2 tons
Weight in service	93.5 tons
Weight with tender	144 tons
Water capacity	6,800 gallons
Coal capacity	7 tons
Horsepower	1,700
Maximum speed	62mph (later raised to 75mph)

Weight diagram

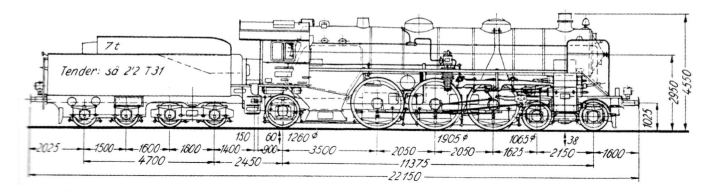

Statistics

Several Saxon 18.0 Pacifics spent long periods in store after the early 1960s, before decisions were taken to withdraw them officially from traffic.

Loco No.	Built	Stored (z)	Withdrawn (+)	Scrapped (++)
196 (18.001)	1917	1/61	2/67	2/68
197 (18.002)	1917	4/45	8/45 Destroyed by bomb	
198 (18.003)	1917	Unknown	2/67	7/69
199 (18.004)	1917	12/47	12/51 Spare parts for 18.0s	
200 (18.005)	1917	4/63	2/68	
201 (18.006)	1917	5/65	7/65 Stationary boiler from 6/62	
202 (18.007)	1917	4/63	2/67	2/68
203 (18.008)	1917	Unknown	2/67	7/69
204 (18.009)	1918	12/61	7/67	12/69
205 (18.010)	1918	5/65	3/67	2/74

The *Deutsche Reichsbahn* two-cylinder 01 & DR (East German) 01.5

Dimensions
Standard 01

Coupled wheels diameter	6' 7"
Bogie wheels diameter	2' 9" (3' 3" from 01.102)
Cylinders (2)	23.6" x 26"
Boiler pressure	227lbpsi
Grate area	47.4sqft
Heating surface	2,554 or 2,658sqft (from 01.077)
Superheater	1,075sqft or 914sqft (from 01.077)
Axle-load	20.2 tons
Weight	108.9 tons
Tender coal capacity	10 tons
Tender water capacity	7,000 or 7,500 gallons
Tractive effort	33,510lb
Horsepower	2,240
Maximum speed	75mph (from 01.102, 81mph)

01 with feedwater heater (01.042/046/112/154/192 - DB)

As above, except:

Bogie wheels diameter	3' 3"
Grate area	46.3sqft
Heating surface	2,324sqft
Superheater	1,021sqft
Axle-load	19.9 tons
Weight	111.1 tons
Horsepower	2,450

01 with all-welded boiler (DB)

As standard 01, except:

Bogie wheel diameter	3' 3"
Grate area	42.6sqft
Heating surface	2,076sqft
Superheater	1,081sqft
Axle-load	19.8 tons
Weight	108.3 tons
Horsepower	2,330

01.5 (DR)

As standard 01, except:

	3' 3"
Grate area	52.4sqft (coal-burners only)
Heating surface	2,413sqft
Superheater	1,048sqft
Weight	111 tons
Horsepower	2,450 or 2,500 (oil-burners)
Tender capacity	3,000 gallons fuel oil (oil-burners)

Weight Diagrams
Standard 01

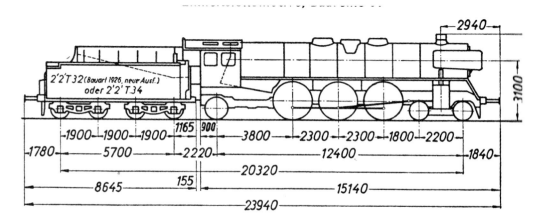

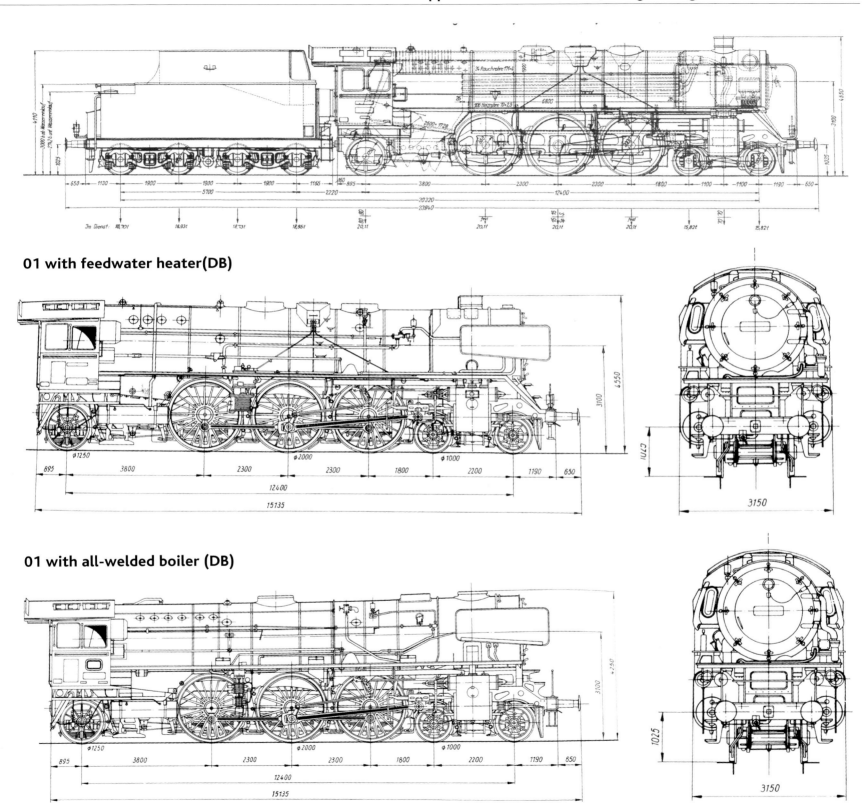

01 with feedwater heater(DB)

01 with all-welded boiler (DB)

01.5 (DR)

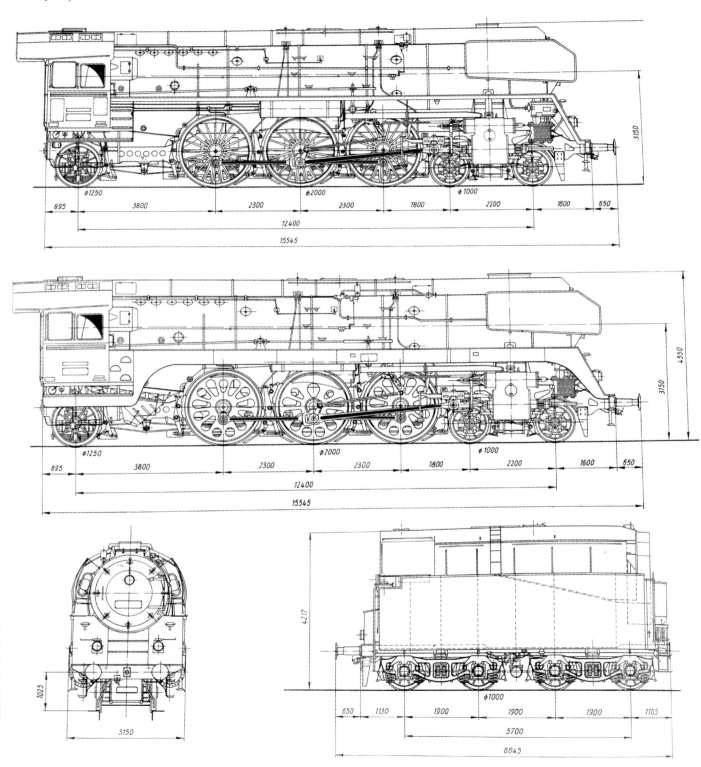

Statistics

Loco No.	Built	Post-1945 All-welded boiler Rebuilt 01.5	Stored (z)	Withdrawn (+)
01.001	1/26	DB	11/58	2/59
01.002	2/26	DB	8/59	6/60
01.003	2/26	DB	3/60	9/60
01.004	3/26	DB	9/59	9/60
01.005	3/26	DR	2/69	12/74 Preserved
01.006	3/26	DB	10/65	3/66
01.007	4/26	DB	4/64	3/65
01.008	1/26	DB	11/73	Preserved
01.009	12/26	DB	2/66	6/66
01.010	7/26	DB	2/66	6/66
01.011	9/37	DB*	1/64	11/64
01.012	-/28	DB	5/60	9/60
01.013	-/28	DB	8/62	3/65
01.014	-/28	DR	9/75	7/76 Heizlok
01.015	-/28	DB	6/64	11/64
01.016	-/28	DR	8/77	10/77 Heizlok
01.017	-/28	DB	12/66	2/67
01.018	-/28	DR	6/73	11/73
01.019	2/28	DB	3/67	7/67
01.020	2/28	DB	2/66	9/66
01.021	-/28	DB	5/66	8/66
01.022	-/27	DR	6/72	8/76
01.023	-/27	DR	4/68	8/69
01.024	-/27	DR		3/68 Heizlok
01.025	-/27	DR	6/72	11/75
01.026	-/27	DR	12/48	12/50 War damage
01.027	-/27	DR	8/73	8/74 Heizlok
01.028	-/27	DR	4/68	7/69
01.029	-/27	DR	1/80	9/80 Heizlok
01.030	-/27	DR	10/48	10/50 War damage
01.031	12/27	DB	10/62	7/64
01.032	12/27	DB	3/64	7/64
01.033	12/27	DB	12/64	3/65
01.034	12/27	DB	12/66	5/67
01.035	-/27	DR	1947	6/56 War damage
01.036	-/27	DR	6/72	11/75
01.037	12/27	DB	12/66	5/67
01.038	1/28	DB		5/48 War damage
01.039	-/28	DB	7/70	9/70
01.040	-/28	DB	9/64	11/64
01.041	-/28	DB	8/66	11/66
01.042	6/28	DB	5/57	8/57 accident
01.043	7/28	DB	4/68	10/68
01.044	8/28	DB	1/60	9/60
01.045	9/28	DB	3/64	7/64

Loco No.	Built	Post-1945	All-welded boiler	Rebuilt 01.5	Stored (z)	Withdrawn (+)
01.046	9/28	DB			5/67	10/68
01.047	10/28	DB			3/68	10/68
01.048	10/28	DR			5/75	4/76
01.049	11/28	DB			10/64	3/65
01.050	-/29	DR			2/78	8/80
01.051	2/29	DB			5/68	10/68
01.052	-/29	DB			3/68	6/68
01.053	1/28	PKP as Pm1-1			11/46 War damage – to PKP?	
01.054	1/28	DR			6/73	7/73
01.055	1/28	DB			4/64	3/65
01.056	1/28	DB			5/65	9/65
01.057	1/28	DR			12/75	6/76
01.058	1/28	DB			9/67	3/68
01.059	1/28	DB			3/67	3/70
01.060	2/28	DB			11/65	3/66
01.061	2/28	DB			9/68	12/68
01.062	2/28	DB			6/70	9/70
01.063	2/28	DB			1/67	7/67
01.064	-/28	DB			2/66	6/66
01.065	-/28	DR			4/81	6/81 *Heizlok*
01.066	-/28	DR			2/78	5/78 Preserved
01.067	-/28	DB			8/69	12/69
01.068	7/28	DB			6/64	3/65
01.069	-/28	DR			2/78	11/80
01.070	8/28	DB			7/64	3/65
01.071	8/28	DB			1/67	5/67
01.072	9/28	DB			97/65	/65
01.073	9/28	DB			2/71	6/71
01.074	10/28	DB			4/64	3/65
01.075	10/28	DB			12/62	5/63
01.076	11/28	DB			3/67	7/67
01.077	-/30	DB			9/66	11/66
01.078	4/30	DB			5/65	3/66
01.079	5/30	DB			11/66	5/67
01.080	5/30	DB			10/66	5/67
01.081	5/30	DB			3/69	9/69 accident
01.082	-/30	DB			10/68	3/69
01.083	6/30	DB			12/67	3/68
01.084	-/30	DR			3/75	5/75
01.085	-/30	DR			6/72	7/73
01.086	6/30	DB			9/67	3/68
01.087	11/30	DB			12/63	12/63
01.088	11/30	DB			6/73	8/73
01.089	-/30	DR			10/69	9/71
01.090	12/30	DB			5/67	11/67
01.091	1/31	DB			2/66	6/66

Loco No.	Built	Post-1945	All-welded boiler	Rebuilt 01.5		Stored (z)	Withdrawn (+)
01.092	1/31	DB				10/67	3/68
01.093	1/31	DB				2/66	6/66
01.094	2/31	DB				10/62	5/63
01.095	-/31	DB				9/67	3/68
01.096	3/31	DB				11/65	3/66
01.097	-/31	DB				2/59	7/59
01.098	5/31	DB				1/67	5/67
01.099	6/31	DB				9/64	9/65
01.100	6/31	DB				311/64	/65
01.101	7/31	DB				11/58	11/58 accident
01.102	11/34	DB				1/69	7/69
01.103	12/34	DB	11/61			1/73	4/73
01.104	-/34	DB	7/59			9/68	12/68
01.105	11/34	DB				11/67	3/68
01.106	11/34	DB				11/68	3/68
01.107	-/34	DR		01.517	11/63	8/82	3/89
01.108	-/34	DB				1/69	7/69
01.109	12/34	DB				11/67	3/68
01.110	-/34	DR				1947	11/50 War damage
01.111	11/34	DB				11/73	3/74 Preserved
01.112	-/34	DB				6/67	11/67
01.113	12/34	DB	10/60			7/68	10/68
01.114	12/34	DR				4/84	6/85 *Heizlok*
01.115	12/34	DB	6/59			1/68	6/68
01.116	?12/34	DR		01.533	12/64	2/84	4/84 Preserved
01.117	?12/34	DR		01.516	9/63	11/77	1/78 accident
01.118	?1/35	DR				10/81	11/81 Preserved
01.119	?1/35	DR		01.528	9/64	4/80	2/81 *Heizlok*
01.120	?1/35	DR				3/79	8/79 *Heizlok*
01.121	?1/35	DR		01.505	11/62	9/80	5/81
01.122	1/35	DB	6/58			3/65	9/65
01.123	1/35	DB				8/68	12/68
01.124	2/35	DB	6/60			7/68	10/68
01.125	3/35	DB	7/61			1/67	10/68
01.126	2/35	DB	9/58			3/72	8/72
01.127	-/35	DR		01.506	11/62	9/78	2/81
01.128	-/35	DB				8/70	11/70
01.129	-/35	DR		01.524	6/64	11/81	9/83
01.130	-/35	DB	11/59			5/67	10/68
01.131	3/35	DB	1/66			6/73	8/73
01.132	3/35	DB	1/61			1/67	10/68
01.133	3/35	DB	8/60			10/71	12/71
01.134	4/35	DB	4/59			4/67	7/67
01.135	-/35	DR		01.532	12/64	4/80	2/81 *Heizlok*
01.136	-/35	DR		01.507	12/62	4/80	2/81 *Heizlok*
01.137	-/35	DR				3/81	Preserved

Loco No.	Built	Post-1945	All-welded boiler	Rebuilt 01.5		Stored (z)	Withdrawn (+)
01.138	6/35	DB	11/60			9/68	12/68
01.139	-/35	DR		01.510	2/63	11/81	3/89
01.140	-/35	DB				11/65	6/66 accident
01.141	3/35	DB				10/66	2/67
01.142	-/35	DR		01.503	10/62	7/80	6/81
01.143	-/35	DR		01.509	2/63	9/82	6/85 Preserved
01.144	-/35	DR		01.521	3/64	11/81	9/83
01.145	6/35	DB				1/47	War damage
01.146	6/35	DB	9/61			2/67	7/67
01.147	6/35	DB				7/67	3/68
01.148	7/35	DB	10/61			7/67	11/67
01.149	7/35	DB	4/59			1/69	7/69
01.150	-/35	DB				11/73	11/73 Preserved
01.151	-/35	DB				5/68	10/68
01.152	-/35	DR		01.513	4/63	1/82	3/89
01.153	-/35	DR		01.508	2/63	5/81	9/81
01.154	10/35	DB				6/66	9/66
01.155	-/35	DB				11/46	War damage
01.156	-/35	DR		01.535	5/65	8/80	10/81 *Heizlok*
01.157	-/35	DR		01.502	9/62	3/82	6/82
01.158	11/35	DR		01.531	11/64	2/84	Preserved
01.159	11/35	DB	11/58			9/68	12/68
01.160	-/35	DR		01.515	7/63	6/79	10/79
01.161	12/35	DB				2/70	6/71
01.162	-/35	DR		01.520	4/64	11/81	9/83
01.163	-/35	DR		01.526	7/64	11/79	12/82
01.164	1/36	DB	8/60			5/71	12/71 Preserved
01.165	1/36	DR				9/77	10/77
01.166	1/36	DB	9/61			4/67	7/67
01.167	-/36	DB				9/68	12/68
01.168	2/36	DB				6/73	8/73
01.169	2/36	DB	8/61			3/71	12/71
01.170	-/36	DB				3/67	5/67
01.171	-/36	DB				7/68	12/68
01.172	-/36	DB	7/60			7/68	12/68
01.173	-/36	DB				11/73	12/73 Preserved
01.174	-/36	DR		01.501	4/62	11/80	3/81
01.175	-/36	DR		01.512	3/63	11/85	11/85 *Heizlok*
01.176	5/36	DB				12/65	8/66
01.177	5/36	DB	10/60			10/66	10/68
01.178	5/36	DB	8/59			3/69	9/69
01.179	5/36	DB				9/69	12/69
01.180	5/36	DB	6/60			5/73	8/73 Preserved
01.181	6/36	DB	5/60			11/72	12/72
01.182	6/36	DB	11/61			5/67	10/68
01.183	6/36	DB	2/59			2/69	12/69

Loco No.	Built	Post-1945	All-welded boiler	Rebuilt 01.5	Stored (z)	Withdrawn (+)
01.184	-/36	DR		01.522 4/64	1/82	9/83
01.185	-/36	DR		01.518 12/63	3/81	5/81
01.186	-/36	DR		01.519 2/64	1983	3/91 Preserved
01.187	6/36	DB	2/61		1/73	4/73
01.188	6/36	DB			11/65	6/66 accident
01.189	7/36	DB			1/69	7/69
01.190	7/36	DB	11/60		8/71	12/71
01.191		DR		01.523 5/64	2/82	5/82
01.192`	1/37	DB	10/58		7/72	11/72
01.193	12/36	DB	8/60		4/68	6/68
01.194		DB	9/59		2/67	5/67
01.195	1/37	DB			2/66	6/66
01.196	1/37	DB	10/61		2/67	7/67
01.197	-/37	DB	12/60		1/67	5/67
01.198	2/37	DB			9/68	12/68
01.199	2/37	DB	12/61		1/72	4/72
01.200	3/37	DB	7/59		4/71	9/71
01.201	3/37	DB			4/46	War damage
01.202	3/37	DB			2/73	4/73 Preserved
01.203	-/37	DR		01.534 5/65	3/84	6/84 *Heizlok*
01.204	-/37	DR			3/81	6/82 Preserved
01.205	-/37	DR		01.529 9/64	2/83	7/83 *Heizlok*
01.206	6/37	DB	9/60		11/68	3/69 accident
01.207	-/37	DR			2/78	12/78
01.208	-/37	DR		01.514 6/63	5/83	5/84 Preserved
01.209	7/37	DB	3/59		4/67	7/67
01.210	8/37	DB	5/61		4/71	9/71
01.211	9/37	DB	5/59		4/73	8/73
01.212	9/37	DB			5/68	10/68
01.213	5/37	DB			12/68	3/69
01.214	5/37	DR			8/45	10/50 War damage
01.215	5/37	DB			7/67	3/68
01.216	5/37	DB	6/58		9/67	3/68
01.217	5/37	DB	5/58		5/71	9/71
01.218	-/37	DR		01.511 3/63	11/85	11/85 *Heizlok*
01.219	-/37	DR		01.525 6/64	8/80	11/80
01.220	6/37	DB	8/59		5/68	10/68 Preserved
01.221	-/37	DR		01.530 10/64	8/80	9/81
01.222	-/37	DB			10/66	5/67 accident
01.223	7/37	DB	7/58		3/68	10/68
01.224	?-/37	DR		01.504 10/62	6/81	7/81
01.225	?-/37	DR		01.527 8/64	6/82	12/84 *Heizlok*
01.226	?-/37	DR			6/73	7/73
01.227	4/38	DB	1/61		1/73	4/73
01.228	5/38	DB	12/61		12/67	3/68
01.229	5/38	DB	11/58		3/72	8/72

Loco No.	Built	Post-1945	All-welded boiler	Rebuilt 01.5	Stored (z)	Withdrawn (+)
01.230	6/38	DB	9/60		2/72	4/72
01.231	6/38	DB	5/60		8/68	12/68
01.232	7/38	DB	9/59		6/67	11/67
01.233	-/38	DB*			5/65	9/65
01.234	9/38	DB*			6/72	11/72
01.235	11/38	DB*			5/68	10/68
01.236	9/38	DB*			11/65	3/66
01.237	11/39	DB*			11/65	3/66
01.238	7/40	DB*			3/45	4/46 War damage
01.239	7/41	DB*			11/65	3/66
01.240	10/42	DB*			5/68	10/68
01.241	11/42	DB*			10/62	11/62

* Rebuilt from class 02   *Heizlok* = Stationary boiler

01.5 (DR)

Several 01.5 Pacifics were taken out of store in the early 1980s and drafted to Saalfeld to cover a period of oil shortage. Some were retained on the books afterwards, although stored out of use as a strategic reserve, and were not scrapped for several years. Certain locomotives were retained as heritage engines during this period until purchased by private individuals or societies and some were reconverted to coal burning (01.519, 01.531 and 01.533). Some locomotives were used as stationary boilers and the date at which they ceased to be operational in traffic is not clear – the official 'z' dates are possibly the dates on which they became active as '*Heizloks*' rather than the date at which they were stored out of traffic. It is reported that the last two 01.5s in active service other than heritage events were the coal-burners 01.1511 and 01.1512 in the autumn of 1982.

Statistics	Rebuilt from	Date	Oil-burning	Stored (z)	Withdrawn (+)	Scrapped (++)
01.501	01 174	4/62	6/65	11/80	3/81	6/81
01.502	01.157	9/62	7/65	3/82	6/82	10/88
01.503	01.142	10/62	9/65	7/80	6/81	12/81
01.504	01.224	10/62	2/65	6/81	7/81	2/82
01.505	01.121	11/62	3/66	9/80	5/81	7/81
01.506	01.127	11/62		9/78	2/81	4/81
01.507	01.136	12/62	12/65	4/80	5/81 *Heizlok*	7/81
01.508	01.153	2/63	2/66	5/81	9/81 *Heizlok*	11/81
01.509	01.143	2/63	10/65	9/82	6/85	Preserved
01.510	01.139	2/63	1/66	11/81	3/89	1990
01.511	01.218	3/63		Autumn 1982	11/85 *Heizlok* 1/86	
01.512	01.175	3/63		Autumn 1982	11/85 *Heizlok* 12/85	
01.513	01.152	4/63	4/66	1/82	3/89	1/90
01.514	01.208	6/63		5/83	5/84	Preserved
01.515	01.160	7/63		6/79	10/79	5/89
01.516	01.117	8/63		12/77	1/78 Boiler explosion	
01.517	01.107	11/63	2/65	8/82	3/89	10/89
01.518	01.185	12/63		3/81	5/81	5/81
01.519	01.186	2/64	2/64	1983	3/91	Preserved
01.520	01.162	4/64	4/64	11/81	9/83	10/83

Statistics	Rebuilt from	Date	Oil-burning	Stored (z)	Withdrawn (+)	Scrapped (++)
01.521	01.144	3/64	3/64	11/81	9/83	12/83
01.522	01.184	4/64	4/64	1/82	9/83	12/83
01.523	01.191	5/64	5/64	2/82	5/82	4/87
01.524	01.129	6/64	6/64	11/81	9/83	10/83
01.525	01.219	6/64	6/64	8/80	11/80	2/81
01.526	01.163	7/64	7/64	11/79	12/82	3/83
01.527	01.225	8/64	8/64	6/82 *Heizlok*	12/84	1/85
01.528	01.119	9/64	9/64	4/80 *Heizlok*	2/81	4/81
01.529	01.205	9/64	9/64	2/83 *Heizlok*	7/83	9/83
01.530	01.221	10/64	10/64	8/80	9/81	10/82
01.531	01.158	11/64	11/64	2/84 * Traditionlok		Preserved
01.532	01.135	12/64	12/64	4/80 *Heizlok*	2/81	5/81
01.533	01.116	12/64	12/64	2/84	4/84	Preserved
01.534	01.203	4/65	4/65	3/84 *Heizlok*	6/84	8/84
01.535	01.156	5/65	5/65	8/80 *Heizlok*	10/81	2/82

The *Deutsche Reichsbahn* four-cylinder compound 02

Dimensions

Coupled wheels diameter	6' 7"
Bogie wheels diameter	2' 9"
Cylinders (2) Low-pressure	28.4" x 26"
Cylinders (2) High-pressure	18" x 26"
Boiler pressure	227lbpsi
Grate area	48.4sqft
Heating surface	2,554sqft
Superheater	1,075sqft
Axle-load	20.2 tons
Weight	113.5 tons
Tender capacity (coal)	10 tons
Tender capacity (water)	6,500 gallons
Horsepower	2,300
Maximum speed	75mph

Weight Diagram

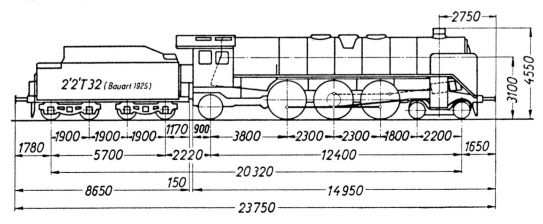

Statistics	Built	Rebuilt to class 01
02.001	10/25	9/37 to 01.011
02.002	1926	11/39 to 01.237
02.003	1926	9/38 to 01.234
02.004	1926	11/42 to 01.241
02.005	1926	-/38 to 01.233
02.006	1926	7/41 to 01.239
02.007	1926	9/38 to 01.237
02.008	1926	10/42 to 01.240
02.009	1926	7/40 to 01.238
02.010	1926	11/38 to 01.235

The *Deutsche Reichsbahn* three-cylinder 01.10
Dimensions

	As built	New boiler	Oil firing
Coupled wheel diameter	6' 7"		
Cylinders (3)	19.7" x 26"		
Boiler pressure	227lbpsi		
Grate area	46.4sqft	42.4sqft	
Heating surface	2,654sqft	2,220sqft	
Superheater	925sqft	1,034sqft	1,011sqft
Axle weight	20.4 tons		20.8 tons
Weight in service	192 tons		196.5 tons
Water capacity	8,360 gallons		
Coal capacity	10 tons		13.5 tons oil
Tractive effort	34,848lb		
Horsepower	2,100	2,350	2,470
Maximum speed	94mph	87.5mph	87.5mph

Weight diagram

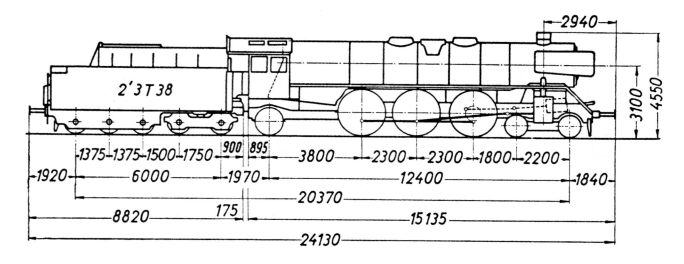

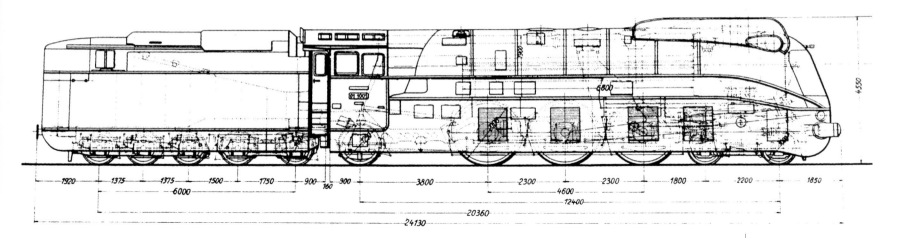

Statistics

Loco No.	Built	De-streamlined	New boiler	Oil Firing	Stored (z)	Withdrawn (+)
01.1001	8/39	4/49	4/54	8/57	9/72	12/72
01.1052	1/40	8/50	12/53	6/58	2/72	4/72
01.1053	1/40	5/49	11/54		4/68	6/68
01.1054	2/40	5/49	4/54	11/57	3/72	8/72
01.1055	2/40	7/49	9/54	11/57	5/75	7/75
01.1056	2/40	3/49	8/54		4/71	Preserved
01.1057	2/40	6/49	11/54	10/57	8/71	2/71
01.1058	2/40	4/49	2/54	9/57	12/72	4/73
01.1059	2/40	6/49	6/55	9/57	12/70	9/71
01.1060	2/40	7/49	12/53	11/57	6/72	11/72
01.1061	2/40	5/49	1/54	10/57	6/75	Preserved
01.1062	2/40	8/50	2/54		2/73	4/73
01.1063	2/40	9/49	7/54	6/58	6/75	Preserved
01.1064	3/40	7/49	7/54	9/57	10/72	12/72
01.1065	3/40	5/49	10/54		6/71	9/71
01.1066	3/40	6/49	2/54	11/57	6/75	Preserved
01.1067	3/40				1945	5/48 Collision damage
01.1068	3/40	6/49	12/54	11/57	1/74	6/74
01.1069	3/40	6/49	11/55		6/69	9/69
01.1070	3/40	9/50	11/56		1/70	11/70
01.1071	3/40	3/49	11/55	6/58	5/73	8/73
01.1072	3/40	6/50	12/53		9/72	12/72
01.1073	3/40	3/49	9/55	8/57	4/72	8/72
01.1074	4/40	3/49	5/54	9/57	10/72	12/72
01.1075	8/40	5/49	6/54	9/57	6/75	Preserved
01.1076	4/40	8/49	3/54	8/57	5/71	12/71
01.1077	4/40	3/51	3/54	6/57	9/73	3/74
01.1078	4/40	6/49	12/55		8/69	12/69
01.1079	4/40	8/49	3/56	9/57	11/67	3/68 Accident damage
01.1080	4/40	4/49	12/53	10/57	1/75	5/75

Loco No.	Built	De-streamlined	New boiler	Oil Firing	Stored (z)	Withdrawn (+)
01.1081	4/40	11/49	12/55	6/57	6/75	Preserved
01.1082	4/40	9/49	10/56	8/57	9/74	Preserved
01.1083	4/40	6/49	5/54		2/69	7/69
01.1084	5/40	6/49	12/54	6/57	4/73	8/73
01.1085	5/40	8/49	3/54	6/57	9/71	12/71
01.1086	5/40	5/49	6/54		9/68	3/69 Accident damage
01.1087	5/40	2/50	2/54		4/68	10/68 Accident damage
01.1088	5/40	6/49	7/55	10/57	11/69	11/70
01.1089	5/40	9/49	9/54	10/57	5/68	10/68
01.1090	5/40	12/49	1/54		5/69	9/69
01.1091	6/40	5/49	8/55		9/71	12/71
01.1092	6/40	6/49	9/54	10/57	6/73	8/73
01.1093	6/40	7/50	4/54		3/70	6/70
01.1094	7/40	8/49	8/54		8/68	12/68
01.1095	7/40	1/50	3/62		3/68	6/68
01.1096	7/40	5/51	4/55		4/69	9/69
01.1097	7/40	3/50	1/54		5/69	9/69
01.1098	6/40	12/49	5/54		5/70	6/70
01.1099	6/40	12/49	11/54		10/68	3/69
01.1100	7/40	6/49	7/56	7/56	6/75	Preserved
01.1101	7/40	7/50	5/54	5/57	7/74	12/74
01.1102	7/40	9/50	6/54	5/57	12/72 Preserved (streamlined)	
01.1103	8/40	11/49	4/54	5/57	5/72	8/72
01.1104	8/40	3/50	3/54	5/57	5/74	Preserved
01.1105	9/40	2/50	12/53	5/57	9/72	12/72

The *Deutsche Reichsbahn* two-cylinder 03

Dimensions	
Coupled wheel diameter	6′ 7″
Bogie wheel diameter	2′ 9″ (3′ 3″ from 03.123)
Cylinders (2)	22.5″ x 26″
Boiler pressure	227lbpsi
Grate area	42.7sqft
Heating surface	2,171sqft
Superheater	752.5sqft
Axle-load	18.2 tons
Weight	100.3 tons
Horsepower	1,980
Maximum speed	75mph (81mph from 03.123 & 87.5mph for selected locos)

Weight Diagram

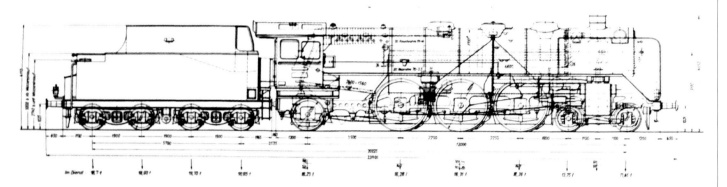

Statistics	Built	Post-1945	Stored (z)	Withdrawn(+)
03.001	6/30	DR	3/69	Preserved
03.002	7/30	DR	11/80	Shell preserved as 03.193 streamlined
03.003	8/30	DB	Not known after 1945, presumed destroyed in war	
03.004	11/31	PKP Pm2-1		4/71
03.005	12/31	DB	6/63	8/63
03.006	12/31	DB	5/65	9/65
03.007	12/31	USSR		
03.008	12/31	DB	11/61	7/62
03.009	1/32	PKP Pm2-12		6/73
03.010	2/32	DB	4/65	9/65
03.011	2/32	DB	3/66	10/66
03.012	3/32	DB	1/63	6/63
03.013	3/32	DB	8/65	1/66
03.014	4/32	DB	5/67	11/67
03.015	5/32	DB	4/65	9/65
03.016	11/31	DB	3/65	6/65
03.017	11/31	DB	6/63	8/63
03.018	11/31	PKP Pm2-16		4/71
03.019	12/31	DR	4/77	Sold for spare parts
03.020	12/31	PKP Pm2-2		10/73
03.021	12/31	DR	6/78	1/80
03.022	12/31	PKP Pm2-3		6/78
03.023	1/32	DR	1945	1/54 Bomb damage
03.024	1/32	PKP Pm2-4		2/76
03.025	1/32	DR	1/78	5/78
03.026	1/32	PKP Pm2-5		1/57
03.027	2/32	PKP Pm2-35 (after 03.253 z)		12/72
03.028	2/32	DR	1/78	5/78
03.029	2/32	PKP Pm2-6		8/58
03.030	8/31	DR	11/78	1/80
03.031	8/31	PKP Pm2-17		7/71

Statistics	Built	Post-1945	Stored (z)	Withdrawn(+)
03.032	8/31	DB	7/65	3/66
03.033	8/31		1/45	10/45 Bomb damage
03.034	8/31	DB	7/69	12/69
03.035	9/31	DB	8/63	11/63
03.036	9/31	DB	3/62	7/62
03.037	9/31	DB	11/66	3/67
03.038	9/31	USSR		
03.039	9/31	USSR		
03.040	9/31	USSR		
03.041	9/31	DR	1959	
03.042	9/31	DR	4/68	6/74
03.043	-/31	USSR		
03.044	-/31	DB	11/64	3/65
03.045	10/31	DB	2/65	6/65
03.046	10/31	DB	11/65	10/66
03.047	10/31	DB	9/64	3/65
03.048	-/31	DB	5/59	9/59 Derailment damage
03.049	-/31	PKP Pm2-18		10/77
03.050	11/31	DR	7/75	11/75
03.051	11/31	USSR		
03.052	7/31	PKP Pm2-13		11/78
03.053	8/31	DB	1/62	6/63
03.054	8/31	DB	4/66	10/66
03.055	8/31	DB	7/68	12/68
03.056	8/31	DB	12/62	6/63
03.057	9/31	DB	6/65	9/65
03.058	9/31	DR	10/80	1983 Purchased for spare parts
03.059	10/31	PKP Pm2-14		11/73
03.060	11/31	DR	11/77	12/83
03.061	11/31	DB	2/67	6/67
03.062	12/31	DB	3/67	7/67
03.063	11/31	DB	7/69	12/69
03.064	11/31	DB	9/66	12/66
03.065	11/31	PKP Pm2-7		11/70
03.066	-/31	DB	3/67	7/67
03.067	-/31	DR	2/79	8/80
03.068	12/31	DB	9/64	12/64
03.069	-/32	PKP Pm2-8		11/78
03.070	4/32	DR	7/68	10/73
03.071	5/32	DB	3/66	7/66
03.072	5/32	DB	9/69	12/69
03.073	5/32	DB	2/62	7/62
03.074	5/32	DB	10/66	12/66
03.075	6/32	PKP Pm2-9		5/78
03.076	8/32	DB	5/67	11/67
03.077	8/32	DB	2/69	7/69

Statistics	Built	Post-1945	Stored (z)	Withdrawn(+)
03.078	9/32	DB	10/64	3/65
03.079	9/32	DB	11/64	3/65
03.080	9/32	PKP Pm2-15		5/75
03.081	9/32	DR	5/76	2/80
03.082	9/32	PKP Pm2-10		4/77
03.083	9/32	DR	6/79	9/80
03.084	-/32	PKP Pm2-11		5/75
03.085	5/32	DB	1955 ?	
03.086	5/32	DB	3/66	8/66
03.087	6/32	DB	1/69	7/69
03.088	6/32	DB	9/72	2/73
03.089	6/32	DB	1/66	6/66
03.090	8/32	DB	9/68	12/68
03.091	5/32	DB	9/65	1/66
03.092	6/32	DB	12/66	7/67
03.093	7/32	DB	2/66	6/66
03.094	4/33	DB	8/67	3/68
03.095	5/33	DR	12/79	9/83
03.096	5/33	DR	6/79	9/83
03.097	5/33	USSR		
03.098	6/33	DR	11/78	Preserved
03.099	6/33	DR	1957	
03.100	7/33	DR	8/76	2/77
03.101	7/33	DB	11/65	1/66 Accident damage
03.102	2/33	DB	2/65	9/65
03.103	4/33		6/46	Bomb damage
03.104	5/33	DB	9/66	6/67
03.105	5/33	DR	4/79	7/83
03.106	6/33	DB	11/67	3/68
03.107	6/33	DB	8/67	3/68
03.108	7/33	DB	9/64	12/64
03.109	7/33	DB	4/66	10/66
03.110	3/33	USSR		
03.111	3/33	DB	12/70	6/71
03.112	3/33	DB	12/67	3/68
03.113	-/33	ŐBB/DB	5/66	10/66
03.114	4/33	DB	12/69	9/70
03.115	4/33	USSR		
03.116	4/33	DB	5/67	11/67
03.117	4/33	DR	9/80	12/83
03.118	-/33	DR	12/77	Used for spare parts
03.119	6/33	DR	10/77	10/81
03.120	8/33	DR	7/68	5/75
03.121	-/33	DR	12/77	2/78
03.122	8/33	DB	2/66	6/66
03.123	11/33	DR	1/79	12/80

Statistics	Built	Post-1945	Stored (z)	Withdrawn(+)
03.124	11/33	USSR		
03.125	11/33	DR	1958 ?	
03.126	12/33	DR	4/78	8/83
03.127	12/33	DB	12/68	3/69
03.128	12/33	DR	1/81	7/81
03.129	11/33	DB	1/65	6/65
03.130	11/33	DB	11/67	4/68
03.131	11/33	DB	5/72	Preserved
03.132	11/33	DB	3/67	7/67
03.133	11/33	DR	3/76	5/77
03.134	11/33	DB	3/68	8/68
03.135	12/33	DR	5/76	4/77
03.136	12/33	DB	6/67	11/67
03.137	1/34	DB	12/64	6/65
03.138	-/34	DB	6/66	10/66
03.139	12/33	DB	2/67	6/67 Collision damage
03.140	1/34	DB	1/66	6/66
03.141	2/34	DB	9/67	7/68
03.142	3/34	DR	11/75	4/76
03.143	3/34	DR	11/77	9/83
03.144	3/34	DB	9/65	1/66
03.145	4/34	DB	5/66	10/66
03.146	-/34	USSR		
03.147	-/34	PKP Pm2-20		5/68
03.148	-/34	DR	6/78	1/80
03.149	6/34	DB	11/67	3/68
03.150	7/34	DR	5/78	11/82
03.151	2/34	DR	1/78	7/83
03.152	2/34	PKP Pm2-21		11/78
03.153	2/34	DR	2/80	7/85
03.154	3/34	DR	5/79	12/83
03.155	3/34	DR	5/79	Preserved
03.156	3/34	DR	1/78	1/80
03.157	3/34	DR	1/79	12/83
03.158	3/34	DR	12/68	4/74
03.159	-/34	USSR		
03.160	4/34	DB	5/70	9/70
03.161	4/34	PKP Pm2-19		7/76
03.162	4/34	DR	6/78	3/82
03.163	9/34	PKP Pm2-24		3/77
03.164	9/34	DB	2/68	8/68
03.165	-/34	DB	1/47	Cannibalised
03.166	12/34	DB	9/64	3/65
03.167	12/34	DB	8/65	1/66 Accident damage
03.168	1/35	DB	6/71	9/71
03.169	12/34	DB	5/68	10/68

Statistics	Built	Post-1945	Stored (z)	Withdrawn(+)
03.170	1/35	DB	1/65	9/65
03.171	12/34	USSR		
03.172	12/34	DR	12/78	2/81
03.173	1/35	PKP Pm2-23		6/78
03.174	1/35		3/39	Boiler explosion
03.175	4/35	PKP Pm2-30		10/73
03.176	5/35	DR	11/79	8/83
03.177	5/35	DR	3/77	9/83
03.178	6/35	USSR		
03.179	6/35	DB	7/71	12/71
03.180	6/35	DR	7/77	8/83
03.181	8/35	PKP Pm2-26		5/76
03.182	8/35	DB	9/68	12/68
03.183	9/35	PKP Pm2-27		6/75
03.184	10/35	DB	3/69	7/69
03.185	1/35	DB	1/67	6/67
03.186	1/35	DR	12/77	8/83
03.187	-/35	USSR		
03.188	2/35	DB	9/69	12/69 Preserved
03.189	-/35	PKP Pm2-22		10/77
03.190	3/35	USSR		
03.191	-/35	USSR		
03.192	-/35	USSR		
03.193	9/35	DB	8/66	4/68
03.194	12/35	DB	5/66	10/66
03.195	1/36	DR	5/77	7/77
03.196	1/36	DB	8/68	12/68
03.197	1/36	DB	2/67	6/67
03.198	2/36	DB	10/64	3/65
03.199	2/36	DB	3/67	7/67
03.200	2/36	DB	10/64	3/65
03.201	2/36	USSR		
03.202	3/36	DR	4/76	10/77
03.203	3/36	DR	6/77	8/83
03.204	4/36	DR	8/76	Preserved
03.205	4/36	DR	2/77	7/77
03.206	5/36	DR	12/76	10/77
03.207	6/36	DR	4/78	12/83
03.208	10/35	USSR		
03.209	10/35	DB	8/66	12/66 Accident damage
03.210	10/35	DB	1/67	6/67
03.211	11/35	DB	5/67	11/67
03.212	11/35	DR	8/75	2/77
03.213	12/35	DB	10/64	3/65
03.214	11/35	DR	12/77	11/82
03.215	1/36	USSR		

Statistics	Built	Post-1945	Stored (z)	Withdrawn(+)
03.216	2/36	DR	3/45	1951 Bomb damage
03.217	2/36	DB	1/45	8/51 Bomb damage
03.218	2/36	DB	9/66	12/66
03.219	3/36	DB	1/68	7/68
03.220	1/36	DB	9/70	3/71
03.221	2/36	DB	1/68	8/68
03.222	2/36	DB	3/70	7/70
03.223	3/36	DB	8/66	12/66 Accident damage
03.224	3/36	PKP Pm2-28		5/78
03.225	3/36	DB	1/66	10/66
03.226	3/36	DB	6/60	12/61 Accident damage
03.227	3/36	PKP Pm2-29		1/77
03.228	4/36	DR	6/77	8/77
03.229	5/36	PKP Pm2-25		12/71
03.230	5/36	DB	7/67	4/68
03.231	5/36		11/46	War damage
03.232	5/36	DB	9/65	10/66
03.233	5/36	DB	7/66	12/66
03.234	6/36	DR	1/78	8/80
03.235	6/36	DR	6/79	7/83
03.236	6/36	DR	3/78	3/82
03.237	6/36	DR	12/77	7/78
03.238	7/36	USSR		
03.239	7/36	DR	7/75	10/77
03.240	8/36	DB	1/67	6/67
03.241	8/36	DB	1/65	9/65
03.242	8/36	DR	6/77	11/83
03.243	8/36	DR	4/81	Purchased for spare parts
03.244	9/36	DB	3/67	7/67
03.245	7/36	DB	5/64	9/65
03.246	7/36	DB	3/71	6/71
03.247	7/36	DB	1/67	6/67
03.248	8/36	DB	6/71	9/71
03.249	8/36	DB	5/67	11/67
03.250	10/36	DR	10/77	11/79
03.251	10/36	DB	3/71	6/71
03.252	10/36	DB	10/69	3/70
03.253	11/36	PKP Pm2-35		1/48
03.254	5/36	DR	4/79	8/83
03.255	-/36	PKP Pm2-31		6/78
03.256	6/36	DR	5/78	7/85
03.257	7/36	DR	4/77	9/83
03.258	7/36	DB	11/64	3/65
03.259	8/36	DB	3/69	7/69
03.260	9/36	DB	10/69	3/70
03.261	-/36	PKP Pm2-32		12/76

Statistics	Built	Post-1945	Stored (z)	Withdrawn(+)
03.262	9/36	DB	3/70	3/71
03.263	10/36	DB	10/69	3/70
03.264	10/36	USSR		
03.265	10/36	DR	11/77	4/78
03.266	11/36	DB	7/68	12/68
03.267	11/36	DB	5/67	11/67
03.268	11/36	DB	1/72	4/72
03.269	12/36	DR	1/77	7/77
03.270	1/37	DR	2/76	2/77
03.271	1/37	USSR		
03.272	1/37	PKP Pm2-33		10/75
03.273	2/37	PKP Pm2-34		11/78 Preserved Poland
03.274	2/37	DR	5/76	4/77
03.275	3/37	DB	3/69	7/69
03.276	6/37	DB	10/71	12/71
03.277	6/37	DR	11/76	6/77
03.278	6/37	DR	8/78	11/82
03.279	6/37		10/44	1947 War damage
03.280	6/37	DB	5/67	11/67
03.281	7/37	DB	7/71	12/71
03.282	7/37	DB	4/67	7/67
03.283	7/37	DB	10/67	3/68
03.284	8/37	DB	8/68	12/68
03.285	8/37	DB	5/69	3/71
03.286	8/37	DR	10/77	11/79
03.287	9/37	DB	3/68	10/68
03.288	10/37	DB	6/66	10/66
03.289	10/37	DB	3/67	7/67
03.290	11/37	USSR		
03.291	11/37	DB	9/67	7/68
03.292	11/37	DB	4/67	7/67
03.293	11/37	DB	9/65	1/66
03.294	12/37	DB	5/66	10/66
03.295	12/37	DR	3/78	Preserved
03.296	12/37	DB	10/69	3/70
03.297	1/38	DR	12/77	9/83
03.298	12/37	DR	3/78	11/83

The *Deutsche Reichsbahn* three-cylinder 03.10
Dimensions

Coupled wheels diameter	6′ 7″
Bogie wheel diameter	3′ 3″
Cylinders (3)	18.5″ x 26″
Boiler pressure	227lbpsi
Grate area	41.8sqft
Heating surface	2,184sqft

Superheater	776.4sqft
Axle-load	18.4 tons
Weight	103.2 tons
Tender capacity (coal)	10 tons
Tender capacity (water)	7,500 gallons
Tractive effort	30,864lb
Horsepower	1,790
Maximum speed	87.5mph

DB Rebuilt 03.10 with all-welded boiler
Dimensions
As above, except:

Grate area	41.6sqft
Heating surface	1,909sqft
Superheater	1,030sqft
Axle-load	19.2 tons
Weight	104.2 tons
Horsepower	1,870

DR Rebuilt 03.10 with new boiler (oil-burner)
Dimensions
As DRG 1940 destreamlined design with DR-designed all-welded boiler:

Horsepower (oil-burners)	2,100

Weight Diagram

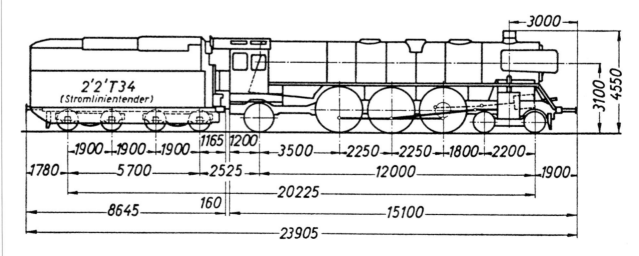

Statistics	Built	Post-1945	New boiler	Oil-burning	Stored (z)	Withdrawn(+)
03.1001	2/40	DB	1957-8		8/66	11/66
03.1002	6/40	PKP				
03.1003	8/40	PKP Pm3-3				
03.1004	8/40	DB	1957-8		4/66	8/66
03.1005	8/40	PKP Pm3-5				
03.1006	9/40	PKP Pm3-6				
03.1007	9/40	PKP Pm3-7				
03.1008	10/40	DB	1958		9/66	11/66
03.1009	10/40	DB	1957-8		4/66	8/66
03.1010	11/40	DR	2/59	8/67	6/81	Preserved
03.1011	11/40	DB	1958		9/66	11/66
03.1012	12/40	DB	1957-8		9/66	11/66
03.1013	12/40	DB	1956-7		9/66	11/66
03.1014	1/41	DB	1958		7/66	11/66
03.1015	1/41	PKP Pm3-15				
03.1016	2/41	DB	1957-8		11/65	6/66
03.1017	2/41	DB	1958		8/66	11/66
03.1018	3/41	PKP Pm3-18				
03.1019	3/41	DR	1959	1965/6	6/79	6/81
03.1020	4/41	DR	1959	9/72	9/78	7/85
03.1021	4/41	DB	11/59		9/66	11/66
03.1022	5/41	DB	1956-8		3/66	6/66
03.1043	6/40	DB	1958		9/66	11/66
03.1044	8/40	PKP Pm3-44				
03.1045	9/40	DB	1957/8		9/66	11/66
03.1046	10/40	DR	1959	1965/6	6/81	7/81
03.1047	11/40	PKP or USSR (DR -/58 ?)				
03.1048	12/40	DR	1959	3/72	3/82	9/83
03.1049	1/41	DB	1956-8		5/66	8/66
03.1050	2/41	DB	1956-8		9/66	11/66
03.1051	3/41	DB	1957-8		11/65	6/66
03.1052	4/41	PKP Pm3-52				
03.1053	5/41	PKP Pm3-53				
03.1054	6/41	DB	1956-8		9/66	11/66
03.1055	7/41	DB	1956-8		12/65	6/66
03.1056	8/41	DB	3/61		9/66	11/66
03.1057	9/41	DR	1959		1/74	5/75
03.1058	10/41	DR	1959	1965-6	4/81	5/81
03.1059	11/41	DR	1959	1965-6	6/80	9/81
03.1060	12/41	DB	1957-8		9/66	11/66
03.1073	7/40	DB	1956-8		5/66	6/66
03.1074	7/40	DR	1959	8/65	6/79	6/81
03.1075	7/40	DR	1959	1965-6	7/80	10/81
03.1076	8/40	DB	1957-8		9/66	11/66
03.1077	8/40	DR	6/66	1965-6	2/80	7/81
03.1078	8/40	DR	1959	1965-6	m6/77	7/77 Accident

Statistics	Built	Post-1945	New boiler	Oil-burning	Stored (z)		Withdrawn(+)
03.1079	8/40	DR			7/50	4/51	Cannibalised
03.1080	8/40	DR	1959	1970	8/80		11/82
03.1081	8/40	DB	1956-8		9/66		11/66
03.1082	9/40	DB	1956-8		11/65		6/66
03.1083	9/40	PKP Pm3-83					
03.1084	9/40	DB	1956-8		9/66		11/66
03.1085	9/40	DR	1959	9/65	7/80		6/81
03.1086	10/40	PKP or USSR					
03.1087	10/40	DR	1959		10/71		7/75
03.1088	10/40	DR	6/66	1965-6	3/78		
03.1089	10/40	DR	1959	1965-6	7/77		9/77
03.1090	10/40	DR	1959	1965-6	11/79		Preserved
03.1091	10/40				5/44		
03.1092	11/40				8/44		War damage

The *Deutsche Reichsbahn* 04 four-cylinder compound
Dimensions

Coupled wheels diameter	6' 7"
Bogie wheel diameter	3' 3"
Cylinders (2 inside High-pressure)	13.8" x 26"
(2 outside Low-pressure)	20.5" x 26"
Boiler pressure	330lbpsi
Grate area	44sqft
Heating surface	2,223sqft
Superheater	909sqft
Axle-load	18.9 tons
Weight	106.3 tons
Tender capacity (coal)	10 tons
(water)	7,000 gallons
Maximum speed	81mph

Statistics

Loco No.	Built	Converted to 02	Withdrawn	Scrapped
04.001	1932	02.101 1935	4/39 boiler explosion	1940
04.002	1932	02.102 1935	1939	1940

The *Deutsche Bundesbahn* three-cylinder class 10 (Oil-burning)
Dimensions

Coupled wheels diameter	6' 7"
Bogie wheels diameter	3' 3"
Cylinders (3)	18.9" x 28.4"
Boiler pressure	256lbpsi
Heating surface	2,326sqft
Superheater	1,147sqft

Axle-load   22.4 tons
Weight   118.9 tons
Tender capacity(water)   8,800 gallons
Horsepower   2,500
Maximum speed   87.5mph

Weight Diagram

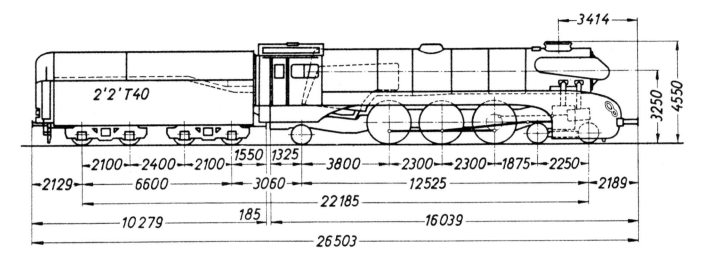

Statistics	Built	Oil- burning	Stored (z)	Withdrawn (+)
10.001	1956	1/58	10/67	Preserved
10.002	1957	Built as oil-burner	11/67	Stationary boiler until 1971

T18 Turbine Pacific Locomotives
Dimensions

Krupp T18.1001
Coupled wheels diameter   5' 5"
Bogie wheel diameter   3' 3"
Boiler pressure   213lbpsi
Main turbine revolutions   6,800 per minute
Grate area   33.3sqft
Heating surface   1,666sqft
Superheater   709.5sqft
Weight   112.4 tons
Condensing tender capacity   4,290 gallons
Horsepower   2,000
Maximum speed   69mph

Maffei T18.1002

Coupled wheels diameter	5′ 9″
Bogie wheel diameter	2′ 9″
Boiler pressure	312lbpsi
Main turbine revolutions	8,800 per minute
Grate area	37.6sqft
Heating surface	1,717sqft
Superheater	548sqft
Weight	104 tons
Condensing tender capacity	5,280 gallons
Horsepower	2,000
Maximum speed	75mph

Statistics

Loco No.	Built	Withdrawn	
T18.1001	1924	1941	Bomb damage
T18.1002	1926	10/43	War damage (boiler retained as a test bed for research, Munich-Freimann, until 1954)

High-Speed Test Locomotive 18.201
Dimensions

Coupled wheels diameter	7′ 6 ½ ″
Bogie wheel diameter	3′ 7″
Cylinders (3)	20.5″ x 26″
Boiler pressure	227lbpsi
Grate area	245.5sqft
Heating surface	2,218sqft
Superheater	901sqft
Weight	112.2 tons
Tender capacity (coal)	10 tons
(water)	7,500 gallons
Horsepower	1,590
Maximum speed	100mph

Statistic

Loco No.	Built	Oil-burning Withdrawn
18.201	1961 (rebuild of 61.002/45.024) 1967	Preserved

BIBLIOGRAPHY

Allen, Cecil J., *Locomotive Practice and Performance in the Twentieth Century*, W.Heffer & Sons Ltd., 1949

Asmus C. & Bufe S., *Dampflokomotiven im Allgäu*, Hermann Merker Verlag, 1976

Ball, M.G., *European Railway Atlas, Denmark, Germany, Austria, Switzerland*, 1992

Bellingrodt, Carl, *Reichsbahn-Dampflokomotiven*, EK Verlag, 1977

Benet, F.O., *Reichsbahn-Dampf 1970-1980*, Ferrovia Verlag, 1982

Cook, Thomas, *European Timetable*, August 1998

Ebel, Jürgen-Ulrich, *Die Baureihe 01.10*, EK Verlag, 2010

Eisenbahn Kurier Special, *Museumsbahnen in Deutschland*, EK-Special 17, 1990

Eisenbahn Kurier Special, *Die Geschichte der Baureihe 03.10*, EK-Special 117, 2015

Eisenbahn Journal, *Die Bay. S3/6*, Sonder-Ausgabe, 2002

Eisenbahn Journal, *Legendäre Baureihe 01*, Konrad Koschinski, Sonder-Ausgabe, 2006

Fischer, Siegfried, *Dampflokomotiven bei der DB*, Franckh'sche Verlag, 1980

Garvin, Brian & Fox, Peter, *German Railways, Part 2: Private Railways & Museums*, Platform 5, 2004

Gottwaldt, Alfred & Bündgen, Eduard, *Der Rheingold Express,* Motorbuch Verlag Stuttgart, 1977

Gottwaldt, Alfred, *Meisterfotos der Reichsbahnzeit II*, Franckh'sche Verlag, 1977

Heinrich, Peter, *Die sächsischen Schnellzuglokomotiven*, EK Verlag, 1985

Kenning Verlag, *Triebfahrzeuge der Deutschen Reichsbahn* (Ost) 1945/46, 1996

Kühne, Klaus-Jürgen, *Alles über Einheits-Dampfloks*, Transpress, 2010

Lüdecke, Steffen, *Die Baureihe 18.4-6*, EK Verlag, 1984

Lüdecke, Steffen, *Die Baureihe 18.3*, EK Verlag, 1990

Maedel, Karl-Ernst, *Deutschlands Dampflokomotiven*, Gestern und Heute, VEB Verlag Technik Berlin, 1957

Maedel, Karl-Ernst, *Geliebte Dampflok*, Frankh'sche Verlag, Stuttgart, 1967

Maidment, David, *European Railways Magazines*, Nos.160, 163, 166, 169, 172, 175, 176, 177, 178 Travellines, articles on journeys in continental Europe, Atlantic Publishers, 2004 – 2008

Merkbuch fur die Schienenfahrzeuge der Deutschen Bundesbahn, Eisenbahn Kurier Verlag, 1953, new edition, 1977.

Obermayer, Horst J., *Taschenbuch Deutsche Dampflokomotiven*, Franckh'sche Verlagshandlung, 1969

Paulitz, Udo, *Dampf auf der Emslandstrecke*, Frankh'sche Verlag, 1988

Pieper, Oskar, *Lokomotivverzeichnis der Deutschen Reichsbahn, DB und DR, Band 1*, Gustav Rohr, 1968

Scherer, Thomas, *Die Baureihe 18.1*, EK Verlag, 1986

Tauber, Helmut & Lüdecke, Steffen, *Die legendäre bayerische S3/6,* Eisenbahn Kurier Verlag, 2008

Troche, Horst, *Die Baureihe 03*, EK Verlag, 2006/2012

Weisbrod, Manfred & Petznick, Wolfgang, *Baureihe 01*, Hermann Merker Verlag, 1979

Baden Railway locomotives 1895 – 1905, 14, 15

INDEX